"This book is a valuable contribution to our understanding of Behavioural Public Finance with chapters by distinguished scholars focusing on decision-making, public policy, regulation and tax compliance and covering both theoretical insights and important empirical research."
— Simon James, Honorary Associate Professor in Economics
at the University of Exeter Business School, UK

"*Behavioural Public Finance* is a must-read for anyone who is interested in public finance and taxation. The original, intelligent and thoughtful chapters written by international experts represent an important and influential contribution to the field."
— John Hasseldine, Professor of Accounting & Taxation,
University of New Hampshire, USA

"I suppose Adam Smith would have been very happy if he could have seen how the powerful arguments from his famous 1759 book *Theory of Moral Sentiments* are reflected 250 years later in this beautiful volume on the economic psychology / behavioural economics of public finance, regulation and tax compliance."
— Henk Elffers, Professor Emeritus, Department of Criminal
Law and Criminology, VU University, Amsterdam, Netherlands

"It is really praiseworthy that a key part of this book is devoted to tax compliance behaviour."
— Gaetano Lisi, Associate Professor in Economic Policy,
University of Cassino and Southern Lazio, Italy

"This book is an excellent introduction to the interesting field of Behavioural Public Finance. It provides a comprehensive overview of this discipline with a strong emphasis on regulation, tax compliance, and how the tax revenue can be achieved. The editors did a tremendous job in gathering some of the most highly respected scholars, which makes this volume a valuable read for scientists, students, and practitioners."
— Stephan Muehlbacher, Professor of Work, Organizational, and
Economic Psychology, Karl Landsteiner University of
Health Sciences, Krems, Austria

"A valuable resource for behavioural economists, economic psychologists and policymakers, this book collects original studies on innovative topics, such as the history of taxation for the plutocrats, the effect of media on public finance behaviours, along with several case studies on behavioural responses to regulations. A must-read for those interested in behavioural aspects of public finance."
— Edoardo Lozza, Professor of Economic Psychology,
Università Cattolica, Milan, Italy

"A thought provoking and contemporary contribution to the Behavioural Public Finance literature. This book is essential reading for students, scholars and anyone interested in gaining a wider appreciation of this expanding area of public finance."

– Adrian Sawyer, Professor of Taxation, UC Business School, University of Canterbury, Christchurch, New Zealand

"Many of the ideas and approaches explored, discussed, and utilized in this book may, over time, lead to further fruitful explorations of this still new terrain, enriching and improving our understanding of this important dimension of the relationships between state and society, which have come increasingly to shape how people everywhere in the world go about the ordinary business of their lives ... Students, scholars, and analysts can all find material for thought and some suggestions and lessons to guide future work in this book."

– Richard Bird, Professor Emeritus of Economic Analysis and Policy, Rotman School of Management, University of Toronto, Canada

Behavioural Public Finance

This book tackles political, social, and behavioural aspects of public finance and fiscal exchange. The book combines conventional approaches toward public finance with new developments in economics such as political governance, social and individual aspects of economic behaviour. It colligates public finance and behavioural economics and gathers original contributions within the emerging field of behavioural public finance.

The book addresses public finance topics by incorporating political, social, and behavioural aspects of economic decision-making, assuming the tax relationship is shaped by three dimensions of decision-making. Thus, it aims not only to reflect the interdisciplinary nature of public finance by bringing together scholars from various disciplines but also to examine public finance through the lens of political, social, and behavioural aspects. The book scrutinizes the relationship between political institutions, governance types, and public finance; it investigates the impact of social context, social capital, and societal cooperation on public finance; it explores behavioural biases of individual fiscal preferences.

This book is of interest to scholars, policymakers, tax professionals, business professionals, financers, university students, and researchers in the fields of public policy and economics.

M. Mustafa Erdoğdu is Professor of Economics at Marmara University, Istanbul, Turkey, where he is head of the Financial Economics division. He received his MA and PhD in development economics from Manchester University, UK. His research interests are economic development, public finance, international political economy, institutions, financial crises, sustainability, and renewable energies.

Larissa Batrancea is Associate Professor of Corporate Finance at Babes-Bolyai University, Cluj-Napoca, Romania. Her research addresses tax behaviour, experimental economics, neuroeconomics, and financial analysis. She acted as principal investigator/member in 16 international/national research grants. She has been awarded 12 prizes for excellence in research and teaching.

Savaş Çevik is Professor in the Department of Economics at Selçuk University in Turkey. He received his MS and PhD degrees in public finance from Marmara University. His research interests are in public economics, the economics and politics of taxation, and behavioural economics.

Routledge International Studies in Money and Banking

Money, Inflation and Business Cycles
The Cantillon Effect and the Economy
Arkadiusz Sieroń

Public Value Theory and Budgeting
International Perspectives
Usman W. Chohan

Venture Capital Performance
A Comparative Study of Investment Practices in Europe and the USA
Keith Arundale

Complexities of Financial Globalisation
Analytical and Policy Issues in Emerging and Developing Economies
Tony Cavoli, Sasidaran Gopalan and Ramkishen S. Rajan

Capital and Finance
Theory and History
Peter Lewin and Nicolás Cachanosky

Democracy and Money
Lessons for Today from Athens in Classical Times
George C. Bitros, Emmanouil M. L. Economou, Nicholas C. Kyriazis

Monetary Policy after the Great Recession
The Role of Interest Rates
Arkadiusz Sieroń

Behavioural Public Finance
Individuals, Society, and the State
Edited by M. Mustafa Erdoğdu, Larissa Batrancea, and Savaş Çevik

For more information about this series, please visit: www.routledge.com/
Routledge-International-Studies-in-Money-and-Banking/book-series/
SE0403

Behavioural Public Finance
Individuals, Society, and the State

Edited by
M. Mustafa Erdoğdu, Larissa Batrancea,
and Savaş Çevik

LONDON AND NEW YORK

First published 2021
by Routledge
2 Park Square, Milton Park, Abingdon, Oxon OX14 4RN

and by Routledge
52 Vanderbilt Avenue, New York, NY 10017

Routledge is an imprint of the Taylor & Francis Group, an informa business

© 2021 selection and editorial matter, M. Mustafa Erdoğdu, Larissa Batrancea, and Savaş Çevik; individual chapters, the contributors

The right of M. Mustafa Erdoğdu, Larissa Batrancea, and Savaş Çevik to be identified as the authors of the editorial material, and of the authors for their individual chapters, has been asserted in accordance with sections 77 and 78 of the Copyright, Designs and Patents Act 1988.

All rights reserved. No part of this book may be reprinted or reproduced or utilised in any form or by any electronic, mechanical, or other means, now known or hereafter invented, including photocopying and recording, or in any information storage or retrieval system, without permission in writing from the publishers.

Trademark notice: Product or corporate names may be trademarks or registered trademarks, and are used only for identification and explanation without intent to infringe.

British Library Cataloguing-in-Publication Data
A catalogue record for this book is available from the British Library

Library of Congress Cataloging-in-Publication Data
Names: Erdoğdu, M. Mustafa, 1962– editor. |
Batrancea, Larissa, editor. | Çevik, Savaş, editor.
Title: Behavioural public finance: individuals, society, and the state /
edited by M. Mustafa Erdoğdu, Larissa Batrancea and Savaş Çevik.
Description: 1 Edition. | New York: Routledge, 2020. |
Series: Routledge international studies in money and banking |
Includes bibliographical references and index.
Identifiers: LCCN 2020026799 (print) | LCCN 2020026800 (ebook)
Subjects: LCSH: Finance, Public. | Fiscal policy. |
Economics–Psychological aspects. | Human behavior–Economic aspects.
Classification: LCC HJ141.B424 2020 (print) |
LCC HJ141 (ebook) | DDC 336–dc23
LC record available at https://lccn.loc.gov/2020026799
LC ebook record available at https://lccn.loc.gov/2020026800

ISBN: 978-0-8153-6430-6 (hbk)
ISBN: 978-1-351-10737-2 (ebk)

Typeset in Bembo
by Newgen Publishing UK

Contents

List of figures	ix
List of tables	x
List of contributors	xii
Foreword	xv
RICHARD BIRD	
Book overview	xviii
M. MUSTAFA ERDOĞDU, LARISSA BATRANCEA, AND SAVAŞ ÇEVIK	

PART I
Theoretical considerations on behavioural public finance   1

1   Behavioral public finance in a populist world   3
VITO TANZI

2   Smart decision-makers, institutional design and x-efficient
(real-world optimal) public finance   16
MORRIS ALTMAN

3   Behavioral economics and public policy   38
JULIA DOBREVA

PART II
Behavioural responses to regulations   51

4   Financial decisions and financial regulation: three concepts of
performance-based regulation   53
UWE DULLECK

5   Behavioral biases and political actors: three examples from
US international taxation   80
REUVEN S. AVI-YONAH AND KAIJIE WU

viii *Contents*

6 Varieties of general anti-avoidance legislation 93
JOHN PREBBLE

PART III
Tax compliance behaviour: cases 123

7 Political economy of tax compliance behavior: an analysis of
three cities in Turkey 125
M. MUSTAFA ERDOĞDU AND OSMAN GEYIK

8 Incidental emotions, integral emotions, and decisions to
pay taxes 157
JANINA ENACHESCU, ŽIGA PUKLAVEC, CHRISTIAN MARTIN BAUER,
JEROME OLSEN, ERICH KIRCHLER, AND JAMES ALM

9 Moral concerns and personal beliefs regarding tax evasion:
empirical results from Germany, Romania, Turkey, and the
United Kingdom 178
LARISSA BATRANCEA, ANCA NICHITA, CARLA STARTIN,
IOAN CHIRILA, IOAN BATRANCEA, ROBERT W. MCGEE,
SERKAN BENK, AND TAMER BUDAK

10 Paying is caring? Prosociality and gender in fiscal compliance 197
JOHN D'ATTOMA, CLARA VOLINTIRU, AND ANTOINE MALÉZIEUX

11 Tax compliance theories and fiduciary taxes: do the shoes fit? 222
ELAINE DOYLE, BRIAN KEEGAN, AND EOIN REEVES

12 How to tax the powerful and the sophisticated? 233
PAUL FRIJTERS, KATHARINA GANGL, AND BENNO TORGLER

13 Starbucks and media allegations of tax avoidance:
an examination of reputational loss 253
YINGYUE DING, JANE FRECKNALL-HUGHES, AND JA RYONG KIM

14 The effect of media on tax compliance: hypothetical
scenarios study 277
N. TOLGA SARUÇ, ÇIĞDEM BÖRKE TUNALI, HAKAN YAVUZ,
AND TUNÇ İNCE

Names index 290
Subject index 300

Figures

2.1	Tax compliance and economic theory: the role of non-economic variables	22
2.2	The economic impact of taxation	23
2.3	Average costs, x-inefficiency, and labour benefits	28
2.4	Higher labour benefits and unemployment	29
2.5	Behavioural theory of the firm and the Phillips Curve	30
2.6	Implications of the small agent-based rationality narrative for policy	34
4.1	Dominated choices	57
8.1	Geneva Emotion Wheel	160
8.2	Determinants and consequences of immediate and expected emotions	162
8.3	Experimental procedure	165
8.4	Tax compliance by conditions and experimental rounds	168
10.1	Screen capture of the clerical task	204
10.2	Screen capture of the reporting screen	204
10.3	Distribution of tax compliance	209
10.4	Effects of SVO on tax compliance	210
10.5	Bar chart of tax compliance by gender and country	211
10.6	Cumulative distributions for the SVO angle	212
10.7	Schematic diagram of mediation analysis results	217
13.1	Process of thematic analysis	262
13.2	Frequency of the terms "tax avoidance" and "Starbucks", 2006–2015	262
13.3	Returns and abnormal returns	264
13.4	Cumulative abnormal returns	265

Tables

3.1	MINDSPACE	45
4.1	Basic savings products of one Australian bank in April 2018	72
7.1	General budget city revenues in Turkey, 2018	136
7.2	Well-being index rankings and values for the three cities, 2015	137
7.3	Demographic, social, and educational status of participants	138
7.4	Average response by city	139
7.5	Taxes in return for public services	140
7.6	Perception of non-compliance behavior – 1	140
7.7	Perception of non-compliance behavior – 2	141
7.8	Fairness of the Turkish tax system	141
7.9	Ensuring the rights of taxpayers	142
7.10	Satisfaction with the services provided by the tax administration	142
7.11	Perception of tax amnesties	143
7.12	Trust in government policies	143
7.13	Trust in the Parliament	144
7.14	Accountability of the tax administration	144
7.15	The quest for information on spending tax money	145
7.16	Efficiency of public spending	145
7.17	Waste perception in public spending	146
7.18	Averages of TS and PPAT by city	147
7.19	ANOVA – PPAT – by city	148
7.20	ANOVA – PPAT – by education level	150
8.1	Sample socio-demographic statistics	164
8.2	Positive and negative mood scores by condition	166
8.3	Manipulation check regression models for positive and negative mood scores	167
9.1	Demographics and statistical results by country for participants included in the analyses of Part 1	186
9.2	Demographics and statistical results by country corresponding to the survey items included in Part 2	189
10.1	Description of experimental treatments	205
10.2	Social Value Orientation allocation decisions (example)	206

List of tables xi

10.3	Descriptive statistics	208
10.4	Individual level models and mediation analysis	213
10.5	Mediation analysis with Structural Equation Modeling	216
13.1	Returns and abnormal returns	264
13.2	Public reactions after the Reuters report	266
13.3	Starbucks' response to the crisis	269
14.1	Predicted results of the model	286

Contributors

James Alm is Professor and Chair of the Department of Economics at Tulane University, New Orleans, USA.

Morris Altman is Professor and Dean of the University of Dundee School of Business, Dundee, UK.

Reuven S. Avi-Yonah is Professor at the University of Michigan Law School, Ann Arbor, USA.

Ioan Batrancea is Professor in the Faculty of Economics and Business Administration, Babeş-Bolyai University, Cluj-Napoca, Romania.

Larissa Batrancea is Associate Professor in the Faculty of Business, Babeş-Bolyai University, Cluj-Napoca, Romania.

Christian Martin Bauer is Assistant Professor in the Faculty of Psychology, University of Vienna, Vienna, Austria.

Serkan Benk is Professor in the Department of Public Finance, İnönü University, Malatya, Turkey.

Richard Bird is Professor Emeritus at the Rotman School of Management, University of Toronto, Toronto, Canada.

Tamer Budak is Professor in the Department of International Trade, Alanya Alaaddin Keykubat University, Alanya, Turkey.

Savaş Çevik is Professor in the Department of Economics, Selçuk University, Konya, Turkey.

Ioan Chirila is Professor in the Faculty of Orthodox Theology, Babeş-Bolyai University, Cluj-Napoca, Romania.

John D'Attoma is Lecturer at the University of Exeter Business School and Tax Administration Research Centre, University of Exeter, Exeter, UK.

Yingyue Ding is a postgraduate student at Nottingham University Business School, Jubilee Campus, Nottingham, UK.

List of contributors xiii

Julia Dobreva is Associate Professor in the Department of Economics, VUZF University Bulgaria, Sofia, Bulgaria.

Elaine Doyle is Senior Lecturer at Kemmy Business School, University of Limerick, Limerick, Ireland.

Uwe Dulleck is Professor at the Centre for Behavioural Economics, Society and Technology (BEST), Queensland University of Technology, Brisbane, Australia; Crawford School of Public Policy, Australian National University, Canberra, Australia; and CESifo, Ludwig Maximilian University, Munich, Germany.

Janina Enachescu is Pre-doc Research Assistant in the Faculty of Psychology, University of Vienna, Vienna, Austria.

M. Mustafa Erdoğdu is Professor in the Faculty of Economics, Marmara University, Istanbul, Turkey.

Jane Frecknall-Hughes is Professor at Nottingham University Business School, Jubilee Campus, Nottingham, UK.

Paul Frijters is Professor at the Centre for Economic Performance, London School of Economics and Political Science, London, UK.

Katharina Gangl is Researcher at the Institute for Advanced Studies, Vienna, Austria.

Osman Geyik is Lecturer in the Faculty of Economics and Administrative Sciences, Dicle University, Diyarbakır, Turkey.

Tunç İnce is Research Assistant in the Faculty of Political Sciences, Sakarya University, Serdivan, Turkey.

Brian Keegan is Director of Public Policy and Taxation, Chartered Accountants Ireland, Chartered Accountants House, Dublin, Ireland.

Ja Ryong Kim is Lecturer at the Nottingham University Business School, Jubilee Campus, Nottingham, UK.

Erich Kirchler is Professor in the Faculty of Psychology, University of Vienna, Vienna, Austria.

Antoine Malézieux is Assistant Professor at the Burgundy School of Business, Université Bourgogne Franche-Comté, Besançon, France.

Robert W. McGee is Associate Professor at the Broadwell College of Business and Economics, Fayetteville State University, Fayetteville, USA.

Anca Nichita is Assistant Professor in the Faculty of Economic Sciences, "1 Decembrie 1918" University of Alba Iulia, Alba Iulia, Romania.

Jerome Olsen is a post-doc at the Max Planck Institute for Research on Collective Goods, Bonn, Germany.

xiv *List of contributors*

John Prebble is a barrister and Emeritus Professor of Law at Victoria University of Wellington, Wellington, New Zealand; Gastprofessor, Institut für Österreichisches und Internationales Steuerrecht, Wirtschaftsuniversität, Vienna, Austria; Adjunct Professor of Law, Sydney School of Law, The University of Notre Dame, Sydney, Australia.

Žiga Puklavec is Pre-doc Research Assistant in the Faculty of Psychology, University of Vienna, Vienna, Austria.

Eoin Reeves is Professor and Head of the Department of Economics, Kemmy Business School, University of Limerick, Limerick, Ireland.

N. Tolga Saruç is Professor in the Faculty of Economics, Istanbul University, Istanbul, Turkey.

Carla Startin is Associate Lecturer in the Department of Psychology, University of York, UK.

Vito Tanzi has served as Chief of the Tax Policy Division and Director of the Fiscal Affairs Department with the IMF, President of the International Institute of Public Finance (IIPF), State Secretary for Economy and Finance in the Italian Government and Senior Consultant for the Inter-American Development Bank.

Benno Torgler is Professor at the School of Economics and Finance and Centre for Behavioural Economics, Society and Technology (BEST), Queensland University of Technology, Brisbane, Australia.

Çiğdem Börke Tunalı is Associate Professor in the Faculty of Economics, Istanbul University, Istanbul, Turkey.

Clara Volintiru is Associate Professor in the Department of International Business and Economics (REI), Bucharest University of Economic Studies (ASE), Bucharest, Romania.

Kaijie Wu is an SJD candidate at the University of Michigan Law School, Ann Arbor, USA.

Hakan Yavuz is Assistant Professor in the Faculty of Political Sciences, Istanbul University, Istanbul, Turkey.

Foreword

"Economics is a study of mankind in the ordinary business of life", as Alfred Marshall famously said in the first sentence of his 1890 treatise. Even when simply going about the ordinary business of life, however, people are complex. Everyone is of course similar in an important respect because they are all human beings. But everyone is also unique because each has been shaped by a unique combination of genetics, their specific natural, social, and community environments, their family and life experiences, and their own past choices.

To deal with the economic behaviour of this inherently heterogeneous population, economists long ago simplified reality to a model that they could analyse in a meaningful way. Contrary to what some critics still occasionally assert, they did not simply assume that everyone always acts in a fully rational way to maximize the extent to which their defined, stable, and transitive set of preferences are satisfied. No one who lives in this world could ever believe that this proposition was true. What economists did was instead to realize that assuming that this condition might be roughly satisfied on the average and over time for any large enough group provided a good base case to begin to understand, analyse, and sometimes even predict how people – heterogeneous and imperfect as they are – might behave when faced with the resource allocation decisions that are the central concern of economic analysis. For most of the last century, economists developed this framework with an ever-increasing degree of mathematical and empirical sophistication and produced demonstrably useful results.

However, since economists too are human, they do not all agree about anything, and over the years many prominent economists have suggested various modifications in this basic paradigm to improve our understanding of people's economic decisions. To mention only a few Nobel Prize winners as examples, Herbert Simon's concept of "satisficing" instead of maximizing, Joseph Stiglitz's emphasis on information asymmetry, Daniel Kahneman's exploration of the biases and heuristics shaping how people make decisions, and most recently Richard Thaler's work on "nudging" have all in different ways and to different extents contributed to the recent development of what is now usually called "behavioural economics" – an approach that recognizes more explicitly that

xvi *Foreword*

people are not perfectly rational calculators but a diverse group of imperfect decision-makers living in an uncertain and changing world.

As the studies collected in this book convincingly demonstrate, public finance, like other branches of economics, has been enriched in recent years by a range of studies reflecting this new broader approach to understanding and analysing how the diverse people who make up any institutional or political grouping manage to cope with change, uncertainty, and conflicting interests. To paraphrase another famous person, Winston Churchill, we are definitely not yet at the end of the development of "behavioural public finance". Nor, indeed, are we likely near the beginning of the end. But perhaps we may now be at least close to the end of the beginning. Many of the ideas and approaches explored, discussed, and utilized in this book may, over time, lead to further fruitful explorations of this still new terrain, enriching and improving our understanding of this important dimension of the relationships between state and society, which have come increasingly to shape how people everywhere in the world go about the ordinary business of their lives.

Many years ago a well-known public finance expert of the day, Gerhard Colm, in a 1948 essay in the *National Tax Journal*, called public finance a "borderline science" because it sat at the intersection of a number of disciplines and required some knowledge of each in order to be properly understood. To be a good public finance analyst or scholar, he suggested that one had to be knowledgeable about at least some aspects of political science, public administration, sociology, management, and accounting in addition to economics. Interestingly, although Colm also mentioned the need for some knowledge of psychology and the importance of a sound historical understanding of how and why institutions developed and work the way they do, he did not add these disciplines to his suggested tool kit. As the scope of the essays included in the present book suggests, however, a diligent student of public finance and especially of its recent behavioural shift should ideally add not only these two subjects to their toolkit but also be well advised to have at least some knowledge of philosophy and law. Since anyone trained in economics these days must also be well acquainted with mathematics and statistics, few if any public economists are likely ever to be fully equipped with all the tools ideally necessary.

In the future, as in the past, perhaps even the best policy analyst can usefully – as Esther Duflo memorably said recently – be thought of as similar to a good plumber faced with a mysterious leak. Whether plumber or public finance analyst, the first thing to do is to observe as closely and diligently as possible all features that seem relevant to understanding how the problem arose and exactly why it is a problem. Often, certainly if one is working for a government or an international organization, the problem turns out to be not what they told you it was when they assigned you the task. Nor is it necessarily what even the (usually very different) people at the "front end", those who deliver or receive whatever the output is supposed to be, think it is. In any case, the first task is always to decide what the problem really is. The next step – the required analysis – is of course then to figure out what needs to be done and how to do it. Sometimes an appropriate answer can be found simply by applying the tools at hand, drawing on the traditional economics tool kit; sometimes the ideas and techniques emerging from the behavioural literature may be more helpful. Often, however, even if the analyst is, as is seldom the case, both willing and able to engage directly and persistently in the usually lengthy and complex process of decision-making and implementation required to fix the problem, not even a second- or third-best solution may prove acceptable to those responsible for making the relevant decisions. The reason may be because they do not understand the analysis, they do not agree with some of the assumptions made, or they do not want to make the required changes because they cannot sell them to their political base or they do not have sufficient capacity or resources to do so. Many good policy analyses remain unread in the files of governments everywhere.

Whether the particular problem at hand is solved or not, however, an important lesson one can draw from the burgeoning literature on behavioural public finance is that one can always learn something from close examination of problems and processes that may help develop a better approach to the next problem – and perhaps a useful contribution to the literature. Similarly, one can always learn something from reading studies in behavioural public finance like those in this book. What one learns may not always be new, immediately useful, or even correct: but a good "public financier" never stops learning. Students, scholars, and analysts can all find material for thought and some suggestions and lessons to guide future work in this book.

Richard Bird
Professor Emeritus of Economic Analysis and Policy
Rotman School of Management, University of Toronto, Canada

Book overview

M. Mustafa Erdoğdu, Larissa Batrancea, and Savaş Çevik

Background

Political and social contexts, as well as individual behaviour, are important determinants not only for decisions that change the life of the individual but also for the economic performance of nations. Recent developments in economics facilitate the analysis of the impact of behavioural motivations, social context, and political governance on economic results and individual decisions. While social economics introduces topics such as social capital, social norms, identities, cooperation, collective action, and the analysis of individual utility function to the field of economics, behavioural economics extends the limits of the rationality assumption by introducing cognitive biases into decision-making processes.

As McCaffery and Slemrod (2006, p. 4) highlight, "public finance has been a principal concern of economics at least since Adam Smith". The discipline lays out the welfare implications of various alternative government actions and changes in tax systems that may shape societal and political relationships. Although tax regimes define the ability of states to achieve social goals, they can also be seen as a reflection and one of the central areas of social and political interactions that go beyond the ability to raise public funds. The fiscal relationship between the state, society, and the individual can play a central role in building and maintaining state power. It can shape the ties with society by establishing a social contract and stimulating the strengthening of institutions, thereby approving the formation of democratic states. The relationship between good governance and a public funding system is a two-way street. On one hand, better governance supports citizen participation in collective actions to finance the state by improving tax compliance. On the other hand, an effective and sustainable tax system may help to improve the quality of governance and political institutions.

This edited volume deals with political, social, and behavioural aspects of public finance and fiscal exchange. It engages with the core questions of public finance with a particular focus on human behaviour. The "rational" decision-making model has been the traditional lens through which public finance decisions and results have been examined. According to this model, when different options are offered to people under the conditions of scarcity, they would choose the option that maximizes their welfare. This model assumes that people can make rational decisions by effectively evaluating the costs and benefits of each option available to them. The rational person has self-control and is unaffected by external factors and emotions, and hence knows what is best for herself/himself. Risk and uncertainty are assessed by using objective weights that represent the likelihood of events, and thus produce risk-adjusted measures of potential results. However, we all know from our personal experiences that those assumptions are a poor match for reality. People do not always act purely out of self-interest; their behaviours are also shaped by social norms, beliefs, and biases. As a natural consequence, recent work in behavioural economics has challenged the rationality assumption.

Classical and neoclassical economists did incorporate certain psychological explanations for economic behaviour. But in general, psychology did not try to sort out the concept of homo economicus, whose behaviour was fundamentally rational. After economic psychology surfaced in the 20th century, that perspective started to change. In the 1960s cognitive psychology began to shed more light on internal mental processes. Psychologists in this field like Amos Tversky and Daniel Kahneman started to work together in the early 1970s and compared their cognitive models of risky decision-making and uncertainty with economic models of rational behaviour.

Among other economists, Richard Thaler joined them in the early 1990s. Mainly due to these scholars, the assumption of rationality in decisions started to be challenged more widely. Experiments, initially run by psychologists and later by (experimental) economists like Vernon Smith, suggested that, when faced with particular choices or decisions, individuals do not always act rationally. Tversky and Kahneman (1973) and, later, Thaler (1991) revealed that human behaviour sometimes deviates significantly from the assumptions put forward by generations of economists. They proposed a different theoretical framework to understand how individuals make decisions known today as behavioural economics. It needs to be acknowledged, however, that political scientist Herbert A. Simon dealt with decision-making much earlier than the aforementioned scholars. As Barros (2010, p. 459) identified, he coined the famous term "bounded rationality" in 1957 as an alternative basis for the mathematical modelling of decision-making. Thanks to their contribution to behavioural economics, three of these scholars earned a Nobel Prize in Economics.[1]

Behavioural economics combines the normative backbone of economics with insights from behavioural sciences (Kahneman, 2011). The general assertion of behavioural economics is that the common assumptions made in economics about how individuals form and express preferences — that they

---

1 Herbert A. Simon in 1978, Daniel Kahneman in 2002, and Richard Thaler in 2017 earned a Nobel Prize in Economics. It appears that the reason why Amos Tversky could not earn the Nobel Prize is related to his untimely death in 1996.

xx *Book overview*

are perfectly rational, that they are perfectly self-interested, and so on – are not precise representations of how individuals think and choose (Congdon, Kling, & Mullainathan, 2009, p. 377). People are not always rational and self-interested in pursuing the outcome of their economic activity. Behavioural economics emphasizes that, due to the overwhelming complexity of evaluating outcomes and probabilities, economic actors approach uncertain decisions using heuristics. In essence, the weights used in the decision-making process of the behavioural approach are determined rather subjectively and influenced by the selection of the heuristic.

Behavioural economics provides a new lens for examining public policies. It examines different facets of economic life and asks how behavioural research can improve public well-being. As Alm and Sheffrin (2017, p. 1) suggest, the influence of behavioural economics on public economy has been very strong in areas such as compliance, savings incentives, tax incidence, time-consistent policies, and social insurance. It is possible to say that after more than a decade has passed from the publication of the pioneering *Behavioral Public Finance* book edited by Edward J. McCaffery and Joel Slemrod, we now have a rapidly developing subfield of public economics. McCaffery and Slemrod prefer to use the term "behavioural public finance" for this new discipline[2] that applies behavioural economics principles to the role of government in defining economic and social policy. They highlight that "behavioural public finance can contribute to an understanding of citizen compliance with the tax system as well as other fiscal measures to the extent that compliance decisions depend on factors beyond the rational self-interested calculus" (McCaffery & Slemrod, 2006, p. 18).

One of the most extensive applications of behavioural economics in the field of public finance has been the study of tax compliance and tax evasion decisions. Based on Becker's (1968) theory of economic crime, the Allingham-Sandmo (1972) deterrence model or standard model of tax evasion sees the taxpayer as a wealth-maximizer who weights the costs and benefits of tax evasion. Maintaining rational decision-making principles lies at the heart of this approach, which usually suggests employing frequent checks and heavy fines as political tools to enforce compliance. The deterrence model has dominated tax evasion and avoidance explanations. The deterrence model conceives taxpaying as a decision that people make by comparing the financial gain derived from the non-payment of taxes with the loss derived from the imposition of sanctions (Braithwaite & Wenzel, 2008, p. 305). However, the prevailing theories of tax compliance behaviour cannot describe or predict empirically established compliance levels. As Alm, McClelland, and Schulze (1992) indicate, because of relatively low fines and audit probabilities in most countries, taxpayers should evade more than they do. This creates a puzzle.

---

2 James Alm and Steven M. Sheffrin in their 2017 review paper prefer to use the term "behavioral public economics" instead.

It appears that people are not only after financial gain when they make their tax compliance decisions. As Feld and Frey (2007, p. 103) point out, they are influenced by government policy, by the behaviour of tax authorities and public institutions, which all in turn influence tax morale. Moreover, psychologist Erich Kirchler suggested in his 2007 book *The Economic Psychology of Tax Behaviour* that the climate of interaction between taxpayers and tax authorities is important and that coordination of power and trust in a holistic approach to understanding and regulating tax behaviour is the key. The following year, Kirchler, Hoelzl, and Wahl developed the "slippery slope framework" of tax compliance. According to this framework, tax compliance behaviour is influenced by two main dimensions, namely trust in authorities and power of authorities. Depending on the levels of trust and power, either voluntary tax compliance or enforced tax compliance is likely to be a behavioural outcome.

Behavioural economics has suggested that a guiding role of the government could be developed, a role that, at little cost to taxpayers and with little or no coercion on citizens, could improve their lives and the well-being of the society. According to Thaler and Sunstein (2008, pp. 5–6), "a nudge is any aspect of the choice architecture that alters people's behaviour predictably without forbidding any options or significantly changing their economic incentives". They argued that individuals can be nudged into making decisions that are in their best interest and the interest of society at large. The practice of behavioural insights in public policy has come a long way over the last decade. It is now increasingly used to inform and develop policy interventions. An OECD (2017, p. 12) publication identifies that behavioural insights can improve policy-makers' understanding of the behavioural drivers of tax compliance and can help them develop more effective policies to tackle tax compliance. Currently, many countries around the world have been adopting various behaviourally informed tools and methodologies to improve the way policies and interventions are formulated and delivered. Leicester, Levell, and Rasul (2012) suggest that perhaps the most visible application of behavioural economics has been the development of "nudge" policies. Such policies emphasize a change in how decisions are presented or a change in the environment where decisions are made, thus triggering significant behavioural shifts.

With contributions from leading academics from a variety of countries and backgrounds, this book examines taxation, public spending, and public policy-making from the perspective of the behavioural, political, and social contexts that generate them. The book aims to create interaction among academics from different areas of economy and other related social sciences. Contributors examine public finance through the lenses of behavioural, political, and social aspects that go beyond traditional allocation, redistribution, and stabilization approaches. The chapters scrutinize behavioural biases of individuals on taxes and investigate the impact of social context, social capital, and societal cooperation on public finance. They reflect combinations of theoretical and empirical approaches that together can provide solid qualitative and quantitative rules

xxii *Book overview*

for optimal policies. We believe that the book will stir the interest of academic researchers, graduates in behavioural economics, economic psychology, tax professionals, practitioners, policy-makers, and the general public alike.

Organization of the book

This volume revisits core issues of public finance by making use of a psychologically richer perspective on human behaviour. Chapters constitute an intersection between behavioural economics and public finance. They examine either theoretically or empirically different dimensions of public finance. Moreover, chapters analyse fundamental questions regarding the mechanisms of public finance and tax compliance models through a behavioural lens. The book consists of three parts: theoretical considerations on behavioural public finance; behavioural responses to regulations; cases of tax compliance behaviour.

Part I

Theoretical considerations on behavioural public finance

The first part provides a theoretical basis for the behavioural approach and presents an overview of the field. In Chapter 1, **Vito Tanzi** sets the stage indicating that in recent decades various economists and psychologists identified systematic acts of irrational behaviour, which led to the creation of "behavioural" and "experimental" economics. Although Tanzi acknowledges that governments can play a tutorial role to promote rational behaviour and public welfare, he does not expect an automatic positive outcome. The author cautions about such a role because governments may not always necessarily act in the best interest of the citizens.

In Chapter 2, **Morris Altman** addresses some key public finance questions through the lenses of a smart agent with bounded rationality. He argues that core behavioural and institutional assumptions made by conventional literature are typically not consistent with facts. According to him, more realistic assumptions yield the prediction that government expenditure for productive usage can have a long-lasting positive impact on the economy and society. Of course, this depends on rational and smart agents.

In Chapter 3, **Julia Dobreva** introduces behavioural economics on a conceptual level. She discusses the role that behavioural economics has in shaping modern policies for decision-making. The author also examines the main perspectives of the interrelation between behavioural economics and public policy, focusing particularly on public health and education policies. She concludes that the behavioural elements of each policy are tightly related to the individual decision-making process, which ultimately affects public choice and its social consequences.

Part II

Behavioural responses to regulations

This part addresses the behavioural dimension of international taxation and regulations. Authors apply behavioural insights to the issues that are covered.

In Chapter 4, **Uwe Dulleck** discusses the fundamental concepts of implementing performance-based measures to financial regulation. Drawing on empirical methods and insights from the field of behavioural economics, he describes regulatory approaches that are not based on mandatory content and/or mandatory forms of financial services provided. Although this discussion is focused on the Australian context, Dulleck illustrates that legal obstacles to such regulatory approaches are unlikely to be insurmountable and can be implemented in most countries.

In Chapter 5, **Reuven S. Avi-Yonah** and **Kaijie Wu** examine three examples of availability heuristic that affect political actors and the unwanted consequences of their reactions. All examples come from US international tax regulations. The authors therefore document the foreign investment in real property tax act, the exit tax on US expats, and the enforcement of withholding tax on dividend equivalents. They suggest that conventional "rational actor" approaches inspired by "economic" versions of rationality need to consider own biases of political actors.

In Chapter 6, **John Prebble** inquires whether behavioural economics can help a legislature decide whether to enact a general anti-avoidance rule and, if so, whether discipline enables citizens to predict the form of the rule that will be enacted. The discussion in this chapter suggests that there is little, if any, useful role for behavioural economics in identifying principles that could be applied to determine certain legal policy. Despite this, however, the author suggests that behavioural economics may provide insights for governments to clamp down on tax avoidance.

Part III

Tax compliance behaviour: cases

The chapters in this part address the behavioural dimensions of the economics of taxation, particularly focusing on their revenue-raising aspect. Authors aim to provide evidence from the psychology and behavioural economics literature.

In Chapter 7, **M. Mustafa Erdoğdu** and **Osman Geyik** examine state–society–individual relations to shed further light on interactions between tax compliance determinants. The chapter focuses particularly on taxpayers' fairness assessment of their burdens and their trust in governing institutions. Findings of the case studies carried out in the Turkish cities of Istanbul, Şanlıurfa, and Diyarbakır suggest that taxpayers' fairness perception of the tax system and their

xxiv *Book overview*

satisfaction derived from public services play a much larger role than the one generally assumed in the literature addressing voluntary tax compliance.

Because taxes have a significant psychological component, **Janina Enachescu, Žiga Puklavec, Christian Martin Bauer, Jerome Olsen, Erich Kirchler,** and **James Alm** discuss psychological perspectives concerning tax behaviour in Chapter 8. Initially, authors present an investigation of the role that emotions play in tax compliance decisions. They introduce various emotion theories that show different ways in which emotions can potentially influence tax decisions. Next, they present an experimental study that examines the impact of positive and negative sentiments on tax compliance. Finally, authors suggest that a fruitful path for future research would be to integrate emotions into the slippery slope framework of tax compliance.

In Chapter 9, **Larissa Batrancea, Anca Nichita, Carla Startin, Ioan Chirila, Ioan Batrancea, Robert W. McGee, Serkan Benk,** and **Tamer Budak** explore insights into the moral concerns and personal beliefs surrounding tax evasion of participants from Germany, United Kingdom, Romania, and Turkey. As a result of the cross-cultural study they carried out, the authors suggest that in countries where the vast majority of taxpayers favour compliance, authorities should provide high-quality public goods to reward their cooperative stances and therefore increase tax compliance levels. The more a large number of citizens believe that tax evasion is always unjustifiable and that taxpaying should be the norm for everybody, the more compliance levels might increase. Such an outcome would benefit individuals and the overall society in the long run.

In Chapter 10, **John D'Attoma, Clara Volintiru,** and **Antoine Malézieux** make an empirical contribution to the literature by examining whether gender differences in tax compliance are due to increased prosociality among women. In their cross-national tax compliance experiment in Italy, UK, USA, Sweden, and Romania, they find that women are not more prosocial than men. They conclude that the differences in prosociality between men and women appear to be contextual, but the differences in tax compliance are much more consistent.

In Chapter 11, **Elaine Doyle, Brian Keegan,** and **Eoin Reeves** explore conceptually whether the existing tax compliance theories are appropriate since tax systems from developed countries rely heavily on fiduciary tax collection mechanisms. Authors suggest that a focus on individual taxpayers' compliance decisions in the context of their direct engagement with revenue authorities needs to be broadened out in order to increase the contribution of fiduciary taxes to the overall tax yield.

In Chapter 12, **Paul Frijters, Katharina Gangl,** and **Benno Torgler** focus on ways to tax the powerful and the sophisticated, particularly the biggest non-state organizations and the wealthiest individuals. The authors first present a brief and stylized history of taxation, then summarize different forms of taxation (*i.e.*, recurrent, incidental, seigniorage, tribute, and accounting-based tax) and present examples of how plutocrats were taxed in the past. Based on this

Book overview xxv

review, the tribute tax is suggested to be an old strategy suitable for today's plutocrats.

In Chapter 13, **Yingyue Ding, Jane Frecknall-Hughes**, and **Ja Ryong Kim** examine the impact of media reports on tax avoidance in the UK using Starbucks as a case study. Based on stakeholder theory, they contribute to the literature on corporate tax avoidance by assessing how media may trigger reputational loss for a company that engages in tax avoidance and on its subsequent tax compliance behaviour. Their findings have a practical implication in that media reports can act as a means of amending tax avoidance behaviour, which may be useful for tax authorities.

In Chapter 14, **N. Tolga Saruç, Çiğdem Börke Tunalı, Hakan Yavuz**, and **Tunç İnce** analyse media effect, especially the effect of newspaper news about taxes on people's tax compliance decisions. Their results indicate that news about frequent tax amnesties and large amounts of tax evasion have a negative effect on tax compliance. Therefore, the authors suggest that when considering to enact a new tax amnesty, its potential effect on trust and tax duty amongst taxpayers should be carefully taken into account by tax authorities.

References

Allingham, M. G., & Sandmo, A. (1972). Income tax evasion: A theoretical analysis. *Journal of Public Economics, 1*, 323–338.

Alm, J., McClelland, G. H., & Schulze, W. D. (1992). Why do people pay taxes? *Journal of Public Economics, 48*, 21–38.

Alm, J., & Sheffrin, S. M. (2017). Using behavioral economics in public economics. *Public Finance Review, 45*(1), 4–9.

Barros, G. (2010). Herbert A. Simon and the concept of rationality: Boundaries and procedures. *Brazilian Journal of Political Economy, 30*(3), 455–472.

Becker, G. S. (1968). Crime and punishment: An economic approach. *Journal of Political Economy, 76*(2), 169–217.

Braithwaite, V. A., & Wenzel, M. (2008). Integrating explanations of tax evasion and avoidance. In: A. Lewis (Ed.), *The Cambridge handbook of psychology and economic behaviour* (pp. 304–333). Cambridge: Cambridge University Press.

Congdon, W. J., Kling, J. R., & Mullainathan, S. (2009). Behavioral economics and tax policy. *National Tax Journal, 62*(3), 375–386.

Feld, L. P., & Frey, B. S. (2007). Tax compliance as the result of a psychological tax contract: The role of incentives and responsive regulation. *Law & Policy, 29*(1), 102–120.

Kahneman, D. (2011). *Thinking, fast and slow*. New York: Farrar Straus and Giroux.

Kirchler, E. (2007). *The economic psychology of tax behaviour*. Cambridge: Cambridge University Press.

Kirchler, E., Hoelzl, E., & Wahl, I. (2008). Enforced versus voluntary tax compliance: The "slippery slope" framework. *Journal of Economic Psychology, 29*, 210–225.

Leicester, A., Levell, P., & Rasul, I. (2012). *Tax and benefit policy: Insights from behavioural economics*. London: Institute for Fiscal Studies.

McCaffery, E., & Slemrod, J. (Eds.) (2006). *Behavioral public finance*. New York: Russell Sage Foundation.

xxvi *Book overview*

OECD (2017). *Behavioural insights and public policy: Lessons from around the world.* Paris: OECD Publishing.

Simon, H. A. (1957). *Models of man, social and rational: Mathematical essays on rational human behavior in a social setting.* New York: John Wiley and Sons.

Thaler, R. H. (1991). *Quasi-rational economics.* New York: Russell Sage Foundation.

Thaler, R. H., & Sunstein, C. R. (2008). *Nudge: Improving decisions about health, wealth, and happiness.* New Haven, CT: Yale University Press.

Tversky, A., & Kahneman, D. (1973). Availability: A heuristic for judging frequency and probability. *Cognitive Psychology, 5,* 207–232.

Part I

Theoretical considerations on behavioural public finance

1 Behavioral public finance in a populist world

Vito Tanzi

Introduction

The traditional approach to public finance, as it was best described by Richard Musgrave's classic 1959 book, *The Theory of Public Finance*, assumed that a group of individuals, within a given geographical area, establishes a governing body to promote the social or community goals of the individuals who make up the group. Because of free-rider and other problems, these social goals are difficult to promote and achieve through the uncoordinated actions of the individual members. A governing body is needed to promote these goals, by producing public goods, by creating needed institutions, and by coordinating the financing of the public spending. This approach also reflected a particularly optimistic view of the government. The government has been created by the individuals that make up the community, is charged by them with satisfying their social needs, and it will do exactly what is expected of it.

It has been recognized that the government's actions may not always be easy. In democracies it may be difficult to determine what public goods to produce, in what quantity, and how to determine who should pay for them. See on this the classic works by Arrow (1951) and Downs (1957). The government may also make honest mistakes in that pursuit and may be less efficient in its operations than it could theoretically be. However, its ultimate goal is not questioned. In the traditional voluntary-exchange approach, the approach that has characterized traditional public finance literature, that goal has remained the pursuit of the public interest as it is seen by the individuals of the community.

To promote the public interest, the government has available to it particular resources and tools. Of these, the main ones are: taxes, public spending, and regulations, although it may also occasionally rely on less traditional, or less orthodox, tools and resources (see, Tanzi, 2018a, ch. 13 for a fuller listing of government tools and resources). Much of the traditional literature in public finance has dealt with the use (optimal or otherwise) of the above, main, instruments. In more recent decades, however, some concerns were raised by economists from the School of Public Choice, that the tools that governments use might be abused for political purposes, and by economists from the Chicago School

4   *Vito Tanzi*

or the Austrian School, that large public sector activity such as high taxes may interfere with the work of the free market.

Since the publication of Musgrave's book, which systematized public finance economics, the pursuit of the public interest by the government has been decomposed in, or made to depend on, three main areas of concerns: (a) the allocation of resources, to get the best use out of available resources; (b) the distribution of income, to satisfy some community perception of fairness on how different standards of living of the population in the community ought to be allowed to be; and (c) the stabilization of the economy, to ensure that the available resources (labor and capital) are fully employed and do not remain underemployed because of recessions.

The aforementioned traditional approach to public finance generally accepted the assumption that the government works to promote the public interest and that individuals, both those in private sector activities and those working for the government, are rational and act rationally. In their actions, they are not influenced by *irrational* biases, or are guided by *irrational* behavior. Both when they act in what could be defined as their strictly *personal* interests, or when they act in the interest of the whole community, they act *rationally*. Even acts of corruption, or other dishonest or antisocial acts that may occur, are assumed to be guided by rationality, if not always by honesty. In addition, it was accepted that governments have a clear interest in maximizing the welfare of the community, as that welfare is conceived by the individuals who make up the community; and that consumer sovereignty, based on the rationality of the individuals, remains the basis for evaluating public policy (McCaffery & Slemrod, 2006).

Do individuals act rationally?

In the distant past, economists, such as Adam Smith, David Hume, David Ricardo, Vilfredo Pareto, and others, had, at times, discussed psychologically based reactions, as, for example, in the Ricardian Equivalence hypothesis; in Hume's explanation of why governments tended to borrow more than they should, or in the more recent rational expectations theories, to explain particular behaviors by private individuals or by government officials. However, the assumption of rationality on the part of the economic actors continued to be maintained, and it was defended by major economists. That assumption was seen as the best, or the most realistic, to make. And so was the prevailing view of the role of the government.

In 1955, Herbert Simon theorized that "rationality" may be "bounded" so that the assumption of rationality by individuals should be seen as having limits. Other economists, including Katona, in 1975 and Schelling, in 1978, also raised some questions about the assumption of rationality. However, those remained isolated challenges and they attracted limited attention. In more recent years, however, partly because of the initial work by psychologists, especially Amos Tversky and Daniel Kahneman (1974; 1992; Kahneman and Tversky, 1979),

Behavioral public finance in a populist world 5

the assumption of rationality in decisions started to be challenged more widely. Experiments, initially by psychologists and later by (experimental) economists, suggested that, when faced with particular choices or decisions, individuals do not always act rationally. They tend to rely on heuristics, on rules of thumb, that have been largely formed by past experiences. Often, they also give more weight to short run results, compared to, presumably superior, longer run results, and to expected losses compared to objectively superior, expected, gains. It could of course be assumed that the rules of thumb may be rational, in the sense that they may save time and effort, but they may also lead to occasional costly mistakes.

Psychologists and experimental economists have argued that cognition can be affected by biases, just as vision can be affected by optical illusions. Past experiences have made individuals expect particular outcomes, because, in their minds, they have formed models of behavior, or expectations, that they tend to apply to new situations, challenging rational behavior. This is especially the case when the time to make decisions is short (List, 2004; Kahneman, 2011). Past experiences create patterns of thoughts, or expectations that act as filters, when individuals have to make decisions. These filters may lead to non-optimal choices, because they have created biases that favor particular outcomes. Furthermore, it has been argued that the irrationality may, in some ways, have a predictable pattern, because mistakes are repeated (Ariely, 2008).

Such reasoning naturally requires agreement on how to define rationality and rational behavior, and such agreement has not always been accepted and the definition of irrationality has been challenged by some economists (Sugden, 2017). If correct, the finding about systematic irrationality in behavior would be a strong challenge to the fundamental hypothesis of market efficiency. That is the hypothesis that had prevailed among most economists. A strong defender of that assumption had been the late Milton Friedman. It has continued to be strongly defended by economists associated with the Chicago School and the Austrian School.

Not surprising, the finding of significant irrationality, especially in financial markets, has been challenged by some economists, as, for example, by Eugene Fama, a prominent Chicago professor who, in 2013, shared the Nobel Prize in economics with Lars Peter Hansen and Robert J. Shiller. Fama and others, who have continued to believe in the efficiency of the market, have seen behavioral economics as an unconvincing challenge to orthodox economics (Fama, 1970; Fama & French, 2000). It was faith in the market that had characterized the *laissez faire* ideology that had prevailed in the past, has been behind *the efficient market hypothesis*, and that supported the *market fundamentalism* that prevailed in recent decades.

The assumption of irrationality in human behavior is also, inevitably and importantly, an invitation to governments to intervene, to correct for irrational acts of citizens. This is especially the case in the financial market, but it extends to decisions by individuals in other areas. Irrationality can be seen as a special kind of *market failure*. Like traditional market failures, it challenges the work

6   *Vito Tanzi*

and the efficiency of the market, making it less optimal in its results, and invites governments to intervene, with regulations and with other public finance instruments.

An early and significant reference to *irrational behavior* in the financial market was made by Alan Greenspan, in a speech delivered in December 1996 (Greenspan, 2007, p. 177). At that time, Greenspan had become worried by the enormous growth that was taking place in asset prices in the technological sector. He considered that growth excessive, unjustified, and clearly irrational. Other and more articulate cases for the existence of *irrational exuberance*, also in the financial sector, were made, in 1989 and 2000, in important books by Robert Shiller. See also, Kindleberger and Aliber (2005) and Smith, Suchanek, and Williams (1988). Irrationality, and the bubble that it was causing, would lead to the 2007–2008 financial crisis, and to the Great Recession that followed.

Several examples of presumed irrationality in decisions, in areas other than the financial sector (sport, medical field, wealth decisions, choices about foods, etc.) have been reported in recent years by both psychologists and by a growing number of "experimental economists" (Thaler & Sunstein, 2008; Thaler, 2015; Lewis, 2017). Systemic, or "predictably irrational" mistakes, as distinguished from "random" mistakes, are now believed, by behavioral economists, to characterize many individuals' actions. For example, it is maintained that irrational mistakes were made by many of the individuals who bought houses that they could hardly afford given their incomes, with borrowed money, before the 2007–2008 financial crisis; or by those who invested in technological stocks, in the late 1990s (Shiller, 2000; Greenspan, 2007). The minds of these investors had been conditioned by their recent experiences that had made them believe that upward trends of the prices of houses or technological stocks would continue in future years.

While the assumption of rationality in human behavior had been initially challenged mainly by only a few psychologists, it started to attract some economists, and some of them used controlled, or laboratory, experiments, to determine whether individuals acted rationally when they made particular choices. See also, Shiller (1989) and Shleifer (2000). After Daniel Kahneman, a psychologist, and Vernon Smith, an economist, shared the Nobel Memorial Prize in Economic Sciences in 2002 for their separate work on irrational behavior, and after the publication of Shiller's 2000 book, these ideas acquired a larger following among economists. **Behavioral economics and experimental economics** became significant, new, and lively branches of economics.

In recent years, economists have made important contributions to the area of *behavioral economics*, and other economists have earned Nobel Prizes for their contributions to that area. In 2013, Robert J. Shiller received the Prize for having argued that irrationality dominates financial markets. Interestingly, Shiller shared the Nobel Prize with Eugene Fama and Lans Peter Hansen, both strong defenders of the rationality of financial markets. As they had done occasionally in the past, those who confer the Nobel Prize had decided to

Behavioral public finance in a populist world 7

hedge their bets between those who believed in the rationality and those who believed in the irrationality of financial markets.

In 2017, Richard Thaler also earned the Nobel Prize in economics for his more general work in *behavioral economics*. He reported many examples of irrationality in the behavior of individuals in several areas. *These* prizes helped give much publicity to this area. Behavioral economics had attracted the attention of governments and some of them recognized that a new and potentially useful tool for promoting their goals (without the coercive use of taxes, public spending, and regulations) had become available and could be used.

Behavioral economics has attracted a large following among economists but, to some extent, it has remained controversial. There has not been a "Behavioral Economics Revolution" as there had been a "Keynesian Revolution", in the 1940s (Klein, 1947). Both believers and non-believers have been given Nobel Prizes, sometimes, as we saw with Shiller and Fama, in the same year. Over the past two decades, several books and hundreds of articles in professional journals have dealt with this new area and some of the books have become "best sellers". These have included: Shiller (2000); Ariely (2008); Thaler & Sunstein (2008); Akerlof & Shiller (2011); Kahneman (2011); Lewis (2017).

A tutorial role for governments?

If the market fails, because of irrational behavior by those who participate in it, the obvious question is whether, as with other kinds of market failures, the government could play a role in correcting the failures. Behavioral economics has inevitably raised the question of whether some of its findings could not be used, by a caring government, to promote the goal of a better society, and an optimal allocation of resources. Putting it differently, is there a **tutorial role** that could be assigned to governments, to make citizens operate more rationally? In addition to its traditional tools that are available in promoting the public interest, and in correcting for traditional market failures (Bator, 1958), should the government rely on the findings of behavioral economics to promote the public interest?

Behavioral economics has suggested that a **tutorial role** by the government could be developed, a role that, at little cost to taxpayers and with little or no coercion on citizens, could improve their lives and the welfare of society. Such a tutorial role would use "choice architecture" and "nudges" – concepts developed by Thaler and Sunstein (2008) – to induce individuals to make better choices. This behavioral public finance approach has been called **libertarian paternalism**, because it is claimed that significant and desirable social goals can be promoted by the government, without coercion, and with trivial public spending. In this *tutorial role* the government would not use its traditional public finance tools (taxes, public spending, and regulations) to *force* individuals to make changes in directions considered desirable. Rather, it would use **nudges**, that is delicate pushes, to encourage them to make more rational choices.

8 *Vito Tanzi*

The promoters of this approach have claimed that the areas of health, wealth, happiness, and some others could be improved by friendly **nudges**.

Thaler and Sunstein defined nudges as "any aspect of the *choice architecture* that alters people's behavior in a predictable [and desirable] way without forbidding any options, or significantly changing their economic incentives ... [They stressed that] Nudges are not mandates". Individuals would be free to continue to make irrational decisions, if they wanted to. Nudges can be developed from observed anomalies, or from the results of laboratory experiments. The supporters of this approach have maintained that nudges can be useful tools that a democratic, efficient, and caring government could use to promote the well-being of citizens.

This was an offer that governments could hardly refuse. In recent years, several countries' governments, starting with the UK's Cameron government in 2010, seized the opportunity and created what came to be called "Social and Behavioral Sciences'Teams", or "Behavioral Insights Teams". The UK example was followed by that of the USA, Australia, Denmark, South Africa, and a few other countries that also created such teams. Some of these teams have produced annual reports that describe their activities and that provide a list of claimed successes. An example is the US Executive Office of the President, 2015 *Annual Report*, which listed what was attempted and what was achieved.

These teams hired individuals from different fields and backgrounds (psychology, political science, sociology, accounting, economics, statistics, public administration, law, and some others) and attempted to influence, with the use of nudges, the behavior or the choices of citizens, in their roles as consumers, savers, taxpayers, polluters, and others. With nudges, they have tried to encourage individuals to choose more nutritive foods, to save more money for retirement, to smoke or drink less, to exercise more, to pollute less, to comply more with tax obligations, to stay in school, and to promote other presumably healthy, welfare-enhancing, efficient, and environmentally sound actions.

The application of behavioral economics has been wide and, as mentioned, it has addressed several areas of economics, including tax policy and tax collection, economic development, public spending, etc. (McCaffery & Slemrod, 2006; Lewis, 2017; John, 2018; Datta & Mullainathan, 2012; Congdon, Kling, & Mullainathan, 2009; Leicester, Levell, & Rasul, 2012). It has also covered areas outside of economics. Clearly, the more efficient and effective are the "nudges", the more impact they can have on the activities and on the choices that individuals make, and, indirectly, on government spending. For example, if nudges can induce individuals to exercise more and to eat healthier foods, governments might have to spend less on curative public health. If individuals can be made to save more for their retirement, governments may have to spend less on assisting individuals in old age. If bubbles can be avoided, by reducing irrational exuberance in financial decisions, governments would spend less for counter-cyclical fiscal policies, when bubbles lead to recessions, as they did, after 2008. In the rest of this chapter we confine the discussion mainly to the public finance area.

Behavioral public finance in a populist world   9

While strong claims have been made by the advocates of the behavioral approach and about the use of nudges, the concrete evidence, that the new approach has worked in practice and that it has generated noticeable or significant results, is still limited. The evidence available has come mostly from questionable laboratory experiments, or from rather trivial behavioral changes, which have been often repeated and advertised. See James and Edwards (2014) and Hallsworth, List, Metcalfe, and Vlaev (2014). These have included those indicating that letters sent to tax non-filers may induce some increase in tax compliance; those indicating that giving a "default choice" to workers, in voluntary saving programs, may encourage some workers to subscribe to the programs; or that placing vegetables in front of a cafeteria display leads to more eating of vegetables.

Those who have worked in the field of technical assistance to countries (in tax administrations, or in other government programs) have been aware that, to some extent, governments had always used some intuitive, behavioral approaches to encourage desirable behavior on the part of citizens. For example, in the 1970s, the Brazilian government put up many posters all over Brazilian cities' walls. The posters were black and carried the statement that the black represented the *souls* of tax evaders. During World War I, the US government put up many posters (some of which can be seen in the Museum of Fine Arts, Boston) to encourage young men to volunteer for the US Army. In Italy and France, at the beginning of World War II, citizens were encouraged to donate gold, including wedding rings, to the governments to help finance the war effort.

Tax experts have known for a long time that hidden taxes (such as the European value added taxes) are more easily paid than disclosed taxes (*i.e.*, excise taxes of some US states) (Dalton, 1967, p. 33). They have also known that tax withheld at the source, especially if each withholding is small because it is spread over long periods, enjoys more tax compliance. When Ronald Reagan was governor of California he wanted to abolish withholding income taxes at the source, because he hated taxes and wanted to reduce tax revenue and public spending in California. These and similar actions were not supported by behavioral economics, but simply by intuition.

While it may be too early to judge the long-run results of the behavioral approach, there is still too little concrete evidence that it has made a significant (as distinguished from a trivial) difference in the size, the efficiency of public spending, the level and the structure of taxation. Taxes have remained more complicated than they could be, and so have government programs (Tanzi, 2018a). And tax compliance has remained a problem in many countries. As good or even better results might have been achieved by simply promoting more simplicity in public policies (Tanzi, 2017, 2018a, 2018b). Simplicity has not yet been given the importance that it deserves, by economists and by policymakers, and it should be considered a powerful, general nudge, or a more efficient alternative to many nudges.

Equally, outside of the public finance area in many countries: (a) the incidence of obesity and illnesses related to it, such as diabetes, have been growing;

10 *Vito Tanzi*

(b) the saving rate has been coming down; and (c) private debt has continued to rise. Impressionistic evidence does not indicate that the health and the degree of happiness of the populations have improved. Recent evidence has indicated that the score for happiness in the USA has fallen. Other expected and significant beneficial effects from nudges do not seem to have occurred, except in limited cases, or in laboratory experiments. However, in all fairness, it must be repeated that a final judgment on the value of behavioral public economics, and of libertarian paternalism, to achieve desirable outcomes, may have to wait more years. It can be argued that without the nudges the situation would have worsened even more.

Recent evidence also indicates that the initial enthusiasm for the new approach may have abated a little, at least among some governments. For example, the Trump government eliminated the "Behavioral Team" that had been installed in the White House by the Obama Administration to promote "libertarian paternalism" (Stillman, 2017). There has been much less news coming from the British team in recent years, as compared with the period when the Cameron government had been in place.

Use of nudges in authoritarian governments

Perhaps, an important question to ask is whether the behavioral, or libertarian approach that has been promoted by behavioral economists, and that would use government *nudges*, would necessarily generate desirable results in an era when governments are becoming more populist and more authoritarian, when it has become increasingly difficult to distinguish correct and objective news or facts, from "fake news" or "fake facts". In such a world, governments might use not only "good" nudges but also "bad" or "fake nudges". Putting it differently, would the behavioral approach depend on the kind of government in power? This is a different question from the, also important, question of whether people want to be nudged (see, Sugden, 2017, for the latter). This question has not been raised.

To some extent, we are facing a situation somewhat similar to the one that was faced in the 1940s and 1950s, when discoveries by economists of an increasing number of "market failures", combined with a new, optimistic view of what *democratic and well-intentioned* governments could do to raise the welfare of the populations, led to large, rapid, and not always wise increases in public spending and in taxes in advanced countries, and it led to the creation of "welfare states". That development also led, in time, to the rise of the School of Public Choice, a school that argued that governments' interventions had not always been in the public interest (Mueller, 1993; several works by James Buchanan, 1960, 1975). The view that growing state intervention had not necessarily been desirable led, in turn, to the *market fundamentalism* of the 1980s and 1990s.

Putting it differently, does the discovery by psychologists and experimental economists of some irrationalities in the behavior of individuals always or necessarily justify the use of nudges by governments? Does it justify it, regardless of the type of government in power and the views of the nudged individuals?

Behavioral public finance in a populist world 11

We shall deal with only the first of these questions, by relying on some little-known Italian literature of the early part of the last century. That literature was associated with economists such as Pareto, Puviani, Loria, Fasiani, and others.

The Italian "Scienza delle Finanze" relates specifically to the kind of government that different countries may have and to the use that those governments might make of what the Italian literature called *fiscal illusions*. Fiscal illusions may be considered as "bad nudges" or "fake nudges" which, like bad publicity to sell products and services to consumers, may be used to encourage citizens to make bad choices. The advertising industry may contain important messages for behavioral economics.

Governments may use particular situations, or the intentional mis-presentation of data or policies with the objective of reducing taxpayers' resistance to higher taxes, increasing citizens' acceptability of some inefficient public spending, or to "sell" bad policies. These are the fiscal illusions. For examples related to taxes see especially Puviani ([1903] 1973) and Fasiani (1951). A brief description of that literature is available in chapter 1 of Tanzi (2000). Essentially, governments have used particular moments when the attention or the resistance of taxpayers is weakest to impose some taxes. They may also use misleading information to "sell" some spending policies.

The main message that comes from the Italian literature is that it may be naïve to assume an optimistic view of the government role and behavior, the role that came to prevail and to be accepted by the Anglo-Saxon literature, as shown in Groves (1954), Musgrave (1959), and most other books until the advent of the School of Public Choice. Historic reasons may have been behind the attitudes of the Italian public finance economist (Tanzi, 2018c) as they may be behind the fact that Southern "states" in the USA have been much more suspicious of a larger US, federal government role than the "states" in the North.

If governments and the policymakers that make decisions for them aimed only and always at maximizing the public interest; if they did not suffer from biases and irrationality; if there were no or few disagreements on what the public welfare is, and on how to promote it; and if the governments were efficient in their actions, then nudges could be a welcome addition to the ammunitions already available to the governments, to promote policies and behavior that would promote welfare.

Unfortunately, the above conditions are often not met. Furthermore, in recent years, we seem to have entered a period in which (a) the distribution of the national pie (the size of the national income) has become as important, or more important, than the size of the pie, raising questions on how to define the *public interest*, and (b) where some previously accepted fundamental truths, such as the merit of free trade, balanced budgets, fair and progressive taxation, the benefits of a clean environment, pursued with policies that would contain pollution and global warming, and other "truths", are being more widely questioned, even by governments.

In this new anti-scientific environment, *fake, or manipulated, news* has often replaced real, objective news; and fake news or false facts have influenced the

12 *Vito Tanzi*

views of less sophisticated citizens and their votes in democratic countries. In this "brave new world" it has become increasingly difficult to distinguish, or to agree on, what are good policies. It has also become more difficult to assume that the governments in charge would necessarily use nudges to pursue clear and objective interpretations of the public interest. Some governments might prefer to promote the interests of those who, directly or indirectly, are controlling the government, lobbies, and other particular groups. Again the advertising industry may have some important messages for this possibility.

In such a political and social environment, one that seems to be becoming more common, as Albright (2018) has argued in a recent book, the *kind* of government in charge, the one that would use the nudges, becomes an important consideration in judging the wisdom of giving it the use of the new policy instrument. One would be reluctant to give the additional tool provided by nudges to a government that would use it to promote its own interests, and not those of the population.

The Italian literature mentioned above did not have unrealistic expectations. It recognized that governments can differ in fundamental ways, and that some are better than others. That literature assumed that often there are groups that control the reins of governments. The reality was ignored in the Anglo-Saxon literature, until some recent recognition by the School of Public Choice. The School had been influenced by the Italian literature, through James Buchanan, the creator of that school who in the 1950s had spent time in Italy and had studied the Scienza delle Finanze. However, the Public Choice literature has assumed that *all* governments can suffer from particular shortcomings.

The Italian literature had identified three primal or pure types of governments. Each would make a different use of the tools available to them, including fiscal illusions and, now, nudges. The three types are: the *individualistic* state; the *paternalistic* state; and the *monopolistic* state. It should be stressed that the Italian literature recognized that those kinds of governments almost never existed in their pure forms because all governments share some shortcomings. However, real life governments tend to approach in their behavior more of the above primal types than the others.

The *individualistic* state is the one, implicitly or explicitly, closest to the traditional *voluntary-exchange approach*. It is the one assumed by Musgrave (1959) and Groves (1954). As Groves (1954, p. 6) put it, in this state "the individual not only has a voice in determining the role of the state, [but] the *state exists only to serve him*" (italics added). An important characteristics of this first group is that the state is a genuine "democracy" in which the citizens have ways to express their views and to influence the government. In it nudges could be used and, if they were effective, they could have a useful impact on public spending, on tax compliance, and on public welfare in general.

The *paternalistic* state might pay less attention to the wishes of *individual* citizens but still promoted the welfare of the community, as that welfare is interpreted by the policymakers. The paternalistic state would not hesitate to replace the wishes of the individual citizens with those of the government leaders, if the latter think that they are for the good of the country. Thus, in some sense, the government could exhibit authoritarian traits, but it would do so by keeping in mind the interests of the community. There are some governments in the world today, as for example that of Singapore, which approach the paternalistic definition. China may also claim to represent this paternalistic state.

Such a paternalistic state might use nudges, in addition to the other tools, for what it considered to be the good of the citizens. However, the nudges could have more coercion. Also, more often, it might move the choices of the individuals away from what they might have liked. For example, one who enjoyed the pleasure of smoking, or that of eating delicious but unhealthy foods, might have wished to trade a shorter, expected, life expectancy for the current pleasures. A paternalistic government would try to prevent that. For example, by changing the "choice architecture" it might use nudges and more coercive tools to make smoking more difficult and more expensive, for example, by prohibiting smoking in public places, including public parks, or by allowing the sale of cigarettes only in specified places. Presumably these actions would be taken for the benefit of the citizens.

The *monopolistic* state is the kind of government closest to Puviani's own conception of how governments actually operate in the real world. Puviani's conception is more removed from the idealistic Anglo-Saxon, voluntary-exchange conception. In this kind of state, a "ruling class" or a ruling group comes to control the government's apparatus and it uses it not to promote the public interest but to maximize that of the ruling class. In this government, of which there are many examples in today's world, there is little genuine concern for the citizens and their choices are much constrained. However, it may still be politically convenient for the government to use "fiscal illusions" and "fake nudges", rather than direct coercion, to push individuals toward choices that ultimately aim at maximizing the wealth and the welfare of the members of the ruling class.

Concluding comment

Readers of this chapter may have their views of the kind of government that is running the country in which they live. If they live in an *individualistic* state, and believe that their government is efficient and relatively corruption free, they may welcome the recent literature on behavioral economics and the suggested uses of nudges that it has proposed. The nudges would aim at promoting the general welfare. If their assessment is that they live in countries where the two other kinds of governments are in place, they may be less inclined to do so. Especially if they think that their government is of the monopolistic kind, they may wish to think twice before welcoming the use of nudges.

Unfortunately, recent trends seem to indicate that libertarian or even monopolistic governments are becoming more common (Albright, 2018).

14   *Vito Tanzi*

References

Akerlof, G.A., & Shiller R. J. (2011). *Animal spirits: How human psychology drives the economy, and why it matters for global capitalism*. Princeton, NJ: Princeton University Press.

Albright, M. (2018). *Fascism: A warning*. New York: HarperCollins.

Ariely, D. (2008). *Predictably irrational: The hidden forces that shape our decisions*. New York: HarperCollins.

Arrow, K. J. (1951). *Social choice and individual values*. New York: John Wiley and Sons.

Bator, F. M. (1958). The anatomy of market failure. *The Quarterly Journal of Economics*, 72(3), 351–379.

Buchanan, J. M. (1960). La Scienza delle Finanze. In: J. M. Buchanan (Ed.), *Fiscal theory and political economy* (pp. 24–74). Chapel Hill, NC: University of North Carolina Press.

Buchanan, J. M. (1975). Public finance and public choice. *National Tax Journal, 28*, 383–394.

Congdon, W. J., Kling, J. R., & Mullainathan, S. (2009). Behavioral economics and tax policy. *National Tax Journal, 62*(3), 375–386.

Dalton, H. (1967). *Principles of public finance*. New York: Augustus M. Kelley.

Datta, S., & Mullainathan, S. (2012). Behavioral design: A new approach to development policy. CGD Policy Paper 016, Washington, DC: Center for Global Development.

Downs, A. (1957). *An economic theory of democracy*. New York: Harper and Row.

Fama, E. F. (1970). Efficient capital markets: A review of theory and empirical work. *The Journal of Finance, 25*, 383–417.

Fama, E. F., & French, K. R. (2000). Forecasting profitability and returns. *Journal of Business, 73*, 161–175.

Fasiani, M. (1951). *Principi di Scienza delle Finanze*. Torino: G. Giappinelli Editore.

Greenspan, A. (2007). *The age of turbulence: Adventures in a new world*. New York: Penguin.

Groves, H. M. (1954). *Financing government* (4th ed.). New York: Henry Holt and Company.

Hallsworth, M., List, J. A., Metcalfe, R. D., & Vlaev, I. (2014). The behavioralist as tax collector: Using natural field experiments to enhance tax compliance. NBER Working Paper No. 20007.

James, S., & Edwards, A. (2014). The importance of behavioral economics in tax research and tax reform: The issues of tax compliance and tax simplification. University of Exeter Paper No. 07/14.

John, P. (2018). *How far to nudge? Assessing behavioral public policy*. Cheltenham, UK: Edward Elgar.

Kahneman, D. (2011). *Thinking, fast and slow*. New York: Farrar, Straus and Giroux.

Kahneman, D., & Tversky, A. (1979). Prospect theory: An analysis of decision under risk. *Econometrica, 47*(2), 263–291.

Katona, G. (1975). *Psychological economics*. New York: Elsevier.

Kindleberger, C. P., & Aliber, R. (2005). *Manias, panics, and crashes: A history of financial crises* (5th ed.). Hoboken, NJ: John Wiley and Sons.

Klein, L. R. (1947). *The Keynesian revolution*. New York: Macmillan.

Leicester, A., Levell, P., & Rasul, I. (2012). Behavioral economics and tax reform. IFS Working Paper W11/10.

Lewis, M. (2017). *The undoing project: A friendship that changed our minds*. New York and London: W. W. Norton & Company.

List, J. (2004). Neoclassical theory versus prospect theory: Evidence from the marketplace. *Econometrica*, *72*(2), 615–625.

McCaffery, E., & Slemrod, J. (Eds.) (2006). *Behavioral public finance*. New York: Russell Sage Foundation.

Mueller, D. C. (1993). *Public choice II* (Revised edition). Cambridge: Cambridge University Press.

Musgrave, R. (1959). *The theory of public finance*. New York: McGraw-Hill.

Puviani, A. ([1903] 1973). *Teoria dell' illusione finanziaria. A cura di Franco Volpi*. Vicenza: ISEDI.

Schelling, T. C. (1978). Egonomics, or the art of self-management. *American Economics Review*, *68*(2), 290–294.

Shiller, R. J. (1989). *Market volatility*. Cambridge: MIT Press.

Shiller, R. J. (2000). *Irrational exuberance*. Princeton, NJ: Princeton University Press.

Shleifer, A. (2000). *Inefficient markets: An introduction to behavior finance*. Oxford: Oxford University Press.

Simon, H. A. (1955). A behavioral model of rational choices. *Quarterly Journal of Economics*, *69*(1), 99–118.

Smith, V. L., Suchanek, G. L., & Williams, A. W. (1988). Bubbles, crashes and endogenous expectations in experimental spot asset markets. *Econometrica*, 1119–1151.

Stillman, S. (2017). Can behavioral science help in Flint? *The New Yorker*, January 16.

Sugden, R. (2017). Do people really want to be nudged towards healthy lifestyles? *International Review of Economics*, *64*(2), 113–123.

Tanzi, V. (2000). *Policies, institutions and the dark side of economics*. Cheltenham, UK: Edward Elgar.

Tanzi, V. (2017). Taxation, complexity and tax evasion. *e Journal of Tax Research*, *15*(2), 144–160.

Tanzi, V. (2018a). *The termites of the state: Why complexity leads to inequality*. Cambridge and New York: Cambridge University Press.

Tanzi, V. (2018b). Welfare systems and their complexity. Paper presented at the 2018 IIPF Congress in Tampere, Finland, August 23.

Tanzi, V. (2018c). *Italica: L'unificazione difficile tra ideali e realtà*. Fasano, Italy: Schena Editore.

Thaler, R. H. (2015). *Misbehaving: How economics became behavioral*. London: Allen Lane.

Thaler, R. H., & Sunstein, C. R. (2008). *Nudge: Improving decisions about health, wealth and happiness*. New Haven, CT and London: Yale University Press.

Tversky, A., & Kahneman, D. (1974). Judgement under uncertainty: Heuristics and biases. *Science*, *185*(4157), 1124–1131.

Tversky, A., & Kahneman, D. (1992). Advances in prospect theory: Cumulative representation of uncertainty. *Journal of Risk and Uncertainty*, *5*(4), 297–323.

US Executive Office of the President (2015). Social and behavioral sciences team. *Annual Report*, September.

2 Smart decision-makers, institutional design and x-efficient (real-world optimal) public finance

Morris Altman

Introduction

The main focus of this chapter is to examine aspects of public finance in terms of the modelling assumptions that are made with regard to human behaviour and the decision-making environment of economic agents. We incorporate traditional economics' focus on income and price as drivers of decision-making. We also recognize that, as important as these variables are, they are not the sole determinant of the decision-making across a range of domains inclusive of tax compliance, taxation, government expenditure, labour market behaviour, which is a vital bedrock of macroeconomic policy, and firm responsiveness to changes in wages, where the latter is impacted by government policy. Apart from price and income, also of critical importance are non-economic considerations such as sociological, institutional, and psychological variables; neurological factors can also be highly significant. Also vital are the mental models that decision-makers use to engage in decision-making. Bad mental models generate bad analyses and bad public policy (Altman, 2014).

In addition, we recognize that critical to decision-making across all decision-makers is the decision-making capabilities of individuals and the decision-making environment within which decisions are made. This impacts on the decision-making process, decisions made, and the responses to the decisions made. Therefore, a starting point of our analysis is, following Simon, the assumption that decision-makers and economic agents live in a world of bounded rationality and public finance can be understood only given this assumption (Altman, 1999, 2006b; Simon, 1987). Moreover, to better understand all aspects of public finance and to generate robust analyses (including causal analyses) in this domain, one's modelling assumptions must be realistic, albeit necessarily simplistic – here too following upon the critical methodological understandings of Simon in his appreciation and deconstruction of conventional economic methodology. In this chapter we exemplify this specifically bounded rationality approach to public finance. From this perspective, many of the foundational theoretical conclusions of conventional public finance, which have significant public policy implications, are found to be seriously wanting. Given the focus of this chapter, a more robust theory suggests that tax compliance is not all about economic incentives, rational

Institutional design, x-efficient public finance 17

individuals should not be expected to behave in a manner that neutralizes the impact of government fiscal and monetary policy, real wages cuts are not the penultimate solution to unemployment problems, and government policy that improves the wellbeing and capabilities of workers should not reduce the supply of labour, nor should it negatively impact on the wealth of nations.

Different modelling perspectives

The conventional wisdom assumes that we behave as if we live in a world of unbounded rationality. And in this world, individuals are dominated by concerns about prices and income or wealth, especially with regard to utility and profit maximization. Moreover, it is assumed that we are economically efficient – there is no problem in this domain. Conventional economics makes the assumption, therefore, that within the firm, members are working as hard and smart as they can. On top of this, it is assumed that workers and potential employees prefer leisure over work – leisure is a normal good. In addition, it is assumed that consumers typically make choices that are utility maximizing, allowing them to realize their preferred preferences. More generally, the conventional wisdom assumes that one can model decision-makers such that best practice decision-making involves a careful marginal calculation of costs and benefits (with a focus on material considerations), perfect knowledge of pertinent information, predicting the future implications of current decisions, and, relatedly, no regret about current decisions. One assumes that decision-makers behave as if they approach the decision-making process in the above manner and also that they should behave in accordance with these behavioural norms to generate optimal results in the domain of consumption and production, as well as with regard to non-economic domains.

I argue that these assumptions are either wrong or misleading and generate ambiguous, equivocal, or even false analyses and public policy recommendations that can be damaging to the human condition; the overall wellbeing of members of our communities and economies. Therefore, robust public finance requires robust modelling assumptions and aspects of behavioural economics can contribute to the latter.

In this chapter, I argue that the behaviour of economic agents (decision-makers) can be assumed to be rational, smart, not irrational, and not systemically biased. Errors are typically corrected by learning (Bayesian updating, learning-by-doing) and by improving the decision-making environment. Being rational is not the same thing as engaging in detailed calculating behaviour and search behaviour. This behaviouralist approach is consistent with the bounded rationality approach articulated by Simon.

Simon (1986, p. S211) argues:

[I]f we accept the proposition that knowledge and the computational power of the decision maker are severely limited, then we must distinguish

18   *Morris Altman*

between the real world and the actor's perception of it and reasoning about it ... we must construct a theory (and test it empirically) of the processes of decision. Our theory must include not only the reasoning processes but also the processes that generate the actor's subjective representation of the decision problem, his or her frame ... The rational person of neoclassical economics always reaches the decision that is objectively, or substantively, best in terms of the given utility function. The rational person of cognitive psychology goes about making his or her decisions in a way that is pro-cedurally reasonable in the light of the available knowledge and means of computation [it is context dependent].

A close associate of Simon, March (1978, p. 589), clearly articulates this ration-ality approach to decision-making, where decision-making is contextualized in the framework of the decision-making environment. March argues that one should first assume that choice behaviour is smart, sensible, and therefore rational even when choice behaviour significantly deviates from conventional economic behavioural norms:

Engineers of artificial intelligence have modified their perceptions of efficient problem solving procedures by studying the actual behavior of human problem solvers. Engineers of organizational decision-making have modified their models of rationality on the basis of studies of actual organizational behavior ... Modern students of human choice behavior frequently assume, at least implicitly, that actual human choice behavior in some way or other is likely to make sense. It can be understood as being the behavior of an intelligent being or group of intelligent beings.

In this approach, the rationality norms of conventional economics can result in sub-optimal choices and outcomes, as this approach does not assume that decision-making takes place in a world of perfect and symmetric informa-tion (Akerlof, 1970). This is a point articulated by Gigerenzer (2007; Todd & Gigerenzer, 2003) and associates in their fast and frugal heuristic approach. From this perspective, non-conventional decision-making norms are developed, which yield choices and outcomes that tend to be superior to those generated when decision-makers abide by neoclassical behavioural norms. But then what becomes critically important is to determine when and under what conditions the adopted heuristics are relatively efficient, being more effective than abiding by conventional behavioural norms or, more importantly, relative to available heuristics. Adopting a heuristic does not necessarily mean that it is the most effective and efficient one amongst alternative heuristics in a given, what one might refer to as, heuristic possibility set. This relates to a determination of which heuristic works best in a particular public finance context and what the implications of using an x-inefficient or sub-optimal heuristic are.

Apart from heuristics, what is critically important is to best understand the nuanced process of decision-making as it actually takes place. This allows one

Institutional design, x-efficient public finance   19

to better predict how decision-makers will most probably respond to particular policies and changes in policy. This incorporates understanding which heuristic a decision-maker is most likely to choose in a particular context. This Simon, bounded rationality approach clearly distinguishes behavioural economics from the conventional narrative wherein it assumes that behaviour takes place in a particular fashion, without testing empirically the validity of the conventional narrative's simplifying assumptions. But if one's assumptions are wrong, then our predictions about the effect of policy on socio-economic outcomes, mediated by decision-makers' choices will be wrong (Simon, 1978, 1986, 1987).

This particular bounded rationality perspective, which is a smart people or smart agent perspective (Altman, 2017b), seriously overlaps with one of the assumptions of conventional economics, that people are rational and smart decision-makers. In other words, let's not assume that decision-makers can be fooled and deceived when designing and implementing policy and that this deception can persist over time. This relates, for example, to some of the macroeconomic policy discourse (especially in the "Keynesian" space) where 'money' illusion appears to be critical to increasing employment. This is a form of practical rationality, which is consistent with smart behaviour and incorporates the notion that one "satisfices" – doing the best one can with the information in hand (Simon, 1978). But, of course, from this behaviouralist perspective, I do not assume that rationality, being smart, means that individuals abide by conventional or neoclassical behavioural norms. And, this has implications for understanding the predicted effect of policy on socio-economic outcomes.

The more recent developments in behavioural economics fuelled initially by the research of Kahneman and Tversky (1979), dubbed as the heuristics and biases approach, rejects the assumption of the conventional wisdom that individuals behave neoclassically, that is in accordance with conventional economic norms. More importantly, this rejection is based on real-world evidence. In other words, the neoclassical or conventional assumption that individuals behave in accordance with neoclassical behavioural norms – or even that they behave as if they are adhering to these norms (Berg and Gigerenzer, 2010) – is found to lack an empirical basis. This simply reinforces the point made by Simon. Nevertheless, conventional economic norms are largely accepted as the gold standard for optimal behaviour, whereas deviations from such norms (*e.g.*, the use of heuristics) result in sub-optimal choices and, therefore, in sub-optimal outcomes.

This has given rise to the nudge perspective, pioneered and championed by Thaler and Sunstein (2008), whereby it is argued that individuals need to be nudged into making decisions that are in their own best interest and in the interest of society at large. This would be the case even if the individual who is being nudged would not agree with the choice that he or she is being nudged to make by the experts in choice determination, referred to as choice architects. The assumption here is that individuals or economic agents are hardwired to make biased and persistently biased and, therefore, sub-optimal decisions. Individual and social utility is enhanced by generating nudged choices informed

20 *Morris Altman*

by choice experts or choice architects, whose choice architecture is somehow immune to the biases to which the general population is assumed to be subject to. The nudge approach does not necessarily have a theoretical foundation in terms of policy recommendations, but it is most concerned about changing behaviour so that the choice architects' understanding of what are the optimum or utility or welfare maximizing outcomes is achieved.

Biased decision-making that must be de-biased is not the only logical outcome to be derived from the evidence that individuals persistently deviate from conventional behavioural norms. As already mentioned, one has the fast and frugal approach to decision-making and more recently one has the slow and fast thinking approach advanced by Kahneman (2011), which is somewhat decoupled from the Kahneman and Tversky heuristics and biases narrative. There is also the possibility that decision-makers can improve their decisions (closer to the optimal frontier) through improvements in the decision-making environment and also through improvements of the decision-making capabilities of decision-makers (Altman, 2017a). In this instance, biases are often errors in decision-making and are based upon sub-optimal decision-making environments and capabilities. This takes us well beyond nudges. And, these relate to issues of institutional design that have implications for public finance policy. Policy will have different outcomes given different decision-making environments and capabilities.

The conventional wisdom has focused on government policy as typically distorting incentives from what they ideally should be, using neoclassical norms as benchmarks for what the world should be like if one is to reap optimal socio-economic outcomes. It also tends to build policy on particular behavioural and institutional assumptions that are methodologically derived as opposed to being empirically derived and institutionally contextualized. In this chapter we examine the implications of "the assumptions-are-important perspective" of behavioural economics, as well as the smart decision-maker-bounded rationality approach to behavioural economics, for public finance narratives.

Especially from the assumptions-are-important-bounded rationality perspective, we examine the impact of taxes on tax compliance and economic efficiency; the Lucas Critique – the widely accepted assumption that real wages must fall to increase employment; the policy implications of an alternative behaviouralist model of the firm for wage and labour market and macroeconomic policy, with implications for Philips curve analyses; and policy implications of a behavioural theory of labour, where what drives labour supply is changing target income and an individual's hierarchy of needs.

Tax compliance

An important contribution of the behaviouralist literature is that tax compliance is not simply about largely penalizing individuals so that they pay their taxes as prescribed by government. It is now clear that tax compliance critically depends on non-economic variables. But this does not mean that the traditional economic variables are unimportant. Both sets of variables must be taken into account (Alm, McClelland, & Schulze, 1992; Alm & Torgler, 2006; Chun, 2019; Feld & Frey, 2002; James, Sawyer, & Wallschutzky, 2015; Kirchler, Maciejovsky, & Schneider, 2003; Kirchler, Hoelzl, & Wahl, 2008; Torgler, 2002, 2007; Wenzel, 2004). This speaks to the importance of the assumptions one makes when modelling tax compliance.

The conventional economic model predicts that increasing penalties for "tax cheats" and enforcing these penalties (audits for example), and making this enforcement known, will increase compliance. In other words, the only reason for non-compliance are too low penalty rates and inadequate enforcement of the penalty rates already in place. Improvements to either of these variables, *ceteris paribus*, should increase compliance. But behavioural economists have focused on issues such as fairness, trust, complexity, tax illiteracy, framing, biases, and relatedly to nudging individuals towards compliance as additional determinants of compliance (see above references). The importance of fairness and trust is referred to as tax morale. This raises the question of whether or not and the extent to which persistent deviations from compliant behaviour is always a form of *intentional* cheating. Also raised here is the issue of institutional parameters as determinants to paying taxes (tax evasion versus tax avoidance).

Two narratives illustrate some of the above points. Firstly, taxpayers in the US (and in many other countries) pay more taxes than the 'rational' conventional economic model predicts they should be paying based on economic incentives alone. In some other countries, taxpayers pay less. The American case is most interesting since Americans are often regarded as very oppositional to taxes. But what the typical American is offended by are unfair taxes and tax cheats – individuals who avoid paying their legal tax obligations. Also, disliked are people who avoid paying taxes and are thereby not paying their fair share of taxes (Williamson, 2017). On the other hand, Swedes are not known as detesting taxes, even though individual tax rates are amongst the highest in the advanced economies. But like the Americans, Swedes value fairness in the tax system. This also relates to a belief (and trust) that government is making good (and fair) use of tax revenues. Greeks, on average, do very poorly on the compliance scale because they do not trust their governments. It is fairness and, relatedly, believing that your government is using your money (what you pay in taxes) for what you think is appropriate, that appears to play a large role in tax compliance.

Ortiz-Ospina and Roser (2019), summarizing findings from an international data set, argue in favour of the strength of political institutions, which speaks to tax morale, as a key independent variable explaining variation in tax compliance across the globe. They argue:

> [T]he data shows that developed countries actually collect much higher tax revenue than developing countries despite comparable statutory taxation rates, even after controlling for underlying differences in economic activity.

This suggests that cross-country heterogeneity in fiscal capacity is largely determined by differences in compliance and efficiency of tax collection mechanisms. Both of these factors seem to be affected by the strength of political institutions.

(para. 5)

A fairness model helps to explain both over- and undercompliance given the conventional model, and the fairness model, thereby, helps to explain how best to improve compliance without increasing penalties and enforcing these penalties. It also helps to explain variations in tax compliance across tax jurisdictions. This behaviouralist model should also help inform the government on how to maintain or even increase compliance whilst increasing the tax rate.

Figure 2.1 illustrates some of these points. We have two neoclassical assumption-based tax compliance curves, one is negatively related to taxes rates, the other one is fixed. The first curve fits with the assumption (not always in line with the evidence) that individuals are more tax compliant as the tax burden diminishes). There are tax morale-tax compliant curves that lie above the neoclassical ones. This is compatible with the fact that increasing tax morale inspires individuals to be more tax compliant for any given set of economic incentives, inclusive of punishment. And, the low tax morale-tax compliant curves illustrate the fact that lower levels of tax morale yield lower levels of tax compliance, for any given set of economic incentives. Government policy that pays heed to the importance of tax morale to tax compliance would work towards increasing tax morale. When in place, it is a highly efficient and effective means of increasing government revenue for any given tax rate.

The second tax narrative relates to an important topic in behavioural economics that broadly falls under the banner of bounded rationality. This has very much to do with the complexity involved in paying taxes. Increasing the complexity of tax forms increases the time or opportunity costs and psychological costs incurred in filing taxes returns. This in itself can result in lowering the rate of compliance. Reducing the support offered by government to taxpayers, both

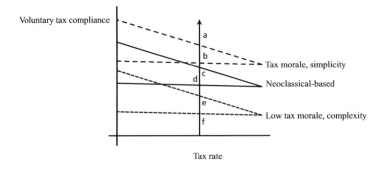

Figure 2.1 Tax compliance and economic theory: the role of non-economic variables

Institutional design, x-efficient public finance 23

online web-based help and live assistance would also be expected to reduce the rate of compliance. In Figure 2.1, this would shift the tax compliance curves downwards, whilst reducing the costs of tax compliance would shift these curves upwards. An important point to note here, efforts to support taxpayers through web-based support, whilst reducing live support, might reduce tax compliance when taxpayers do not have the capabilities or the information to efficiently extract the appropriate data. One should not assume that these capabilities and information are automatically at hand. These assumptions must be tested empirically.

An aspect of taxes that is not much touched upon by behavioural economists from any persuasion is conventional wisdom's prediction that taxes and tax increases necessarily generate welfare loses to society, reflected in relatively higher prices and lower output. Substantively, this takes the form of deadweight loses to society, a form of allocative inefficiency. But this is a static narrative of taxes. It does not take into consideration what might occur when taxes are expended. The implicit assumption being made is that no welfare-improving expenditure will be made with the tax revenue.

The static losses to society, as reflected by changes in prices and output, are illustrated in Figure 2.2 and are given by the shift in the supply curve from S_o to S_{t+1}, where the tax is given, for simplicity, by the vertical difference between the two supply curves. Taxes increase production costs per unit of output, hence the leftward shift in the supply curve. The baseline for economic efficiency and welfare maximization is given by the intersection of D_o and S_o. The introduction of a tax increases the price to $P1$, reducing consumer surplus and reducing output to $Q1$. The deadweight loss is bce. But this should not be the end of this analytical narrative.

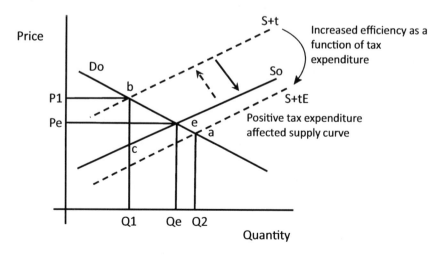

Figure 2.2 The economic impact of taxation

24   *Morris Altman*

One needs to bring into the static model other fundamental variables affected by taxes. This contributes to building a more holistic, realistic, and contextualized understanding of the impact of taxes on society, thereby enriching the important static analytic framework, first developed by Alfred Marshall in the late 19th century. If the tax revenue is expanded productively, then this could have the effect of reducing unit production costs to the firm. By investing in infrastructure, education and training, R&D, and health care, government can contribute to increasing firm productivity, thereby reducing their unit production costs.[1] *Ceteris paribus*, increasing productivity reduces average or unit costs. This is illustrated by an outward shift in the supply curve, whose micro-foundations are built on the cost side of the firm.

The extent of such a shift is an empirical question, but this reasonable possibility needs to be brought into consideration in any analysis of the impact taxes on the socio-economic wellbeing of the affected population. Such a shift can diminish any negative effects of taxes on allocative efficiency. Moreover, a significant enough shift to S_0 (the non-tax supply curve) would eliminate any deadweight losses whilst allowing government to meet its social obligations. A further shift to $S+tE$, for example, would actually reduce unit costs, making firms more competitive, strengthening the position of the economy, and this would be a product of imposing taxes; but also of using the tax revenue wisely.

Ignoring this dynamic part of the tax narrative or assuming that government spending is entirely unproductive presents what appears to be a robust, but is actually a highly distorted, model of the impact of taxes. This could contribute to highly biased policy with negative effects on socio-economic wellbeing.

The Lucas Critique

A critical assumption made by Lucas (1976) is that individuals respond to changes in government policy and related incentives. Individuals cannot be modelled statically, being unable or unwilling to update or change their behaviour given new relevant information and incentives. This is an assumption of rationality consistent with the bounded rationality-smart agent approach taken in this chapter. Lucas argues that this more realistic modelling of the economic agent undermines important policy claims of Keynesian and other forms of interventionist economics. Any theory that assumes static, irrational economic agents in its micro-foundations fails what is referred to as the Lucas Critique. Moreover, such theory cannot be used to predict the impact of policy changes on economic outcomes as it falsely assumes that decision-makers, on average, will not change their behaviour in response to changes in policy. Any policy that is based on tricking or deceiving decision-makers, Lucas argues, fails since rational real-world decision-makers cannot be tricked over the long run. Although the Lucas Critique focuses attention of significant gaps in economic model building, the

---

1 In a simple model, unit production costs can be written as Average Cost = wage/(output/unit of labour input). Increasing productivity here (output/unit of labour input) reduces average cost.

behavioural micro-foundations specified in the Lucas Critique are not always built on solid empirical foundations (Stanley, 2000).

Key aspects of this critique assume that individuals are always neoclassically rational and, therefore, they must behave in a very specific fashion. A core assumption of the Lucas Critique is that economic models must be built on specific assumptions about rational behaviour and the workings of the market economy. Lucas maintains, for example, that economic theorists should assume that rational individuals should have full knowledge and understanding of all information relevant to their decisions. Moreover, theorists should assume that rational individuals behave in accordance with the "true" model of the economy, which is one where all markets, including labour markets, clear continuously (supply and demand will adjust to equality with great speed). Thus, any errors in decision-making are quickly corrected. Importantly, it is assumed that unemployment is caused by real wages being too high, that rational workers know this to be "true", and, therefore, if workers want to secure jobs, they simply need to accept lower real wages. Aggregate demand will automatically adjust to absorb the increased supply of low real wage labour. If real wages do not fall when unemployment is high (without workers being deceived into accepting lower real wages, where deception can only work in the very short run), this means that existing unemployment is voluntary. This narrative presumes that this model is the true model, a claim that has been seriously challenged in the literature.

In fact, individuals often make decisions that are inconsistent with the behavioural assumptions embedded in the Lucas Critique. Related to this, it is not always the case that individuals adjust their behaviour to new information and incentives. These behaviours include maintaining sticky nominal and real wages and sticky prices for good rational reasons. But not adjusting behaviour and price in accordance with Lucas's "true" model can be consistent with rational behaviour in a world of complex (imperfect and asymmetric) information. These behaviours would also be rational if decision-makers are using a different model to inform their decisions.

Akerlof and Shiller (2009), for example, argue that rational agents will not calculate the impact of slow inflation rates on real wages, thereby, allowing government policy to impact the equilibrium rate of unemployment by reducing the real wage without rational workers demanding compensating money wage increases (see also Altman, 2006a). Keynes argues that unemployment can be caused by demand-side shocks to the economy. But given the reality of sticky prices, markets will not clear instantaneously. As a consequence, this type of unemployment needs to be fixed by demand-side policy to avoid unnecessary hardship and social upheaval. Keynes speaks against the view that workers suffer from money illusion. Therefore, they cannot be fooled into accepting lower real wages, even in the 'short' long run. But to the extent that real wages need to fall to increase employment back to pre-negative aggregate demand levels, workers would accept such cuts (as with Akerlof, workers are rational). Basically, Keynes accepts the conventional micro-foundations of a negatively sloped marginal

26 Morris Altman

product of labour curve. Less employment therefore means higher real wages. More employment requires real wages being restored to their initial lower wage equilibrium, given this type of marginal product of labour curve. But this can only be done through government demand-side policy designed to increase employment, which involves an inflationary component. All workers are then subject to the same "fair" relative cut to real wages. These assumptions are all consistent with rational micro-foundations. They are compatible, therefore, with the Lucas Critique. But here, a model of rational agents is consistent with increasing employment after a negative demand-side shock through government fiscal and monetary policy.

To be compatible with the Lucas Critique does not mean that agents will behave as predicted by Lucas. Decisions can be boundedly rational and consistent with solid behavioural micro-foundations. However, these micro-foundations can be quite different from those specified by Lucas as being consistent with rational behaviour. Rational, but pure Lucas Critique inconsistent decisions, have modelling and policy implications different from those flowing from the Lucas Critique. But consistent with the Lucas narrative, models and policy are consistent with rational agents.

Behavioural public finance and the theory of the firm

Behavioural economics, especially most recently, has had little to say about the micro-foundations, theory of the firm, related issues, that play such an important role in informing policy. Further back in time we have had contributions to behavioural theories of the firm related to the work of Cyert and March (1963), Leibenstein (1966) (see also Frantz, 1997), and Williamson (1975), whose work closely relates to that of Coase (1937). But the theory of the firm is critical when assessing the potential impact of government policy, inclusive of macro policy discussed above. I will briefly discuss a rational theory of the firm built upon and extending Leibenstein's (1966) contributions, specifically x-efficiency theory and its implications for an understanding of how labour benefits and other costs to the firm, such as greener policy, might impact on unit production costs (Altman, 2001b, 2002, 2004, 2006a, 2006b, 2009; see also Hirschman, 1970).

The main point here is that the assumptions of the conventional model are quite narrow and not very realistic. More reasonable assumptions allow one to appreciate why policies that might positively impact labour benefits and policies that encourage greener firms need not generate higher unit costs of production. Firms can therefore be cost competitive even whilst employees are made materially better off and the environment becomes greener. In this scenario, from a macro perspective high wages need not be the obstacle to more employment as it is from both a Keynesian and new classical (Lucas Critique) perspective.

Conventional theory presumes that rational economic agents adhering to conventional behavioural norms will be maximizing profits and utility thereby

Institutional design, x-efficient public finance 27

maximizing or optimizing on their effort inputs into the firm's process of production. How this is achieved in reality is not much discussed in the conventional narrative; effort maximization is assumed to be somehow achieved. At a minimum effort input is assumed fixed for analytical purposes – a convenient simplifying assumption. Following from this assumption, any increase in labour benefits will cause unemployment and make firms less competitive as unit production costs would be driven up. It also follows that one is assuming that firms are economically efficient and the only possible economic inefficiency to speak of would be allocative inefficiency, driven by price distortions – deviations from the presumed perfectly competitive neoclassical ideal.

A key point made by Leibenstein (1966) is that firms typically do not optimize on effort inputs, as such effort optimization is not utility maximizing from the perspective of the key firm decision-makers. Leibenstein does not assume that effort maximization is somehow hardwired into preference function and therefore into the brain architecture of firms' decision-makers. And, firms can get away with this behaviour in the typical product market, which is not perfectly competitive. The difference between what the firm can produce, given traditional factor inputs when effort is optimized and when it is not, is a measure of what Leibenstein refers to as x-inefficiency, to be distinguished from allocative inefficiency. X-inefficiency is found to be relatively large, whereas allocative inefficiency is found to be relatively small in terms of GDP (Frantz, 1997; Leibenstein, 1966). A key point in this narrative is that effort is a discretionary variable in the production function. For Leibenstein, effort input is driven by the x-inefficient-related preferences of managers, which yield sub-optimal effort inputs (negatively impacting on productivity) and, thereby, higher unit production costs. I expand his narrative to take into consideration how the work culture of the firm affects effort inputs, how labour benefits affect effort inputs, and how these and related costs impact on innovation and technical change (Altman 2002, 2006b).

In this alternative modelling narrative, improved labour benefits, an improved work environment, and more democratic work cultures incentivize increased effort input. In this scenario, increasing wages, for example, is positively associated with improvements to productivity and lower wages with diminutions in productivity. For this reason, improvements in the work environment, albeit coming at a cost, need not generate higher unit production costs. Associated increases in productivity can offset these increased costs. On the other hand, reducing immediate labour costs need not reduce unit production costs as these might be offset by reductions in productivity.

This point is illustrated in the equation below for a simple economy with one factor input, where AC is average costs, w is labour benefits and related costs, and Q/L is labour productivity. AC will not change as w changes if Q/L changes sufficiently to neutralize or offset changes to w. This model with effort discretion opens the analytical door to the possibility that changes to labour benefits need not affect unit production costs. Of course, in the conventional model, improvements to labour benefits, to the material wellbeing of workers,

28 Morris Altman

increase average costs, negatively impacting employment and the competitive position of the firm.

$$AC = \frac{w}{\left(\frac{Q}{L}\right)} \qquad 1$$

If one is more realistic and introduces other factor inputs into the equation, the extent of increases in productivity to neutralize increases in costs diminishes. In the simple model, for example, a 10% increase in W requires a 10% increase productivity (here based on improvement in the quantity and quality of effort inputs). But if labour represents only 50% of costs, this same percentage increase in w would require only 5% increase in productivity (50% of the 10% increase).

In conventional wisdom and, indeed, in the original x-efficiency narrative increasing labour benefits, working conditions, and the like increases labour costs. But according to my revised rendition of an x-inefficiency model of the firm, going deeper into the black box of the firm, one cannot predict whether improving worker wellbeing will damage the firm competitively and reduce employment. Also, reducing real wages *per se* does not become a necessary condition to increase employment. This has important implications for policy.

These points are illustrated in Figure 2.3. In the conventional model, increasing labour benefits yields higher average costs as per line segment, CON. In our behavioural model increasing labour benefits have no impact on average cost up to point c. Up to this point effort inputs increase sufficiently to offset increases in the costs of labour benefits. Thereafter, one hits a wall of diminishing returns with regard to increasing effort input sufficiently to offset the costs of further increasing labour benefits. Unlike in the conventional model, in the behavioural model increasing labour benefits is not the negative force that it is

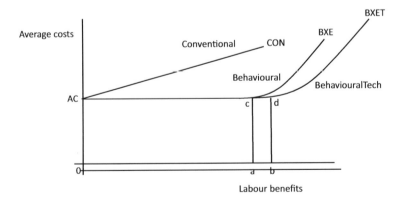

Figure 2.3 Average costs, x-inefficiency, and labour benefits

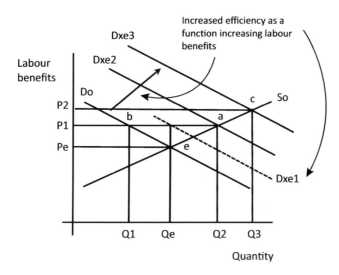

Figure 2.4 Higher labour benefits and unemployment

in the conventional model. Once the wall of diminishing returns is hit, I argue (in a model of endogenous technical change) that increasing labour benefits induces technological change to offset any related costs (Altman, 2009). At a minimum, in this scenario, the firm must innovate to remain competitive. This is illustrated by shifts in our particular average cost curve such as from BXE to BXET. This provides firms with additional degrees of freedom as costs increase. In this modelling scenario, with effort as a discretionary variable, labour benefits can increase without increasing average costs whilst increasing the size of the economic pie.

Figure 2.4 illustrates some of the labour market implications of this modelling. In the conventional model, assuming no effort variation or induced technical change, improvement to labour benefits, such as through improvements in minimum wages, other such forms of government intervention, through unions or other forms of collective action, yielding an increase in benefits from *Pe* to *P1*, should result in measured unemployment of *Q1Q2*, where *QeQ1* is a product of policy induced unemployment. The remainder is a product of more workers entering the formal labour market in search of work. Increased benefits therefore only benefit those who keep their jobs, but also tend to make affected firms less competitive. Evidence suggests that this prediction tends to be highly exaggerated, if not completely wrong (Card & Krueger, 1995; Freeman & Medoff, 1984).

The alternative behavioural model articulated above predicts that, in a dynamic model, these increased benefits will shift the demand curve outward to the right through induced increases in productivity (as the extent of x-efficiency increases) and through induced technical change. A shift in demand from *Do* to

Dxe1 would eliminate the conventional theory's reduction in employment. But a movement to *Dxe2* would also absorb the induced increase in labour supply. A movement to *Dxe3* would simply take this one step further. The extent of the induced shift in demand is an empirical question. Yet, the probability of such a shift should force theoreticians and policy makers to appreciate that efforts to improve the wellbeing of workers need not, and would probably not have the negative economic consequences predicted by conventional economic theory.

From the perspective of macroeconomic policy, with regard to the long run Phillips Curve debate, the implication of this x-efficiency modelling is quite simple. It suggests the possibility that given the existence of x-inefficiency and induced technical change, as discussed above, increasing employment, by increasing aggregate demand, especially moving from the downturn (trough) to recovery, need not require a cut in real wages. This is because of the induced productivity increases compensating for possible increases in real wages. Inflation is not required to cut real wages nor, in this context, is money illusion. Therefore, increases in aggregate demand can be expected to increase employment, up to a point. And, this increase is not causally related to an increase in the rate of inflation (Altman, 2006a; Blanchflower & Oswald, 1995).

This behaviouralist narrative is illustrated in Figure 2.5. In the classic Phillips Curve relationship, increasing aggregate demand must be accompanied by increasing prices for employment to increase, as would be the case along supply curve *SPC*, with demand increasing from *AD1* to *ADo* to *AD2*. But the new classical economists, well exemplified by Lucas, argue that this positive relationship is not possible with rational or smart economic agents. The Phillips Curve should be vertical. Hence, the longer term effect of increasing aggregate

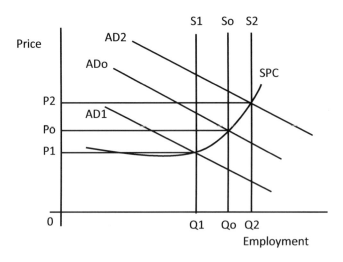

Figure 2.5 Behavioural theory of the firm and the Phillips Curve

Institutional design, x-efficient public finance 31

demand is to generate increasing prices. But in the behavioural modelling scenario, one would also have a vertical Phillips Curve (real wages are unaffected by inflation). In the behaviourist model, induced increases to productivity shift the vertical supply curve to the right as aggregate demand increases and as real wages rise. Hence, the supply-side conditions for increasing employment are met with rational decision-makers. Inflation is only spuriously, but positively, correlated with increasing employment. In this scenario, restoring employment to pre-recession levels, *ceteris paribus*, becomes largely a demand-side issue. And, longer term increases in employment are related to both demand-side factors and accommodating labour market considerations, in part, related to the capability of firms to increase productivity. The latter is facilitated by a positive incentive environment in the firm.

Environmental policy implications of this behavioural theory of the firm, if firms are required to be greener without government dictating how to achieve improved standards, is that the cost of becoming greener is, most likely, greatly exaggerated by the conventional model. In a nutshell, efforts to become greener could at least induce increases in the quality of effort input, since being greener is regarded by many as a utility enhancing activity. Also, this could induce technological change. Increases in effort and induced technical change can also compensate for the increased costs of becoming greener, and this can either neutralize or mitigate the conventional economics' predicted increases to average costs. Moreover, firms facing green challenges are incentivized to develop new products to generate additional income streams to remain profitable (Altman, 2001b).

Conventional economics does not condemn efforts to become greener, but it maintains that there are very hefty opportunity costs involved. The behaviouralist approach, more consistent with evidence, suggests that the conventional model is built upon weak behavioural assumptions. More robust assumptions yield a model predicting that green need not come at the significant immediate opportunity costs suggested by the conventional wisdom. One can move towards greener economies without fearing economic disaster, appreciating that becoming greener requires government and communities to facilitate organizations making the transition to greener methods of production.

Behavioural labour and public policy

The conventional approach to labour supply assumes that work is an inferior good and that leisure is a normal good. Individuals are assumed to prefer not to work and increases in real income, *ceteris paribus*, are used to buy-out work so as to reallocate time to leisure, hence increasing one's utility or level of well-being. Individuals will work more or enter the labour market if the opportunity cost of leisure increases (the substitution effect of increasing the wage rate), but the resulting income effect will generate an increase in the demand for more leisure time. Therefore, social policy that is designed to support the income of the employed, the unemployed, and their families is predicted to

32   *Morris Altman*

generate a reduction in the supply of labour as it allows individuals to purchase leisure. This reduction in labour supply then has the effect of increasing the bargaining power of labour, which would increase real wages and related benefits to workers. In the conventional narrative, where effort is fixed and there is no induced technical change, this increases average costs, making firms less competitive. Overall, interventions on the labour market that provide workers with the opportunity to purchase leisure have negative effects on the economy. Moreover, this assumes that unemployment is a form of leisure activity. Hence, being unemployed is not investigated as an event that can serve to depreciate an individual's human capital stock and damage the unemployed and their families psychologically and financially. The latter would damage the economy in the long run, reducing the wellbeing of those enduring unemployment and their families (Altman, 2001a; Darity & Goldsmith, 1996).

One problem with the conventional model is that it cannot predict changes in labour supply through the interaction of the substitution and income effect and also tends to predict large increases in unemployment to be a product of dramatic changes in the preferences of the formerly employed towards leisure time (this is a core assumption of new classical economics, which is very much associated with Robert Lucas of the Lucas Critique fame).

An alternative behavioural model (Altman, 2001a), based on a target income/ hierarchy of needs approach to labour, better predicts changes in labour supply and is better grounded in our understanding of how economic agents behave. This theory does not deny the importance of the substitution and income effect in some instances. But target income and a hierarchy of needs dominate (the latter concept is borrowed from Maslow, 1943). From this perspective, the supply of labour is conditional upon the target income of the individual and her or his family. It is also simultaneously affected by the relative importance of non-market work activities relative to market-related activities. In addition, it is understood here that the conventional application of the term leisure can be highly misleading as non-market activities comprise not only leisure but also non-market work, such as childcare and household chores. I also reject, based on the evidence, the conventional assumption that leisure is a superior good and work is something to be avoided. Rather, for many individuals, work itself generates utility. This is partially related to the sense of community, friendship, pride, and belonging that it tends to produce.

In this model, providing support to workers and their families, such as social support, free meals for kids, unemployment insurance, health care, and the like, will not reduce labour supply if the worker's and the worker's family's target income is not being met. Indeed, although real income has increased dramatically over the past 120 years, hours of work have not collapsed. And when hours of work have fallen they have only done so when real income increased (Altman, 2001a). Only when target income is met would one predict that increasing income support to workers will reduce the labour supply. Moreover, even increasing real wages cannot be predicted to reduce labour supply (forget about the income and substitution effect) if target income is not met. Dynamically, increasing target income translates into no decrease in labour supply.

Institutional design, x-efficient public finance   33

Introducing the hierarchy of needs framework, one can predict that income support can reduce labour supply even if target income is not met under certain conditions. For example, government income support could facilitate a family member, typically the female, to reduce market work so as to take care of her children in the absence of affordable childcare. Here the labour force is reduced, but not because the mother prefers leisure to work. Reducing such support would attract single-parent mothers into the labour market, but here at the opportunity cost of leaving their kids with no child support or substandard child support.

The bottom line in this scenario is that changes in labour supply can be best explained by determining the target income of workers and their families and where target income is situated in the individual's hierarchy of needs. In this model, working on the labour market is not treated as an inferior good. Given the assumptions of this model, one cannot predict that providing economic support to individuals, in general, will result in a decrease in labour supply. And, cuts to such support could result in economic harm to affected individuals, even if it might increase somewhat the supply of labour. Moreover, this model would not predict that significant recessions are explained by individuals suddenly and dramatically increasing their preference for leisure over work, preferring unemployment to work.

Given that target income has tended to increase over time, this alternative modelling framework would predict that public policy to support workers and their families will not reduce the supply of labour. But it will improve the bargaining power of workers. And, this can incentivize improvements in economic efficiency. Moreover, the quality of human capital will also be enhanced.

Conclusions

I address some key public finance questions through the lenses of a smart agent-bounded rationality approach to behavioural economics. From this perspective, what is vitally important is the realism of the assumptions underlying economic models. Different assumptions yield different causal analyses and analytical predictions.

I pay special attention to an already well-articulated behavioural approach that specifies non-conventional economics conditions for tax compliance. But I go beyond this important issue to examine the implications of introducing more reasonable assumptions about the role of government spending of tax revenue for the predicted efficiency of taxation. Unlike in the static conventional model, in a dynamic model where government spending can generate positive productivity effects, taxation can have positive welfare effects, making the economy better off than it would otherwise be.

Also, I present a critical assessment of the Lucas Critique based upon smart or rational agents, where government interventions can positively affect economic outcomes even when one incorporates rational responses of smart decision-makers to government policy. Introducing a revised version of x-efficiency theory (and a behavioural theory of the firm), one can also argue that real wage cuts should not be considered as the most likely solution to business-cycle-related and persistent unemployment.

Taking this more reasonable modelling narrative one step further, where effort is a variable and technological change is endogenous to the firm, one can argue that policy facilitating higher real wages might very well dynamically incentivize increased productivity through increased levels of x-efficiency and induced technical change. This would suggest that policies that enhance minimum wages and income support, and strengthen unions, might very well have a positive efficiency effect on the economy and should act as a brake on economic growth, development, and employment. This modelling also has implications for government and firm-specific policy on the greening of society. The costly process of becoming green should be expected to induce increasing productivity and new marketable products, which dramatically reduce, if not potentially eliminate within reason, the costs of greening the economy. Becoming green need not come at the severe economic opportunity costs predicted by conventional economics.

With regard to labour supply, in a behaviouralist approach, target income and the hierarchy of needs are as important as the income and substitution effects in determining labour supply. Also, as in reality, leisure is not typically preferred to work. Work itself generates utility. This has significant policy implications, as efforts to improve the material conditions of workers and their families and the unemployed and their families should not be expected to reduce labour supply and cause overall damage to the economy. This can also be expected to have efficiency effects on the economy.

From the critical perspective taken in this chapter, the realism of assumptions drives the robustness of one's models. This has significant implications for public finance issues and policy and should force a reconsideration of policy in a number of significant domains ranging from taxation, macroeconomics, and labour market considerations. Some of these points are illustrated in Figure 2.6,

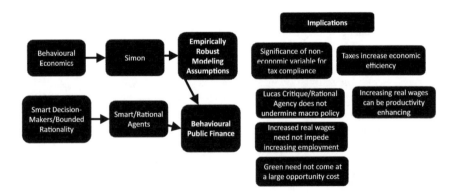

Figure 2.6 Implications of the small agent-based rationality narrative for policy

where we outline the implications of the smart agent–bounded rationality narrative for policy.

Acknowledgements

The author thanks the books editors, Hannah Altman, and Louise Lamontagne for their invaluable comments and suggestions.

References

Akerlof, G. (1970). The market for "lemons": Quality uncertainty and the market mechanism. *The Quarterly Journal of Economics, 84*(3), 488–500.

Akerlof, G. A., & Shiller, R. J. (2009). *Animal spirits: How human psychology drives the economy, and why it matters for global capitalism*. Princeton, NJ: Princeton University Press.

Alm, J., McClelland, G. H., & Schulze, W. D. (1992). Why do people pay taxes? *Journal of Public Economics, 48*, 21–38.

Alm, J., & Torgler, B. (2006). Culture differences and tax morale in the United States and in Europe. *Journal of Economic Psychology, 27*, 224–246.

Altman, M. (1999). The methodology of economics and the survivor principle revisited and revised: Some welfare and public policy implications of modeling the economic agent. *Review of Social Economics, 57*, 427–449.

Altman, M. (2001a). Preferences and labor supply: Casting some light into the black box of income–leisure choice. *Journal of Socio-Economics, 31*, 199–219.

Altman, M. (2001b). When green isn't mean: Economic theory and the heuristics of the impact of environmental regulations on competitiveness and opportunity cost. *Ecological Economics, 36*, 31–44.

Altman, M. (2002). Economic theory, public policy and the challenge of innovative work practices. *Economic and Industrial Democracy: An International Journal, 23*, 271–290.

Altman, M. (2004). Why unemployment insurance might not only be good for the soul, it might also be good for the economy. *Review for Social Economy, 62*, 517–541.

Altman, M. (2006a). Involuntary unemployment, macroeconomic policy, and a behavioral model of the firm: Why high real wages need not cause high unemployment. *Research in Economics, 60*, 97–111.

Altman, M. (2006b). What a difference an assumption makes: Effort discretion, economic theory, and public policy. In: M. Altman (Ed.), *Handbook of contemporary behavioral economics: Foundations and developments* (pp. 125–164). Armonk, NY: M. E. Sharpe.

Altman, M. (2009). A behavioral–institutional model of endogenous growth and induced technical change. *Journal of Economic Issues, 63*, 685–713.

Altman, M. (2014). Mental models, bargaining power, and institutional change. World Interdisciplinary Network for Institutional Research, Old Royal Naval College, Greenwich, London, UK, September 11–14.

Altman, M. (2017a). A bounded rationality assessment of the new behavioral economics. In: R. Frantz, S. H. Chen, K. Dopfer, F. Heukelom, & S. Mousavi (Eds.), *Routledge handbook of behavioral economics* (pp. 179–193). London and New York: Routledge.

Altman, M. (Ed.) (2017b). *Handbook of behavioural economics and smart decision-making: Rational decision-making within the bounds of reason*. Cheltenham, UK: Edward Elgar.

Berg, N., & Gigerenzer, G. (2010). As-if behavioral economics: Neoclassical economics in disguise? *History of Economic Ideas, 18*, 133–166.

36 *Morris Altman*

Blanchflower, D. G., & Oswald, A. J. (1995). An introduction to the wage curve. *Journal of Economic Perspectives, 9*, 153–167.

Card, D., & Krueger, A. B. (1995). *Myth and measurement: The new economics of the minimum wage*. Princeton, NJ: Princeton University Press.

Chun, R. (2019). Why Americans don't cheat on their taxes: The weirdly hopeful story of how the U.S. came to be a leader in tax compliance. *The Atlantic*. Retrieved August 12, 2019, from www.theatlantic.com/magazine/archive/2019/04/why-americans-dont-cheat-on-their-taxes/583222/.

Coase, R. (1937). The nature of the firm. *Economica, 4*, 386–405.

Cyert, R., & March, J. G. (1963). *A behavioral theory of the firm* (2nd ed.). Oxford: Blackwell.

Darity, W. Jr., & Goldsmith, A. H. (1996). Social psychology, unemployment, and macroeconomics. *Journal of Economic Perspectives, 10*, 121–140.

Feld L. P., & Frey, B. S. (2002). Trust breeds trust: How taxpayers are treated. *Economics of Governance, 3*, 87–99.

Frantz, R. (1997). *X-efficiency theory: Evidence and applications* (2nd ed.). Boston, MA, Dordrecht, and London: Kluwer Academic Publishers.

Freeman, R. B., & Medoff, J. L. (1984). *What do unions do?* New York: Basic Books.

Gigerenzer, G. (2007). *Gut feelings: The intelligence of the unconscious*. New York: Viking.

Hirschman, A. O. (1970). *Exit, voice, and loyalty: Responses to decline in firms, organizations, and states*. Cambridge, MA: Harvard University Press.

James, S., Sawyer, A., & Wallschutzky, I. (2015). Tax simplification: A review of initiatives in Australia, New Zealand and the United Kingdom. *eJournal of Tax Research, 13*, 280–302.

Kahneman, D. (2011). *Thinking, fast and slow*. New York: Farrar, Straus and Giroux.

Kahneman, D., & Tversky, A. (1979). Prospect theory: An analysis of decision under risk. *Econometrica, 47*, 263–291.

Kirchler, E., Hoelzl, E., & Wahl, I. (2008): Enforced versus voluntary tax compliance: The "slippery slope" framework. *Journal of Economic Psychology, 29*, 210–225.

Kirchler, E., Maciejovsky, B., & Schneider, F. (2003). Everyday representations of tax avoidance, tax evasion, and tax flight: Do legal differences matter? *Journal of Economic Psychology, 24*, 535–553.

Leibenstein, H. (1966). Allocative efficiency vs. x-efficiency. *American Economic Review, 56*, 392–415.

Lucas, R. (1976). Econometric policy evaluation: A critique. In: K. Brunner & A. Meltzer (Eds.), *The Phillips Curve and labor markets* (pp. 19–46), Carnegie-Rochester Conference Series on Public Policy, Vol. 1. New York: Elsevier.

March, J. (1978). Bounded rationality, ambiguity, and the engineering of choice. *Bell Journal of Economics, 9*, 587 608.

Maslow, A. H. (1943). A theory of human motivation. *Psychological Review, 50*, 370–396.

Ortiz-Ospina, E., & Roser, M. (2019). Taxation. Published online at OurWorldInData. org. Retrieved August 14, 2019, from https://ourworldindata.org/taxation/.

Simon, H. A. (1978). Rationality as a process and as a product of thought. *American Economic Review, 70*, 1–16.

Simon, H. A. (1986). Rationality in psychology and economics. *Journal of Business, 59*, S209–224.

Simon, H. A. (1987). Behavioral economics. In: J. Eatwell, M. Millgate, & P. Newman (Eds.), *The new Palgrave: A dictionary of economics*. London: Macmillan.

Stanley, T. D. (2000). An empirical critique of the Lucas Critique. *Journal of Socio-Economics*, *29*, 91–107.

Thaler, R. H., & Sunstein, C. R. (2008). *Nudge: Improving decisions about health, wealth, and happiness*. New Haven, CT: Yale University Press.

Todd, P. M., & Gigerenzer, G. (2003). Bounding rationality to the world. *Journal of Economic Psychology*, *24*, 143–165.

Torgler, B. (2002). Speaking to theorists and searching for facts: Tax morale and tax compliance in experiments. *Journal of Economic Surveys*, *16*, 657–683.

Torgler, B. (2007). *Tax compliance and tax morale: A theoretical and empirical analysis*. Cheltenham, UK: Edward Elgar.

Wenzel, M. (2004). An analysis of norm processes in tax compliance. *Journal of Economic Psychology*, *25*, 213–228.

Williamson, O. E. (1975). *Markets and hierarchies: Analysis and antitrust implications*. New York: Free Press.

Williamson, V. (2017). *Read my lips: Why Americans are proud to pay taxes*. Princeton, NJ and Oxford: Princeton University Press.

3 Behavioral economics and public policy

Julia Dobreva

Introduction

Economics has been considered as the social science of choice when it comes to defining and developing policies. In this chapter we discuss the role of behavioral economics for enlightening policy-makers, specialized in public policy development. The main reason for which behavioral science should be part of the policy debate is that it provides in some cases a perspective that is vastly different from economics. The most notable difference has to do with assumptions about rationality. Whereas economics assumes that individuals and organizations are rational agents, behavioral science does not. In fact, much of the work in the fields of behavioral decision-making has been aimed at empirically demonstrating deviations from rationality due to cognitive and perceptual aspects of human architecture. Similarly, much work in behavioral economics has been aimed at relaxing these assumptions within the standard economic tools.

For example, economic research emphasizes the importance of retirement savings programs to the future welfare of workers (Ando & Modigliani, 1963). And indeed, many offerings have been created to enable people to act upon their best interests and save money for their retirement period. The common finding, though, is that too many employees without pre-defined pension plans do not save nearly enough for their future (Benartzi & Thaler, 2004). This is despite the obvious economic benefit of doing so. Behavioral researchers have demonstrated many possible reasons for this phenomenon, among them the sheer number of investment options causing inaction (Huberman, Iyengar, & Jiang, 2003) and the intertemporal asymmetry between the costs and benefits of the decision (Thaler & Shefrin, 1981). Understanding some of these behavioral antecedents to individuals' poor decision-making led to the creation of an innovative savings policy called "Save More Tomorrow". In this policy, individuals are not asked to invest a portion of their salary immediately, but to commit to a future saving that would be taken out of a portion of their raise (Benartzi & Thaler, 2004). This way, many of the behavioral (irrational) difficulties of committing a part of one's salary toward some future benefit are mitigated, and a greater proportion of employees save for their future.

Behavioral economics and public policy 39

In this chapter we will examine the main perspectives of the interrelation between behavioral economics and public policy. The main focus will be on public health and education policies.

Behavioral economics and public policy perspectives

Chetty (2015) discusses three ways in which behavioral economics can contribute to public policy: *by offering new policy tools, improving predictions about the effects of existing policies, and generating new welfare implications.* He further illustrates these contributions using applications to retirement savings, labor supply, and neighborhood choice. Central to the study is the question: "How can we increase savings rates?" which incorporates behavioral factors to the extent that they improve empirical predictions and policy decision-making. The applications focus on three major decisions people make over the course of their lives: *how much to save, how much to work, and where to live.* Each application is motivated by a policy question that has been studied extensively using neo-classical models. The objective is to illustrate how incorporating insights from behavioral economics can yield better answers to these longstanding policy questions.

The first application shows how behavioral economics offers new policy tools to increase retirement saving. The US federal government currently spends approximately \$100 billion per year to subsidize retirement saving in 401(k) and IRA accounts. However, evidence suggests that such subsidies have much smaller effects on savings rates than "nudges" (Thaler & Sunstein, 2008) such as defaults and automatic enrollment plans that are motivated by behavioral models of passive choice. These new policy tools allow us to achieve savings rates that may have been unattainable with the tools suggested by neoclassical models. These empirical findings are very valuable irrespective of the underlying behavioral model, although theory remains essential for extrapolation (*e.g.*, predicting behavior in other settings) and for welfare analysis.

The second application illustrates that behavioral models can be useful in predicting the impacts of existing policies even if they do not produce new policy tools. Here, the focus is on the effects of the Earned Income Tax Credit (EITC) – the largest means-tested cash transfer program in the US – on households' labor supply decisions. The EITC provides subsidies that are intended to encourage low-wage individuals to work more. Yet recent evidence shows that individuals living in areas with a high density of EITC claimants have greater knowledge about the parameters of the EITC schedule and, accordingly, are more responsive to the program. These differences in knowledge across areas provide new counterfactuals to identify the impacts of the EITC on labor supply decisions and reveal that the program has been quite successful in increasing earnings among low-wage individuals. These results demonstrate that even if one cannot directly manipulate perceptions of the EITC, accounting for the differences in knowledge across areas is useful in understanding the effects of the existing incentives.

40 Julia Dobreva

The third application shows how behavioral models also provide new insights into the welfare consequences and optimal design of policies. These normative implications are illustrated by considering policies such as housing voucher subsidies, whose goal is to change low-income families' choice of neighborhoods. Recent empirical studies have shown that some neighborhoods generate significantly better outcomes for children, yet do not have higher housing costs. Both neoclassical models and models featuring behavioral biases (*e.g.*, present-bias or imperfect information) can explain why families do not move to such neighborhoods, but these models generate very different policy prescriptions. The neoclassical model says that there is no reason to intervene except for externalities. Behavioral models call for policies that encourage families to move to areas that will improve their children's outcomes, such as housing voucher subsidies or assistance in finding a new apartment.

Overall, the three applications illustrate that incorporating behavioral features into economic models can have substantial practical value in answering certain policy questions. Of course, behavioral factors may not be important in all applications. The decision about whether to incorporate behavioral features into a model should be treated like other standard modeling decisions, such as assumptions about time-separable utility or price-taking behavior by firms. In some applications, a simpler model may yield sufficiently accurate predictions; in others, it may be useful to incorporate behavioral factors, just like it may be useful to allow for time-non-separable utility functions. This pragmatic, application-specific approach to behavioral economics may ultimately be more productive than attempting to resolve whether the assumptions of neoclassical or behavioral models are correct at a general level.

An example for such research is the work on effects of defaults of organ donations (Johnson & Goldstein, 2003), showing that the proportion of people who have organ donor status in countries where the default is that everyone is a donor (and people have to opt out if they do not want to be donors) is over 90%. The proportion of people who have organ donor status in countries where the default is that everyone is a non-donor (and people have to opt in if they want to be donors) is below 20%. There are other cases in which the power of defaults can be harnessed to do good – it can be used to help people contribute to their 401K plans, to their Roth accounts, to enroll people in healthcare, gyms, etc. (again with all the problems related to paternalism).

Another example of possible small interventions could be based on context effects such as the asymmetric dominance effect (Huber, Payne, & Pluto, 1982), and the compromise effect (Simonson & Tversky, 1992). The work looking at context effects has repeatedly demonstrated that the alternatives provided in the choice set, even if they are not chosen, can have substantial effects on the options that are chosen. In the domain of policy, these effects could be used to influence the choices individuals make on a range of topics from healthcare plans, to the selection of public officials, and even to convince people that they are not paying much income tax. A third example could be based on anchoring

Behavioral economics and public policy 41

(Kahneman & Tversky, 1979). It has been repeatedly demonstrated that asking people to answer a question about their willingness to pay (*e.g.*, would you pay an amount equal to the last two digits of your social security number for this box of chocolates?), can have a substantial effect on their true willingness to pay for the good when elicited later using an incentive-compatible procedure. In general, people do not believe that answering a hypothetical question about their willingness to pay can actually change their willingness to pay, and this is why anchoring could also be a part of the small interventions category. In the policy domain, anchoring can be used to "help" people contribute more to charity, increase their savings, etc.

A second direction for policy-oriented behavioral research involves the application of the established arsenal of behavioral effects and results – finding ways to use these ideas to improve existing results or to come up with new policies. For example, past research has shown that when a stack of newspapers is offered for sale using the honor system, asking people to leave the correct amount if they take a newspaper, at the end of the day there are more missing newspapers than money. The results also show that if a mirror is placed behind the stack of newspapers such that the people taking the newspapers can see their reflection, the discrepancy between the amount of missing newspapers and money left is reduced. Using such devices to increase self-awareness could have far reaching implications if we were to apply this principle to driving (reducing the tendency not to obey traffic rules), to personal tax returns (decreasing tax evasion), and to dishonesty at the workplace.

Another example regarding the application of a well-documented result to the policy domain involves an examination of the framing of tax reduction on spending. In their paper, Epley, Idson, and Mak (2006) examined why the effect of the 2002 tax return on the economy was smaller than anticipated. Based on a series of experiments, the authors conclude that if the tax reduction had been framed as a "bonus" rather than a "rebate", people would have spent significantly more of it. More generally, framing can be used in many situations ranging from framing the propositions citizens vote on during election times, to Medicare prescription options, and even to the question of how to trade-off personal freedom for security.

A final example of an application of established results relates to the "hot cold empathy gap" (Loewenstein, 1996). This work has demonstrated that when people are in a "cold" and non-emotional state, they are unable to accurately predict how they themselves would behave if they were in a "hot" emotional state. Drawing on personal experience, it is commonly observed that people who go food shopping while hungry usually buy too much food, and moreover that they do not seem to learn from their past experiences. A more controlled examination of this idea was provided by Ariely and Loewenstein (2006), where they asked subjects to indicate the likelihood that when aroused they will have safe sex, and the likelihood that when aroused they will behave immorally in order to secure sexual gratification. The male respondents who answered these questions in a cold state indicated that they were unlikely

42   *Julia Dobreva*

to take risks of unprotected sex and that they would not engage in morally questionable behavior in order to obtain sexual gratification. On the other hand, when sexually aroused, the same participants gave dramatically different responses. Indicating that they would take risks of unprotected sex and engage in morally questionable behavior in order to obtain sexual gratification. Such "heat of the moment" effects and the intra-personal empathy gap can have substantial implications for policy. In the domain of sexual education, these results question the current practices, suggesting that more effective approaches to safe sex education and to the availability of contraceptives should be considered. A more distant example involves the relationship between actual voting behavior and opinions expressed away from the voting booth. When voting or expressing opinion, people are likely to be less accurate if their emotional state at the time of the opinion expression (which is usually a cold state) is different from the emotional state of the experience in question (which is sometimes a hot state).

A second direction for behavioral policy type of research involves influencing policy via economics. The idea here is to use the established path from economics to policy – attempting to modify economics to be more descriptively accurate, and from there to influencing policy. A prime example for this type of approach is prospect theory (Kahneman & Tversky, 1979), which formalized the idea that judgments and preferences were reference dependent, and has since spurred many applications. One recent example is the abovementioned work by Epley *et al.* (2006) on the effects of the framing of tax returns. As another example, Ariely, Koszegi, and Mazar (2005) provide experimental evidence for the dependence of consumers' maximum willingness to pay (WTP) on the prices they expect to see in the marketplace – challenging the assumption that demand (WTP) is an independent force from production (supply). Their results show that as the price distribution for products increases in magnitude (*i.e.*, a shift in the supply curve), so does consumers' willingness to pay (*i.e.*, shifting the demand curve). They then go further and illustrate how neoclassical economists, who assume that the forces of supply and demand are independent, will be led astray when they calculate the effects of policy changes, such as taxation, on consumption. In particular, they show that the assumption of independence will overestimate the effects of taxation, and that this overestimation will increase as the dependency of supply on demand increases. If these results were to hold more generally, and if this idea were to be incorporated in the economics models attempting to estimate the effects of policy changes, the estimation might be more accurate.

A third direction for behavioral policy type of research involves influencing policy via law. For example, Jolls and Sunstein (2004) consider the potential to amend behavioral biases through corrective regulation. However, as may be apparent by the currently narrow scope of overlap between behavioral research and the field of law, some topics and principles are more easily applicable and useful for informing public policies than others.

Behavioral economics and public policy 43

According to Altman (2008), some of the key points, critical to behavioral economics, to be addressed are:

- Assumptions matter substantively for causal and predictive analysis, be they of a psychological, sociological, or institutional type. It is important to understand why people behave the way they do, with regard to both their cognitive abilities and their environmental constraints.
- It is important to understand how cognitive capacities, information flows, culture, learning, and institutions affect intelligent decision-making.
- A critical component of behavioral economics is building models that better reflect actual behavior. Such behavior can be both rational and intelligent without being neoclassical.
- Related to this, behavioral economists and economic psychologists run experiments and engage in empirical exercises to determine the choices people make and how these choices are made, and to ascertain to what extent these deviate from the conventional mainstream economic wisdom.
- Individuals tend to behave quite differently from what is predicted by the conventional wisdom.
- This suggests that economic theory needs modification from a causal and/ or normative perspective.
- Some important concepts to be discussed are: the survival principle, multiple equilibria, bounded rationality, satisficing, fast and frugal heuristics, x-inefficiency, efficiency wages, prospect theory, framing effects, efficient market hypothesis, social and personal capital, capabilities, and soft or benevolent paternalism.
- Modification of economic theory does not suggest that relative prices, opportunity costs, and incomes play no role in affected behavior – material incentives matter.
- Supply and demand analysis is enriched by the findings and methodology of behavioral economics.
- Introducing non-material variables into one's analytical framework, such as altruism and reciprocity, social and personal capital, relative positioning, capabilities and framing, enriches consumer theory.
- Introducing effort variability, non-material variables, organizational slack, capabilities, and relative positioning enriches production theory.

Bhargava and Loewenstein (2015) contend that policies aspiring to simplify products and incentives, rather than choice environments, aggressively protect consumers from behavioral exploitation. Moreover, such policies apply behavioral economics mechanisms to enhance the design and implementation of traditional policy instruments that offer solutions to contemporary challenges. Case studies in health insurance, privacy, and climate change illustrate the application of these ideas.

44   Julia Dobreva

Behavioral economics and public health policy

Behavioral economics is improving public policy in a number of ways. Recent research shows that it provides an empirically informed perspective on how individuals make decisions, including the important realization that even subtle features of the environment can greatly impact behavior. Matjasko, Cawley, Baker-Goering, and Yokum (2016) highlight the potential for behavioral economics to improve the effectiveness of public health policy at low cost. However, they also point out that, although incorporating insights from behavioral economics into public health policy has the potential to improve population health, its integration into government public health programs and policies requires careful design and continual evaluation of such interventions.

Furthermore, it is well-observed that recently governments worldwide are increasingly incorporating the behavioral economics approach into policymaking. For example, in 2010 the UK Cabinet Office created the Behavioral Insights Team (BIT) dedicated explicitly to such work. Also, the US government created the White House Social and Behavioral Science Team in 2014. Both of these organizations have been referred to as "nudge" units and nudge was defined by Thaler as "any aspect of the choice architecture that alters people's behavior in a predictable way without forbidding any options or significantly changing their economic incentives" (Thaler & Sunstein, 2008, p. 14). Hence, the use of behavioral economics is spreading beyond these individual units and influencing policy throughout government. Other nudge units have been created in Australia, Denmark, and by the World Bank.

A decision-maker should, for example, respond similarly to a description of alternatives to address an outbreak of a new disease expected to affect 600 people, whether it is stated that 200 people would be saved or 400 people would die – the objective risk is identical in both descriptions. Yet, behavioral economics has found that the framing of risks and probabilities matters; people may react differently to positive frames (such as the chance of living) than to negative frames (such as the chance of dying). In one study that involved a hypothetical scenario involving cancer, patients, graduate students, and physicians were all more likely to elect surgery over irradiation if the consequences were framed in terms of the probability of living rather than the probability of dying.

The UK's BIT succinctly describes some of the key lessons of their approach with the acronym MINDSPACE. Some of the concepts overlap with those in Table 3.1 (*e.g.*, time-inconsistent preferences, loss aversion, and social norms), but other concepts are new, such as the importance of the messenger. The BIT argues that simple policy interventions based on these principles have the potential to achieve significant impact at low cost. For example, organ donation rates have been low in countries that require donors to opt in (*i.e.*, take action to be listed as a potential donor). Historically, these low consent rates were interpreted as unwillingness to serve as a donor, but behavioral scientists perceived that it might be the result of inertia or the influence of the default assumption that people do not want to be donors. When an online experiment

Behavioral economics and public policy 45

Table 3.1 MINDSPACE

Acronym	Stands for	Explanation
M	Messenger	We are heavily influenced by who conveys the information
I	Incentives	People respond to incentives, and in particular they exhibit loss aversion
N	Norms	People are influenced by their perception of what others do
D	Defaults	People are heavily influenced by default options
S	Salience	People are particularly influenced by incentives that are visible and new
P	Priming	People can be influenced by subconscious cues
A	Affect	Emotions shape decisions
C	Commitment	People with time-inconsistent preferences may seek pre-commitment devices
E	Ego	People prefer to act in ways that make them feel better about themselves

changed the default, and made default donor status opt-out rather than opt-in, organ donation rates nearly doubled (from 42% to 82%), and a follow-up survey indicated that it raised willingness to serve as a donor (*i.e.*, making it opt-out did not simply force unaware people onto the donor rolls).

Nudges can be effective because people are influenced by stimuli that are visible and new and small changes can lead to behavior modification. Several studies have found that simply prompting (nudging) individuals to make a plan increases the probability of the subject eventually engaging in the prompted health behavior, such as immunizations, healthy eating, and cancer screening. For example, one study found that e-mailing patients' appointment times and locations for their next influenza vaccination increased vaccination rates by 36%. In another example, rather than assigning a date and time for the patient to be vaccinated, patients were simply mailed a card asking them to write down the day or day and time they planned to get the influenza vaccine (they were also sent the day and time of free influenza vaccine clinics). Relative to a control condition (people who only received the information about the day and time of the clinics), those prompted to write down the day and time they planned to get the influenza vaccine were 4.2 percentage points (12.7%) more likely to receive the vaccine at those clinics. Those prompted to write down the date without the time were not significantly more likely to be vaccinated at the clinics. Highlighting descriptive norms among a group of trusted experts, or priming (*e.g.*, 90% of doctors agree that vaccines are safe) can significantly reduce public concern about (childhood) vaccines and promote intentions to vaccinate.

Taking into account the above examples, it becomes clear that behavioral economics can inform the design of interventions to increase the utilization of a covered service that accounts for the complexity of human behavior. In the

46 *Julia Dobreva*

case of prescription drugs for chronic conditions, nudges such as automated text messaging can remind individuals to take their medication. An automatic refill of prescriptions is seen as a way to harness the power of defaults to increase medication adherence. Also automatic refills could be made the default for prescription medications for chronic conditions.

Numerous nudges have also sought to improve diet, physical activity, and obesity. The first example given in Thaler's book *Nudge* (Thaler & Sunstein, 2008) concerns changing the choice architecture (*i.e.*, the environment in which choices are made) in school cafeterias to improve children's diets. Subsequent research has found that minor alterations to school cafeterias to increase the convenience and appeal of healthier options can increase schoolchildren's fruit and vegetable consumption (*e.g.*, changes as simple as giving interesting names to the vegetable options), although there is little information of the durability of these effects. In addition, some restaurant chains have altered the default drinks and side dishes in children's meals to healthier options (*e.g.*, changing the default beverage from soda pop to water, or the default side from French fries to apple slices).

Behavioral economics and education

Of vital importance to institutions of higher education is an understanding of what drives students to apply to a given set of schools, to enroll at one school among several options, to stay in school or leave, and to contribute their time, expertise, and/or money as alumni. Unfortunately, determining the drivers of such key behaviors is often anything but straightforward. At its simplest, one may ask students why they did or did not apply or enroll and ask alumni why they did or did not provide support. However, stated importance can sometimes lead one to miss more subconscious drivers of behavior, which is better ascertained through more sophisticated analyses.

This research contrasts straightforward methods of evaluating student priorities in the college decision process with more advanced methods. While both methods have applicability and value in understanding student choice, the addition of more advanced methods often allows one to attain an even greater understanding of student choice and, as a result, make smarter decisions. In a crowded marketplace, an institution's greater understanding of the drivers of student choice can be a competitive advantage, allowing a college or university to craft more sophisticated marketing and engagement strategies and better achieve their strategic, enrollment, image, and financial objectives.

The most common way to ascertain the importance of a factor is simply to ask. For example, one might use a construction such as: Please rate each of the following items for its importance in your decision to enroll at a particular school using a scale of 1 ("not at all important") to 5 ("extremely important"). Alternatively, one could ask research participants to choose up to three out of a list of perhaps ten possible reasons for their choice. These are just two of many

Behavioral economics and public policy 47

ways to assess stated importance. Regardless of the method, the validity of stated importance rests on at least five assumptions:

1. The true reasons are salient enough in the target audience's mind to stand out.
2. They are self-aware enough to accurately answer the question.
3. They are being honest with themselves.
4. They are being honest with researchers and not answering in a socially desirable manner.
5. They are otherwise rational in the way they conduct their evaluation.

All of these assumptions have been examined extensively via survey and experimental research and found to be potentially misleading in selected instances. "The most important thing that social psychologists have discovered over the last 50 years", writes University of Michigan psychologist Richard Nisbett, "is that people are very unreliable informants about why they behaved as they did, made the judgment they did, or liked or disliked something" (Nisbett, 2007).

Castleman (2015) claims that behavioral economics, in the form of nudges to help students and families make more active and informed decisions has entered the mainstream of American education, guiding practice and policy from when children are barely old enough to toddle all the way through college and beyond. As a result of nudge work over the last decade, school choice information is simpler and more visually digestible; the architecture of school cafeterias subtly encourages children to select healthier eating options; text messages flow in the hundreds of thousands if not millions, prompting parents to sing the ABCs with their children, high school graduates to finalize their financial aid, and college students to meet with their academic advisor.

The infusion of behavioral insights into education holds considerable potential for leveling the decision-making playing field for economically disadvantaged students and their families throughout all stages of schooling. Targeted implementation of behavioral solutions can help compensate for low-income families' lack of access to quality information or advising about their educational options. Well-designed nudges can help students and families make active and informed decisions about the educational pathways they pursue.

Castleman further provides some guiding principles for applying behavioral science to educational choices which include:

1. **Start with critical junctures:** From preschool through college, students and families face a series of transitional decisions that are often complex and hard to navigate, but which can have long-lasting ramifications for how they do in school and whether they pursue additional education. These junctures often occur over a short time frame – a window of only a few months in which students can actively choose which elementary

48 *Julia Dobreva*

school to attend, which high school courses to take, or whether to apply for financial aid for college. Families that stick with the default school or course assignment, or who fail to apply for financial aid by priority deadlines, may miss out on the chance to attend high-quality schools, take college-preparatory coursework, or receive thousands of dollars in additional grant aid.

2. **Prompt active engagement rather than give directions:** Nudges that are overly directive run the risk of distorting the choices students and families make, leading them to make choices that do not align with their goals or interests. An example would be to send students nudges encouraging them to limit how much they borrow for college. On the surface this seems advisable, but what about the student for whom additional loans would allow her to take more costly STEM courses and pursue an engineering degree? Similarly, declarative nudges (*e.g.*, "Make sure you sign up for an after school enrichment program!") can confuse and worry families who thought they had already completed an important task. Nudges should encourage active thinking and decision-making, not tell people what to do. Well-framed and timed questions can also prompt students to reach out for professional guidance when they are struggling with a complicated decision.

3. **View nudges as supplements to, not substitutes for, existing educational investments:** Behavioral interventions often have a creative appeal, and their low cost is alluring to educational leaders and policymakers who often are grappling with tight budgets. But the apparent "bang for the buck" of behavioral interventions should not be used as justification for scaling back spending on other important areas in education. After all, interventions to promote more active and informed decision-making can only be successful if there are quality educational opportunities available to students.

Conclusions

The applications of behavioral economics are numerous and, depending on the contextual environment, they could be very specific. This chapter's main objective was to comment on the most important aspects of behavioral economics and its relation to the development of public policies and their effectiveness. The main applications chosen here are education and public health policies and the results of the observations show that the behavioral elements of each policy are tightly related to the individual decision-making process, which ultimately affects the public choice and its social consequences.

References

Altman, M. (2008). Behavioral economics, economic theory and public policy. *Australasian Journal of Economic Education, 5*(1–2), 1–55.

Ando, A. & Modigliani, F. (1963). The "life cycle" hypothesis of saving: Aggregate implications and tests. *American Economic Review, 53*, 55–84.

Ariely, D., Koszegi, B., & Mazar, N. (2005). Psychology, behavioral economics, and public policy. *Marketing Letters, 16*(3–4), 443–454.

Ariely, D., & Loewenstein, G. (2006). The heat of the moment: The effect of sexual arousal on sexual decision making. *Journal of Behavioral Decision Making, 19*, 87–98.

Benartzi, S., & Thaler, R. H. (2004). Save more tomorrow: Using behavioral economics to increase employee saving. *Journal of Political Economy, Papers in Honor of Sherwin Rosen: A Supplement to Volume 112*, S164–S187.

Bhargava, S., & Loewenstein, G. (2015). Behavioral economics and public policy 102: Beyond nudging. *American Economic Review, 105*(5), 396–401.

Castleman, B. (2015). Knowing when to nudge: Utilizing behavioral economics in education. Retrieved from www.brookings.edu/blog/brown-center-chalkboard/2015/08/06/knowing-when-to-nudge-in-education/.

Chetty, R. (2015). Behavioral economics and public policy: A pragmatic perspective. *American Economic Review, 105*(5), 1–33.

Epley, N., Idson, D., & Mak, L. C. (2006). Bonus of rebate? The impact of income framing on spending and saving. *Journal of Behavioral Decision-Making, 19*, 213–227.

Huber, J., Payne, J. W., & Pluto, C. (1982). Adding asymmetrically dominated alternatives: Violations of regularity and the similarity hypothesis. *Journal of Consumer Research, 9*(1), 90–98.

Huberman, G., Iyengar, S. S., & Jiang, W. (2003). How much choice is too much? Contributions to 401(k) retirement plans. Pension Research Council Working Paper.

Johnson, E. J., & Goldstein, D. (2003). Do defaults save lives? *Science, 302*, 1338–1339.

Jolls, C., & Sunstein, C. R. (2004). Debiasing through law. John M. Olin Law & Economics Working Paper No. 225.

Kahneman, D., & Tversky, A. (1979). Prospect theory: An analysis of decision under risk. *Econometrica, 47*(2), 263–292.

Loewenstein, G. (1996). Out of control: Visceral influences on behavior, *Organization Behaviour and Human Decision Processes, 65*(3), 272–292.

Matjasko, J. L., Cawley, J. H., Baker-Goering, M. M., & Yokum, D. V. (2016). Applying behavioral economics to public health policy. *American Journal of Preventive Medicine, 50*(*Supplement 1*), S13–S19.

Nisbett, R. E. (2007). All brains are the same color. *The New York Times.*

Simonson, I., & Tversky, A. (1992). Choice in context: Trade-off contrast and extremeness aversion. *Journal of Marketing Research, 29*, 281–295.

Thaler, R. H., & Shefrin, H. M. (1981). An economic theory of self-control. *Journal of Political Economy, 89*, 392–401.

Thaler, R. H., & Sunstein, C. R. (2008). *Nudge: Improving decisions about health, wealth, and happiness.* New Haven, CT: Yale University Press.

Part II

Behavioural responses to regulations

4 Financial decisions and financial regulation

Three concepts of performance-based regulation

Uwe Dulleck

Economics and behavioural economics and the performance of financial services and products

Introduction

This chapter[1] develops concepts of performance based on financial services consumer protection regulations and building on Lauren Willis's (2015, 2017a, 2017b) proposal to rely on performance-based measures in financial regulation.

Regulators of financial services aim to ensure that customers "know before they owe" (Sunstein, 2013; Franklin, 2012). That is, markets operate such that consumers have all the information available and therefore, in principle, they are able to make informed decisions.

The challenge relates not only to whether relevant information is available (see, *e.g.*, Jadad & Gagliardi, 1998) but also to whether this information can be processed by consumers (Simon, 1996). In particular, this applies to all consumers – not only those with specialized knowledge or training. If confusion[2] or 'information or choice overload'[3] play a role and are abused by service providers, it is unlikely that consumers will make appropriate decisions[4] – or at least decisions they would feel comfortable with when these decisions are analysed for them. In addition to information overload, there are, of course, a range of additional factors relevant to consumer decision making which may play a role. They include context, biases, and cognitive load. In addition, on the supply side, actions can range from unintentional to intentional manipulation.

---

1 This chapter benefited from extensive discussions and comments from Nicola Howell and Benno Torgler, providing their insights into legal issues and the behavioural economic approach respectively. I am grateful to Jeremy Webb and Harriet Smith for editorial feedback. I would like to thank CESifo for its support and hospitality in December 2019, which allowed me to finish this work.
2 Confusion can be defined as the combination of information and choice overload (Cohen, 1999).
3 For a meta-analysis on choice overload see Scheibehenne, Greifeneder, and Todd (2010).
4 See, *e.g.*, Lee and Lee (2004), who found that online, overload leads to less satisfied, confident and more confused consumers.

54   *Uwe Dulleck*

This chapter outlines regulatory approaches that do not rely on mandated content and/or mandated forms of the financial service provided. Instead of assuming behaviour of consumers to be either rational, in the sense of the homo economicus model, or reasonable, in the sense of the reasonable person assumption in law, the approaches focus just on the choices made by consumers. The *confusion audits* proposed are not asking whether the consumer reasoned or could have reasoned appropriately but looks instead at the choices made. This is designed to capture the performance of a financial service provision in terms of whether observed choices of consumers are transitive. It also captures whether they would stand by their choice when having access to an analysis of their decision.

The proposed approaches rely on choices made by consumers. They use data on consumer decisions measuring the extent to which financial services consumers chose are not dominated by an option from the same service provider.

The approaches chosen rely on empirical methods used in the field of behavioural economics. Specifically, they involve an experimental approach that identifies the effects of different means used to provide a service using a control and a treatment group. The appropriate choices of these groups made under the different concepts will be discussed.

Behavioural economics: theory and data

Behavioural economics combines the normative backbone of economics with insights from the behavioural sciences (Kahneman, 2011). This combination allows situations to be identified in which consumers and decision makers in general deviate from the economic benchmark of rational behaviour. To discuss a bias or deviation, we first need to define what determines a benchmark of rational behaviour. Such a discussion will also explain where the traditional economic argument that governs current financial services regulation comes from.

Basic economic theory considers choices as rational if they can be shown to fulfil a set of basic assumptions. While authors vary on the exact composition of this set and the specificity, usually the set includes: completeness and transitivity.[5]

Completeness simply says that consumers are able to make a choice between any pair of products offered to them. Transitivity requires a consistency of choice, *i.e.*, if one option is preferred over another, then whatever other options are added, this relationship remains. Economic models may be more specific in their characterization of optimal behaviour of individuals. But in almost all cases they assume that (optimal) choices of decision makers need to be complete and transitive to be called rational.

---

5 Any microeconomic textbook can provide an overview of these assumptions or axioms – the terminology academic economists use for these. See, for example, Varian (2014), Mas-Colell, Whinston, and Green (1995) or Bowles (2009).

Financial decisions & financial regulation   55

Gilboa (2010, p. 5) is one of the few authors with a less demanding definition of rational behaviour. In his view behaviour "is rational for a given person [the decision maker] if this person feels comfortable with it, and is not embarrassed by it, even when it is analysed for him [or her]". This definition is helpful as it is evident – and can be shown empirically – that simple choices with assumptions such as completeness and transitivity are the determinants of 'comfort' or 'non-embarrassment' of decisions that we try to justify to ourselves or others.

In law, the concept of rationality has a close counterpart in the concept of a reasonable person.[6] While a reasonable person may not have the capacity to understand and analyse all the information provided, he or she is expected to use all the information that is provided to him or her reasonably. Both the rational and the reasonable decision maker will not be confused by overprovision of information or by the use of unusual concepts.

For many choices, rational or reasonable behaviour would seem to be an acceptable point of comparison for a "good" decision. Simple choices such as choosing between apples and peaches for an afternoon snack, or between a family holiday and a new TV, fall into this category. However, many financial products present a far more involved choice. Financial products do, nevertheless, have one advantage. Some characteristics of these products are easily comparable as they can be represented in monetary terms. The decision is thus cast in the simple terms of "more is better than less". That is, people prefer to have as much money as possible.

Traditional theory of regulation assumes that rationality applies to these decisions as well.[7] But here the definitions lead to different interpretations of rationality. A fundamental assumption-based definition will claim that, as long as individuals have all the information, they must make a rational or reasonable choice. Whereas a rational individual in the sense of Gilboa's definition will say he is comfortable with many choices given the fine print is too much for him or her to have considered in making the choice at hand.

When data relating to financial decisions are examined we ask questions about choices made by consumers and try to benchmark them against optimal choices. While this may be difficult with more complex financial products – for example superannuation funds or hybrid securities – it may be more straightforward in the case of simpler products, such as credit cards or simple saving accounts. We will look for cases where simple dominance relationships between financial product offerings can be found in a category. That is, situations are sought where the returns and benefits are at least as good for one option compared to the other and the costs of this option are lower. Most consumers, when the two options are properly explained, would use the low cost/same or higher benefits option over the alternative option. If we observe choices

---

6 For a discussion of these two concepts and their relationship, see Sibley (1953).

7 For a growing literature that discusses judgement errors of individuals in the context of law and regulations, see, *e.g.*, Sunstein (2000) and Jolls (2007).

56   *Uwe Dulleck*

to the opposite, we will see this as confusion or underperformance. Note that we define confusion in this case as choices that cannot be rationalized easily. We do not necessarily identify the reasons for these choices. In two of our three concepts proposed, the measures can be complemented with instruments to identify reasons for these decisions.

These approaches do not consider whether consumers are able to identify specific characteristics of products. Are consumers able to correctly understand product information provided? To provide a simple illustration of the case not covered by the proposed approaches, consider the 2011 floods in Queensland, Australia. Many consumers were caught out by not being aware of the difference between inundation – water rising from below – and floods – water rushing through a property. While many affected residents were not covered for inundation, they were for floods. For most people, however, these two phenomena were essentially the same. In other words, what is referred to as the Brisbane flood, was largely an inundation event, against which the majority of consumers were not insured. This type of confusion is not covered by the present proposals.

Dominated choices – measuring confusion

The three main concepts proposed in this chapter and described below are based on violations of transitivity. In respect to financial services, a simple explanation of transitivity lies in the observation that customer choices for financial products should follow the rule that under the assumption that all non-monetary characteristics of a product "are equal" the consumer chooses the product that leaves more money in his or her pocket – *i.e.*, a simple "more is better than less" heuristic applies. That is, if the benefits of a product are the same, we expect a customer to choose the cheaper product – for example fees on a credit card or interest paid on a savings product. If the costs are the same – fees or interest on money owed – we expect a customer to choose the product that offers more benefits – interest earned on savings or additional services such as insurance offerings. This is a quite restrictive measure as it is rare that benefits in the first case, or the costs in the second, are exactly the same. Nonetheless, it would apply when the benefits are better or the same and the costs are lower, or when costs are the same or lower and services are better.

More importantly, the concept can also apply to a wider range of the dimensions of costs and benefits. Figure 4.1 illustrates the case.

Each dot in the diagram represents an offering for a financial product. For now, we ignore the shading and thus we consider products that vary in only two dimensions. These are a benefits dimension varying from low to high shown on the horizontal axis and a costs dimension varying from low to high shown on the vertical axis. Our assumption for a rational choice is based on customers' preference for more benefits and lower costs, all things being equal. In this case, product A is a dominated choice given product B offers higher benefits.

Financial decisions & financial regulation 57

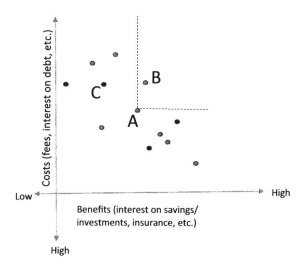

Figure 4.1 Dominated choices – product B, which offers higher benefits with lower costs, thus dominates products A and C. If different shades represent other product characteristics, such as brand or non-financial aspects like accessibility of services, we may argue that B only dominates A because B and C cannot be compared.

These could be assumed to be in the form of higher interest on savings as well as lower costs in the form of annual fees. If only these two dimensions matter when a customer chooses product A over B, it is very likely that this customer would want to change this choice if he or she has the advantages of B explained. If A and B are offerings from the same financial service provider, we could question whether the service, including advice provided, performs in the interests of the consumer given it is most likely this customer was not directed to option B. Given the offers are from the same financial service provider and no other factors are relevant, access to branches and other service variables cannot matter.

To illustrate the restrictiveness and limitation of this approach, no such statement could apply to choices A and C. C offers lower benefits at lower costs compared to A. Thus there will be customers that prefer C to A while others will prefer the converse. Our dominance argument applies only when options are to the right of and above the option considered. In this diagram, C would also be dominated by B as well as by the option to the north-east of point C.

How does this argument change with additional dimensions? While each additional characteristic takes away some of the power to classify offers as dominating or dominated, the principle argument still applies. Consider the shading of the dots. Assume that the dark and light dots represent different options and,

58   *Uwe Dulleck*

for now, assume the dark ones are better than the light ones. In this case A is still dominated by B but C cannot be compared to B. Similarly, if the third dimension has no ordering, only lighter and darker dots could be compared but the same basic principle would apply.

The argument made relies on the fact that many financial products have large financial dimensions – in terms of benefits, interest earned, etc. – as well as in cost, fees, and interest paid. These benefits and costs can be ordered in a way that transitivity should apply. Customers who pay more than necessary or take less of a financial benefit than is available, are likely to be confused or act in a non-rational manner. That is, as Gilboa (2010) describes it, they would very likely have changed their mind if they received proper analysis and advice. This is the fact that concepts 1–3 rely on to identify performance of financial services.

In the "Illustration and discussion" section of this chapter we illustrate with examples that such dominance relationships seem to be frequent enough for financial products to use our measure.

Behavioural economics

Behavioural economics is an approach that applies behavioural insights – that is cognitive biases – to help people make better decisions for themselves (Thaler & Sunstein, 2008). Performance-based regulation[8] aims to ensure that financial service providers apply these insights to help their customers make better decisions for themselves. However, performance-based regulation can only present a case for regulating the outcomes of these decisions. On the other hand, can we apply the protocol of behavioural economics to ask financial service providers to provide evidence that their service and communication channels perform with respect to customer decision making?

In his book *Simpler: The Future of Government*, Sunstein (2013) suggests that government policy should always require reporting on the success of a policy intervention using an experimental – control vs. treatment group – approach. In this chapter it is argued that performance-based regulation should operate on the same premise. That is, financial service providers should be asked to provide evidence of the way they provide their services that enable consumers to make appropriate decisions. If not, at the very least they should provide evidence that they do not contribute to consumers' confusion.

Thus, the concepts proposed in this chapter rely on data about choices and behaviours which have been observed. That is, they are firstly based on actual past choices made by consumers of financial service providers and which have been documented in administrative data. They are also choices made by participants in computer-based laboratory experiments that have simulated real problems. And finally, they are choices made by mystery shoppers interacting with financial service providers.

---

8 For an overview on performance-based regulation, see May (2004).

Financial decisions & financial regulation 59

Empirical methods

Behavioural economics relies on identifying where behaviour deviates from a rational or reasonable benchmark. In particular, it relies on evidence supporting certain behavioural interventions which, in this case, can demonstrate that such interventions lead to consumer behaviour that is likely to be closer to the consumers own interest (Thaler & Sunstein, 2008; Camerer, Issacharoff, Loewenstein, O'Donoghue, & Rabin, 2003). The scientific method employed is one that asks for a comparison of different policies or strategies mainly in terms of both an existing "business as usual" model and a new intervention. Comparing these two allows identification of changes in a policy or strategy which leads to better behaviour.

The performance-based regulation concepts presented in this chapter rely on this approach. It is argued that the changes to financial services regulation based on the performance concepts presented can improve the effectiveness of the system. This would be done by requesting financial institutions to provide evidence that changes they intend to make with respect to their services offered will lead to better consumer decisions as measured by these concepts. While such an approach may at first seem unusual in terms of financial service regulation, it is not unusual in other parts of consumer law. In most countries health regulation includes provisions for asking providers of services and products to furnish evidence of safety for consumers. This extends to those covered by public health insurance and even to requiring evidence of the benefits of a medication over existing therapies. In the regulation of vehicles, not only do public regulators rely on specifications but also on the producers of these vehicles to provide evidence that vehicles are safe in expected use situations. This extends to evidence that vehicles operate within predetermined environmental limits. "Safety" aspects in relation to financial products do exist as well in the regulation of financial products, in particular with respect to vulnerable consumers (see, s31A, 32A of the Australian National Credit Code). The approaches presented here thus propose an evidence-based approach to be applied to a broader range of financial products.

Three sources of data – three concepts

Data to inform measurements of performance can come from three sources: existing administrative reporting or accounting data; observed decisions in a controlled or (computer) laboratory environment; and observed decisions in a field experiment. Concept 1 is based on the use of existing data. (Behavioural) economists refer to these as natural experiments if some quasi-experimental variation can be observed in the conditions under which choices were made. The experiment we can employ is the choices consumers have made with one service provider. We can compare these choices among all the institution's consumers and identify how often a consumer chose a product sub-optimally. This analysis will rely on identifying situations where the available choice set

60   *Uwe Dulleck*

of a consumer has dominance relationships that allow such a measurement. An experimental perspective applied to this data relies on changes to the system or the environment that are – in the best case – exogenous to decision making by the financial service provider. For example, unpredicted shocks, such as an international financial crisis (see, *e.g.*, Puri, Rocholl, & Steffen, 2011) or a news report that changes demand behaviour of consumers, can serve as a quasi-natural experiment.

Concept 2 is based on simulated decision situations in a controlled environment such as a computer lab (Kagel & Roth, 1995). In this situation we can apply the communication[9] and service strategy of a financial service provider and observe the choices made. We can also study whether consumers make decisions that they understand. To incorporate an experimental approach we compare a business as usual scenario as a control group with an alternative new strategy put forward by the financial service provider. Another alternative to illustrate any deviation is to compare choices of a highly financially literate group as a control to a more representative consumer group.

Concept 3 relies on interactions in the field (Harrison & List, 2004). We can vary the demand that consumers – in this case mystery shoppers (participants that are asked to shop for a certain product category) – have when they interact with a service provider. We can then observe whether the behaviour that providers show leads to appropriate choices by the consumers. Different service policies – where there are different providers – can be observed. Our experimental variation could, for example, be based on different scenarios, including the demanded financial product or background information about potential financial needs in the near future, and education levels of mystery shoppers. A natural benchmark may be the choices made by a highly financially literate customer group compared to a more normal audience.

Alternative conventional measures

How are these measures or concepts different from more traditional approaches? In discussing this question, a comparison and contrast can be made to approaches and measures that rely on economic reasoning and which explicitly cover the incentives of service providers or on measures that rely on explicitly measuring the potential creation of confusion. Confusion may be created by communication[10] or the way services are provided. Regulation in this context would focus on capturing incentive structures or ways to evaluate potential confusion created by communication and service channel design. Such measures are not unknown: regulations now forbid the use of bonus payments to financial advisors. This is an example of an intervention informed by the analysis of

9 See also ASIC Report 428 (Dulleck, Koessler, Schaffner, & Torgler, 2015), http://download. asic.gov.au/media/3040748/rep428-published-18-march-2015.pdf.

10 For an interesting case study showing how consumers cope with confusion derived by overload in information and choice, see Kasper, Bloemer, & Driessen (2010).

incentives. Similarly, with respect to the creation of confusion, style guides for disclosure documents try to regulate using a similar philosophy to what will be discussed as a comparison in this chapter.

The theory of credence goods (Darby & Karni, 1973; Dulleck & Kerschbamer, 2006) provides a framework with which to analyse the incentives of financial service provider employees to recommend appropriate products. An index measuring a "culture to confuse" would look for indications in the incentive structure of these employees that may encourage them to confuse consumers – that is, that lead to choices not in the best interest of consumers. While such an approach could be effective, it may require more onerous regulatory interventions. A simpler approach would be to ask financial service providers to provide direct evidence of appropriate choices by consumers.

Another alternative for a confusion audit would be to ask financial service providers to implement new measures of clarity, simplicity of communication, and disclosure for customers. In recent times computational linguistics (Miller, 2010; Vajjala, Meurers, Eitel, & Scheiter, 2016) have been employed to achieve greater readability of documents. Such an approach could be added to content and form regulation and explicitly be used to complement consumer surveys in order to ensure consumer communication and disclosure are not confusing. If this approach takes the length of a document into account it may even provide some protection against an information overload strategy (Moy, Chan, & Torgler, 2018). This approach would ensure that the information not only meets the condition of the rational or reasonable consumer but also allows for it to be absorbed without specialist knowledge. However, there is no mechanism to ensure that the information is used appropriately by the consumer. The measure would capture the performance or non-confusion of communication or disclosure provided but not the performance or non-confusion of the decision maker. Achieving this would require an outcome-based measure – *i.e.*, a measure capturing whether the communication or disclosure evaluated leads to better decisions by consumers.

Three concepts of performance-based regulation

Concept 1: Using existing data – what have customers chosen in the past?

Description of the concept

Customers continuously choose among financial service provider product offers. These choices will depend both on their specific needs and wants (*i.e.*, their preferences) and on the way they are served by employees of the institution.

Concept 1 relies on a systematic analysis of the choices a specific institution's customers make. In particular, the aim is to measure how often consumers choose a product from this provider that is dominated either in terms of the cost to the consumer without offering additional benefits, or in terms of the benefit – without any additional costs – by another option the financial provider

62 *Uwe Dulleck*

offers. By restricting the offers made by an individual provider, it cannot be argued that sale channels, other services of this provider, or the location of branches make a difference for customers. The only difference is that some consumers may not be aware of or find a better option. It can be expected that good performance of financial services would ensure that consumers are able to choose the option that is most financially advantageous to them.

More formally, consumers may purchase a financial product – which may be a savings product or a credit card – and have several options on offer that differ in a limited number of characteristics. They might be fees, interests owed or earned, and limitations on access to funds. In most cases these characteristics can be clearly ordered: higher interest earned on savings is better than low interest; higher interest owed on debt is worse than low interest owed on debt; low fees are better than higher fees. A rational or reasonable person will always prefer the better option. In terms of economic theory, if they choose the opposite they violate the assumption of transitivity as they prefer less over more. Concept 1 counts the cases of customers choosing dominated options among the portfolio offer by a financial provider in a specific class. Looking at all consumers making a choice, **the ratio of consumers making suboptimal to optimal choices can be used as a confusion index**.

Natural experiments: how would "confusion audits" work?

Financial service providers would be asked to report on consumer decisions among their product classes as well as to report on what options the financial service provider had available at the moment in time the consumer made the decision. This data would be available to financial service providers given the concept does not rely on the set of options from which consumers chose. Rather, it relies on the set of all options that would have been available from the provider at the time. Financial reporting data is likely to be available to satisfy regulatory requirements and to provide appropriate support to customers. These decisions can then be aggregated and the confusion ratio can be calculated and compared across institutions.

The control and treatment group in this case is stylized. Thus it can be said that a neutral environment – for example a consumer picking his or her product via a well-organized market survey such as that provided by third party ratings – allows for optimal choices. Against this benchmark the identified ratio will show the level of deviation due to the financial provider's particular strategy used for the majority of consumers and employing the services of the institution. Alternatively, recent developments using methods of artificial intelligence and empirical approaches to so called Big Data could be employed to identify dominance relationships in existing administrative data of financial service providers.

What would a "confusion auditor" look like?

The auditor could be internal or external to a financial market regulator. The index or ratio depends purely on truthfully reported data. The auditor needs to aggregate this data (most likely treat it as commercially in confidence) and calculate the ratios, and only the aggregated data would need to be made public.

To be able to calculate the ratios, the auditor needs to classify products and identify dominance relationships. This should be doable for those with a high level of financial literacy. A university-qualified auditor with some experience in empirical research will be able to conduct such an analysis. Given that the methods and data are well defined, the audit could be easily verified by regulated entities as well as by the interested public. As for academic research, anonymous data and the code used in the analysis can be published to ensure credibility and transparency.

Observations on limitations, risks, and challenges

One limitation that applies throughout the three behavioural economic approaches presented in the chapter is the reliance on the dominance relationship between different offers in a product class. Even simple products, such as a credit card or a savings contract, may have dimensions such as non-direct transfers or extras, which are of high value to the customer. The most obvious examples are frequent flyer points with airlines or other consumer loyalty programmes as well as insurance components. If this is the case, the group of dominated products may become very limited. The following presents three solutions to address this issue.

First, the regulator can opt to provide an unedited audit that takes even small variations in products as separate dimensions and thus limiting the number of dominance relationships that can be identified. This will reduce the measured value of the confusion index. However, given that this measure is compared to a value set by the regulator, the regulator would be able to increase or decrease this required value to partially address this limitation. A stronger limitation is the likely strategic reaction of financial service providers. Providers are likely to issue a greater number of extras and a much wider variety in order to create seemingly non-comparable options.

Second, instead of considering all consumers and all offers in a product class, the regulator can opt to consider only consumer decisions in product classes that are clearly comparable and where dominance relationships exist. This would substantially reduce the number of data points that can be considered. However, given that this measure attempts to capture confusion that the provider may intend to create for consumers, the index should provide a reliable measure. The measure in this case would always show a lower level of performance compared to the original concept as the measure is defined as a ratio and the number of cases considered is reduced to cases where a dominated option exists. Again, the regulator can adopt the critical value that a provider needs to achieve.

Third, based on either informed experts or consumer research, some of these extras being offered can be classified as valuable and relevant or as comparable. These changes open up criticism of the choice of what still constitutes a dominance relationship that is at the heart of the approaches presented. But, as long as the auditor is transparent about the decisions made about dominance

64   *Uwe Dulleck*

relationships, consumers will receive valuable information. Classification of non-direct transfers can be easily evaluated by a skilled auditor. This could be carried out by conducting a simple survey that classifies each extra on some scale that can be converted to a monetary equivalent. Adding to this method, a more targeted approach would include determining a consumer's willingness to pay for the product extra. This context-sensitive method uses a decision framework in either a direct or indirect setting to derive a value for the non-monetary good. Such a technique is extensively used in microeconomic analysis (see, *e.g.*, Kopp, Pommerehne, & Schwarz, 1997).

The direct risks of this technique to customers are minimal as only past decisions are studied. The main risk may be political pressure from financial service providers, in particular large financial service providers like major banks. This is because, the larger the institution, the more likely it is that some products that are frequently sold are dominated by other products offered by the same institution. The index would make such large organizations likely to receive lower scores. An index could be scaled to acknowledge this effect.

Another limitation is that targeted regulation is required to ensure financial service providers grant access to the relevant data. For some financial products this may already be required for other aspects of financial regulation. For others, additional safeguards may be needed.

Apart from further development of this concept their dynamic limitation needs to be considered. If such a regulation is implemented it is likely to lead to strategic behaviour by financial service providers. The main challenge is that, while an index based on this concept would provide a good indication of behaviour in the past, it will lead institutions to ensure that offers do not fulfil the dominance relationships indicated. In this case, further regulation may be needed to ensure that products offered are standardized to the extent that competition takes place only on the limited set of characteristics. The long-term effect of the policy could be that financial service providers avoid offering clearly dominated products. This should be seen as a successful outcome for the index.

Concept 2: Laboratory experiments – simulated choices using real-world communication and online services

Description of the concept

Laboratory experiments in economics are situations where participants make decisions in a controlled and computerized environment. Economists put a lot of emphasis on how participants are rewarded for their efforts. In particular, the decisions made should influence the rewards in a way that participants would expect (Friedman & Sunder, 1994; Smith & Walker, 1993; Hertwig & Ortmann, 2001). Thus, the controlled environment simulates real-world decisions in terms of the effects on payments, albeit on a much smaller scale. That is, it is more or less as it would happen with larger sums in the real world.

Financial decisions & financial regulation   65

In the case of a performance index based on this concept, participants representing usual customer groups of a certain financial product can be asked to make a decision from options the financial providers offer. The easiest illustration may be a situation where participants are asked to use the internet interfaces of financial providers to choose a product for a specific use. From these choices it can be determined whether the internet interface leads participants to the right option or not.

This concept can test for two aspects of financial service performance. Similar to concept 1, it can identify whether choices are optimal in the sense that no dominated options should be chosen. In this case, an index or ratio similar to concept 1 can be calculated based on data collected within the laboratory environment and which produces controlled decisions.

Second, whether participants understand what they chose can be part of the empirical strategy – *i.e.*, whether information provided is interpreted correctly can be checked. Here, an index could measure the number of correctly identified characteristics of a marketing study. Participants could be enrolled either from a specific pool maintained by the auditor, or from a market research sample, or those found through an advertising campaign. They would then be asked to complete the choice experiments online or in a computer lab. Choices of the participant group will have an effect on audit results. But, at least over time, the changes in behaviours of financial service providers will be easily identifiable with this method. In general, evidence shows that the exact size of an effect is difficult to identify in a laboratory experimental setting. However, the qualitative effect – *i.e.*, the changes that result from a change in the relevant environment – carries over, independent of other factors affecting the participant pool. After making decisions about which products to use, participants can be surveyed regarding their understanding of the product (if this is part of the index) and, as such, can be tested for behavioural biases. Organizing the data collection, the logistics for this index are – naturally – higher than in the first case but still within a reasonable range.

Extension: surveying participants' understanding of products

In the context of a confusion index, the choice environment of the computer laboratory allows the auditor to conduct a survey of consumers' understanding of his or her decisions. This survey would be conducted after the computer-based simulated choice has been carried out and would take the form of a quiz on the characteristics of the options chosen by the participant. The questions could range from simple product characteristics: "What are the annual fees of the service you have chosen?" or "How high is the interest you earn on the invested sum?" to more specific questions asking for reasons why the participant preferred his or her choice over an alternative. The latter would help to identify whether choices were made for the correct reasons.

The survey-based index can be read in a similar manner to a school test. It can be rated by the number of mistakes that are made, but alternatively by

66   *Uwe Dulleck*

identifying critical mistakes. An example would be consistent evidence that participants confuse interest earned on credit and interest to be paid on debt for an account.

Such a survey, given that it is conducted in a simulated, computer-based environment, would be ethically acceptable as the choices are part of an experiment, *i.e.*, choices made are non-binding. Participants can receive feedback, providing a learning opportunity.

The limitation of this survey-based measure would be that only specific product classes will be considered instead of a larger set of products.

What would a "confusion auditor" look like?

Concept 2 could be implemented by a confusion auditor who is either internal or external to the financial regulator. To use the choice-based index (similar to concept 1's index), the auditor would need financial literacy to identify cost and/or benefit dominance relationships. Some programming capacity would be needed as would a computer lab or an online facility to conduct the experiments. It would be recommended participants be paid based on their choices to ensure validity of the results.

A performance index based on measuring an understanding of products involved would require expertise to develop. It would require creation of surveys that provide insights into what participants know or understand after they have made decisions about which products to choose. Once such knowledge of the products is obtained the index again becomes an aggregate of the level of understanding the participants displayed in the survey. This would be similar to the results of a standardized exam used in the context of education.

Observations on limitations, risks, and challenges

Concept 2 will have to rely on a limited set of products to be considered at any audit. The products need to be those for which the service provision can be simulated in a laboratory environment. This may work particularly well to represent some customers whose journey to a choice is a pure online journey. For the broader public, the journey may be more extensive. In their case the experimental setting focuses only on the online offering and audits its performance. While this approach is an easy way to audit online offerings, cases where more direct, personal advice is involved would be much more difficult to implement in an audit of this kind. Engagement with online and traditional offline communication channels, including disclosure documents, would lend themselves to this type of audit. Such engagement could be generated in virtual environments, for example by video recordings. Risks in this type of audit are limited. Most participants will feel only minor discomfort in participating and may benefit from acquiring financial knowledge.

The index is calculated, similar to that of concept 1, by counting the number of choices where the lab participant chooses sub-optimally and comparing this

Financial decisions & financial regulation 67

number to the overall number of choices. Financial service providers may again have an incentive to artificially avoid products where such dominance relationships exist. This in itself may be more of an advantage of the concept than a challenge. Additionally, it can be asked whether such decisions correctly represent the attention consumers give to these decisions in the field. In this regard concept 2 is richer in the information it provides about service performance but lacks the real-world decision making that is captured by concept 1.

The problem of identifying dominance relationships discussed in the previous section applies here as well. To some extent, this limitation can be mitigated by the product class chosen for the experiment. Auditors could clearly specify that extras are not to be considered.

Concept 3: Randomized controlled trials or field experiments – mystery shoppers

Description of the concept

Randomized controlled trials or field experiments vary specific parameters in decisions where behaviours are observed (Harrison & List, 2004).[11] Given that a performance index or a confusion audit is about measuring the performance or behaviour of financial service providers, the experiment providing information for this audit should include a variety of customer cases. Concept 3 will achieve this by using mystery shoppers, *i.e.*, agents, actors, or simulated customers, who are instructed to shop for a certain product and engage with the financial service provider. Mystery shopping[12] is a qualitative method for observing a service interaction in a real market setting. The advantage of this method is that researchers can control the information flow on one side of the interaction and monitor the consequent behaviour of the financial service employee on the other side.[13] This method is used extensively worldwide as a diagnostic tool and in all types of service markets.

Unlike other methods of evaluation – such as satisfaction surveys – mystery shopping captures the process of the decision making by providers (Wilson, 2001). Note, these agents could be simply briefed consumer representatives told to shop for a particular product or actors with a prepared case. The trade-off here is between more control to reveal the operation of financial service providers, versus greater insight into how these services affect information

---

11 For a practical guide to running randomized control trial evaluations, see Glennerster and Takavarasha (2013).
12 Depending on the industry environment participants are also referred to as pseudo-clients, simulated consumers, mystery buyers, or standardized patients.
13 For further discussion on practical application of mystery shopping in financial markets, see Lubin (2011, pp. 80–89). Smith *et al.* (2019) present a mystery shopping experiment on performance of service provision by pharmacies.

acquisition and, potentially, the nature of representative consumers' confusion. These agents will be asked to make decisions based on this interaction. If the agents are representative consumers, their decisions can then be compared to benchmark decisions made by professionals or well-trained financially literate individuals.

Similar to concept 2, these audits can be complemented with surveys or questionnaires on product characteristics now known by the agent. If agents are well informed, a memory protocol could be employed to determine whether relevant information was provided. But relying on memory protocols will have its own set of shortcomings and potential biases. These are likely to be unrelated to the audit measure. Another alternative to overcome the memory problem would be to focus on interactive online channels, chat functions, or on telephone services and keep a record of the conversations that took place. This concept relies on agents acting as consumers and engaging with the service channel of financial service providers. Depending on the number and training of agents, decisions can be seen as a direct measurement of service performance or as a measurement of the extent to which information is provided reliably. Furthermore, it is an assessment mechanism of which offers were actually considered or recommended by the financial service provider or its employees.

Field experiments: how would "confusion audits" work?

Concept 3 relies on a set of mystery shoppers interacting with financial service providers. A likely annual audit might pick a small set of products (say three to five), and ask participants to interact with financial service providers to inquire about the products. While the "needs" of customers would be well specified in a brief these mystery shoppers receive, training them on what to look for in the interaction with the financial service provider could be avoided. If the audit is conducted this way, concept 3 could employ the strategies of concepts 1 and 2 in order to identify the ratio of optimal choices. It could also survey and document the correct understanding of characteristics of the products chosen. If untrained participants are chosen as mystery shoppers, the extension of survey questions can still be applied. In this case it may be worthwhile to employ quantitative as well as qualitative surveys. To note: there is also a discussion on this extension in "Illustration and discussion" section of this chapter.

Alternatively, the mystery shoppers could be actors trained to perform certain conversations. These conversations should lead to the recommendation of specific offers of the financial service provider. A brief in this case would try to prepare for a full conversation with an advisor or agent from the financial service provider. In this way, the audit focuses on how close the final recommendation is to the identified best option and whether the conversation meets performance criteria.

Financial decisions & financial regulation   69

What would a "confusion auditor" look like?

In terms of the design used to implement this concept, this would be the most resource intensive of all audits outlined. Clearly, it would need to be conducted by a specialized unit within the financial regulator or by a skilled independent agent.

While the data collection process would require detailed preparation, data aggregation would be of similar complexity to the other concepts. Thus, the preparation of briefs would require educated professionals with good to very good market expertise. Data could be collected by either trained actors or by agents that are representatives of the general population or financial services customers. In the case of actors, they would be prepared with standard briefs and a set of questions and answers to be exchanged with the financial service provider and are asked to record recommended services. Alternatively if data is collected by representative customers, these should not receive particular training but instructed to seek a certain product and report back what was recommended (and potentially discussed). In both cases the observations can be compared to the benchmarks.

Observations on limitations, risks, and challenges

The main limitation of this process is that financial service providers may prepare for the exact design of the mystery shopper engagement given that the potential stakes in the audit are high and the observation size will be limited. This implies special safeguards will be needed to keep the exact audit cases secret and so avoid strategic behaviour by financial service providers. If this is possible, this process may provide the most effective performance measure as it studies real-world cases and allows mystery shoppers to engage with the full suite of communication services provided. As indicated above, the costs of this audit may be a limiting factor. The industry backlash may be substantial and involve raising ethical concerns. Service personnel will not be aware of being subject to an audit and there will be imposed, but not planned for, costs of the mystery shopper interactions. These concerns are important with respect to the costs of the regulation. The auditing will not only require the time and effort of the regulator but also of the financial service provider, potentially taking away resources that would have otherwise been devoted to customer service. These costs require a judgement on the benefit that can be derived from such a process and it can be argued that the benefits outweigh these costs if the number of interactions is limited. Another concern is that the exact data on interactions can potentially lead to consequences for provider personnel. This should be addressed with strict confidentiality arrangements to limit ethical risks.

There would necessarily be an annual change in the cases audited to prevent a learning effect. This would pose a challenge given that it limits audit comparability over time.

70 *Uwe Dulleck*

Illustration and discussion: credit cards, savings, and insurance products

Credit cards

A quick review of credit card offerings of the major banks in most countries immediately raises suspicion that some of these products must dominate others. Indeed rating agencies – for example Canstar in Australia[14] – usually have more than one offer from a specific institution on their lists comparing similar products, even when one keeps other product characteristics largely identical. These types of lists can be used to identify performance of consumer choice across financial provider products.

Using existing data, regulation would require the type and characteristics of cards, accounts, or insurance products offered by a financial service provider at any point in time and the choices made by consumers signing up to an offer at that time. Offers that are seen as dominant, *i.e.*, lower fees and interest rates on debt or higher benefits (holding other components of the product constant or dominating in other dimensions as well) serve as the benchmark. The performance index captures the share of new consumers that chose these "optimal" offers over the total number of new credit card consumers.

An even more demanding analysis could additionally look at legacy consumers. If new products are offered which dominate old ones, this could be captured by looking at whether or not the financial institution succeeds in switching the consumer to the new and better product, or vice versa if new products are dominated by legacy products, whether consumers remain with the old product. The application of concept 2 – decisions are made in a simulated, computer-based, controlled environment – involves asking real-world participants to make choices in a laboratory environment. The performance of the online service a financial provider offers is the ratio of the participants in these experiments that choose the dominant product over the other products. Additionally, a survey of the characteristics of the product on which participants decide could measure to what extent the information provided is absorbed and understood.

The field experiment for this concept would require mystery shoppers to engage with a financial institution after being briefed about some product inquiry. For example, a case may involve a mystery shopper being told that he or she will always repay their credit card on or before the due date and to approach a financial institution with this information. Again, after the decision a survey could help to illuminate some of the product characteristics for these mystery shoppers. If a benchmark for good consumer interaction exists, whether this is fulfilled can be examined.

---

14 Canstar is one of Australia's biggest financial comparison sites – see www.canstar.com.au/ for examples and more information, including how this particular site aims to solve conflict of interest problems.

Savings products

The offering of financial institutions to consumers that involves choosing among simple savings options is at least as large and confusing as offers for credit cards. In this case, bonus rates for the first weeks or months, early withdrawal fees or interest payments (or fees) depending on minimum monthly savings, lead to a large set of choices. Naturally, some of these will be dominated and the methodology proposed in this article would apply.

Similar to the case of credit cards, the data needed to measure performance of a financial provider is the information regarding the choices available at the time and the decisions made by consumers. If we assume rational consumer behaviour, an index could even match ex-post saving behaviour to the option chosen. This version of the index would be more demanding and, without well-defined parameters, could overestimate the level of confusion at the time of decision making. That is, it would be based on the assumption that consumers have perfect foresight about behaviours in the time period considered. In laboratory experiments as above, interaction with the web interface of the financial service provider would be an option to see whether participants choose reasonably in the sense that they avoid dominated options. The necessary brief for participants could be the availability of a certain amount of funds to be saved over a fixed amount of time.

Similarly, mystery shoppers could be equipped with a clear savings plan and a protocol of how to answer questions on the likelihood of withdrawal. A post-interaction survey could test awareness of hidden costs and risks involved in the choices recommended by the financial service provider that relate to uncertainty regarding interest rate payments.

Detailed case study: savings products

To illustrate the three approaches discussed in this chapter, the following will consider a simple savings decision. This involves offers for a cash deposit with a major Australian bank (NAB). Table 4.1 summarizes the three products, as offered by the bank in April 2018.

This example illustrates some of the difficulties but also the potential of the approach. All products can be compared through interest rate levels. But apart from the bottom two interest rate levels, their form of product offering can confuse consumers. Conditional interest, which may depend either on a deposit or on a new contract, makes it difficult to compare products. While fees play a role for many products, in this case they are nil in all four cases.

Among this set of options, it is obvious that the NAB Trade High Interest account offer dominates the iSaver option with and without bonuses. Both accounts are the same in terms of accessing the accounts via automated teller machines (ATM) or via vendor payment terminal access (referred to as EFTPOS in Australia). Adding assumptions, or observing consumer deposit behaviour, allows the auditor to find similar relationships for other options. For example,

72 *Uwe Dulleck*

Table 4.1 Basic savings products of one Australian bank in April 2018

Name	Base interest	Conditional interest	Fees	Conditions
Reward Saver	0.50%	2.0%	0	Bonus interest only paid with monthly deposit; branch access; no ATM; no EFTPOS
iSaver	0.80%	1.1%	0	Bonus interest only new customers, first four months; no branch access; no ATM; no EFTPOS
Cash Manager	1.00%	0.0%	0	Branch access; ATM; EFTPOS; only product with cheque facility
High Interest (NABtrade)	2.15%	0.0%	0	No branch access; no ATM; no EFTPOS

a consumer making a one-off deposit should choose the Cash Manager over the Reward Saver if he or she values branch access. If branch access is not important, the iSaver should be chosen if the expected time the money is left in the account is less than two years. For a period of more than two years a calculation of the interest received reveals that the Cash Manager dominates the iSaver. While the comparison of these options needs to be made carefully, the choices observed by consumers can be compared – either based on previous behaviour in a simulated/laboratory environment (concept 2), or by a mystery shopper. In this way it becomes obvious that dominance relationships between the products exist.

By limiting the considered choices to only one financial provider, we consequently have a confusion audit for this provider. In principle, an advisor of this provider should know all the options the provider offers and would inform consumers about them. Furthermore, access to branches and services offered – on and offline – are comparable, limiting arguments about differences resulting from different providers.

Survey questions for participants in simulated/laboratory choices and participants in the mystery shopper experiments (*i.e.*, untrained individuals) can be posed regarding the interest rate they are paid for a one-off deposit of $1,000 over a 12-month period. Indicators for confusion would be if consumers in the survey instrument state that base plus conditional interests is the long-term interest rate in the case of the Reward Saver as well as the iSaver; or if they state for any product but the Cash Manager offer that ATM and EFTPOS access is included as a service.

This example is conservative in that it restricts the products considered to only those that allow daily withdrawal of the funds. Term deposits could be added as an example in order to consider the option of a one-off deposit over a

Financial decisions & financial regulation 73

12-month period. Even more advanced financial options could be considered, but such considerations would then clearly lead to questions as to whether products with respect to their other characteristics are comparable.

Insurance products

Insurance products are the most complex products in the examples discussed in this section. To that extent, they may serve as an example of the difficulty in generalizing about these proposed measures. In this case it may be harder to identify dominance relationships, particularly given that services provided may differ between different brands offered by the same insurance company. Nonetheless, it is likely that such relationships exist and, if that is the case, the concepts presented can be applied. More importantly, these limitations apply particularly to the use of existing data where some assumptions may need to be made when specific characteristics can be seen as the same. As an example, the availability of a telephone channel to lodge a claim may be an important aspect of service delivery. This would be especially so when online and branch lodgement are offered for two products that otherwise involve the same service and coverage. For concepts 2 and 3, the brief prepared and the choices made can be compared relatively easily. In this case we control for what consumers were asked to purchase and compare whether the chosen option is the best of those that the insurance provider has on offer at the time. Within the mystery shopping concept, even the communication can be planned and described allowing for further control of variables.

Where existing data is used, the establishment of clear dominance relationships between products becomes difficult. That is because the way in which products can differ in the insurance space are much more numerous than in the case of credit cards or savings products. This diversity will lead to fewer cases of clearly dominated products and there may be instances where a "sort of" dominance can be identified. This product class, as with many more complex products, may hence require one of the other concepts to be considered. In the case where a clear dominance is present, for example where the risks covered are exactly the same but fees differ, the concept still applies and can provide some insight into financial service provision. The main problem arising here is that the number of observations may be significantly lower and hence the index would lose some of its reliability.

Laboratory experiments face a larger problem whereby services decided upon are not so much derived from a web interface or a stylized choice situation, but from an environment that relies on some form of consultation and advice. Where this advice is provided through an online channel, such as a chat function on a webpage, the concept can still be applied. However, it is not clear to what extent generalizing from these findings would be possible.

On the other hand, field experiments/randomized controlled trials using mystery shoppers do not struggle with the above limitations. Given that mystery

74　*Uwe Dulleck*

shoppers would be briefed with what they are asked to shop for, a follow up of choices made available by the financial provider would provide a means of determining the quality of advice.

Discussion

The examples discussed in this section provide some evidence as to why the concepts are substitutes as well as complements. The more standardized the product, as in the case of savings products and to some extent credit cards, the easier it will be to derive a confusion or performance index based on existing large data sets. The more complex the product offering, the more an auditor will be required to make assumptions about consumer needs and the comparability of specific aspects of a product. Where this applies to experimental concepts – either laboratory or field – complexity can be controlled for by carefully designing cases or briefs for participants. For the concept based on existing data there is a trade-off between the availability of consumer data and the extent to which assumptions are made about products offered by financial service providers.

Good financial services should be measured by the personalization of financial solutions for consumers. Thus, experimental methods (concepts 2 and 3) are more likely to allow for measurements of more specialized aspects of financial services. These two concepts would also allow the auditor to keep the measurement up to date in the sense that the index would depend each year on specific products to measure service performance. While this keeps the measure current, it reduces comparability over time.

What works for which market?

As already indicated in discussion of the examples, the type of products will inform the concept best suited to the needs. The discussion also revealed that the use of existing data as a comparable measure for highly standardized products may be the most cost effective and reliable over time. Performance regulation in these cases can be conducted based on consumer decisions in the past and can be compared across different periods of time. For more complex and specialized solutions there is a need to control the interaction with financial service providers using experimental techniques. These will provide quite targeted feedback on performance in specific cases.

Considering the requirement of regulating based on such measures, it may be necessary to determine how comparable the measure or index needs to be over time. Regulation could require minimum performance or even improvement of performance. This may imply that cases and products to be considered have to be specified and the measures need to be fixed. While this may well be possible for some products, it will be more challenging for others, especially if we allow for strategic behaviour of financial service providers. Keeping a constant protocol over time is very likely to lead to strategic behaviour of financial service providers in the cases and product classes used for analysis. This can be seen as a learning effect. However, the index may be misleading in the sense that financial service providers may avoid confusion in the measure implemented but do not change behaviour in other classes.

Some of these shortcomings can be accommodated for by varying the products studied but normalizing performance relative to the market. That is, while a different product may lead to other index results, the requirement could be relative to the industry. For example, it may be determined that performance should be above half of the median of the performance ratio, or where feasible, above a certain minimum value.

As an extension, the concepts could also be applied to other service providers relevant to the industry. Price comparison services, such as the Cannex service, could be evaluated using these concepts with or without fees or commissions paid to them.

Naming confusion audits

The confusion audits discussed vary in the way the data is collected. But they all rely to a large extent on a benchmark of a rational or reasonable choice. To this extent the name *confusion index* is quite appropriate as the concepts discussed indicate that services provided yield behaviour that many consumers would want to change if they receive all the information and a reasonable analysis of their decision. More importantly, the indices could easily allow creation of subindices, *e.g.*, the *savings confusion index*, the *credit card confusion index*. This would allow financial service providers to differentiate with the type of service in which they excel.

The complementary information collected through concepts 2 and 3 could be well named the *consumer understanding index*. If the focus is on minimum clarity, a star system could be used where each star or tick indicates aspects of a product that a sufficient number of consumers need to understand. All of these measures would allow financial service providers to compete on the quality of their services and not just on the financial aspects of products that currently seem to be easily used to confuse consumers. Bonus interest rates for limited periods of time are a good example of the intentional use of confusion. This can be captured by an index showing the level of understanding consumers have of chosen products.

Regulation and confusion audits

The confusion audits or indices can serve as a basis for financial service regulation. This would be similar to the requirement that a newly registered car needs to fulfil certain fuel efficiency requirements. In the case of new financial products and services, they would need to pass a test which shows consumers are able to choose these products correctly and indicates the level of understanding required by regulation. The operationalization of the indices

76   Uwe Dulleck

would allow for the setting of minimum standards and the setting of protocols governing testing conditions.

Conclusions

This chapter introduced concepts to regulate the performance of financial services. The concepts rely on the one hand on empirical approaches – natural experiments, laboratory experiments, and randomized controlled trials – in the form of mystery shopper experiments – taken from behavioural economics, on the other hand they apply a simple concept of dominated options in choice set – which we argue applies particularly well when financial products are considered.

All of these concepts are straightforward to implement. Considering the Australian case, where financial services are regulated by the Australian Securities and Investments Commission (ASIC), the regulator would be well able to conduct such an analysis.

With respect to the first concept, ASIC has powers to require financial services providers to produce books about financial products (ASIC, Act s31) or financial services (ASIC, Act s32A). Such powers can be used for the performance or exercise of any of ASIC's functions and powers under the corporations legislation (ASIC, Act s 28(a)). Thus, using its information-gathering powers to collect data for creating performance benchmarks would be consistent with ASIC's functions and powers in relation to promoting consumer protection. Similarly, wide-ranging information-gathering powers are included in the credit and corporations legislation. For example, under the National Consumer Credit Protection Act 2009 (Cth) ("NCCPA"), ASIC can require a credit licensee to provide a written statement containing specified information about the credit activities engaged in by the person (NCCPA, s49).

With respect to the third concept, involving the collection of data using mystery shopping or shadow shopping, ASIC has previously conducted or commissioned a number of shadow shopping exercises in the course of its investigations (see, for example, ASIC Report 279 Shadow shopping of retirement advice (March 2012)). A shadow shopping exercise can be completed (or commissioned) by ASIC without needing to rely on its information-gathering powers. Instead, ASIC could secure this information directly from shadow shopping participants (whether they be genuine consumers or professional actors). This could include any relevant documents created for the purpose of the transaction (for example, Statements of Advice) or provided to the 'consumer' during the transaction.

In both cases ASIC is subject to confidentiality obligations in relation to information that it collects or receives in carrying out its functions. However it is permitted to disclose summaries of information or statistics that do not identify individual consumers (s 127(1A) ASIC Act). In addition, ASIC can disclose information with the permission of the relevant person (s 127(3A) ASIC Act). While this discussion is limited to the Australian context, it illustrates that legal

Financial decisions & financial regulation 77

barriers to such approaches to regulation are likely not to be insurmountable and in most jurisdictions – Australia included – they could be implemented even without a change of legislation.

For an economist, such performance-based regulation would allow the regulator to enable competition by providing consumers with information on the performance of financial service providers. Even without regulating certain minimum performance levels, providing ratings on the extent to which a service provider advises its customers to buy inferior products – in particular when limited to the set of products offered by this service provider – enables customers to exert the right level of caution when a service provider claims to be interested in the customer's best interest. Compared to a regulation of incentives, informed, for example, by the theory of credence goods (Dulleck & Kerschbamer, 2006; Dulleck, Kerschbamer, & Sutter, 2011), customers are not only informed about the provider's incentives for its agents but about the actual outcome for customers. Such a measure could be used by services providers to incentivize its executive to align it with – an often claimed – customer focus.

References

Bowles, S. (2009). *Microeconomics: Behavior, institutions, and evolution*. Princeton, NJ and Oxford: Princeton University Press.

Camerer, C., Issacharoff, S., Loewenstein, G., O'Donoghue, T., & Rabin, M. (2003). Regulation for conservatives: Behavioral economics and the case for "Asymmetric Paternalism". *University of Pennsylvania Law Review, 151*(3), 1211–1254.

Cohen, M. (1999). Insights into consumer confusion. *Consumer Policy Review, 9*(6), 210–213.

Darby, M. R., & Karni, E. (1973). Free competition and the optimal amount of fraud. *Journal of Law and Economics, 16*(1), 67–88.

Dulleck, U., & Kerschbamer, R. (2006). On doctors, mechanics, and computer specialists: The economics of credence goods. *Journal of Economic Literature, 44*(1), 5–42.

Dulleck, U., Kerschbamer, R., & Sutter, M. (2011). The economics of credence goods: An experiment on the role of liability, verifiability, reputation, and competition. *American Economic Review, 101*(2), 526–555.

Dulleck, U., Koessler, A.-K., Schaffner, M., & Torgler, B. (2015). Improving communication with directors of firms in liquidation. ASIC Report 428.

Franklin, E. H. (2012). Mandating precontractual disclosure. University of Miami Law Review, *67*, 553–593.

Friedman, D., & Sunder, S. (1994). *Experimental methods: A primer for economists*. Cambridge: Cambridge University Press.

Gilboa, I. (2010). *Rational choice*. Cambridge, MA: The MIT Press.

Glennerster, R., & Takavarasha, K. (2013). *Running randomized evaluations: A practical guide*. Princeton, NJ: Princeton University Press.

Harrison, G. W., & List, J. A. (2004). Field experiments. *Journal of Economic Literature, 42*(4), 1009–1055.

Hertwig, R., & Ortmann, A. (2001). Experimental practices in economics: A methodological challenge for psychologists? *Behavioral and Brain Sciences, 24*(3), 383–403.

78 *Uwe Dulleck*

Jadad, A. R., & Gagliardi, A. (1998). Rating health information on the Internet: Navigating to knowledge or to Babel? *Jama, 279*(8), 611–614.

Jolls, C. (2007). Behavioral law and economics. NBER Working Paper No. 12879.

Kagel, J. H., & Roth, A. E. (Eds.) (1995). *The handbook of experimental economics.* Princeton, NJ: Princeton University Press.

Kahneman, D. (2011). *Thinking, fast and slow.* New York: Farrar, Straus and Giroux.

Kasper, H., Bloemer, J., & Driessen, P. H. (2010). Coping with confusion: The case of the Dutch mobile phone market. *Managing Service Quality: An International Journal, 20*(2), 140–160.

Kopp, R. J., Pommerehne, W. W., & Schwarz, N. (Eds.) (1997). *Determining the value of non-marketed goods: Economic, psychological, and policy relevant aspects of contingent valuation methods.* New York: Springer Science.

Lee, B. K., & Lee, W. N. (2004). The effect of information overload on consumer choice quality in an on-line environment. *Psychology & Marketing, 21*(3), 159–183.

Lubin, P. C. (2011). *Protecting main street: Measuring the customer experience in financial services for business and public policy.* New York: Routledge.

Mas-Colell, A., Whinston, M. D., & Green, J. R. (1995). *Microeconomic theory.* New York: Oxford University Press.

May, P. J. (2004). Performance-based regulation and regulatory regimes: The saga of leaky buildings. *Law & Policy, 25*(4), 381–401.

Miller, B. P. (2010). The effects of reporting complexity on small and large investor trading. *Accounting Review, 85*(6), 2107–2143.

Moy, N., Chan, H. F., & Torgler, B. (2018). How much is too much? The effects of information quantity on crowd funding performance. *PloS One, 13*(3), e0192012.

Puri, M., Rocholl, J., & Steffen, S. (2011). Global retail lending in the aftermath of the US financial crisis: Distinguishing between supply and demand effects. *Journal of Financial Economics, 100*(3), 556–578.

Scheibehenne, B., Greifeneder, R., & Todd, P. M. (2010). Can there ever be too many options? A meta-analytic review of choice overload. *Journal of Consumer Research, 37*(3), 409–425.

Sibley, W. M. (1953). The rational versus the reasonable. *Philosophical Review, 62*(4), 554–560.

Simon, H. A. (1996). *The sciences of the artificial.* Cambridge, MA: The MIT Press.

Smith, H., Whyte, S., Chan, H. F., Kyle, G., Lau, E. T., Nissen, L. M., …, & Dulleck, U. (2019). Pharmacist compliance with therapeutic guidelines on diagnosis and treatment provision. *JAMA network open, 2*(7), e197168–e197168.

Smith, V. L., & Walker, J. M. (1993). Monetary rewards and decision cost in experimental economics. *Economic Inquiry, 31*(2), 245–261.

Sunstein, C. R. (Ed.) (2000). *Behavioral law and economics.* Cambridge: Cambridge University Press.

Sunstein, C. R. (2013). *Simpler: The future of government.* New York: Simon & Schuster.

Thaler, R. H., & Sunstein, C. R. (2008). *Nudge: Improving decisions about health, wealth, and happiness.* New Haven, CT: Yale University Press.

Vajjala, S., Meurers, D., Eitel, A., & Scheiter, K. (2016). Towards grounding computational linguistic approaches to readability: Modeling reader-text interaction for easy and difficult texts. *Proceedings of the Workshop on Computational Linguistics for Linguistic Complexity,* 38–48.

Varian, H. R. (2014). *Intermediate microeconomics: A modern approach* (9th ed.). New York: W. W. Norton & Co.

Willis, L. E. (2015). Performance-based consumer law. *The University of Chicago Law Review, 82*(3), 1309–1409.

Willis, L. E. (2017a). Performance-based remedies: Ordering firms to eradicate their own fraud. *Law and Contemporary Problems, 80*(3), 7–41.

Willis, L. E. (2017b). The consumer financial protection bureau and the quest for consumer comprehension. *The Russell Sage Foundation Journal of the Social Sciences, 3*(1), 74–93.

Wilson, A. M. (2001). Mystery shopping: Using deception to measure service performance. *Psychology and Marketing, 18*(7), 721–734.

5 Behavioral biases and political actors

Three examples from US international taxation

Reuven S. Avi-Yonah and Kaijie Wu

Introduction

The literature on behavioral public finance has tended to focus on the biases of taxpayers. However, politicians and government agents are human as well and can be expected to show the same biases to which the public are all subject. Few works have studied empirically the heuristics applied by political elites, such as members of cabinet, party leaders, or members of Congress, and they rarely focused on the field of public finance (Vis, 2019; Böhmelt, Ezrow, Lehrer, & Ward, 2016; Kropp, 2010; Weyland, 2007; Laver & Sergenti, 2012). This chapter intends to make a contribution by conducting several case studies from US international taxation.

Instead of comprehensive cost–benefit calculation, people rely on cognitive shortcuts in some cases. The availability heuristic is one of the most common cognitive shortcuts. People employ the availability heuristic when they assess how likely it is that something occurs by focusing on the ease with which they can think of occurrences of it (Tversky & Kahneman, 1973). If certain risks are easy to recall, people are inclined to regard them as more serious and thus advocate for solutions (Sunstein, 2000). These easy-to-recall risks, however, are not necessarily risks with higher probability and greater harm than other risks. For instance, people tend to overestimate the risks of nuclear accidents due to media reports. Therefore, the availability heuristic helps people to arrive at decisions, but often causes overall misperceptions and behavioral biases, leading to bad policy decision-making.

Once the availability heuristic has drawn decision-makers' attention to certain issues, the representativeness heuristic shapes assessments of potential solutions' quality and promise (Weyland, 2007). This cognitive shortcut causes people to overestimate the extent to which a small sample represents true population values, and thus draw excessively firm conclusions from a limited set of data. Even though a solution only works well under certain circumstances, the representativeness heuristic persuades people to ignore the premises and overly induces the solution's applicability.

While voters and taxpayers are subject to these cognitive heuristics, politicians may also encounter the same problem. Theoretically, we can distinguish a

Behavioral biases and political actors   81

situation in which politicians are rationally following the biases of the electorate (Noll & Krier, 2000) from situations in which their own biases come into play. Despite that political actors often possess more information and resources than common people, they also face more issues and have limited time, and thus tend to rely on cognitive heuristics for decisions without comprehensive cost–benefit analysis (Kingdon, 1989). Politicians' own biases could be a more serious problem because they not only would be incapable of correcting the biases of the electorate, but also might make undemocratic and irrational policy decisions that rational voters or taxpayers might not intend to.

This chapter argues that political actors are subject to the availability heuristic in their decision-making. To make this argument, this chapter examines three examples of availability heuristic arguably influencing political actors and the unintended consequences of their reactions. The examples are all from US international tax rules: the Foreign Investment in Real Property Tax Act (FIRPTA) (1980), the exit tax on US citizens who expatriate (2008), and the enforcement of withholding tax on dividend equivalents (2010).

The Foreign Investment in Real Property Tax Act (FIRPTA) (1980)

FIRPTA was enacted to tax foreign investors on their profits from disposition of US real properties. Before the enactment of FIRPTA, if American citizens, residents, or nonresidents who engaged in a US trade or business invested in US real property, their gains upon disposition of that real property was usually taxable as capital gains.[1] In contrast, certain foreign investors who did not engage in a US "trade or business" were exempt from tax on their US-source capital gains, including gains derived from sales of US real estate. That was the dichotomy FIRPTA abolished. Under FIRPTA, real estate profits are now taxable, no matter how limited a foreign investor's US contacts may be. FIRPTA provided that gains realized by a nonresident alien individual or foreign corporation on the disposition of an interest in US real property would always be income "effectively connected" with the conduct of a US trade or business, and thus would be subject to regular rates of tax.[2]

Cognitive heuristic

The lawmaking behind FIRPTA revealed the cognitive heuristic of political actors. FIRPTA was enacted on the background of widespread concern over foreign ownership of US real property. In the 1970s, foreign ownership of US real property became the focus of widespread concern and intense debate

---

1 Internal Revenue Code (I.R.C.) §§ 871(b)(1), 882(a)(1), 1001(c) (1976 & Supp. V 1981). For nonresidents, the gain must also be "effectively connected" with the taxpayer's United States trade or business. I.R.C. § 864(c)(1)(A), (2) (1976).

2 I.R.C. § 897(a)(1). See Taylor (2013).

82   Reuven S. Avi-Yonah and Kaijie Wu

(Crowe, 1978; Rubin, 1978; Samuelson, 1978; Drinkhall & Guyon, 1979). This increased concern was related to the perceived considerable expansion of such ownership at that time (Kaplan, 1983). Although foreign investors had long been attracted to US investment, this attraction became especially strong in the 1970s due to the concentration of more investable funds, a decline in the dollar value of real estate, the rise of local destabilizing events overseas, and other factors (Fry, 1980; Kaplan, 1983).

Availability and representativeness heuristics induced people to make some high-profile foreign acquisitions of US real estate and to overestimate the significance of such acquisitions. Before FIRPTA's enactment, there were media reports of Japanese and Arab investors making money with the acquisition of prime US real estate like the Rockefeller Center (Paul, 1980). They acquired the US real estate at the time when the US economy was in bad shape because of the decline of the auto industry (Chrysler bankruptcy in 1980) blamed on Japanese competition and soaring oil prices blamed on the OPEC oil embargo following the Iranian revolution. The stated concern was that these pieces of real estate were being bought at artificially low prices by the very same people who caused their decline in value, and that when the economy rebounded the foreign investors would reap a windfall gain and escape taxation because of the source rule (capital gains sourced by residence of the seller).

Such concern over foreign investors earning windfall profits led to the ill-advised tax policy in FIRPTA. Taxing foreign investors on their US real property profits under FIRPTA is an excessive and irrational response due to the availability heuristic. As Kaplan said, "FIRPTA is an ineffective solution to a nonexistent problem" (Kaplan, 1983, p. 1095).

First, though foreign investors in US real property were exempt from capital gain tax under certain circumstances, the "loophole" is limited (Kaplan, 1983). Before the enactment of FIRPTA, foreign investors would be taxable on their US real estate income if a foreign investor's real estate activities constituted a "trade or business".[3] The scope of "trade or business" was quite expansive in a real estate context. While the Code provides no comprehensive definitions, the Tax Court's decision in *Lewenhaupt v. Commissioner* suggested that activities "beyond the scope of mere ownership of real property" constituted engaging in a business.[4] As largely passive activities were deemed as "beyond the scope of mere ownership" in *Lewenhaupt*, many foreign investors probably are engaging a "trade or business" and thus their real property gains are already taxable without FIRPTA.

Second, the intention to close the "loophole" is problematic. The legislative history of FIRPTA suggested that pursuing horizontal equity between taxed domestic investors and untaxed foreign investors, who did not engage

3 I.R.C. § 871(b) (nonresident alien individuals); § 882(a)(1) (foreign corporations).
4 20 T.C. 151, at 163 (1953), affirmed, 221 F.2d 227 (9th Cir. 1955).

in a US "trade or business", was the primary intention.[5] But such different treatment is justified on the ground that domestic taxpayers enjoy protections and benefits of US law and participation in US commercial life, while foreign investors having no US "trade or business" do not (Kaplan, 1983; Taylor, 2013). Moreover, it seems strange to tax capital gains on real estate that cannot be moved elsewhere and not on stock in subsidiaries that are valuable because of intangibles that can be moved out of the US (Kaplan, 1983).

Notwithstanding the stated purpose of horizontal equity, FIRPTA was at least also intended to discourage foreign investment in US real estate. This could be seen from the fact that the equalization between foreign and domestic investors was limited to real estate gains, but not gains derived from listed securities, commodities, bonds, or any capital asset other than real estate.[6] However, FIRPTA is unlikely to affect foreign investment in US real property. Foreign investments in US real property take place for many important reasons other than tax exemption, including this country's stable political system, relatively low rates of inflation, clearly articulated respect for private property, relatively inexpensive land prices, and good prospects for capital appreciation (Katz, 1979). In comparison, a tax upon disposition has no impact on foreign investors unless they dispose of the property. In fact, it turned out that the expected gains rarely materialized due to long-time holding and other reasons, for instance, the Rockefeller Center bankruptcy in 1992.

Third, FIRPTA is an ineffective solution to its own intentions. The resulting statute is complex. It is difficult to enforce, and it can be avoided by using a foreign holding corporation to own US real property. It imposes unneeded burdens on regular sellers of portfolio stock in US companies where there is a possibility that over 50% by value is real estate. For instance, it happens when the company is doing badly in business but its Manhattan headquarters building is very valuable – this was true of IBM at one point. It may also cause double taxation (Taylor, 2013).

Politicians' own biases

The analysis above shows that the availability heuristic caused concern regarding foreign investments in US real property earning windfall without taxation, leading to the enactment of FIRPTA. The next question is whether, in proposing and voting for FIRPTA, politicians were responding to public pressure (so rationally maximizing their re-election chances) or to their own biases and frustration about the state of the economy. Evidence supports the latter explanation.

---

5 The Committee Report tried to eschew any motive other than erasing this inequality of tax treatment and justified this single objective by invoking the principle of "horizontal equity". See Senate Report No. 504, 96th Congress, 1st Session 6 (1979). This report accompanied the bill that was subsequently enacted as FIRPTA.

6 See I.R.C. §§ 871(a)(2), 881(a), 897(a)(1) (1976 & Supp.V 1981).

84 *Reuven S. Avi-Yonah and Kaijie Wu*

First, the public did not condemn the tax code for the increase in foreign investment in US real property. The increasing foreign investment generated public concerns like windfall gains from the disposition of US real property, but no evidence shows that tax exemption of such dispositions also caused wide public concerns. Lack of public pressure could be explained by the fact that the tax "loophole" issue is too technical for the public to pay attention to. Determining the "loophole" is a technical issue demanding case-by-case analysis (Kaplan, 1983). Though foreign investors could acquire considerable capital gains from investment in US real property, not all such gains were exempt from US taxation without FIRPTA. Foreign investors in US real property were already subject to the capital gains tax if their activities constituted a US "trade or business". The determination of "trade or business", however, demands detailed information sources and professional legal expertise beyond the access of the public. Even if such factual information and legal analysis could be disclosed to the public, the technical nature of such issues would not generate strong public pressure on politicians.

Second, some Congressmen advocated the closure of the 44-year-old "loophole" in view of high-profile foreign purchases. Politicians like Senator Wallop of Wyoming, who opposed such investments, came to blame the tax code for the increasing investment and introduced legislation to close the "loophole".[7] He argued that favored tax treatment for foreign investors in US real property provided "an incentive for land investment and speculation that [was] neither necessary nor desirable", and "place[d] domestic farmers at a competitive disadvantage".[8] With Senator Wallop's efforts, the original bill had the support of over 30 senators, and then attracted more than 50 cosponsors when Senator Wallop introduced an amendment.[9] In proposing a similar bill later, Senator Bumpers supported Senator Wallop's previous ideas and additionally stated that "this equalization of the tax treatment of foreign and domestic investors in US property is especially necessary now, because the depressed value of the dollar is attracting much greater foreign investment".[10]

Third, FIRPTA did not simply respond to public pressure as it did not state discouraging foreign investment in US real property as its objective. The Committee Report said that the purpose of FIRPTA was to correct a breach of "horizontal equity" for domestic and foreign investors. But the real intention of the statute was to discourage foreign investment in US real property (Kaplan, 1983). Had the statute been enacted to follow the public will, legislators would have preferred to explicitly announce popular goals in the text or the legislative

---

7 See S. 3414, 95th Cong., 2d Sess., 124 CONG. REC. 26,140 (1978). The bill is reprinted as amendment 3988 to H.R. 13,511. 124 CONG. REC. at 34,604.

8 See Amendment No. 3988 to S. 3414, 95th Cong., 2d Sess., 124 CONG. REC. 34,604, 34,605 (1978) (reprinted as amendment 3988 to H.R. 13,511).

9 See Amendment No. 3988 to S. 3414, 95th Cong., 2d Sess., 124 CONG. REC. 34,604, 34,604 (1978) (reprinted as amendment 3988 to H.R. 13,511).

10 See S.192, 96th Cong., 1st Sess., 125 CONG. REC. 795, 796 (1979).

Behavioral biases and political actors 85

history. Therefore, politicians arguably enacted FIRPTA on the basis of their own preference to curtail foreign investment.

The exit tax on US citizens who expatriate (2008)

The 2008 exit tax on US citizens who expatriate is another example of cognitive heuristic driven by news reports of expatriations. On June 17, 2008, President Bush signed into law the Heroes Earnings Assistance and Relief Tax Act of 2008 (HEART Act).[11] The HEART Act imposes a so-called exit tax on expatriates who voluntarily give up their US citizenship or status as permanent residents of the US. The exit tax is a mark-to-market tax, treating most assets held by the expatriate as being sold the day before the date of expatriation.[12] The effect of the new tax system is to accelerate the tax due on the built-in gain on such assets, even though no actual sale or other disposition of the asset has taken place.

The exit tax was the latest in a series of measures applied to US citizens or residents who relinquished their citizenship or terminated their residency. The previous one was the amendment to I.R.C. Section 877 in the Health Insurance Portability and Accountability Act of 1996 (HIPAA),[13] driven by Senator Moynihan of New York. In its 2003 report examining the then-present law concerning the tax and immigration treatment of expatriates, including the 1996 HIPAA amendment, the Staff of the Joint Committee on Taxation (JCT) indicated that Congress primarily intended to eliminate unintended tax consequences for relinquishment of citizenship or termination of residency (JCT, 2003).[14]

Cognitive heuristic

Legislators employed the cognitive heuristic in enacting the exit tax. First, the temporal proximity of memorable events influenced the legislators' decision. Before the enactment of the 1996 HIPPA amendment, there were media reports of rich people expatriating, like Ron Lauder of the Estée Lauder

---

11 Heroes Earnings Assistance and Relief Tax Act of 2008, Pub. L. No. 110–245, 122 Stat. 1624 (codified in scattered sections of 26 USC.) (West 2008) [hereinafter "HEART Act"].
12 I.R.C. § 877A.
13 Health Insurance Portability and Accountability Act of 1996, Pub. L. No. 104–191.
14 The Staff of the Joint Committee on Taxation also considered the adoption of a special tax system applicable to expatriates for the following purposes: (1) expressing official disapproval of tax-motivated citizenship relinquishment or residency termination; (2) deterring or punishing tax-motivated citizenship relinquishment or residency termination; (3) removing unintended tax incentives for relinquishing citizenship or terminating residency, thereby achieving tax neutrality in the decision to take such actions; (4) taxing appreciation and asset value that accrues while a person is a US citizen or resident; (5) ensuring that individuals cannot enjoy any tax benefits that may arise from relinquishing citizenship or terminating residency while still maintaining significant ties to the country; and (6) combinations of and variations on these purposes.

86 Reuven S. Avi-Yonah and Kaijie Wu

cosmetics empire, while continuing to spend as many days as possible in the US. On February 6, 1995, a Treasury Department press release also described an individual who relinquished US citizenship but continued to carry a US passport and driver's license (Treasury, 1995). Due to these vivid reports, the availability heuristic induced legislators to pay disproportionate attention and assigned excessive importance to expatriations.

Second, the exit tax was not a result of rational and comprehensive evaluation, but only worked in a limited scope of cases. Despite the intent of Congress to reduce expatriations, the exit tax had the unintended consequence of increasing expatriations. Since its implementation, the average expatriation rate went up from 477 individuals per year between 1998 and 2008 to 1443 individuals per year between 2009 and 2013 (Avi-Yonah, 2015; Ahn, 2015). The reason for this increase is that the exit tax actually diminished costs of expatriation by converting a moral choice to a choice with a price tag. After 2008, expatriation was no longer a shameful act, but an act with a price set by the government. For many rich people, expatriation is an economically rational decision because the present value of future US income and estate tax liabilities is higher than the exit tax (especially with valuation disputes), taking into account the likely future trend of US tax rates and the tax rate in the new resident country. This unintended consequence of increasing expatriation shows that the representativeness heuristic exaggerated the effect of the exit tax.

Politicians' own biases

As the cognitive heuristic has influenced the legislators' decision on the exit tax, the next question is whether there was public pressure or whether politicians were responding to their own biases. Evidence shows that legislators came up with their own idea to eliminate unintended tax consequences for relinquishment of citizenship or termination of residency.

First, Congress, under no strong public pressure, recognized the existence of tax incentives for citizenship relinquishment or residency termination. Before the 1996 HIPPA enactment, Congress directed the Joint Committee staff to conduct a study of issues presented by certain proposals to modify the tax treatment of expatriation.[15] Respondent subcommittees of both the Senate and the House of Representatives held hearings on the tax treatment of Americans who renounced their citizenship (Lenzner & Mao, 1994).[16] Through press reports and hearings, Congress became informed that a small number of very

---

15 See the Self-Employed Person's Health Care Reduction Extension Act of 1995, Pub. L. No. 104–7, sec. 6 (1995).

16 US Senate Committee on Finance, Subcommittee on Taxation and IRS Oversight, Hearing on the Administration's Proposal to Impose a Tax on Individuals Who Renounce Their US Citizenship, Mar. 21, 1995; US House of Representatives Committee on Ways and Means, Subcommittee on Oversight, Hearing to Examine the Administration's Proposal Relating to the Tax Treatment of Americans Who Renounce Citizenship, Mar. 27, 1995.

wealthy individuals each year relinquish their US citizenship for the purpose of avoiding US income, estate, and gift tax in spite of section 877 (JCT, 2003).

Second, some Congress members, in their own judgment, deemed such citizenship relinquishment or residency termination for tax avoidance as unfair and advocated for imposing a tax. A primary argument is that expatriates should continue to be taxed as US citizens or residents for maintaining significant ties with the US. Senator Daniel Patrick Moynihan, in supporting the stricter taxation of expatriates, argued that

> even after renunciation, these individuals can maintain substantial connections with the US, such as keeping a residence and residing in the US for up to 120 days a year without incurring US tax obligations. Indeed, reports indicate that certain wealthy individuals have renounced their US citizenship and avoided their tax obligations while still maintaining their families and homes in the US, being careful merely to avoid being present in this country for more than 120 days each year.[17]

Another rationale for taxing expatriates is that US citizens and residents should pay a price for having enjoyed the benefits of US citizenship or the benefits of having assets located in the US (JCT, 1995). Senator Moynihan said that wealthy expatriates "avoid paying taxes on gains that accrued during the period that they acquired their wealth and were afforded the myriad advantages of US citizenship".[18] In introducing the bill with Senator Moynihan, Senator Bradley also stated that "the bill is fair to those who enjoyed the benefits of US citizenship to make billions and are now attempting to avoid paying tax on such gain".[19]

The enforcement of withholding tax on dividend equivalents (2010)

The third example of cognitive heuristic is the enforcement of withholding tax on dividend equivalents in 2010. Before 2010, payments of US-source dividends to nonresident stockholders generally were subject to a 30% US withholding tax without tax treaties, under which dividend withholding was reduced to 15% for portfolio dividends and 5% for direct dividends (Avi-Yonah, 2008). By contrast, payments under most equity derivatives historically were not subject to withholding tax, even if the derivatives were contingent upon US-source dividends (Miller & Schwartz, 2016). The background rule was that payments

---

17 Statement of Senator Daniel Patrick Moynihan (D-NY) upon introduction of legislation affecting the taxation of expatriates, 141 Cong. Rec. S5443 (April 6, 1995).
18 Statement of Senator Daniel Patrick Moynihan (D-NY) upon introduction of legislation affecting the taxation of expatriates, 141 Cong. Rec. S5443 (April 6, 1995).
19 See Statement of Senator Bradley upon introduction of legislation affecting the taxation of expatriates, 141 Cong. Rec. S5447 (April 6, 1995).

88 *Reuven S. Avi-Yonah and Kaijie Wu*

on derivatives were sourced to the residence of the foreign recipients and thus not subject to US withholding tax.[20] Therefore, foreign investors could avoid withholding tax on dividends by receiving dividend equivalents through equity swaps or stock loans.

In 2010, Congress enacted I.R.C. section 871(m), extending dividend withholding to dividend equivalents under derivatives that reference US equity securities. This rule was the result of the availability heuristic targeting financial transactions designed for dividend tax dodging purposes.

Cognitive heuristic

Before the enactment of section 871(m), increasing non-US stockholders were known to escape from the dividend taxes that they owed. In the early 2000s, several banks entered into so-called "yield enhancement", "dividend enhancement", and "dividend uplift" strategies with foreign hedge funds that used derivatives to eliminate dividend withholding on US equities (PSI, 2008). One main scheme was equity swaps. Under equity swaps, a foreign hedge fund transferred its US stock to a bank shortly before the stock's ex-dividend date, and then entered into an equity swap with the bank that referenced the stock, thereby preserving the fund's economic position with respect to the stock (Avi-Yonah, 2008). This permitted the fund to receive substitute dividend payments under the equity swap free of withholding and to reacquire the stock shortly after the dividend payment.

The availability of the dividend tax dodging problem caught attention and led to congressional action. On September 11, 2008, the Senate's Permanent Subcommittee on Investigation (PSI) organized a hearing and issued a bipartisan Staff Report (PSI Staff Report) on dividend tax dodging (PSI, 2008).[21] PSI recognized the Government Accountability Office's determination that about $42 billion in dividend payments were sent abroad, but the IRS only received less than 4.5%, or $1.9 billion (GAO, 2007). The PSI investigation found that part of the reason for unpaid dividend taxes is that, for more than ten years, US financial institutions have been helping non-US clients dodge dividend taxes with equity swaps.[22] But in fact, this abuse of derivatives could be successfully

---

20 See Reg. §1.863–7(b)(1) (source of swap income generally determined by reference to the residence of the recipient); Reg. §1.1441–4(a) (3)(1) (no withholding on swaps); Reg. §1.1441–2(b)(2)(i) (gains from the sale of property, including option premium and gains from the settlement of a forward contract, are not "fixed or determinable annual or periodical income" subject to withholding).

21 For a complete record of this hearing including the PSI Report, see Dividend Tax Abuse: How Offshore Entities Dodge Taxes on US Stock Dividends, Hearing before the Permanent Subcommittee on Investigation of the Committee on Homeland Security and Governmental Affairs, US Senate of the 111th Congress 2nd Session (Sept. 11, 2008) www.gpoaccess.gov/congress/index.html (hereafter "PSI Hearing Record").

22 For instances, Morgan Stanley enabled its clients to dodge payment of $300 million in US dividend taxes from 2000 to 2007. Lehman Brothers estimated that in one year alone, 2004,

attacked by the IRS on substance over form and economic substance grounds, therefore it did not require changing the law. Nevertheless, the hearing led to the enactment of I.R.C. section 871(m).

Due to the availability and representativeness heuristics, the attention of the legislature was misplaced to ignore more profound issues. Section 871(m) applies to all dividend equivalents on notional principal contracts regardless of their purposes and is very complex. Though the dividend tax dodging is clearly a problem and could be addressed by section 871(m), that section imposed unnecessary burden on derivative transactions without the intent of tax dodging. In addition, a related and more fundamental issue is whether dividends should be subject to withholding at all. In this sense, the underlying policy of section 871(m) is mistaken because it makes no sense to insist on withholding dividends which are not deductible while not imposing any tax on deductible interest and royalties. Being not deductible, dividends are subject to double taxation on both the corporate level and withholding level. This problem was ultimately addressed by the Base Erosion Anti-Abuse Tax (BEAT) and the new I.R.C. section 163(j) during the 2017 tax reform.

Politicians' own biases

The analysis above shows that cognitive heuristics influenced the enactment of 871(m). In making this decision, political actors were subject to their own biases instead of following public pressure. Politicians' anger at the bad actors as shown in the PSI investigation led to bad lawmaking, with no public pressure.

First, dividend tax dodging was not a high-profile public issue and was too technical to generate public pressure. Under the cover of complex financial transactions, the dividend tax dodging issue does not have simple and accessible fact patterns for the public to form strong opinions. Understanding the dividend dodging issue demands a distinction between financial transactions with the sole purpose of tax dodging, and financial transactions that are used for legitimate purposes, including swaps and stock loans that facilitate capital flows, reduce capital needs, or spread risks.[23] To identify the tax dodging purpose, the public needed to understand the complicated transactions and see through the tricks, which demanded considerable information support and professional analysis. Without the resources available to politicians, the general public are unlikely to pay attention to such technical issues.

---

it helped clients dodge perhaps $115 million in US dividend taxes. For UBS, the figure is $62 million in unpaid dividend taxes over a four-year period, from 2004 to 2007. One hedge fund adviser, Maverick Capital, calculated that, from 2000 to 2007, its offshore funds used so-called dividend enhancement products from multiple firms to escape dividend taxes totaling nearly $95 million. In 2007, Citigroup surprised the IRS by paying $24 million in unpaid dividend taxes on a select group of swap transactions from 2003 to 2005, where no dividend taxes had been paid (PSI, 2008).

23 Opening Statement of Senator Levin, PSI Hearing Record, at 6.

90   *Reuven S. Avi-Yonah and Kaijie Wu*

Second, it was the anger at perceived abuses by politicians that drove a response that was dubious from a tax policy perspective. During the PSI hearing, PSI chairman Carl Levin and his Ranking Member Senator Coleman explicitly expressed their opposition to the dividend tax dodging acts, but their opposition was based on professional judgment of inappropriate dividend tax avoidance acts. Senator Levin said that, "What I oppose is the misuse of financial transactions to undermine the tax code, rob the US Treasury, and force honest Americans to shoulder the country's tax burden".[24] Senator Coleman described the abusive financial transactions as "shameless and cynical abuse of US tax policy", and condemned that "inappropriate tax avoidance by a privileged few force[d] millions of honest American taxpayers to shoulder a disproportionate share of the tax base".[25]

What made them even angrier is that many of these "foreign investors" are not truly foreign, but US persons investing through tax havens and avoiding their tax liability on dividends. As Senator Levin said,

> it adds insult to injury when hedge fund managers who live in the United States, enjoy all its benefits, protections and prosperity and use US markets to make money, arrange tax dodges so their offshore hedge funds escape the minimal US tax obligations they are supposed to pay.[26]

They were unsatisfied that "for the last 10 years, as dividend tax dodging took hold and became an open secret among market insiders, the US Treasury Department and the IRS sat on their hands",[27] and thus decided to take legislative action to stop it.

Conclusion

These three case studies show that political actors deviated greatly from the principles of comprehensive rationality and applied cognitive heuristics as shortcuts in deliberating on US international tax rules. In all three cases, political actors employed the availability heuristic and the representativeness heuristic. They paid disproportionate attention to the vivid and dramatic events, and thus failed to conduct rational investigations of the issues. They also rushed to solutions without comprehensive evaluation of their benefits and costs, leading to their failure in solving the issues. More importantly, the three case studies display the role of political actors' own biases. The public did not ask for the tax laws due to their technical and complicated nature; instead political actors enacted the laws on the basis of their own biases. The third example clearly shows that politicians were not just paying attention to voter biases, but made

24 Opening Statement of Senator Levin, PSI Hearing Record, at 6.
25 Opening Statement of Senator Coleman, PSI Hearing Record, at 7–8.
26 Opening Statement of Senator Levin, PSI Hearing Record, at 3.
27 Opening Statement of Senator Levin, PSI Hearing Record, at 6.

Behavioral biases and political actors 91

their own judgment in enacting irrational laws. In view of these findings, conventional rational-actor approaches inspired by "economic" versions of rationality need to take political actors' own biases into consideration.

References

Ahn, J. J. E. (2015). The HEART act of 2008: To deter expatriation, but why more expatriation. *North Carolina Journal of International Law and Commercial Regulation, 40*(4), 1021–1084.

Avi-Yonah, R. S. (2008). Enforcing dividend withholding on derivatives. *Tax Notes*.

Avi-Yonah, R. S. (2015). And yet it moves: Taxation and labor mobility in the twenty-first century. In: R. S. Avi-Yonah & J. Slemrod (Eds.), *Taxation and migration*, Series on international taxation, Vol. 54 (pp. 45–56). Alphen aan den Rijn: Wolters Kluwer Law & Business.

Böhmelt, T., Ezrow, L., Lehrer, R., & Ward, H. (2016). Party policy diffusion. *American Political Science Review, 110*(2), 397–410.

Crowe, K. (1978). *America for sale*. New York: Doubleday.

Drinkhall, J., & Guyon, J. (1979). Real-estate purchases by foreigners climb, stirring wide debate. *Wall Street Journal*, September 26, at 1, col. 1.

Fry, E. H. (1980). *Financial invasion of the USA: A threat to American society?* McGraw-Hill.

GAO (2007). Tax compliance: Qualified intermediary program provides some assurance that taxes on foreign investors are withheld and reported, but can be improved, Government Accountability Office, Report No. GAO-08-99.

JCT (1995). Staff of Joint Committee on Taxation, 104th Congress, Issues presented by proposals to modify the tax treatment of expatriation.

JCT (2003). Staff of Joint Committee on Taxation, 108th Congress, Review of the present law tax and immigration treatment of relinquishment of citizenship and termination of long-term residency.

Kaplan, R. L. (1983). Creeping xenophobia and the taxation of foreign-owned real estate. *Georgetown Law Journal, 71*, 1091–1128.

Katz, J. L. (1979). Foreign direct investment in the United States: Advantages and barriers. *Case Western Reserve Journal of International Law, 11*(3), 473–486.

Kingdon, J. W. (1989). Decision problems and information. In: J. W. Kingdon (Ed.), *Congressmen's voting decisions* (3rd ed.) (pp. 227–241). Ann Arbor, MI: The University of Michigan Press.

Kropp, S. (2010). German parliamentary party groups in Europeanised policymaking: Awakening from the sleep? Institutions and heuristics as MPs' resources. *German Politics, 19*(2), 123–147.

Laver, M., & Sergenti, E. (2012). *Party competition: An agent-based model*. Princeton, NJ: Princeton University Press.

Lenzner, R., & Mao, P. (1994). The new refuges. *Forbes*, November 21.

Miller, D. S., & Schwartz, J. (2016). New 871(m) regulations finalize dividend-equivalent payment withholding rules for equity derivatives. *International Tax Journal*, January – February, 17–28.

Noll, R. G., & Krier, J. E. (2000). Some implications of cognitive psychology for risk regulation. In: C. R. Sunstein (Ed.), *Behavioral law and economics* (pp. 325–354). Cambridge: Cambridge University Press.

Paul, R. (1980). Arabs buying up US? For now, at any rate, they aren't interested. *Wall Street Journal*, August 18, at 1, col. 6.

PSI (2008). Staff of US Senate Permanent Subcommittee on Investigations, dividend tax abuse: How offshore entities dodge taxes on US stock dividends.

Rubin, H. (1978). The selling of California. *California Journal*, 9, 409–411.

Samuelson, J. (1978). Make way: The foreign investors are coming. *National Journal*, 10, 664.

Sunstein, C. R. (2000). Introduction. In: C. R. Sunstein (Ed.), *Behavioral law and economics* (pp. 1–10). Cambridge: Cambridge University Press.

Taylor, W. B. (2013). Suppose FIRPTA was repealed. *Florida Tax Review*, 14(1). Retrieved from https://ssrn.com/abstract=2234713.

Treasury (1995). Clinton offers plan to curb offshore tax avoidance. Department of the Treasury, Treasury News, RR-54.

Tversky, A., & Kahneman, D. (1973). Availability: A heuristic for judging frequency and probability. *Cognitive Psychology*, 5(2), 207–232.

Vis, B. (2019). Heuristics and political elites' judgment and decision-making. *Political Studies Review*, 17(1), 41–52.

Weyland, K. (2007). *Bounded rationality and policy diffusion: Social sector reform in Latin America*. Princeton, NJ and Oxford: Princeton University Press.

6 Varieties of general anti-avoidance legislation

John Prebble

I. Introduction	94
II. Categories of tax minimisation	94
A. Mitigation	94
1. Measures to promote favoured industries	94
2. Measures to stimulate the economy as a whole	95
3. Measures to promote social welfare	95
B. Avoidance	95
C. Evasion	96
III. Example of tax avoidance: *Bowater Property Developments*	96
IV. Problems with the analytical framework	97
V. Second example of tax avoidance	98
VI. Specific anti-avoidance rules	99
VII. General anti-avoidance rules (GAARs)	100
VIII. Fictional transactions	102
IX. Abuse of law	103
X. Operation and history of GAARs	104
XI. Questionable qualities of GAARs	105
XII. The "Investor" example of tax avoidance	106
XIII. International tax planning	107
XIV. Fictions in the Investor (plus Parent Company and Subsidiary) example	108
XV. Specific anti-avoidance regimes revisited	109
XVI. GAARs and economics	110
XVII. An example from the common law: Australia and New Zealand	112
XVIII. Other examples of similarities and dissimilarities between GAARs	113
A. Length and complexity contrasted with conciseness	113
B. Contrasts between GAARs of common law jurisdictions	114
C. Significance of the criterion of economic substance	117
XIX. Conclusion: lessons from differences between GAARs	119
XX. References	120

94   *John Prebble*

I. Introduction

People prefer not to pay taxes. For instance, importers become smugglers to evade customs duties or value added taxes; rich people give their property away during their lives to avoid death duties. Most states punish the former. States that impose taxes on death generally enact measures to frustrate or at least to minimise the latter. For example, states may tax inter-vivos gifts or may claw property given away within a specified time before death back into the taxable estate of the deceased.

This chapter addresses another form of state exaction: income tax. People's behaviour when faced with income tax is often the same as their reaction to customs duties or to death taxes, that is, to endeavour not to pay it. We may call measures to pay less tax "minimisation". As used in this chapter, the term "minimisation" implies no value-judgment. Minimisation may involve a range of activities from measures promoted by the legislature to actions that are punished as illegal. It is useful to think of minimisation as including three categories.

One category of tax minimisation is known as "tax avoidance", which is explained in the following section of this chapter. To counter tax avoidance, legislatures often promulgate what are known as "general anti-avoidance rules", also to be explained. This chapter asks whether the discipline of behavioural public finance can help a legislature to decide whether to enact a general anti-avoidance rule, and, if so, whether the discipline enables us to predict the form of the rule that will be enacted.

II. Categories of tax minimisation

There is no universally accepted vocabulary of tax minimisation. This chapter adopts a tripartite analytical framework that is reasonably widely accepted, though some may employ different terminology. The categories are:

A. Mitigation

The chapter uses "mitigation" to refer to measures that taxpayers may take to reduce tax, being measures of kinds that are encouraged, or at least tolerated, by government policy. The classic example is a donation to, say, a hospital where the legislature exempts income that taxpayers give to charity. There are many other examples. Many tax scholars, including the present author, disfavour these kinds of incentive as apt to distort economic decisions, but they happen, nevertheless. Categories include:

1. Measures to promote favoured industries

A state that favours agriculture may permit farmers to deduct the cost of tractors in the year of purchase rather than capitalising that cost. Or a state may tax an industry at a preferentially low rate, or relieve an industry from any taxation at all, as was formerly the position in respect of gold mining in Australia.[1]

2. Measures to stimulate the economy as a whole

In order to stimulate a sluggish economy, a state may allow a swathe of capital expenditure across the whole economy to be deducted in calculating taxable income as if it were revenue expenditure.

3. Measures to promote social welfare

Some states use the tax system to distribute benefits that might otherwise be delivered by way of a social welfare system. For instance, individual taxpayers may be permitted to deduct personal medical expenses as if they were costs related to earning income.

Generally speaking, taxpayers who take advantage of such incentives or allowances are not thought of as "avoiding" tax, even though the result of their actions is to reduce their taxable income in the year in question.

B. Avoidance

Both journalism and scholarly writing contain many definitions and descriptions of tax avoidance. The following from Andrew Woodcock captures most of the salient points:[2]

> All [methods of avoidance] are alike in that they are definitely contrary to the spirit of the law. All are alike in that they represent a determined effort on the part of those who use them to dodge the payment of taxes which Congress based on ability to pay. All are alike in that failure to pay results in shifting the tax load to the shoulders of those less able to pay.

More succinctly, in announcing a forthcoming work by Christine Osterloh-Konrad,[3] the Max Planck Institute for Tax Law and Public Finance described tax avoidance arrangements as "cases in which the result of applying a legal rule is at odds with the rule's justification".[4] Most crucially, avoidance does not involve breaking the law unless the state in question has legislated to penalise the practice. But these generalisations take us only so far. The point can be made only with an example, which will be appear in section III, below.

---

1 Income Tax Assessment Bill 1924 (Australia), s3.
2 Woodcock, A. (2009, September 22). Darling Blitz on "morally wrong" tax avoidance, *The Scotsman*. Retrieved from www.scotsman.com/latestnews/Darling-blitz—on-.5666457.jp.
3 Osterloh-Konrad, C. (2019). *Die Steuerumgehung–Eine rechtsvergleichende und rechtstheoretische Analyse*. Tübingen: Mohr Siebeck, summarising page 745.
4 Max Planck Institute for Tax Law and Public Finance (2019). *MPI Insights*, 8.

96   *John Prebble*

C. *Evasion*

Evasion is conceptually simpler than avoidance. The term is generally used to refer to minimisation of tax by means that are illegal, such as under-declaring one's income. Most techniques of evasion are relatively simple, such as pocketing cash receipts rather than putting them through the till, or failing to lodge a return at all. Some are more sophisticated, such as generating false invoices for goods or services that were not supplied. But all necessarily involve an element of deceit.

III. Example of tax avoidance: *Bowater Property Developments*

To help to recognise avoidance, consider an example used in a previous paper, *Inland Revenue Commissioners v. Bowater Property Developments*, a United Kingdom case that the House of Lords decided in 1988.[5] That case involved development land tax, a kind of capital gains tax that applied to land sales if the development value component of the sale was greater than £50,000.[6] In a transaction potentially caught by the tax, Bowater proposed to sell land for more than £250,000 to a company called Milton Pipes Limited.[7]

Instead of selling in one parcel, Bowater segmented the land into five undivided shares.[8] It sold one share to each of five sibling companies in the Bowater group for £36,000 per share.[9] Land in each of the undivided shares looked just as it had before being segmented; there was no subdivisional survey nor any separate titles.[10] The five Bowater companies owned the land under one title, just as a married couple may own their home in one title.[11]

The Bowater companies resembled a modern marriage between five spouses who share all their property. These five sales had no effect on the beneficial ownership of the land.[12] Both before and after the sales, the ultimate owners were the shareholders in the Bowater group.[13] The five companies then sold their undivided shares to Milton Pipes for £52,000 each.[14] That is, each company bought for

---

5   *Sub nom Craven v. White*, [1989] A.C. 398 (H.L.) (Eng.), discussed in Prebble, R., & Prebble, J. (2010). Does the use of general anti-avoidance rules to combat tax avoidance breach principles of the rule of law? A comparative study, *Saint Louis University Law Journal*, 55, 21–45, Sanford E. Sarasohn Memorial Conference on Critical Issues in International and Comparative Taxation, 24–25, Victoria University of Wellington Legal Research Paper No. 8/2012.

6   Id. at 499.

7   Id. at 430.

8   Id. at 499.

9   See id. at 496.

10   See id. at 429.

11   Id.

12   See id. at 407 (using "beneficial" in its substantive sense rather than with the meaning that obtains in trust law).

13   Id.

14   See id. at 496.

Varieties of anti-avoidance legislation 97

£36,000 and sold for £52,000, earning a profit of £16,000, well under the capital gains tax threshold of £50,000.

Legally, there were five separate sales from Bowater to the sibling companies and five more sales to Milton Pipes. Economically, there was just one sale from Bowater to Milton Pipes, or, more precisely, from the shareholders in the former to their counterparts in the latter. Ignoring this economic reality, however, the House of Lords treated the transactions not only as legally genuine, which they were, but as effective for tax purposes.[15] Bowater accordingly escaped development land tax.[16] That result would not, or at least should not, obtain in a jurisdiction with an effective general anti-avoidance rule.

IV. Problems with the analytical framework

The tripartite analytical framework just presented is attractive, but deceptively so. It gives rise to a number of problems, of which this chapter discusses two: first, that the lines dividing avoidance from the other two categories are blurred and secondly, that some language used to describe avoidance can be vulnerable to arguments that the words so used are not apt to catch all kinds of arrangement that from a policy point of view should be caught.

Turning to the first problem: at first impression, one would not expect much difficulty in distinguishing between avoidance and evasion. The absence of deceit in the former, and the presence of deceit in the latter, seem to create a sharp line. But that line is elusive. Suppose that an arrangement that minimises tax involves only legally effective transactions. Nevertheless, the transactions and the overall structure are artificial and lack economic rationale; in short, they amount to avoidance. On the face of it, the arrangement amounts to avoidance at worst. But suppose that the arrangement is so obviously artificial that it would clearly fail if discovered and challenged, or suppose even that there is a good chance that this is so. In these circumstances, it is arguably dishonest for the taxpayer to rely on the arrangement when returning income to the Commissioner. The author has argued elsewhere that such an arrangement, apparently no more than avoidance, is in fact evasion.[17] That is, not only is the line between avoidance and evasion blurred, but the two concepts in a sense overlap.[18]

Turn to the second problem that arises in respect of the tripartite analytical framework identified above, viz., language that is not adequate to capture all kinds of arrangement that may entail tax avoidance. A good example of such

15 Id. at 401.

16 Id.

17 Prebble, J. (1996b). Criminal law, tax evasion, shams, and tax avoidance: Part I – Tax evasion and general doctrines of criminal law. *New Zealand Journal of Taxation Law and Policy*, 2, 3–16, and Prebble, J. (1996c). Criminal law, tax evasion, shams, and tax avoidance: Part II – Criminal law consequences of categories of evasion and avoidance. *New Zealand Journal of Taxation Law and Policy*, 2, 59–74.

18 Id.

98 *John Prebble*

language may be the word "abuse". For instance, Part 5 (General Anti-Abuse Rule) of the United Kingdom Finance Act 2013 impugns:[19]

> … arrangements the entering into or carrying out of which cannot reasonably be regarded as a reasonable course of action in relation to the relevant tax provisions, having regard to all the circumstances ….

"Abuse" certainly covers some forms of avoidance, but possibly not all forms. In terms of the definition offered by the Max Planck Institute, quoted above,[20] whereby tax avoidance entails "cases in which the result of applying a legal rule is at odds with the rule's justification",[21] the concept of abuse is apt to describe cases where a particular provision has been used for purposes that Parliament cannot have intended. Indeed, many avoidance transactions are of this nature, typically abusing legislation that is calculated to promote the kinds of public policy described above, being policy to promote a particular industry, or to promote the economy in general, or to advance one social goal or another.[22] This point is best explained by an example. Take *Barclays Mercantile Business Finance Ltd v. Mawson (Inspector of Taxes)*, again from the United Kingdom House of Lords.[23] We may call the taxpayer "BMBF".

V. Second example of tax avoidance

Barclays Mercantile[24] involved the calculation of taxable income. In this process, tax systems usually allow businesses to deduct allowances to represent the decline in value of their capital assets through use or obsolescence, often called "depreciation". Most tax regimes try to set depreciation allowances at sums that reflect the true periodic decline in value of the assets in question as well as can be estimated. To encourage industries to make more capital investment, legislation sometimes permits taxpayers to deduct more than the annual estimated decline in value. The effect is to deliver a subsidy through the tax system. An example was section 24 of the United Kingdom Capital Allowances Act 1990, which, broadly speaking, allowed "a person carrying on a trade [who had] incurred capital expenditure on the provision of machinery or plant" to write its cost off against revenue over four years even if the plant or machinery was expected to last much longer.

BMBF came to know that Bord Gáis Éireann, or "BGE", an Irish statutory corporation responsible for the supply, transmission, and distribution of natural gas in the Republic of Ireland, was having a pipeline built to transport

---

19 Finance Act 2013, s 216(2).
20 Text accompanying footnote 4, above.
21 Max Planck Institute for Tax Law and Public Finance (2019). *MPI Insights*, 8, s.
22 Section II.A above.
23 [2005] 1 AC 684 (HL).
24 Id.

gas from Scotland to Ireland. Even assuming that the 1990 United Kingdom statute was intended to confer tax benefits on an Irish statutory corporation (which was not explored in the judgments) BGE would have been unable to take advantage of the accelerated, or of any, capital allowances in respect of the pipeline because BGE was in loss. The solution was for BMBF to buy the pipeline from BGE for £91million and for BMBF, not BGE, to claim the allowances. The transaction thus transferred the benefit of the capital allowances from BGE to BMBF. No doubt the price reflected a sharing of the benefit between the parties. The question was, was BMBF entitled to deduct capital allowances in calculating its taxable income?

The Crown argued that section 24 of the Capital Allowances Act 1994 was intended to benefit industrial taxpayers, not financiers. To translate the Crown's argument into modern terms, the arrangement was artificial and was arguably an abuse of section 24. Nevertheless, their Lordships allowed BMBF's claim. The decision might have been otherwise had the United Kingdom GAAR then been enacted.

As an example of avoidance, the importance of *Barclays Mercantile* rests not in the outcome (which might well be different today or in a different jurisdiction) but in the manner whereby the facts map closely onto the concept of "abuse" of a particular law, in this case of section 24.

So much for an example of a case of avoidance that clearly involves abuse. The position is less clear in respect of, say, *Bowater Property*,[25] the example discussed earlier, where there was clearly avoidance, but where it is hard to point to any particular provision that was "abused". Of course, the Crown could make a broad argument that *Bowater Property* abused rules to the effect that the tax system deals with separate companies and with separate lots of land separately, even if they are all beneficially owned by the same people, but the arrangement is not so clearly able to be stigmatised as an abuse of a particular law.

VI. Specific anti-avoidance rules

Bowater Property[26] and *Barclay's Mercantile*[27] are only two of the many avoidance cases, from many jurisdictions, that illustrate the frustration that the authorities, both officials and lawmakers, have experienced for decades when they have moved against tax avoidance. Authorities' responses depend on the place, the time, and the severity of the problems that reveal themselves. This chapter focuses on the enactment of legislative responses, of which there are two principal models: specific anti-avoidance rules and general anti-avoidance rules.

---

25 *Inland Revenue Commissioners v. Bowater Property Developments, sub nom Craven v. White*, [1989] A.C. 398 (H.L.) (Eng.).

26 Id.

27 *Barclays Mercantile Business Finance Ltd v. Mawson (Inspector of Taxes)* [2005] 1 AC 684 (HL) (Eng.).

100   John Prebble

Specific anti-avoidance rules are the most obvious measure. These are rules that target the particular kind or form of arrangement that taxpayers have adopted to circumvent the policy of the legislature. For instance, if the avoidance arrangement in question abuses a particular rule in the manner seen in the *Barclays Mercantile* case, the legislature may adopt a rule that in effect provides that if an arrangement uses the rule in specified ways then parties to the arrangement are denied relevant tax benefits.[28] Alternatively, or in addition, the legislature may repeal or modify the rule. Similar responses may follow when the avoidance is structural rather than targeted at a particular rule. For instance, the practice of businesspeople employing their spouses at inflated salaries in order to increase their own deductible expenses (and thus to reduce their taxable income) may provoke a legislative response of denying deductions for salaries paid to spouses unless the amount is approved by the revenue authorities.

Specific anti-avoidance rules are useful, but they suffer from a shortcoming: parliaments can draft and enact specific rules only if they can first identify or predict the behaviours or transactions that they wish to target. Such are the multifarious structures and transactions available to businesses that legislation can never be exhaustive. This is the reason for general anti-avoidance rules, or GAARs, which are the primary subject of this chapter.

VII. General anti-avoidance rules (GAARs)

Since tax avoidance poses broadly the same challenges for all jurisdictions, and since all income tax legislation must grapple with similar challenges, one might expect that GAARs would all adopt broadly similar language, or, at least, that GAARs would be similar in jurisdictions that are within the same family of laws, such as common law or civil law.

In respect of their *effect*, in the case of most GAARs this expectation is not far from reality. Generally, and by way of gross over-simplification, GAARs provide that revenue authorities may disregard arrangements made by taxpayers to avoid tax and may impose tax on the basis of the underlying substance of the transactions in question. But while this may be the effect of GAARs, their language and modus operandi vary greatly. We may take the GAARs of France and of Germany as examples. Each has broadly the same effect, but they achieve that effect through rather different language. Nevertheless, they are notably similar in one respect: they are both succinct as GAARs go. In France, the GAAR is Article L 64 (1) of the Code of Tax Procedure, le Livre de Procédure Fiscale.[29] It reads in translation:

---

28 See, *e.g.*, *Commissioner of Inland Revenue v. Challenge Corp Ltd* [1986] NZPC 1, [1987] WLR 24.

29 1. Afin d'en restituer le véritable caractère, l'administration est en droit d'écarter, comme ne lui étant pas opposables, les actes constitutifs d'un abus de droit, soit que ces actes ont un caractère fictif, soit que, recherchant le bénéfice d'une application littérale des textes ou de décisions à

Varieties of anti-avoidance legislation   101

In order to restore the true nature [of an arrangement], the [tax] administration may (which power may not to be invoked against the administration) re-characterise actions that constitute an abuse of rights, whether those actions are of a fictional character or the actions seek to benefit from a literal application of rules or decisions that are contrary to the objectives pursued by the authors [of the rules or decisions], if the said actions have been inspired by no other motive than to avoid or mitigate the tax burden that the person would normally have borne in view of his situation or his real activities if the actions had not been passed or carried out.

In Germany, Section 42 of the General Tax Code: Abuse by tax planning schemes, or § 42 AO (Abgabenordnung) Missbrauch von rechtlichen Gestaltungs-möglichkeiten,[30] reads in translation:

(1) It shall not be possible to circumvent tax legislation by abusing legal options for tax planning schemes. Where the element of an individual tax law's provision to prevent circumventions of tax has been fulfilled, the legal consequences shall be determined pursuant to that provision. Where this is not the case, the tax claim shall in the event of an abuse within the meaning of subsection (2) below arise in the same manner as it arises through the use of legal options appropriate to the economic transactions concerned.

(2) An abuse shall be deemed to exist where an inappropriate legal option is selected which, in comparison with an appropriate option, leads to tax advantages unintended by law for the taxpayer or a third party. This shall not apply where the taxpayer provides evidence of non-tax reasons for the selected option which are relevant when viewed from an overall perspective.

---

l'encontre des objectifs poursuivis par leurs auteurs, ils n'ont pu être inspirés par aucun autre motif que celui d'éluder ou d'atténuer les charges fiscales que l'intéressé, si ces actes n'avaient pas été passés ou réalisés, aurait normalement supportées eu égard à sa situation ou à ses activités réelles.

30 (1) Durch Missbrauch von Gestaltungsmöglichkeiten des Rechts kann das Steuergesetz nicht umgangen werden. Ist der Tatbestand einer Regelung in einem Einzelsteuergesetz erfüllt, die der Verhinderung von Steuerumgehungen dient, so bestimmen sich die Rechtsfolgen nach jener Vorschrift. Anderenfalls entsteht der Steueranspruch beim Vorliegen eines Missbrauchs im Sinne des Absatzes 2 so, wie er bei einer den wirtschaftlichen Vorgängen angemessenen rechtlichen Gestaltung entsteht.

(2) Ein Missbrauch liegt vor, wenn eine unangemessene rechtliche Gestaltung gewählt wird, die beim Steuerpflichtigen oder einem Dritten im Vergleich zu einer angemessenen Gestaltung zu einem gesetzlich nicht vorgesehenen Steuervorteil führt. Dies gilt nicht, wenn der Steuerpflichtige für die gewählte Gestaltung außersteuerliche Gründe nachweist, die nach dem Gesamtbild der Verhältnisse beachtlich sind.

VIII. Fictional transactions

By way of example, and without comprehensively identifying and analysing the differences between the two GAARs, it is notable that the targets of the French GAAR include "actions ... of a fictional character", whereas the German GAAR does not mention fictions. In this respect, the form of the German GAAR is virtually standard; apart from the French GAAR, the author knows of no GAAR that mentions fictions except Article 50 of the General Tax Code of Burundi, which, despite Burundi's Belgian heritage, appears to be a fairly close copy of the French version.

In the context of tax law, "fictional transaction" may have one of two meanings. The first is a transaction that never exists in law or in fact. By "fictional transactions" the French GAAR, and this section of this chapter, mean this kind of transaction, that is, a transaction that does not exist at all. It may be documented, but the documents represent nothing: neither an economic transaction nor even a transaction that has a legal form but no economic substance.

Secondly, the term "fictional transaction" is sometimes used in this latter sense, that is, in the sense of a transaction that has a legal form but no substance. This and following sections of this chapter discuss such transactions. In the present context, we return to transactions that are wholly fictional. Why do GAARS not target fictional transactions? After all, fictional transactions are common enough ploys in attempts to reduce tax. Take as an example claims to subtract deductions in calculating one's taxable income where the deductions are fictional expenses that are evidenced by no more than fraudulent invoices, or possibly by only the taxpayer's imagination. Fullagar J. gave the answer in the High Court of Australia:[31]

> The [GAAR] is not aimed at fraudulent conduct or at pretended as distinct from real transactions. Such cases need no statutory provision. It is aimed at transactions which are in themselves real and lawful but which the Legislature desires to nullify so far, and only so far as they may operate to avoid tax.

To put the matter another way, taxpayers who rely on fictional transactions in calculating their income are guilty of fraud, that is, of evasion, in terms of the tripartite framework explained in section II of this chapter. Fiscal authorities fight evasion by investigation, reassessment, and penalties. There is no need to turn to a GAAR. In fact, this is presumably the case in France and, indeed, in Burundi. It would be odd for any legal system to honour fictional transactions, either by enforcing them or by recognising them for tax purposes. Bearing in mind the difficulty of establishing a negative, such research as the author has been able to undertake indicates that, despite the apparent assumption of the drafter of

---

31 *Federal Commissioner of Taxation v. Newton* (1957) 96 C.L.R. 578, 647, upheld by the Judicial Committee of the Privy Council, [1958] A.C. 450.

the French GAAR, French law follows the logic of the law of everyone else and does not recognise fictional transactions, except no doubt to penalise or to punish their authors, perhaps for fraud, if they try to rely upon them.

IX. Abuse of law

It is notable that both GAARs operate when there has been an "abuse" of law (Germany) or of [legal] rights (France), which amounts broadly to the same thing. An immediate question arises. The legal systems of both France and Germany recognise and act on the principle of abuse of law, meaning, broadly speaking, that the law prohibits legal agents from abusing their legal rights to the detriment of others.[32] Considering this doctrine, why was it necessary for France and Germany (and, indeed, for many other civil law jurisdictions) to enact GAARs? Why did the fiscal authorities not simply rely on basic doctrine? In fact, historically, revenue authorities in at least some civil law jurisdictions have challenged tax avoidance successfully on the basis of the abuse of law doctrine. For example, on 23 December 2008 the Italian Corte Suprema di Cassazione delivered judgment in two cases where tax planners had attempted to contrive that their clients could extract dividends in effect tax free by techniques known as "dividend washing" (judgment 30055) and "dividend stripping" (judgment 30057.) The Italian court applied the doctrine of *abuso di diritto*, not as a doctrine of tax law but as a principle that flows naturally from Article 53 of the Italian constitution, which reads: "Everyone shall contribute to public expenditure in accordance with his means, [and] The system of taxation shall be based on criteria of progression".[33]

The logic of the argument is that if taxpayers succeed in avoiding tax on what is in substance their income they will neither contribute according to their means nor pay the correct amount of tax, as measured by the Italian progressive scale. Nevertheless, by 2015 Italy had enacted a general anti-abuse rule in respect of taxation, namely Article 10-*bis* of Law 212/2000, which addresses in its first paragraph: "operations lacking economic substance that, although complying in form with fiscal rules, essentially realize undue tax advantages".[34]

For some years, the European Court of Justice has taken an approach similar to that of the Italian Corte Suprema di Cassazione. That is, the Court of Justice holds that European law includes a general anti-abuse of law principle.[35] That

---

32 See generally, Bolgár, V. (1975). Abuse of rights in France, Germany, and Switzerland: A survey of a recent chapter in legal doctrine. *Louisiana Law Review, 35*(5), 1015–1036.

33 See further, Galdieri, E. et al. (2009). The limits to tax planning, minimizing taxes and corporate social responsibility. *Eucotax Wintercourse 2009*, 37. Retrieved 22 October 2019, from https://core.ac.uk/download/pdf/54549463.pdf.

34 Legislative Decree 128/2015, Italy.

35 E.g., two cases in 2016 before the European Court from Denmark on treaty shopping, C–115/16 and C–116/16.

104 *John Prebble*

principle appears to apply even where there is a relevant GAAR.[36] Since 1 January 2019, if the taxpayer is a corporation this in effect means "always", in that, pursuant to Article 6 of the Anti Tax Avoidance Directive, or "ATAD", of 12 July 2016, the domestic law of all states of the Union must include a GAAR in respect of tax on corporations, labelled in the Directive a "general anti-abuse rule".[37]

The reasons for a state, and for the European Union, to enact a GAAR even though the state recognises and acts upon the doctrine of abuse of law no doubt include concerns about the scope of the doctrine and a desire to take a belt and braces[38] approach to fighting tax avoidance.

X. Operation and history of GAARs

The foregoing three headings address three aspects of GAARs: their general effect, their relationship to fictional transactions, and their relationship to doctrines that address the abuse of law. These aspects serve to illustrate that as a category of law GAARs are different from most of the rest of law in general, and from most of the rest of tax law in particular.

This difference is explained by considering the nature of tax law. In general, tax law comprises rules that compel people to pay (usually money) in circumstances that the rules specify. In addition to the *presence* of these rules of compulsion are rules that specify procedures for calculation, collection, and enforcement. In some ways the *absence* of a rule compelling payment can be as important as the *presence* of a rule that is found in the statute. By ordinary rules of interpretation, the absence of a rule that compels payment means that citizens have no obligation to pay, even if officials take the view that, in the circumstances, they should pay. For instance, the absence of a rule requiring rich people to contribute more to the state means that the fact alone that one is rich does not mean that one must pay some extra bounty or other to the state.

---

36 For a comprehensive discussion, see Haslehner, W. et al., (2018). General anti-avoidance rules in EU law. *Cahiers de Droit Fiscal International, 103A,* 55–85. Retrieved 11 December 2019 from https://orbilu.uni.lu/handle/10993/35771.

37 The terms of the GAAR that the ATAD mandates are:

1. For the purposes of calculating the corporate tax liability, a Member State shall ignore an arrangement or a series of arrangements which, having been put into place for the main purpose or one of the main purposes of obtaining a tax advantage that defeats the object or purpose of the applicable tax law, are not genuine having regard to all relevant facts and circumstances. An arrangement may comprise more than one step or part.

2. For the purposes of paragraph 1, an arrangement or a series thereof shall be regarded as non-genuine to the extent that they are not put into place for valid commercial reasons which reflect economic reality.

3. Where arrangements or a series thereof are ignored in accordance with paragraph 1, the tax liability shall be calculated in accordance with national law.

38 An English saying that uses, as a metaphor, cautious people who wear both belt and braces, or suspenders, to hold their trousers up.

General anti-avoidance rules, on the other hand, have a different effect. They require people to pay tax even if their actions *do not fall* within the letter of any particular exaction. Specific anti-avoidance rules have a similar, though narrower, effect. For instance, a specific rule may target attempts to exploit a particular tax benefit, or the rule may attempt to frustrate a particular category of transaction, being a transaction that contrives to minimise tax. By way of illustration, a specific rule may provide that where a transaction avoids tax by exploiting a particular facultative regime, tax will apply, though, by implication, not if the transaction takes advantage of the regime in some manner that the legislation allows.[39] Thus, both general and specific anti-avoidance rules are different from the rest of tax law because anti-avoidance rules apply to impose tax *even though* the taxpayer stays outside the tax net according to the strict terms of the legislation.

XI. Questionable qualities of GAARs

To put the matter in the terms of the previous section of this chapter, GAARs can result in citizens being compelled to pay tax even though there exists no rule that on its face compels them to do so. This feature of general anti-avoidance rules has a number of consequences:

- First, GAARs appear to breach the principle identified by Aristotle and expounded by Kelsen, that legal regimes should not contain internal contradictions.[40]
- Secondly, GAARs seem to breach the rule-of-law principles identified by Raz and Fuller, among others, that law should serve to guide us.[41]
- Thirdly, if, contrary to this second point, GAARs do offer guidance, then that guidance is at least to some extent in terrorem, which is an eccentric form of guidance.[42]

As a result, taxpayers may, for instance, eschew structures that are thought to amount to legitimate and beneficial tax and business planning, for fear that the Commissioner will attack those structures as avoidance. Apart from punishments

---

39 *E.g.*, Income Tax Act 1976 s 191 (NZ) as considered by the Judicial Committee of the Privy Council in *Commissioner of Inland Revenue v. Challenge Corp Ltd* [1987] AC 155. [1986] NZPC 1, [1986] 2 NZLR 513 (PC).

40 Prebble, J. (2017). Kelsen, the principle of exclusion of contradictions, and general anti-avoidance rules in tax law. In: M. Bhandari (Ed.), *Philosophical foundations of tax law* (pp. 79–98). Oxford: Oxford University Press.

41 Prebble, R., & Prebble, J. (2010). Does the use of general anti-avoidance rules to combat tax avoidance breach principles of the rule of law? A comparative study. *Saint Louis University Law Journal*, 55, 21–45 (Symposium Issue, Sanford E. Sarasohn Memorial Conference on Critical Theory in Taxation). Amplified version in S. Frankel (Ed.) (2011). *Learning from the past, adapting for the future: Regulatory reform in New Zealand.* Wellington: LexisNexis.

42 Id., *Saint Louis University Law Journal*, 21, 31.

106   John Prebble

threatened by the criminal law, when we speak of the desirability that law should guide people, we do not usually think in terms of guidance by threats.

The author has argued elsewhere that despite the contradictory nature of GAARs and despite their uncertainty, the unusual nature of tax law in general, and of income tax law in particular, and tax law's peculiar vulnerability to avoidance and abuse, legislatures are justified in turning to GAARs to buttress the tax system.[43] A less than adequate summary of the cause of this problem starts with the observation that many of the most significant foundations of tax law are fictions. Secondly, tax law is often removed from the facts that are its subject matter, in ways that (a) make tax law different in kind from other law and (b) offer innumerable opportunities for avoidance. The example below is followed by an explanation of how it illustrates the points just made.

XII. The "Investor" example of tax avoidance

Almost any instance of tax avoidance or of aggressive tax planning could be chosen to illustrate the arguments just mentioned. Take as an example an unadorned prototype of one of the many structures that exploit the distinction between debt and equity. The example makes its points especially clearly where the funder of both debt and equity is the same person, say an individual investor who establishes a parent company that in turn establishes a subsidiary. For purposes of this chapter, let us call this example the "Investor" example.

Generalising, and ignoring many exceptions, from a practical point of view in a structure of this kind it often does not matter to the investor or to the subsidiary whether the parent company funds the subsidiary by equity, typically shares, or by debt, typically debentures. The reason is that in the investment chain of investor, parent company, subsidiary, there is in substance only one natural person, who owns everything: the investor. Other things being equal, it makes no difference to the investor how the law describes the relationship between the investor, at the start of the chain, and the subsidiary, which holds the property at the end of the chain. But from a tax point of view the difference is usually significant. If the funds come to the subsidiary in the form of debentures the subsidiary can deduct interest payments in calculating its taxable income, but if the funds are in the form of shares most tax systems deny

---

43 Prebble, J. (1994b). Ectopia, formalism, and anti-avoidance rules in income tax law. In: W. Krawietz, N. MacCormick, & G. H. von Wright (Eds.), *Prescriptive formality and normative rationality in modern legal systems, festschrift for Robert S. Summers* (pp. 367–383). Berlin: Duncker and Humblot; Prebble, J. (1995). Philosophical and design problems that arise from the ectopic nature of income tax law and their impact on the taxation of international trade and investment. *Chinese Yearbook of International Law and Affairs, 13*, 111–139, reprinted as Ectopia, tax law, and international taxation (1997), *British Tax Review, 5*, 383–403; Prebble, J. (1996a). Can income tax law be simplified? *New Zealand Journal of Taxation Law and Policy, 2*, 187–200; Prebble, J. (1998). Should tax legislation be written from a "principles and purpose" point of view or a "precise and detailed" point of view? *British Tax Review, 2*, 112–123; see also, Prebble, J. (1994a). Why is tax law incomprehensible? *British Tax Review, 4*, 380–393.

subsidiaries (or, indeed, companies in general) any deduction for sums paid as dividends to parent companies or to other shareholders.

The rationale for the difference is that interest is an expense incurred during the earning of earning income, whereas dividends are distributions of profits after income is ascertained. The distinction is often unimportant where subsidiary and parent are resident in the same jurisdiction and operate under the same tax system. If the subsidiary enjoys a deduction for interest the parent will pay tax on interest derived. If paying a dividend has no tax implication for a subsidiary, receipt of the dividend will be taxable to the parent (apart from rules to mitigate multiple bites of tax on the same income as it moves along a chain of companies). But the position may be otherwise if the two companies are taxed by different tax systems, particularly if they are resident in or operate in different jurisdictions with different rates of tax.

XIII. International tax planning

The phenomena described in the previous paragraph are the basis of much international tax planning. Suppose, for instance, that the Investor example relates to two jurisdictions, the states of Moolah and of Indigent, with similar tax systems to each other. Investor and Parent Company are both resident in Moolah. Parent wishes to establish Subsidiary in Indigent to carry on business. Rather than own Subsidiary directly, it might suit Parent to establish Conduit,[44] an intermediate holding company, in another state, in particular, in Devious, a state that is a tax haven that charges no tax on income coming from foreign sources or going to foreign destinations. Further, the state of Devious has a treaty with the state of Indigent whereby neither jurisdiction charges tax on outbound dividends or interest that flow to the other.

One way of avoiding tax on profits made by Subsidiary would be for its holding company, Conduit, to capitalise Subsidiary by interest-bearing debt. Subsidiary's interest burden could be contrived to wipe out the profit from its business. Further, because of the treaty between the states of Devious and Indigent, Indigent cannot tax the interest that flows from Subsidiary to Conduit. In short, there would be little income for Indigent to tax. Then there is a further possible tax liability to address, in respect of payments by Conduit to Parent.

This possible liability arises because at some point Investor will want the benefit of the interest to come into her hands. The obvious first step is for Conduit, after deriving interest from Subsidiary, to pay dividends or interest to Parent. The drawback is that Parent would then have to pay tax to Moolah. In principle. Conduit and Parent could avoid this tax if, instead of paying dividends, Conduit simply lent the same funds to either Parent or Investor, by

---

44 International tax planning sometimes uses "conduit" or "conduit company" as terms of art with specific meanings. This chapter uses "conduit" simply to refer to a company that stands between two other companies, in this case Parent and Subsidiary, via which investment proceeds one way and returns proceed the other.

108   *John Prebble*

way of an indefinite loan without interest. Since Investor owns the whole structure and thus through the companies owns all the property and, in fact, all of Parent, Conduit, and Subsidiary and their assets, it does not matter to Investor whether the funds are in her hands, or in the hands of Parent, whether by way of loan or absolutely. Since Investor owns the lender (Conduit) through Parent, Investor can decide if or when Conduit asks for repayment.

Readers who are familiar with international tax planning will protest that the simplistic structure just described could not survive the attentions of the fisc in modern times. Specific tax rules, or, if not specific rules, GAARs, of either Moolah or Indigent or both would frustrate the plan. However, modifications and added complexity would ordinarily achieve at least some of the tax minimisation described. The basic structure has been, for instance, the model for much investment from capital-exporting countries into India and Indonesia, by way of conduit companies in Mauritius. Sometimes examples reach the courts, such as *Union of India and anr v. Azadi Bachao Andolan and anr* (Supreme Court of India)[45] and *Indofood International Finance Ltd v. JP Morgan Chase Bank NA London Branch* (Court of Appeal of England and Wales).[46] The latter case involved financing for Indofoods, an Indonesian company, arranged by the London branch of an American bank. The funds came to Indofoods via its subsidiary in Mauritius. But the Investor example discussed in this chapter has been simplified and stylised to illustrate both how this kind of tax planning works and the fictions on which it is based.

XIV. Fictions in the Investor (plus Parent Company and Subsidiary) example

This and following paragraphs use "fiction" to describe a state of facts where economic reality differs from the law's description of that reality. This is a different use from the meaning in section VIII of this chapter, where "fiction" is employed to mean something that has no basis in fact at all, neither in economic fact nor in legal form.

To return to the Investor example, from a substantive and economic point of view the whole structure is a fiction. In substance, Investor, resident in the state of Moolah, invests in a business in the state of Indigent. Either Moolah or Indigent ought to tax the profit that arises from the business and flows in different legal forms up the chain of companies, or the two states should share the tax on the profit. Nothing happens in Conduit, where there should be no tax effect either positive or negative. But that is not how the law works. The reason is that in order to tax a profit a state must describe the profit, albeit only in wide generic terms. This description can only be by law. The legal description of the investment chain in the Investor example gains a life of its own, and the state finds itself taxing not an economic profit but a legal simulacrum of

45 (2003) (2004) 10 SCC 1, 263 ITR 3 706, 132 Taxman 373 (SC).
46 [2006] EWCA Civ 158, [2006] S.T.C. 1195, [2006] B.T.C. 8003, 8 I.T.L. Rep. 653 (EWCA).

an economic profit, that is, something that is not only at least partly fictional in that it has no economic substance, but something that is separated from its original.

Within this overall fiction there are several smaller fictions. An incomplete list includes:

- Legally, ownership of Investor's funds passes from Investor to Parent to Conduit to Subsidiary. But substantively the funds are Investor's throughout.
- Legally, Conduit lends capital to Subsidiary, but since Investor owns both companies Investor is in substance lending to herself. The advances and the promises to repay cancel one another to leave no substantive transaction at all.
- Legally, Subsidiary pays interest to Conduit, but since Investor owns both companies these payments have no more substantive effect than if Investor had taken the money from her pocket and put it into her purse.

These transactions may well be fictions, but, as mentioned, the law cannot tax their underlying substance. It can tax only the legally described simulacra that they are in law. Indeed, calling the tax subjects "simulacra" is an exaggeration. A true simulacrum, while it is a distorted image, is still a distorted image of *something*. The interest passing from Subsidiary to Conduit is a simulacrum of nothing, because there is no underlying reality to distort. Moving money from your pocket to your purse has no more substance than a shell game, and a simple one at that, in that there are only two shells involved. But clothing the payment as a legal, documented transaction, between companies that are in law separate legal persons, converts the shell game into something that the tax system has little choice but to respect: emperor's clothes that do in effect exist, if not in substance then in law.

This description of the role of fictions in tax law shows that taxpayers can exploit fictions to engage in avoidance transactions. In the example, nothing of substance happens in the state of Devious, and anything that appears to be going on in a transaction where Conduit is the recipient is negated by a countervailing transaction where Conduit is the payer.

For a second example, take the interest that Subsidiary pays to Conduit. As explained, from an economic point of view this payment has no more substance than moving money between the owner's pocket and her purse. But from a legal point of view the payment has a significant effect: for Subsidiary the interest is deductible as an expense of doing business. As a deduction, the payment reduces or eliminates Subsidiary's taxable profit and thus the tax that Subsidiary pays to Indigent.

XV. Specific anti-avoidance regimes revisited

The avoidance techniques that Investor uses in the example just discussed are relatively crude. Most tax legislation of any sophistication includes specific

110   *John Prebble*

regimes to counteract these particular techniques. In the case of Investor's example, controlled foreign company and thin capitalisation regimes are among the most relevant.

A controlled foreign company, or "CFC", regime operates by attributing the income of a foreign company that a domestic taxpayer controls to that taxpayer. In the present case, a CFC regime of Moolah would attribute the income of Conduit to Parent, a Moolah resident, making the income vulnerable to tax in Moolah even though it is foreign-source income of a foreign entity.

Thin capitalisation regimes attack companies that are "thinly" capitalised, that is, companies that, like Subsidiary in the Investor example, are funded disproportionately by debt, often with the consequence of reducing taxable income. Often, but not necessarily, thinly capitalised companies have the same ownership as the funder who supplies the loan, as in the Investor example, where Parent and Subsidiary both have Investor as their ultimate owner. Thin capitalisation regimes limit the amount of interest that borrowing companies can deduct in calculating their income.

While CFC or thin capitalisation regimes would probably put paid to the tax benefits of the Investor scheme, more complex or more subtle schemes often avoid these and similar targeted anti-avoidance regimes. There are several reasons. One is that legislators must limit the scope of targeted regimes in order not to penalise legitimate investment structures. Another is that business affairs are extremely varied. Policymakers and legislators cannot predict all the ideas that may occur to tax planners. For these sorts of reasons legislators enact broad-spectrum GAARs, though they have been relatively slow to do so, considering the scope that tax law affords to those who would go in for avoidance.

XVI. GAARs and economics

It is possible, though it may not be particularly illuminating, to account for the enactment of GAARs as a logical response of states driven by economic imperatives. For this purpose, it is helpful to think of the state both as representing the body of taxpayers and as an umpire between, on one hand, individual taxpayers who aim to avoid paying some or all of their tax and, on the other hand, the body of taxpayers that will either have to pay more tax to make up for tax avoided by their fellow citizens, or, if collections are not made up, have to make do with smaller sums in the coffers of the state. To put it another way, some taxpayers will aim to maximise their welfare by avoiding such tax as they can manage, while the rest of the taxpaying public will, through the state, try to protect their own welfare by precautionary measures. Individuals cannot protect their welfare by preventing other individuals from avoiding tax, but states do what they can on behalf of the generality of citizens by enacting GAARs.

Unpacking the motivation for enacting GAARs in this manner may not add much to the explanation elsewhere in this chapter of why legislatures who wish to protect the tax base are forced to adopt GAARs. Indeed, the purpose of

Varieties of anti-avoidance legislation 111

the explanation is otherwise: it is advanced by way of ground-clearing before questioning whether behavioural public finance sheds light on the reason for enacting GAARs. The answer to this latter question seems to be "no". For a state to enact a GAAR seems to be an entirely rational measure when we think of the state in its dual roles of (a) representing taxpayers who do not avoid tax and (b) acting as an umpire between taxpayers who argue that their assessments are too high and the body of taxpayers who suffer if others pay less than coherent tax policy requires.

So far, so obvious. Neither classical economics nor behavioural public finance seems to tell us much about the rationale for state action in enacting GAARs that is not already tolerably plain. But there is another angle that is not without interest. This is that the form of GAARs seems to vary much more between states, and much more randomly, than the form of tax law in general. If this conclusion is correct, it is curious. All states face the same challenges in fighting tax avoidance; so why is it that their GAARs vary so much from one another? Rosenblat and Tron offer a plausible explanation: "[E]very GAAR is unique, a product of a tax system's history, culture, effectiveness, approach to statutory interpretation, tax morale and so forth".[47]

Most scholars would no doubt agree with Rosenblat and Tron. Although all GAARs are enacted to address the same challenge, they vary, influenced by the factors listed. Nevertheless, there are certain curiosities. First, one would have thought that if tax systems, culture, and so on influence the form of GAARs, then countries where those factors are similar would have similar GAARs. This expectation is frequently falsified, but also often borne out. For instance, Benin,[48] Burkina Faso,[49] Chad,[50] Niger,[51] and Senegal[52] are all former colonies of France in Africa. Their GAARs are each so similar to one another that they belie the assertion that "every GAAR is unique". Though oddly dissimilar to the GAAR of France,[53] all are similar to Chad's:[54]

> Any transaction concluded in the form of a contract or a legal act disguising a realisation or a transfer of profits or income made directly or through intermediaries cannot be contested against the Tax Administration which has the right to reclassify the operation in its real character and to determine the consequences for corporate and individual income tax base.

---

47 Rosenblat, P., & Tron, M. E. (2018). Anti-avoidance measures of general nature and scope: GAAR and other rules, General Report. *Cahiers de Droit Fiscal International* (International Fiscal Association, Rotterdam), *103A*, 9, 16.
48 Benin General Tax Code, Article 1102.
49 Burkina Faso Tax Code, Article 136.
50 Chad General Tax Code, Article R 32.
51 Niger Repression de L'Abus de Droit (Income Tax Act), Article 345.
52 Senegal General Tax Code, Article 610.
53 France Livre de Procédure Fiscale (French Code of Tax Procedure), Article L 64.
54 Chad General Tax Code, Article R 32.

112   *John Prebble*

On the other hand, as mentioned in section VIII, Burundi,[55] a former colony of Belgium, appears to have copied the GAAR of France. The comparison of the GAARs of former French and Belgian colonies leads us to a second curiosity: while a tax system's history, culture, effectiveness, and so on certainly do influence the form of that system's GAAR, the influence of these factors appears often to be random. Ex post, we can link cause and effect, to show how one factor or another influenced the form of a current GAAR. But ex ante it would be very difficult to predict the provisions of a country's GAAR by looking at factors that might or might not influence its form. That is, while Rosenblat and Tron in one sense are close to being correct in postulating that "every GAAR is unique", the factors to which they point do not help us to determine *how* a particular GAAR came to achieve its own brand of uniqueness. We may illustrate this point by comparing and contrasting certain features of a number of GAARs.

XVII. An example from the common law: Australia and New Zealand

Consider Australasian GAARs, the world's oldest, their predecessors dating from 1877[56] and 1878.[57] The legal systems of Australia and New Zealand are similar. Both developed from English common law. The countries' tax systems and law are also similar, with most of Britain's Australasian colonies, including New Zealand, enacting income taxes, including GAARs for the most part, in the 1890s. But current Australian and New Zealand GAARs could hardly be more dissimilar. The Australian GAAR is almost certainly the world's longest and most detailed. It has over 8500 words, spread over 15 to 30 pages, depending on fount and size of stock. It occupies a whole part of its statute, namely Part IVA of the Income Tax Assessment Act of 1936.[58] In all these respects, the Australian GAAR is very different from its New Zealand counterpart, which is short and drafted essentially in terms of principle. The core of the New Zealand GAAR reads simply: "A tax avoidance arrangement is void as against the Commissioner for income tax purposes".[59]

A definition amplifies the meaning of "arrangement" to include virtually any imaginable disposition, whether binding or not.[60] A second definition amplifies "tax avoidance arrangement" to mean:[61]

---

55 Burundi Procedural Tax Code, Article 50.
56 Land Tax Act 1877 (Victoria) s 55.
57 Land Tax Act 1878 (New Zealand) s 62.
58 There is a parallel Australian statute, the Income Tax Assessment Act 1997. The 1997 Act contains legislation that has been re-written as part of a progressive updating of the language of the statute, together with most new income tax legislation as it is enacted. The GAAR and other parts of the 1936 Act will in due course be revised and moved to the 1997 Act.
59 Income Tax Act 2007 s BG 1(1).
60 Income Tax Act 2007 s YA 1.
61 Ibid.

Varieties of anti-avoidance legislation 113

an arrangement, whether entered into by a person affected by the arrangement or by another person that directly or indirectly–

(a) Has tax avoidance as its purpose or effect; or

(b) Has tax avoidance as 1 of its purposes or effects, whether or not any other purpose of effect is referable to ordinary business or family dealings, if the tax avoidance purpose or effect is not merely incidental.

There is little more to the New Zealand rule apart from procedural provisions and provisions that address aspects of its relationship to other sections of the Act.

The explanation for the difference relates more to the personalities of judges and, in particular, to that of Sir Garfield Barwick, who was Chief Justice of Australia from 1964 to 1981, than to any sweep of history, of culture, or of the other factors that Rosenblat and Tron mention. The Australian and New Zealand GAARs had almost identical legislative origins and were very similar for most of their histories. But in the 1960s and 1970s the Australian High Court, under the leadership of Barwick CJ, began a practice of not enforcing the GAAR, even in egregious cases of tax avoidance.[62] The reaction of the Australian Parliament was to pass the extraordinarily complex regime that now exists. Let us consider a number of other random and almost inexplicable similarities and dissimilarities between various GAARs.

XVIII. Other examples of similarities and dissimilarities between GAARs

A. Length and complexity contrasted with conciseness

Consider again the German and French GAARs, quoted in section VII, above. Their language varies, and, as explained in section VIII, the French GAAR refers to fictions, whereas the German GAAR does not. But the similarities between the two rules are much more notable than their differences. Broadly speaking, both attack an arrangement that is "contrary to the objectives" of the rules in question (France) or that "leads to tax advantages unintended by law" (Germany). The two tests appear to amount to the same thing.

The differences between the French and the German rules can mainly be accounted for by the fact that the German § 42 was revised in 1977 and takes then recent thinking into account, whereas the French Article L 64 was enacted in the Vichy era. For instance, Article L 64 requires that the arrangement in question should "have been inspired by no other motive than to avoid or mitigate the tax burden" whereas the corresponding words in the German rules are that the GAAR "shall not apply where the taxpayer provides evidence of

---

62 E.g., *Cridland v. Federal Commissioner of Taxation* (1977) 140 CLR 330 (HCA, FC), an unashamed and artificial tax shelter.

114   John Prebble

non–tax reasons for the selected option which are relevant when viewed from an overall perspective".

The outcome seems to be that the German GAAR recognises that tax avoidance is often carried out within an overall context of an arrangement that has some underlying business or economic rationale. An example might be a genuine export–import transaction, but a transaction that is routed through a tax haven in order to increase the costs of landing the goods in the country of destination, and thus of reducing taxable profits. With its more holistic approach, the German GAAR may be a more effective weapon against this kind of tax planning than the French GAAR, which requires avoidance to be the only motive for the impugned transaction.

Another example of the relatively unrefined approach of the French GAAR is its reference to fictions, which was discussed in section VIII, above. But, as mentioned, the similarities between the two rules are much more notable than the differences, which is what one might expect from two civil law jurisdictions in close geographical proximity to one another. Of course, their respective histories differ, but a relevant part of those histories is shared, viz. the influence of Napoleonic and other codification, which one would expect to have a similar effect on the legislation of both jurisdictions.

What is remarkable, however, is the close similarity between the Franco–German rules, on one hand, and the New Zealand GAAR on the other. As mentioned, all three are essentially principle-based and concise. It is certainly counterintuitive that the New Zealand legislation is closer to that of Germany than it is to that of Australia. That is, although the factors that Rosenblat and Tron list would seem to point to some sort of pattern, this is often not so.

B. Contrasts between GAARs of common law jurisdictions

The difference between the New Zealand and Australian GAARs is but one example of similar differences between common law countries in general. In short, the GAARs of some common law countries are similar to the GAAR of New Zealand, whereas the GAARs of others have much more in common with the length and complexity of the GAAR of Australia, without reaching its 8500 words. Examples of the former include Hong Kong,[63] Singapore,[64] the Solomon Islands,[65] and Sri Lanka,[66] and of the latter, in addition to Australia, India (1888 words),[67] South Africa (1818 words),[68] and the United Kingdom

---

63 Hong Kong Inland Revenue Ordinance, Cap.112, sections 61 and 61A.

64 Singapore Income Tax Act, section 33.

65 Solomon Islands Income Tax Act, Article 25.

66 Sri Lanka Income Tax Act, Article 103.

67 India Income Tax Act 1961, Chapter XA: General Anti Avoidance Rules, sections 95, 96, 97, 98, 99, 100, 101, and 102.

68 South Africa Income Tax Act No. 58 1962, sections 80A, 80B, 80C, 80D, 80E, 80F, 80G, 80H, 80I, 80J, 80K, and 80L.

Varieties of anti-avoidance legislation   115

(3600 words).[69] The GAAR of Canada (1055 words)[70] falls between the two groups.

India (GAAR implemented 2017) and the United Kingdom (2013) have in common that they came relatively late to the idea of enacting a GAAR. Australia, also, should possibly be classified as a late adopter. At least, although Australia, like New Zealand, traces its GAAR back to the 19th century, the current Australian GAAR, enacted in 1980, is so different from the form that it took for most of its history that its prolixity evidences a new approach, rather than a revision of previous law.

Any attempt to assess why, for example, certain common law GAARs are far more prolix than the general body of common law GAARs must be speculative, but, to the present author, any such exercise leads to the conclusion that differences are explained more by almost random historical circumstances than by any broad trends or characteristics of the societies or legal systems that enact particular GAARs. Section XVII, above, mentions the influence of Chief Justice Barwick in Australia.[71] One has the impression that the Australian Federal Parliament was determined to make its new GAAR work, and kept adding words until it thought that the purpose was achieved.

In contrast, the prolixity of the United Kingdom GAAR may have another explanation. Parliament enacted the rule in only 2013;[72] so we shall not know until litigation has worked through to the higher courts just how effective it will be. But several aspects of the rule suggest that the United Kingdom GAAR may well not live up to the hopes of its drafters. The first is that the GAAR targets not "avoidance" but "abuse", which is a narrower concept. Neither word is a term of art, but it is probably fair to say that all abuse is avoidance, but not all avoidance is abuse.[73] Secondly, the legislation imposes procedural requirements on the tax authorities that are not insignificant. Thirdly, the legislation is finely grained. An abundance of specific detail can be an advantage to the authorities if the detail leads to the case in question fitting squarely within one or other of the terms of a rule, but in general granulated drafting is potentially more favourable to the taxpayer, who has more chance of planning around it than with principle-based GAARs.[74]

Whether these features of the United Kingdom GAAR turn out to be shortcomings and, if so, why they came about, would require an extensive study, but with some trepidation the author offers the theory that United Kingdom anti-avoidance policy and practice have become subject to some degree of

69 United Kingdom General Anti-Abuse Rule Finance Act 2013, Part 5, sections 209, 210, 213, 215, 216, and schedule 43–43C Finance Act 2013, and National Insurance Contributions Act 2014, section 10.
70 Income Tax Act 1985, Part XVI Tax Avoidance, sections 245 and 246(1).
71 See section XVII.
72 Finance Act 2013, s 216(4)(a) and (b) (UK).
73 See also the discussion in section IV of this chapter.
74 For a similar view, see Littlewood, M. (2019). Legislating against tax avoidance. *New Zealand Law Journal, 8*, 295, 296.

116   *John Prebble*

agency capture. The following circumstances and examples are offered as possible, rather than positive, evidence; it is not argued that they are conclusive.

The first is that the overall culture of official circles in the United Kingdom is somewhat more tolerant of fairly aggressive tax planning than is the culture in some other countries. This may be the result of (a) a reaction against the extraordinarily high income tax rates that prevailed in years during and following the Second World War[75] and (b) a belief that it behoves the United Kingdom to promote the City of London as a financial centre even at the expense of tolerating some level of tax minimisation.[76]

The second example is more specific, namely the relationship between a certain Guernsey company,[77] Mapeley Limited, formerly listed in London, and Her Majesty's Revenue and Customs, or "HMRC". In 2001, Mapeley bought most of the tax offices in the country from HMRC, being about 600 properties, some freehold and some leasehold. The purchase was the first move in what became known as the "STEPS" deal, a private finance initiative by sale and lease-back planned to last 20 years.[78] The STEPS deal has been controversial ever since. After one of many investigations, in 2017 the House of Commons Public Accounts Select Committee reported that: "HMRC told us that it now had significant doubts over whether the fundamentals of the STEPS deal ... could ever be demonstrated to be value for money".[79]

More significantly in the present context, the British company, Mapeley Limited, was not a party to the STEPS deal. The contracting parties on Mapeley's side were two of its subsidiaries, Mapeley Steps Contractors Limited, which was to be paid for maintaining the Revenue's and then HMRC's offices, and Mapeley Steps Limited, a Bermuda-based company that bought the buildings for £220m.[80] At the time, Mr Robin Priest, the chief executive of Mapeley Limited, claimed:[81]

> It's not that we won't pay tax, what we have done is sought to mitigate our capital gains position because this is a very tight contract on an operating basis so most of the value for us is in 20 years' time.

---

75 Scheve, K., & Stasavage, D. (2016). *Taxing the rich: A history of fiscal fairness in the United States and Europe*. Princeton, NJ: Princeton University Press; Atkinson, A. (2007). The distribution of top incomes in the United Kingdom 1908–2000. In: A. Atkinson and T. Piketty (Eds.), *Top incomes over the twentieth century: A contrast between continental Europe and English-speaking countries* (pp. 82–140). Oxford: Oxford University Press. For primary sources see the *Reports of the Commissioners of His Majesty's Inland Revenue* (various years).

76 See, *e.g.*, Shaxson, N. (2011). *Treasure islands: Tax havens and the men who stole the world*. London: Palgrave Macmillan.

77 https://en.wikipedia.org/wiki/Mapeley, Retrieved 22 November 2019.

78 www.mapeley.com/OurApproach/Customers/HMRC.aspx, Retrieved 22 November 2019.

79 https://publications.parliament.uk/pa/cm201617/cmselect/cmpubacc/891/89108.htm para 25, Retrieved 22 November 2019.

80 www.theguardian.com/politics/2002/sep/24/uk.economy, last consulted 22 November 2019.

81 http://news.bbc.co.uk/2/hi/business/2263208.stm, last consulted 22 November 2019.

Whether that is so, or whether there are other tax benefits, is impossible to check. But from one perspective it is hard to think of a more vivid example of agency capture than that of a fisc with its landlord based in a tax haven, particularly where the landlord chose the location with this very tenancy in mind. When people speak of agency capture they do not ordinarily mean that the agency in question is a tenant of someone who has done the capturing, but in the case of HMRC the situation seems to have come about through naivety and a lack of conceptual thinking that are regrettable in a tax authority.

The author will not mention other indications of this particular agency capture, since they involve individuals, but is happy to discuss the evidence with interested scholars.

C. Significance of the criterion of economic substance

Drafters of GAARs in common law countries have an uncomfortable relationship with the concept of economic substance. On one hand, in broad summary the effect of GAARs is to cause arrangements to be taxed not according to the form of the language or of legal institutions that the arrangements use but according to the arrangements' economic substance. On the other hand, many judgments of high authority emphasise that tax is imposed according to law, not according to economic effect or substance.[82] Possibly because of these judgments, GAARs in common law countries are usually drafted using indirect language and shy from stipulating directly that transactions must be taxed according to their substance rather than according to their form. There is a minor exception in the United Kingdom GAAR, which lists departure from economic substance as an indication that a transaction may be abusive.[83] In contrast, civil law GAARs commonly go directly to their target, explicitly citing lack of or departure from economic substance as a significant element in an avoidance transaction. The example of the German GAAR was quoted above.[84]

Against this background, the GAAR of the United States of America[85] is an outlier. More directly even than most GAARs of civil law countries it simply enacts into law a pre-existing judge-made rule that it calls by its most common name, the "economic substance doctrine" and defines as:[86]

> [T]he common law doctrine under which tax benefits under subtitle A with respect to a transaction are not allowable if the transaction does not have economic substance or lacks a business purpose.

---

82 *E.g.*, *Europa Oil (NZ) Ltd v. Commissioner of Inland Revenue* [1976] 1 NZLR 546 (PC).
83 *E.g.*, Finance Act 2013, s 216(4)(a) and (b) (UK).
84 See Section 42 of the General Tax Code, quoted in section VII.
85 26 US Internal Revenue Code, Section 7701(o), inserted March 2010.
86 26 US Internal Revenue Code, Section 7701(o) (5).

118   John Prebble

This language is closer to, say, the GAAR of Kazakhstan than it is to any other common law GAAR. The relevant language of the Kazakhstan GAAR mandates the tax authorities to ignore a transaction that:[87] "(a) lacks economic substance and (b) causes a decrease in tax liability".

The American GAAR departs so dramatically from its common law counterparts because of the circumstances of its enactment, which did not occur until as late as 2010. For decades, scholars and policymakers had debated whether the United States should enact a statutory GAAR.[88] Congress had not done so for two reasons. First, the matter seemed less urgent than in other countries. America already had the judge-made substance-over-form rule that has been mentioned. That rule operated far from perfectly, but it meant that in the struggle to defeat tax avoidance the United States was at an advantage over any common law jurisdiction that lacked a GAAR. Secondly, there are the arguments that any GAAR breaches principles of the rule of law, which were influential in America as elsewhere.[89]

In 2010, these considerations became outweighed by overall fiscal needs, in particular by the costs expected to be incurred by the enactment of the new public health system that came to be called "Obamacare". Pursuant to a process known as "scoring", to comply with the Statutory Pay-As-You-Go-Act 2010,[90] procedures managed by the Congressional Budget Office require that spending bills must be accompanied by proposals that show the sources of the funds that will be required to offset the new spending.[91] The promoters of the Obamacare legislation settled on, among other sources, a new idea for raising money: penalties for tax avoidance. Until 2010 there was no legislative authority to impose penalties in respect of transactions that breached the economic substance doctrine. Where the Commissioner successfully challenged an avoidance arrangement the result was simply an order to pay the tax. The advantage of imposing penalties was twofold: (a) penalties would deter tax avoidance and (b) fines collected as penalties for avoidance could help to fund Obamacare. Congress therefore included the United States GAAR as part of the statute that enacted Obamacare. Standard procedures then moved the GAAR from the Obamacare legislation into the Federal Tax Code.[92]

---

87 Kazakhstan Tax Code, Article 556–1.

88 See, *e.g.*, Cooper, G. (2001). International experience with general anti-avoidance rules. *SMU Law Review, 54*, 83–130.

89 See, *e.g.*, Prebble, R., & Prebble, J. (2010). Does the use of general anti-avoidance rules to combat tax avoidance breach principles of the rule of law? A comparative study. *Saint Louis University Law Journal, 55*, 21–45, Sanford E. Sarasohn Memorial Conference on Critical Issues in International and Comparative Taxation, 24–25, Victoria University of Wellington Legal Research Paper No. 8/2012.

90 Title I of Pub.L. 111–139, H.J.Res. 45.

91 Overview of Scoring Legislation, US Office of Management of the Budget Circular No. A–11, §21 (2016), available at https://obamawhitehouse.archives.gov/sites/default/files/omb/assets/a11_current_year/s21.pdf, last consulted 11 December 2019.

92 26 US Internal Revenue Code, Section 7701(o), inserted March 2010.

XIX. Conclusion: lessons from differences between GAARs

The questions that this chapter attempts to address are: does the science of behavioural public finance help us to identify principles that could be applied to determine certain legal policy, namely:

1. Whether a jurisdiction should bolster its tax regime by adding a general anti-avoidance rule to its tax legislation; and, if so,
2. What form of rule is likely to be the most effective; or,
3. Where a jurisdiction proposes to enact a GAAR, could behavioural public finance help to predict the form that the GAAR will take?

The discussion in this chapter suggests that there is little if any useful role for behavioural public finance in addressing these questions. Earlier sections of this chapter study the GAARs of a number of jurisdictions. The study is not comprehensive, but the examples chosen are varied enough to demonstrate that in comparing the provisions of different GAARs we can rarely find patterns that are predictable. (As explained in section XVI of this chapter, the GAARs of several former French colonies in Africa constitute a rare exception.)

It is a major objective of behavioural public finance to discover predictabilities in what seem to be irrational patterns. Bearing this objective in mind, and putting question 2 above in different terms, consider the question whether behavioural public finance can help us to discern meaningful patterns among the varieties of drafting of GAARs. Although classical economics easily explains that it is usually sensible for states to enact GAARs, an exercise to compare the drafting of different GAARs struggles to discern patterns that can be explained logically. We can usually explain individual oddities, such as the GAAR of the United States of America that has been discussed. But such explanations do not yield useful general principles.

This conclusion is not altogether surprising. General anti-avoidance rules are examples of what is sometimes called "lawyers' law". "Lawyers' law" is not a precise term. Broadly, it refers to law that deals with matters that are technical in a legal sense and, in general, that must be reformed by legally technical legislation.

Take a non-tax example, say the common law doctrine of privity of contract. Privity refers to the principle that, ordinarily, someone who is not a party to a contract cannot enforce it. For instance, if the fathers of an engaged couple agree to give wedding presents to their children one father can enforce the agreement as a contract if the other reneges, but the bride and groom cannot do so because they are not parties to the agreement.[93] People may come to the view that certain consequences of the doctrine of privity are harsh or undesirable, perhaps even this particular consequence. As a result, parliaments

---

93 *Tweddle v. Atkinson* (1861) 1 B & S 393.

120 John Prebble

may legislate to change some of the rules about privity. However, this legislation comes about not as a result of behavioural analysis but simply by virtue of concluding that the law is unfair and legislating to reform it. The change may affect people's behaviour, but only in the sense that almost any legislation may affect behaviour, and is probably designed to do so. There is no subtlety that must be measured by behavioural public finance rather than by ordinary economic analysis.

A general anti-avoidance rule is similar. It is lawyers' law, telling us, in effect, that aggressive tax planning will not work. Analysing a transaction in terms of a GAAR is a task in legal analysis, not in behavioural public finance.

None of this is to say that behavioural public finance necessarily has no relevance to tax avoidance. It probably does. For instance, if a government can plausibly persuade citizens that very few people avoid taxes it may well be that the social proof principle will nudge behaviour away from avoidance. But this is a hypothetical example of how one might promote behaviour that is desired, a different matter from the legalistic questions of whether to enact a GAAR and, if so, of what form it should take.

XX. References

Atkinson, A. (2007). The distribution of top incomes in the United Kingdom 1908–2000. In: A. Atkinson & T. Piketty (Eds.), *Top incomes over the twentieth century: A contrast between continental Europe and English-speaking countries* (pp. 82–140). Oxford: Oxford University Press.

Bolgár, V. (1975). Abuse of rights in France, Germany, and Switzerland: A survey of a recent chapter in legal doctrine. *Louisiana Law Review, 35*(5), 1015–1036.

Cooper, G. (2001). International experience with general anti-avoidance rules. *SMU Law Review, 54*, 83–130.

Galdieri, E., Gianni, L., Liotine, V. G., Piccinni, R., Plantamura, P. M., & Sabia, R. (2009). The limits to tax planning, minimizing taxes and corporate social responsibility. *Eucotax Wintercourse 2009*. Retrieved 22 October 2019, from https://core.ac.uk/download/pdf/54549463.pdf.

Haslehner, W., García Prats, A., Heydt, V., Kemmeren, E., Kofler, G., Lang, M. … & Valente, P. (2018). General anti-avoidance rules in EU law. *Cahiers de Droit Fiscal International, 103A*, 55–85. Retrieved 11 December 2019 from https://orbilu.uni.lu/handle/10993/35771.

Littlewood, M. (2019). Legislating against tax avoidance. *New Zealand Law Journal, 8*, 295.

Max Planck Institute for Tax Law and Public Finance (2019). *MPI Insights,* 8, s.

Osterloh-Konrad, C. (2019). *Die Steuerumgehung – Eine rechtsvergleichende und rechtstheoretische Analyse.* Tübingen: Mohr Siebeck.

Prebble, J. (1994a). Why is tax law incomprehensible? *British Tax Review, 4*, 380–393.

Prebble, J. (1994b). Ectopia, formalism, and anti-avoidance rules in income tax law. In: W. Krawietz, N. MacCormick, & G. H. von Wright (Eds.), *Prescriptive formality and normative rationality in modern legal systems, festschrift for Robert S. Summers* (pp. 367–383). Berlin: Duncker and Humblot.

Prebble, J. (1996a). Can income tax law be simplified? *New Zealand Journal of Taxation Law and Policy*, 2, 187–200.

Prebble, J. (1996b). Criminal law, tax evasion, shams, and tax avoidance: Part I – Tax evasion and general doctrines of criminal law. *New Zealand Journal of Taxation Law and Policy*, 2, 3–16.

Prebble, J. (1996c). Criminal law, tax evasion, shams, and tax avoidance: Part II – Criminal law consequences of categories of evasion and avoidance. *New Zealand Journal of Taxation Law and Policy*, 2, 59–74.

Prebble, J. (1997). Ectopia, tax law, and international taxation. *British Tax Review*, 5, 383–403.

Prebble, J. (1998). Should tax legislation be written from a "principles and purpose" point of view or a "precise and detailed" point of view? *British Tax Review*, 2, 112–123.

Prebble, J. (2017). Kelsen, the principle of exclusion of contradictions, and general anti-avoidance rules in tax law. In: M. Bhandari (Ed.), *Philosophical foundations of tax law* (pp. 79–98). Oxford: Oxford University Press.

Prebble, R., & Prebble, J. (2010). Does the use of general anti-avoidance rules to combat tax avoidance breach principles of the rule of law? A comparative study. *Saint Louis University Law Journal*, 55(1), 21–45.

Rosenblat, P., & Tron, M. E. (2018). Anti-avoidance measures of general nature and scope: GAAR and other rules, General Report. *Cahiers de Droit Fiscal International* (International Fiscal Association, Rotterdam), *103A*, 9, 16.

Scheve, K., & Stasavage, D. (2016). *Taxing the rich: A history of fiscal fairness in the United States and Europe*. Princeton, NJ: Princeton University Press.

Shaxson, N. (2011). *Treasure islands: Tax havens and the men who stole the world*. London: Palgrave Macmillan.

Woodcock, A. (2009, September 22). Darling Blitz on "morally wrong" tax avoidance, *The Scotsman*. Retrieved from www.scotsman.com/latestnews/Darling-blitz—on-.5666457.jp.

https://en.wikipedia.org/wiki/Mapeley, Retrieved 22 November 2019.

http://news.bbc.co.uk/2/hi/business/2263208.stm, last consulted 22 November 2019.

https://publications.parliament.uk/pa/cm201617/cmselect/cmpubacc/891/89108.htm, Retrieved 22 November 2019.

www.mapeley.com/OurApproach/Customers/HMRC.aspx, Retrieved 22 November 2019.

www.theguardian.com/politics/2002/sep/24/uk.economy, last consulted 22 November 2019.

Part III

Tax compliance behaviour

Cases

7 Political economy of tax compliance behavior

An analysis of three cities in Turkey

M. Mustafa Erdoğdu and Osman Geyik

Introduction

Tax non-compliance is a key challenge since it is an unfair and illegal confiscation of value that is designed to meet social needs. Tax compliance or the economic deterrence model by Allingham and Sandmo (1972) has guided most academic research and public policies. In this model, taxpayers are assumed to be unethical realistic economic evaders who assess the likely costs and benefits of tax evasion (Alm *et al.*, 2012, pp. 33–34). Based on this premise, the model predicts that increasing the likelihood of detection and/or more severe fines will result in better tax compliance while increasing the tax rate will result in less tax compliance.

Although this model has provided valuable insights, it soon became apparent that the model cannot explain or predict empirically established compliance levels. The main problem here is that tax compliance behavior is difficult to explain by purely financial considerations. There are other motivations, emotions, and interactions that go beyond narrow financial considerations. In this respect, behavioral economics that suggests human rationality is bounded provides invaluable insights.

Behavioral economics combines the normative backbone of economics with insights from behavioral sciences (Kahneman, 2011). It relies on identifying where behavior deviates from a rational or reasonable benchmark (Thaler & Sunstein, 2008). The trend in tax compliance behavior research suggests a shift in the understanding of taxpayers as selfish individuals who try to maximize their benefit to individuals with a sense of community, who are willing to work together if everyone contributes to creating a climate of mutual trust (Alm *et al.*, 2012, p. 34).

The "slippery slope framework", which is proposed by Kirchler (2007) and Kirchler, Hoelzl, and Wahl (2008) to combine the main tax compliance theories, is probably the best approach available to understand tax compliance. This framework distinguishes the "power" of authorities and taxpayers' "trust" in authorities. Power depends on the ability of authorities to identify and punish tax evaders. Trust stems from taxpayers' understanding of tax laws, attitudes towards taxation and taxes, beliefs that tax rules are transparent, and beliefs that society accepts rules and adheres to the law (Gangl *et al.*, 2019).

The slippery slope framework takes into account the relationship between authorities and citizens and the climate of interaction: antagonistic vs. synergistic. If taxpayers consider a tax system to be legitimate, they will comply with it. On the contrary, if the taxpayer is indifferent to the power of the tax authority and/or the taxpayer does not trust that the authority works for the common good, tax compliance rates will decline (Doyle, Keegan, & Reeves, this volume). To explain the dynamics between power and trust, the original slippery slope framework has recently been extended by distinguishing the power of tax authorities into coercive and legitimate power and trust in tax authorities into reason-based and implicit trust (Gangl *et al.*, 2019).

It is essential to understand why people behave the way they do, in terms of both cognitive abilities and environmental constraints in order to select a strategy (Dobreva, this volume). The slippery slope framework and the extended slippery slope framework are invaluable to understanding tax compliance behavior, particularly in advanced countries. Nevertheless, this framework probably has less explanatory power in developing countries. Because governing institutions in these countries hardly respond to the demands of the general public. It follows that burdens and benefits would not be distributed as fairly as they are in advanced countries. As a result, taxpayers feel cheated and tend to develop negative emotions towards governing institutions. As will be seen in the following sections, there are complex social and political interactions between different groups in society that affect tax compliance in developing countries.

The rest of the chapter is organized as follows. The following section identifies the interests and conflicts of different actors related to tax compliance behavior in a society. This section particularly focuses on issues like fairness perception of taxpayers regarding their tax burden, their trust in governing institutions, and effective use of tax revenues by governing authorities. The next section explains the methodology used in the study, presents the empirical results, interprets them, and discusses their policy implications. The final section provides concluding remarks.

The political economy of tax compliance behavior

Bird (2007, p. 47) makes the critical point that

> [t]ax policy decisions are not made in a vacuum. Nor are they made by a benevolent government. Instead, they reflect the outcome of a set of complex social and political interactions between different groups in society in an institutional context established by history and state administrative capacity.

In other words, "[p]aying taxes is, like avoiding or evading them, a form of political interaction" (Sossin, 1992, p. 179). The tax system of a country reflects

Political economy of compliance behavior 127

the distribution of power in society and political interactions between rulers and citizens (Çevik, 2016). Tax structure defines how to distribute the costs of public services and, in combination with a transfer system, has a decisive effect on the form of the distribution of income and wealth (Head *et al.*, 1993).

A tax authority is generally influenced by the specific organizational, socio-economic, and political conditions in which it operates. Political opportunism, organized interests, and demands of voters play important roles in designing tax policies. The influence of certain groups allows them, through legal means, to control the tax system, transferring the burden to others. As Pierre Moscovici, who has served as finance minister in France, claimed, "a tax system will be lost to vested interests without public pressure" (ICIJ, 2018, January 15). Thus, it is important to understand how key actors and elites are likely to use institutions and regulations in their favor and put pressure on policy-making and implementation.

The taxation process provides opportunities for decision-makers to use public resources for their purposes and in a way that citizens do not approve of (Alt, Preston, & Sibieta, 2009, p. 1209). Setting the agenda and making political decisions can give politicians a central role in coordinating special interests (Ilzetzkiy, 2018, p. 198). One way to do this is to tax influential groups lightly. Groups that benefit from preferential arrangements naturally conduct lobbies to influence the development and implementation of tax policies (Daude, Gutiérrez, & Melguizo, 2014, p. 10).

Frijters, Gangl, and Torgler (this volume) highlight that "[t]hroughout the history of civilization, it is rare to find a tax system in which the powerful and rich did not distort it to their advantage". They label the powerful and rich "Plutocrats" and suggest that they actively play the political landscape and the tax system for their advantage. As Daude, Gutiérrez, and Melguizo (2014, p. 11) clarify, the main characteristic of the elite is the ability not only to bypass the institutional structure but also to work within the institutional structure to ensure that "right" decisions are made. Frijters, Gangl, and Torgler (this volume) indicate that during the Roman Empire, for example, tax privileges were granted to a small but extremely wealthy senatorial order, which was also enriched at the expense of the state by obtaining excessive profits from monopolized offices. In recent decades, Plutocrats have increasingly managed to avoid taxes through various accounting tricks and/or moving all properties over a barren rock in the Pacific or declaring a charity at unusually high costs.

There are many ways to create advantages for special interests. One such way is to leave tax loopholes for powerful people and companies to reduce their tax bills. Another way is to provide special tax incentives or tax breaks for privileged companies.[1] A different way to create advantages for special interests is to implement *tax amnesties*, which are used particularly in developing countries to increase the number of votes for politicians or to finance the government's

---

1 ActionAid (2013) revealed that 138 billion USD is lost due to corporate tax exemptions that poor countries grant to multinationals every year.

128   M. Mustafa Erdoğdu and Osman Geyik

budget deficit in the short run. The frequent application of tax amnesties can have very degenerative effects on tax compliance (Erdoğdu *et al.*, 2016). Having a "lax" *tax reconciliation institution out of the judicial process* is another way. As a result of this arrangement, one of the two taxpayers, equal in all aspects under the law, pays less tax. Such a situation deeply harms tax justice, since tax is perceived as a negotiation issue. Similarly, the *tax information confidentiality principle* tends to form a legal excuse for the tax administrations to hide tax data from the public domain. Such a principle may function as an armor to protect tax evaders.

Probably the worst way to create advantages for special interests is to provide excessive tax incentives to multinational companies. Such incentives are generally harmful to an economy because governments tend to give more away to the company in tax than the country receives in national benefits. Moreover, multinational companies, as Frijters, Gangl, and Torgler (this volume) point out, use the diverse possibilities of the international tax system to exploit inconsistencies among national tax rules.

Common needs, collective goods, and reciprocity

The emergence of the state can be seen as meeting the common needs of social life that cannot be obtained individually. As LaPorta *et al.* (1999, p. 227) point out, "institutions are created whenever the social benefits of doing so exceed the costs". Political institutions − and governments in particular − are the only institutions that can bring solutions to the problems of social life and work for the common good. Some of the main problems of social life can be identified as:

1. Ensuring fairness through rule of law and equal opportunities for each citizen;
2. Ensuring human rights, political rights, and democratic representation;
3. Provision of merit goods and gender-responsive quality public services;
4. Redistributing wealth fairly to reduce inequalities.

We may assume that there is an unwritten social contract between ordinary citizens and the government to bring solutions to the problems of social life and provide collective goods (social or public goods). A collective good[2] is a product or a service that one individual can consume without reducing its availability to others and from which no one is deprived. Collective goods, such as clean water, clean air, sewers, parks, law enforcement, national defense, etc.

---

2 Collective goods have two characteristics that distinguish them from private goods. They are non-excludable in supply, which means that it is not easy to prevent someone from accessing your consumption. Collective goods also provide non-rival benefits, which means that consumption of one agent does not affect the availability of the good for others (UNIDO, 2008, p. 7).

Political economy of compliance behavior   129

have positive effects on society and they are generally good for most, if not all. Goods that are accessible to all people provide a shared realm. Such goods, as Kallhoff (2014, p. 635) identifies, "contribute to social inclusion, they support the generation of the public, and they strengthen a shared sense of citizenship".

It is in the common interest that the state brings solutions to the problems of social life in exchange for citizens to commit themselves to pay taxes. In other words, "[p]ublic service benefit is a manifestation of reciprocity principle" (Mangoting *et al.*, 2015, p. 969). It is a joint commitment to make collective achievements available to each citizen (Kallhoff, 2014, p. 648). A contractual relationship implies duties and rights for each contractual partner. The fiscal exchange between the state and its citizens requires that in return for tax payments, citizens should receive a decent and adequate level of public service (Feld & Frey, 2007, p. 4).

Taxes are the most reliable and sustainable source of government revenue and governments operate with tax revenues. Therefore, tax compliance is essential for governments to provide collective goods and redistribute wealth (James & Alley, 2002, p. 28). However, due to the notorious free-rider problem, collective goods tend to be underfunded and undersupplied. The issue here is to share the cost of collective action. Problems that arise in the provision or maintenance of collective goods typically involve a mismatch between personal and social incentives.

The theory of social exchange postulates that the relationship between parties is based on cost and benefit and, to continue, it must be worthwhile for all parties (Alabede, Ariffin, & Kamil, 2011, pp. 129–130). There is a basic expectation of reciprocity. Citizens support the government in its responsibilities by providing finance in the form of tax payments. The return received by the taxpayer for the payment of the tax is decent standards of public services (Mangoting *et al.*, 2015, p. 969). By investing in infrastructure, public health care, education and training, and R&D a government can have a positive impact on society's well-being and make the economy better than otherwise (Altman, this volume). If the taxpayers perceive that the government has failed to maintain its commitment to the contract, voluntary compliance deteriorates. It is important to note that voluntary tax compliance also depends on the existence of reliable democratic institutions and a relationship of trust between citizens and the state. Torgler (2005) found convincing evidence that direct democracy has a significant impact on tax morale. Institutions that respect citizens' preferences will receive more support from the people than a state that acts like a Leviathan.

Fairness perception of tax burden, social norms, and attitudes

As a key concept for all human beings, fairness can be described as the quality of making judgments that are free from discrimination. Fairness is seen as a fundamental human right in social and economic organizations. Rawls (1971, p. 3) identifies fairness as "the first virtue of social institutions". Dimitrakakis *et al.* (2018, p. 1) suggest that "[f]airness is a desirable property of decision rules applied to a population of individuals". Fairness is a basic entitlement and it requires benefits and burdens among members of the society distributed fairly. Instances of perceived unfairness may lead to intense personal emotions and emotions tend to shape decisions (Siahaan, 2012).

Public perception is one of the factors that can shape tax compliance. Perception is closely linked to belief. Once the beliefs associated with a particular behavior are developed, they form the basis for subjective norms and attitudes that, in turn, constitute particular intention and behavior (Fishbein & Ajzen, 2010). Since perception is a reality for affected people, the perception of fairness can have a strong influence on behavior.

Social psychologists Tankard and Paluck (2016, p. 181) suggest that individuals' perceptions of norms guide their behavior. A social norm is composed of a rule of socially defined behavior based on shared values. Norm obedience may follow from the internalization of the norm and the values upon which it is founded, and/or from an effective system of sanctions (Edlund & Åberg, 2002, pp. 203–204). Bobek, Hageman, and Kelliher (2013, p. 465) suggest that "[p]ersonal norms play a much stronger role than any other type of social norm". The intended norms become widespread once a certain threshold is reached (Rosid, Evans, & Tran-Nam, 2018).

Bird (2016, pp. 21–22) points out that attitudes in a social context are formed by factors such as the level of perceived tax evasion, the perceived fairness of the tax structure, its complexity and stability, its administration, the value that people place on government activities, and the legitimacy of the government. Policies that affect any of these factors can affect the attitudes of taxpayers, and, therefore, their tax compliance. Cummings *et al.* (2009, p. 456) add that social norms are also influenced by the tax regime and the ability of the government to respond to the wishes of the citizens.

Taxpayers' perception of fairness is probably the most critical determinant of tax compliance except for effective tax enforcement. Batrancea *et al.* (2016, p. 251) identify that citizens tend to comply more when the tax system is fair. Similarly, findings of Etzioni (1986), Bradley (1994), Siahaan (2012), and Bellemare, Deversi, and Englmaier (2019) show that tax fairness may positively affect compliance behavior. The reverse is also true. The feeling of an unfair tax system increases the propensity for tax evasion. It is difficult to achieve cooperative behavior in highly unequal environments. Therefore, it is important that taxpayers feel tax liabilities are not determined arbitrarily and the taxation process is managed fairly.

As Bird (2016, p. 11) suggests, "[t]axation that is widely perceived to be unfair and administered capriciously and corruptly may not only bring the tax system into disrepute but weaken trust in government and even the legitimacy of the state". Fairness is also related to the behaviors of other taxpayers. Wenzel (2003, p. 58) highlights that an honest taxpayer is annoyed with others who betray society and get away with it. They may find the situation unfair, and consider that their sense of responsibility is disrespected or ridiculed. In

Political economy of compliance behavior 131

other words, as Mangoting *et al.* (2015, p. 970) indicate, tax evasion becomes a justification for dissatisfied taxpayers if the taxpayer's rights are not fulfilled. If the tax burden of an individual is approximately the same magnitude as that of comparable ones, on the other hand, tax compliance tends to increase (Feld & Frey, 2007, p. 15). This may imply that moral obligations of complying with tax regulations depend on the moral behavior, ethical values, and attitudes of other taxpayers, as well as the behavior of those who handle the taxpayers' money (Ho, Loo, & Lim, 2006).

It is becoming increasingly clear that emotions influence judgments, decisions, and behavior. A taxpayer's decision to comply may vary depending on the emotions that arise during communication with tax authorities or the frustration caused by the complexity of filing a tax return. When the tax administration emphasizes service to facilitate tax payments, combined with a trusting relationship between tax authorities and taxpayers, negative emotions are reduced and people are encouraged to comply with tax laws (Enachescu *et al.*, this volume).

Kirchler, Hofmann, and Gangl (2012) suggest that fairness should be achieved at the distributive, procedural, and retributive levels. Distributive fairness refers to the socially equitable distribution of resources and focuses on results. Procedural fairness is related to the perceptions of procedures, namely to how the tax system works and deals with taxpayers. Retributive justice is distinct from distributive justice and procedural justice. It is the fairness of sanctions and reactions to the violation of social rules and norms (Wenzel, 2003, p. 46).

Two taxation issues are extremely important with regard to distributive justice, namely: (a) tax burdens and (b) tax-funded social benefits. Fairness requires that tax burdens are distributed equitably among members of the society and tax liabilities must be consistent with the ability to pay. As mentioned earlier, perceptions of distributive fairness affect tax compliance. People who experience that their tax burden is higher than others tend to be less compliant with tax laws. Therefore, the state must establish equitable forms of taxation (O'Connor, 2002, p. 203).

Procedural fairness looks at the understanding of the decision-making process and the treatment people receive from decision-makers. Procedural fairness plays an important role in making a decision on whether to comply with tax legislation or not. An important factor in procedural fairness is the quality of interpersonal communication. The way authorities interact with taxpayers affects a person's perception of justice, which in turn affects his/her attitude, trust, and cooperation with relevant authorities (Tyler, 1997). Cooperation is strengthened when taxpayers are happy with their treatment (Uslaner, 2007, p. 6). Experiencing anger-related emotions is associated with low tax compliance. Therefore, it is important to take into account the emotional experiences of taxpayers when developing taxation procedures (Enachescu *et al.*, this volume).

Fairness requires equal opportunity and redistribution of wealth from rich to poor. For redistribution, however, society must consider inequality in the normative sense as offensive. According to Ahrens (2019), those who believe that

132 M. Mustafa Erdoğdu and Osman Geyik

income is achieved unfairly in their country are more supportive of top-down redistribution. The author notes that people generally accept unequal income distributions when inequality is the result of fair processes. However, sometimes there is an unequal distribution of income due to an unfair process. Tax evasion, for example, places an additional burden on obedient taxpayers because they take on the higher tax burden to offset unpaid taxes. Such a situation is not fair and unfairly redistributes wealth. Feld and Frey (2007) warn that tax evasion increases if taxpayers believe they will lose with redistribution. As with tax evasion, we may say that tax amnesties tend to redistribute wealth unfairly. Therefore, it is necessary to be avoided.

Trust in governing institutions and the level of corruption perceptions

Trust means a positive expectation that someone (through words, actions, or decisions) will not take opportunistic action (Robbins, 2001, p. 336). Trust stems from the belief that transparency, fair process, and honesty lead to the binding social norm (Braithwaite, 2003). Lack of integrity destroys trust. In other words, if there is a hidden agenda, there is no trust (Siahaan, 2012). Belief in the honesty of officials is a key element in why people trust the government. The perceived legitimacy of the state, the quality of government, and its performance are equally important. Evans (2008) indicates that trust is initially based on rational considerations and over time it becomes implicit due to positive experiences.

Trust in the government is a key factor in explaining tax compliance. Trust in the judiciary and Parliament also has a very strong effect on compliance (Torgler, Schaffner, & Macintyre, 2007). People expect the tax they pay to be used for public purposes. Trust in government would be compromised if government waste is high (Feld & Frey, 2007). Empirical findings of Torgler (2012) show that increasing the trust of individuals in the government, the judicial system, and the quality of governance has a significant and positive effect on tax morale. A weak legal system, poor service delivery, and corruption lead to a reduced willingness to pay taxes and destroys people's trust in government officials (Torgler, 2007). If a taxpayer frames taxes as a waste of government, then s/he can identify loopholes and various ways to avoid them.

Poorer governance outcomes can facilitate corruption. In an inefficient state where corruption is widespread, citizens will have little trust in authority and, therefore, little incentive to cooperate (Torgler & Schneider, 2009). In other words, the perception of corruption may affect the behavior of taxpayers negatively. According to Uslaner (2007, p. 1) "[t]ax evasion is part of a more general syndrome of corruption, impotent legal systems, shaky economies, and especially inefficient governments that fail to provide essential services". Therefore, countries seeking to increase tax compliance must first reduce corruption (Rosid, Evans, & Tran-Nam, 2018).

Although corruption and tax evasion appear like separate and different issues, they can easily be linked and reinforced. First, corruption not only allows tax evasion by helping taxpayers hide their income, but it also contributes to corruption by creating additional opportunities for corruption to flourish (Alm, Martinez-Vazquez, & McClellan, 2016, p. 146). Second, corruption leads to inefficient tax systems, undermines the legitimacy of tax collection, and reduces the willingness of individuals and companies to pay their fair share of taxes. All of this leads to a reduction in tax revenue (Imam & Jacobs, 2007). Therefore, it makes perfect sense to reduce corruption in order to improve tax compliance.

Transparency is essential if the taxpayer loses trust in the system. Transparency is linked to accountability and participation is an essential part of accountability. Accountability is based on a set of criteria for assessing the performance of public sector institutions (Katsimi & Moutos, 2010, p. 4). It promotes efficiency through its effects on government behavior. In all countries, citizens pay their taxes relatively voluntarily if they know what is going on, if they feel treated fairly, and if they receive something valuable in return (Bird, 2016, p. 22).

If citizens and authorities interact with a sense of collective responsibility through institutional structures, the system can be better managed and policies can be made more effective. In other words, when taxpayers see that their interests are adequately represented in political institutions and they receive an increase in the supply of collective goods, their willingness to contribute increases (Bird, Martínez-Vázquez, & Torgler, 2006). However, if citizens feel cheated, if they believe that corruption is widespread, that their tax money is not properly spent, and that they are not well protected by the law, the incentive to participate in tax evasion increases (Torgler & Schneider, 2009).

Castelfranchi and Falcone (2010) classify trust into reason-based and implicit trust based on the socio-cognitive trust theory. Reason-based trust is identified as an intentional decision to trust tax authorities by the tax authority's objectives, benevolence, perceived competence, motivation, and perceived external support environment. Reason-based trust is related to tax knowledge, perceived competence and goodwill of authorities, as well as perceived institutional quality and corruption level (Gangl et al., 2019).

The extended slippery slope framework suggests a negative relationship between coercive power and implicit trust, which leads to an antagonistic or trust-based climate. In an antagonistic climate, implicit trust is low and coercive power is high. In such a climate, authorities are mainly interested in catching taxpayers who evade taxes. Taxpayers pay their taxes because they are forced to do so by controls and punishments (Braithwaite, 2003). In a trust climate, on the other hand, implicit trust is high and coercive power is low. The interaction between tax authorities and taxpayers is characterized by mutual trust and respect. Therefore, a strong coercive power is not required. In this trust climate, taxpayers feel a commitment to the tax system and consider taxes as their moral obligation (Gangl et al., 2019).

Legitimate power fosters reason-based trust, a service climate, and a willingness to pay taxes (Gangl, Hofmann, & Kirchler, 2015). Legitimate power is defined as the belief that authorities are working on a legitimate basis, with expertise, information, and a good reputation (Raven, Schwarzwald, &

134   *M. Mustafa Erdoğdu and Osman Geyik*

Koslowsky, 1998). An essential prerequisite of a better level of tax effort in developing countries appears as a more legitimate and responsive state (Bird, Martínez-Vázquez, & Torgler, 2006). Findings of McGee and Benk (2016, p. 314) provide support for this position with "[t]he more confidence in government one had the more opposed one was to tax evasion".

Effective use of tax revenues and satisfaction from public services

From a social contract perspective, taxation is based on the quality of government and its performance in managing the country's financial affairs from tax revenue (Mangoting *et al.*, 2015). According to many authors, there is a strong link between the quality of public administration and tax compliance (*e.g.*, see LaPorta *et al.*, 1999; Hanousek & Palda, 2004; Feld & Frey, 2007; Uslaner, 2007; Barone & Mocetti, 2011; Cummings *et al.*, 2009; Alabede, Ariffin, & Kamil, 2011; Mangoting *et al.*, 2015; Erdoğdu *et al.*, 2016; Kiow, Salleh, & Kassim, 2017; and Altman, this volume).

In the taxpayer's cost–benefit calculation, inefficiency means a waste of public resources and it implies a less favorable ratio between the supply of collective goods and the taxes used to finance them (Barone & Mocetti, 2011). Taxpayers will be more compliant if the government uses taxpayer's money wisely or if taxpayers receive appropriate benefits for the taxes they pay in terms of collective goods and social amenities (Kiow, Salleh, & Kassim, 2017, p. 1). Returns received from taxpayers for taxpaying are decent standards of public services. As Uslaner (2007, p. 22) highlights the point, "[i]t's not just that people get what they pay for. They pay for what they get". Poor public service and corruption make people reluctant to pay taxes. In other words, proper management of the country makes taxpayers more willing to pay taxes. The more people trust that tax authorities will take care of their paid taxes and spend them carefully, the more they will comply (Siahaan, 2012).

Good public administration is essential to ensure high-quality public services and the well-being of society. Survey results from Cummings *et al.* (2009, p. 457) demonstrate that the quality of governance has an observable effect on tax compliance. Government performance of a given country may be assessed in part based on collective goods delivery, such as infrastructure, infant mortality, schooling, and literacy. The high quality of these goods, as opposed to high expenditure alone, is a sign of a well-functioning government, which includes democracy – both an end in itself and a mechanism for improving institutions (LaPorta *et al.*, 1999, p. 226).

When considering tax compliance, taxpayers' assessment of government based on proper management, integrity, accountability, transparency, and other virtues is a key factor. The quality of public services is particularly important for tax compliance. Citizens would like to be sure that the money they pay through taxes is used properly. People are more likely to evade taxes if they think that public officials embezzle tax money and they do not receive decent quality public services (Hanousek & Palda, 2004; Uslaner, 2007, p. 2). Therefore,

Political economy of compliance behavior 135

social institutions (demand factors) play a very important role in determining tax efforts (Bird, Martínez-Vázquez, & Torgler, 2006).

An empirical examination of tax compliance behavior in Turkey

Survey design

To examine the effect of regional differences in tax compliance in Turkey, individual interviews with a questionnaire were conducted for this study. The Marmara Region and the Southeastern Anatolia Region were selected for the study mainly because the collective goods and social amenities provided by the government are quite different in these two regions. This is particularly related to the fact that these cities are governed by politicians from different political parties.

The Marmara Region is located in northwestern Turkey. The Southeastern Anatolia Region, on the other hand, is bordered by the Mediterranean Region to the west, the Eastern Anatolia Region to the north, Syria to the south, and Iraq to the southeast. Istanbul is chosen as the representative city of the Marmara Region with 676 participants. This is the most populous city in Turkey and considered as the "financial capital" of the country. More than 15 million residents live in Istanbul (TÜİK, 2019b). This is more than one-fifth of Turkey's population. The right-wing Justice and Development Party (AKP) won the most recent parliamentary elections on June 24, 2018 in Istanbul with 42.7% of the votes (SEC, 2019). Istanbul generates 31% of Turkey's GDP (TÜİK, 2019a). The city is also responsible for more than two-fifths (43.9% in 2018) of the national tax revenues (GİB, 2019, p. 156).

The second city, Şanlıurfa, is located in the Southeastern Anatolia Region with a population of 2 million (TÜİK, 2019b). This city is represented by 338 participants in the study. Şanlıurfa is one of the most solid AKP cities, winning the most recent parliamentary election on June 24, 2018 with 52.7% of the votes (SEC, 2019). The third city, Diyarbakır, is also located in the Southeastern Anatolia Region with a population of 1.7 million (TÜİK, 2019b). This city is represented with 378 participants in the study. Although the ethnic distribution in Diyarbakır is unclear, it is estimated that this is one of the cities with the largest Kurdish populations in Turkey. The left-wing pro-Kurdish Peoples' Democratic Party won the most recent parliamentary election on June 24, 2018 in Diyarbakır with 65.5% of the votes (SEC, 2019). Table 7.1 and Table 7.2 show the general budget city revenues as well as their welfare index ratings and values.

As Table 7.1 makes it clear, Istanbul is Turkey's financial center and accounts for 43.9% of Turkey's tax revenue. This is 113 times and 88 times that of Şanlıurfa and Diyarbakır, respectively. Another striking difference between the three cities is that the share of tax revenues in the total collection is above average in Istanbul, far below in Şanlıurfa, and even lower in Diyarbakır.

136 *M. Mustafa Erdoğdu and Osman Geyik*

Table 7.1 General budget city revenues in Turkey, 2018

	Accrual (TL)	*Collection (TL)*	*Collection Rate*	*Share of Tax Revenues in Total Collection*
Istanbul	389,164,621,240	323,881,322,710	83.22	43.89
Şanlıurfa	3,420,204,002	2,095,751,417	61.28	0.28
Diyarbakır	4,385,135,177	2,453,233,915	55.94	0.33
Total (Turkey)	**906,332,362,485**	**737,954,269,710**	**81.42**	**100.00**

Source: GİB (2019, pp. 156–157). TL = Turkish Lira (national currency).

According to Table 7.2, Istanbul ranks the highest among these cities in terms of well-being. The general index for the well-being of the three cities shows how large the differences are between the Marmara Region and the Southeastern Anatolian Region. While the representative of the former region, Istanbul, has an overall index value of 0.649, the representatives of the Southeast Anatolian Region, Şanlıurfa and Diyarbakır, have a lower value of 0.354 and 0.349, respectively.

There are significant differences between the three cities regarding their access to infrastructure services. In this respect, Istanbul has an index almost three times that of Şanlıurfa and twice that of Diyarbakır. Another difference between the cities is related to life satisfaction. While Istanbul and Şanlıurfa have very similar life satisfaction indices, Diyarbakır has registered an extremely low one. The third major difference between these cities is related to education. Şanlıurfa has an index value less than half that of Istanbul. Although Diyarbakır has a much better education index than Şanlıurfa, its index value is only 67% of that of Istanbul.

Interviews were conducted during the period from April 7 to October 3, 2018. The random sampling method was applied by selecting taxpayers aged 18 and above, with different educational status, who participated in the interviews. Table 7.3 presents the demographic characteristics of the survey sample. In terms of gender, 528 of the participants were female and 824 were male. Regarding marital status, 62.1% of participants were married and 37.9% were single. A significant proportion of the participants were university and secondary school graduates, mostly aged 31–40 years. More than half of the participants had a monthly income from 1551 TL to 4500 TL, which corresponds to approximately 265 USD to 765 USD.

Eighteen questions were designed especially to identify the perceived fairness of the interviewees tax burden and their trust in government institutions regarding the effective use of tax revenue used to provide decent standards for public services. Statements targeted tax awareness (4 items), fairness perception of tax burdens and benefits (5 items), trust in governing institutions and their perceived level of corruption (5 items), taxpayers' feelings of social responsibility and their quest for reciprocity (2 items), public service quality and decent

Table 7.2 Well-being index rankings and values for the three cities, 2015

	Overall Index		Health		Education		Environment		Safety		Access to Infrastructure Services		Life Satisfaction	
	Rank	Index	Rank	Index	Rank	Index	Rank	Index	Rank	Index	Rank	Index	Rank	Index
Istanbul	5	0.6494	29	0.6471	56	0.5163	37	0.6219	73	0.4730	1	0.9592	50	0.4602
Şanlıurfa	73	0.3540	74	0.4324	78	0.2440	63	0.5327	31	0.6626	56	0.3704	56	0.4302
Diyarbakır	75	0.3489	60	0.5252	73	0.3472	67	0.4843	72	0.4757	29	0.5081	79	0.1875

Source: TÜİK (2019a).

138   *M. Mustafa Erdoğdu and Osman Geyik*

Table 7.3 Demographic, social, and educational status of participants

		Istanbul		Şanlıurfa		Diyarbakır		Total	
		No.	%	No.	%	No.	%	No.	%
Gender	Female	263	38.9	131	38.8	134	39.6	528	39.1
	Male	413	61.1	207	61.2	204	60.4	824	60.9
Marital	Married	451	66.7	218	64.5	171	50.6	840	62.1
Status	Single	225	33.3	120	35.5	167	49.4	512	37.9
Education	No primary	12	1.8	38	11.2	1	0.3	51	3.8
Status	education								
	Primary	115	17.0	117	34.6	18	5.3	250	18.5
	Secondary	245	36.2	81	24.0	74.0	21.9	400	29.6
	Tertiary	97	14.3	22	6.5	58	17.2	177	13.1
	University and above	207	30.6	80	23.7	187	55.3	474	35.1
Age	18–30	129	19.1	165	48.8	105	31.1	399	29.5
	31–40	278	41.1	79	23.4	146	43.2	504	37.3
	41–60	246	36.4	71	21.0	78	23.1	395	29.2
	Over 61	22	3.3	23	6.8	9	2.7	54	4.0
Monthly	0–1650	68	10.1	123	36.4	44	13.0	235	17.4
Income	1651–3200	153	22.6	85	25.1	87	25.7	325	24.0
(TL)	3201–4800	254	37.6	61	18.0	81	24.0	396	29.3
	4801–6400	53	7.8	15	4.4	42	12.4	110	8.1
	6401–10,000	102	15.1	27	8.0	47	13.9	176	13.0
	Over 10,001	46	6.8	27	8.0	37	10.9	110	8.1

Source: Researchers' computations.

use of tax revenues (2 items). It is important to note that some of the statements were useful to identify not only one but more perceptions. For instance, some of the statements mainly related to awareness were instrumental also for feelings of social responsibility and their quest for reciprocity.

Results

In this section, we first examine the distribution of responses of survey statements. Then, the relationship between political interactions and attitudes towards taxation is examined through one-way ANOVA, taking into account the level of education and the differences between the cities.

Table 7.4 examines the averages of responses to all survey questions by city. In this table, the first six statements (#1 – #6) are assumed to reflect participants' tax awareness and their social responsibility. Statements from #7 to #11 are assumed to reflect participants' perception of fairness and their emotions toward the tax behavior of others. Statements from #12 to #16 assess taxpayers' trust in governing institutions and their perceived levels of corruption in the public sector. The last two statements (#17 and #18) are assumed to reflect respondents' perceptions of public service quality and decent use of tax revenues.

Table 7.4 Average response by city

Items	Istanbul (N = 676)		Şanlıurfa (N = 338)		Diyarbakır (N = 338)	
	Mean	Std. Er.	Mean	Std. Er.	Mean	Std. Er.
#1 Tax is the equivalent of public services.	2.18	0.861	2.14	0.840	2.38	0.770
#2 What would you think of a taxpayer who did not comply with his/her tax liability? (He or she is dishonest.)	0.57	0.501	0.37	0.484	0.49	0.518
#3 What would you think of a taxpayer who did not comply with his/her tax liability? (It harms the state.)	0.45	0.498	0.28	0.452	0.55	0.738
#4 What would you think of a taxpayer who did not comply with his/her tax liability? (I react.)	0.12	0.320	0.12	0.323	0.18	0.388
#5 What would you think of a taxpayer who did not comply with his/her tax liability? (I do not buy anything from there.)	0.07	0.257	0.07	0.252	0.07	0.247
#6 What would you think of a taxpayer who did not comply with his/her tax liability? (A non-compliant taxpayer is a crafty merchant.)	0.22	0.418	0.19	0.398	0.25	0.431
#7 The tax system in our country is fair.	1.86	0.929	2.43	1.043	2.08	1.201
#8 The government's effort to secure the rights of taxpayers is sufficient.	2.69	1.080	2.48	1.068	2.21	1.018
#9 I am satisfied with the services provided by the tax authorities.	2.98	1.159	2.63	1.149	2.37	1.120
#10 Taxpayers' expectation of amnesty leads to tax evasion.	4.22	0.904	3.27	1.224	3.95	1.021
#11 What would you think of a taxpayer who did not comply with his/her tax liability? (S/he did it because s/he was forced to do so / I think it is okay.)	0.34	0.473	0.23	0.422	0.24	0.523
#12 I trust in government policies.	3.00	1.308	2.78	1.120	2.33	1.328
#13 I trust in the Parliament (Grand National Assembly of Turkey).	3.47	1.205	2.76	1.187	2.57	1.219
#14 I believe that all transactions of the tax administration are accountable.	2.66	1.133	2.70	1.166	2.66	1.191
#15 I would like to know where every cent of tax money is spent.	4.39	0.723	3.57	1.172	4.15	1.064
#16 I would give my vote according to how tax money is spent.	3.99	0.999	3.24	1.235	3.84	1.141
#17 Tax revenues are used effectively and properly.	2.66	1.227	2.72	1.136	2.14	1.167
#18 Do you think there is extravagance/waste in the use of public resources?	1.50	0.951	1.80	0.957	1.36	0.781

140   M. Mustafa Erdoğdu and Osman Geyik

Taxpayers' feelings of social responsibility and their quest for reciprocity

This section aims to identify tax awareness of the taxpayers participating in the interview, their feelings of social responsibility, and their quest for reciprocity.

On average, only 60% of respondents consider taxes to be the equivalent of public services. This is much less than expected. The data in Table 7.5 show that taxpayers in Diyarbakır and Şanlıurfa tend to view taxes as a tribute rather than the equivalent of public services. This finding implies that respondents' trust in governing institutions to provide decent collective goods is not high. Therefore, respondents do not perceive a strong relationship between tax compliance and public services.

According to Table 7.6, only 53.4% of respondents believe that tax non-compliance harms the state. We think that this surprising situation is due to two main reasons. One reason might be the respondent's low level of tax awareness. However, respondents are more likely to be deeply suspicious that authorities would maximize social benefits in exchange for taxes collected.

Table 7.7 shows that respondents tend to legitimize tax evasion as if it were something to praise. This is an alarming result since 78.1% of respondents do

Table 7.5 Taxes in return for public services

City		*"Tax is the equivalent of public services"*					*Total*
		Strongly Disagree	*Disagree*	*Neutral*	*Agree*	*Strongly Agree*	
Istanbul	N	36	152	61	319	108	**676**
	%	5.3	22.5	9.0	47.2	16.0	**100.0**
Şanlıurfa	N	29	83	43	156	27	**338**
	%	8.6	24.6	12.7	46.2	8.0	**100.0**
Diyarbakır	N	30	75	31	153	49	**338**
	%	8.9	22.2	9.2	45.3	14.5	**100.0**
Total	N	95	310	135	628	184	**1352**
	%	7.0	22.9	10.0	46.4	13.6	**100.0**

Table 7.6 Perception of non-compliance behavior – 1

City		*"A non-compliant taxpayer harms the state"*		*Total*
		Yes	*No*	
Istanbul	N	303	373	**676**
	%	44.8	55.2	**100.0**
Şanlıurfa	N	242	96	**338**
	%	71.6	28.4	**100.0**
Diyarbakır	N	177	161	**338**
	%	54.4	47.6	**100.0**
Total	N	722	630	**1352**
	%	53.4	46.6	**100.0**

Political economy of compliance behavior 141

Table 7.7 Perception of non-compliance behavior – 2

City		"A non-compliant taxpayer is a crafty merchant"		Total
		Yes	No	
Istanbul	N	524	152	**676**
	%	77.5	22.5	**100.0**
Şanlıurfa	N	277	61	**338**
	%	82.0	18.0	**100.0**
Diyarbakır	N	255	83	**338**
	%	75.4	24.6	**100.0**
Total	N	1056	296	**1352**
	%	78.1	21.9	**100.0**

Table 7.8 Fairness of the Turkish tax system

City		"The tax system in Turkey is fair"					Total
		Strongly Disagree	Disagree	Neutral	Agree	Strongly Agree	
Istanbul	N	255	334	37	29	21	**676**
	%	37.7	49.4	5.5	4.3	3.1	**100.0**
Şanlıurfa	N	45	189	31	61	12	**338**
	%	13.3	55.9	9.2	18.0	3.6	**100.0**
Diyarbakır	N	137	116	23	46	16	**338**
	%	40.5	34.3	6.8	13.6	4.7	**100.0**
Total	N	437	639	91	136	49	**1352**
	%	32.3	47.3	6.7	10.1	3.6	**100.0**

not appear to see taxes as a social responsibility. A possible explanation for this result may be that responders do not perceive the tax system as fair and they do not trust public authorities will use tax revenue properly.

Perceptions of respondents regarding the fairness of the Turkish tax system, their burden, and their emotions

This section aims to identify the perception of respondents regarding the fairness of the Turkish tax system, their burden, and their emotions toward the behavior of others.

Table 7.8 shows that the vast majority of respondents (79.6%) consider the tax system in Turkey to be unfair. This view is the strongest in Istanbul with 87.1%. It is interesting to note that, while Şanlıurfa and Diyarbakır are located in the same region, there are big differences in respondents' perception about the fairness of the Turkish tax system. This might be due to the fact that a significant number of respondents in Diyarbakır are unsatisfied with the tax

142   M. Mustafa Erdoğdu and Osman Geyik

Table 7.9 Ensuring the rights of taxpayers

City			"The government's effort to secure the rights of taxpayers is sufficient"					Total
			Strongly Disagree	Disagree	Neutral	Agree	Strongly Agree	
Istanbul	N	93		220	201	129	33	**676**
	%	13.8		32.5	29.7	19.1	4.9	**100.0**
Şanlıurfa	N	53		156	54	64	11	**338**
	%	15.7		46.2	16.0	18.9	3.3	**100.0**
Diyarbakır	N	88		137	82	17	14	**338**
	%	26.0		40.5	24.3	5.0	4.1	**100.0**
Total	N	234		513	337	210	58	**1352**
	%	17.3		37.9	24.9	15.5	4.3	**100.0**

Table 7.10 Satisfaction with the services provided by the tax administration

City			"I am satisfied with the services provided by the tax administration"					Total
			Strongly Disagree	Disagree	Neutral	Agree	Strongly Agree	
Istanbul	N	67		212	111	239	47	**676**
	%	9.9		31.4	16.4	35.4	7.0	**100.0**
Şanlıurfa	N	48		149	38	87	16	**338**
	%	14.2		44.1	11.2	25.7	4.7	**100.0**
Diyarbakır	N	81		130	58	58	11	**338**
	%	24.0		38.5	17.2	17.2	3.3	**100.0**
Total	N	196		491	207	384	74	**1352**
	%	14.5		36.3	15.3	28.4	5.5	**100.0**

administration (see particularly Table 7.9 in this regard) and question the legitimacy of the local government.

The data in Table 7.9 show that only 19.8% of respondents believe that government efforts to secure taxpayer rights are sufficient. Those who tend to positively evaluate government efforts are much fewer in Diyarbakır than in Istanbul or Şanlıurfa.

Table 7.10 shows that there is a big difference between the two regions in terms of satisfaction with the services provided by the tax authorities. For instance, the rate of respondents who are not satisfied at all with the tax services in Diyarbakır is more than double the level in Istanbul. Such dissatisfaction is likely to have a very negative impact on tax compliance there.

According to Table 7.11, 77.0% of taxpayers believe that the possibility of a tax amnesty leads to tax evasion. In our view, according to this result, tax amnesty is one of the most important factors that feed tax evasion. A particular

Political economy of compliance behavior   143

attention should be paid to the fact that tax amnesties are an injustice to honest taxpayers and discourage them from paying their fair share of taxes. Tax amnesties undermine the idea that everyone in society is subject to the same laws and rules. They affect not only total tax revenue but also the sense of justice in society. Of course, this will also harm trust in governing authorities.

Trust in government and perceived levels of corruption

This section aims to assess taxpayers' trust in government policies and their perception of levels of corruption in the public sector.

Table 7.12 shows that there are dramatic differences of opinion particularly in Istanbul and Diyarbakır. While a total of 45.9% of those interviewed in Istanbul trust or strongly trust government policy, the corresponding value in Şanlıurfa and Diyarbakır is as low as 31.3% and 22.4%, respectively. Since Şanlıurfa and Diyarbakır exhibit extremely low levels of trust, it would be very surprising to see high levels of voluntary tax compliance in these cities. Indeed,

Table 7.11 Perception of tax amnesties

City		"Taxpayers' expectation of amnesty leads to tax evasion"					Total
		Strongly Disagree	Disagree	Neutral	Agree	Strongly Agree	
Istanbul	N	13	40	20	317	286	**676**
	%	1.9	5.9	3.0	46.9	42.3	**100.0**
Şanlıurfa	N	34	64	69	118	53	**338**
	%	10.1	18.9	20.4	34.9	15.7	**100.0**
Diyarbakır	N	17	14	40	164	103	**338**
	%	5.0	4.1	11.8	48.5	30.5	**100.0**
Total	N	64	118	129	599	442	**1352**
	%	4.7	8.7	9.5	44.3	32.7	**100.0**

Table 7.12 Trust in government policies

City		"I trust government policies"					Total
		Strongly Disagree	Disagree	Neutral	Agree	Strongly Agree	
Istanbul	N	89	221	56	221	89	**676**
	%	13.2	32.7	8.3	32.7	13.2	**100.0**
Şanlıurfa	N	40	119	73	88	18	**338**
	%	11.8	35.2	21.6	26.0	5.3	**100.0**
Diyarbakır	N	110	120	32	39	37	**338**
	%	32.5	35.5	9.5	11.5	10.9	**100.0**
Total	N	239	460	161	348	144	**1352**
	%	17.7	34.0	11.9	25.7	10.7	**100.0**

144   M. Mustafa Erdoğdu and Osman Geyik

Table 7.13 Trust in the Parliament

City		"I trust the Parliament (Grand National Assembly of Turkey)"					Total
		Strongly Disagree	Disagree	Neutral	Agree	Strongly Agree	
Istanbul	N	58	119	62	324	113	**676**
	%	8.6	17.6	9.2	47.9	16.7	**100.0**
Şanlıurfa	N	44	125	66	73	30	**338**
	%	13.0	37.0	19.5	21.6	8.9	**100.0**
Diyarbakır	N	80	94	75	69	20	**338**
	%	23.7	27.8	22.2	20.4	5.9	**100.0**
Total	N	182	338	203	466	163	**1352**
	%	13.5	25.0	15.0	34.5	12.1	**100.0**

Table 7.14 Accountability of the tax administration

City		"I believe that all transactions of the tax administration are accountable"					Total
		Strongly Disagree	Disagree	Neutral	Agree	Strongly Agree	
Istanbul	N	86	272	163	97	58	**676**
	%	12.7	40.2	24.1	14.3	8.6	**100.0**
Şanlıurfa	N	49	127	57	85	20	**338**
	%	14.5	37.6	16.9	25.1	5.9	**100.0**
Diyarbakır	N	75	68	117	54	24	**338**
	%	22.2	20.1	34.6	16.0	7.1	**100.0**
Total	N	210	467	337	236	102	**1352**
	%	15.5	34.5	24.9	17.6	7.5	**100.0**

the share of tax revenues in the total collection are far lower in Şanlıurfa and Diyabakır than in Istanbul The data in Table 7.1 shows exactly this result.

Table 7.13 shows that there are dramatic differences of opinion among respondents in the three cities concerning the Parliament. While 16.7% of respondents in Istanbul express their strong trust in Parliament, this rate falls to 8.9% in Şanlıurfa and further to 5.9% in Diyarbakır. These data can be interpreted as a strong perception of respondents from the Southeastern Anatolia Region that the Parliament is less trusted in their region.

The data in Table 7.14 shows that 50.0% of taxpayers do not believe at all that tax administration transactions are accountable. This result is worrisome and implies that a large number of respondents suspect that the tax administration is corrupt. It is too optimistic to expect voluntary tax compliance from those taxpayers who have such an opinion.

Table 7.15 shows that 83.4% of taxpayers want to know where every cent of tax money is spent. This response is more common in Istanbul (94.1%). The result can be interpreted as follows: citizens living in Istanbul believe that

Political economy of compliance behavior 145

Table 7.15 The quest for information on spending tax money

City		"I would like to know where every cent of paid tax is spent"					Total
		Strongly Disagree	Disagree	Neutral	Agree	Strongly Agree	
Istanbul	N	2	23	15	307	329	**676**
	%	0.3	3.4	2.2	45.4	48.7	**100.0**
Şanlıurfa	N	17	61	52	130	78	**338**
	%	5.0	18.0	15.4	38.5	23.1	**100.0**
Diyarbakır	N	21	5	28	132	152	**338**
	%	6.2	1.5	8.3	39.1	45.0	**100.0**
Total	N	40	89	95	569	559	**1352**
	%	3.0	6.6	7.0	42.1	41.3	**100.0**

Table 7.16 Efficiency of public spending

City		"Tax revenues are used effectively and properly"					Total
		Strongly Disagree	Disagree	Neutral	Agree	Strongly Agree	
Istanbul	N	132	215	133	144	52	**676**
	%	19.5	31.8	19.7	21.3	7.7	**100.0**
Şanlıurfa	N	45	124	71	78	20	**338**
	%	13.3	36.7	21.0	23.1	5.9	**100.0**
Diyarbakır	N	124	112	47	40	15	**338**
	%	36.7	33.1	13.9	11.8	4.4	**100.0**
Total	N	301	451	251	262	87	**1352**
	%	22.3	33.4	18.6	19.4	6.4	**100.0**

if closely monitored, there is a lot of room to improve public spending. In Diyarbakır, however, the situation looks very different in an intriguing way. About less than half of respondents want to know where every cent they paid is spent. This is probably due to the fact that a large number of respondents in Diyarbakır might have lost hope that tax revenues can ever be used effectively and properly.

Perceptions of public service quality and decent use of tax revenues

This section aims to identify whether taxpayers believe that tax revenues are being used effectively and appropriately.

Table 7.16 shows that, on average, 55.7% of respondents disagree that tax revenues are used effectively and properly. This opinion seems to be particularly widespread in the Southeastern Anatolian city of Diyarbakır with 69.8%. In our view, the taxpayers in Diyarbakır believe that public service providers in their city are not selected for merit and that there is widespread corruption in the public sector.

146　*M. Mustafa Erdoğdu and Osman Geyik*

Table 7.17 Waste perception in public spending

| City | | *"Do you think there is waste or extravagance in the use of public resources?"* | | | | *Total* |
		Yes	*No*	*Now and Then*	*Undecided*	
Istanbul	N	523	10	107	36	**676**
	%	77.4	1.5	15.8	5.3	**100.0**
Şanlıurfa	N	181	58	85	14	**338**
	%	53.6	17.2	25.1	4.1	**100.0**
Diyarbakır	N	277	7	49	5	**338**
	%	82.0	2.1	14.5	1.5	**100.0**
Total	N	981	75	241	55	**1352**
	%	72.6	5.5	17.8	4.1	**100.0**

Table 7.17 shows that the vast majority of respondents believe there are waste and extravagance in the use of public resources. As with many other related issues, Diyarbakır is the city where this opinion is most commonly represented. Surprisingly, the respondents in Şanlıurfa, which is in the same region, reflect a completely different picture. Compared to the taxpayers in Diyarbakır, eight times more taxpayers in Şanlıurfa have a much more positive opinion and believe in the proper management of public resources with negligible waste. This difference suggests that the perception of governing institutions in these two cities is completely different. Most likely, respondents in Diyarbakır feel they are negatively discriminated against the other cities and react to this with tax non-compliance.

Political interactions and attitudes towards taxes: how are cities different?

In the literature, trust in public authorities is being associated with tax morale and tax attitudes. We have a different view of the direction of this relationship. In our view, there is no trust without justice. The perception of injustice can lead to intense personal emotions that destroy trust. This is because trust is based on justice. Therefore, to build up trust in public authorities, the enactment of fair practices is a priority. Fairness requires that benefits and burdens among members of society be distributed fairly. Here the tax system enters the scene with its fairness and the way tax revenue is used.

To examine the relationship between tax and political interactions by cities, we conducted an ANOVA with the help of two factors obtained by using four items. The first of these factors is trust in the state (TS) and the other is perception towards public authority and taxes (PPAT). TS is composed of the items "I trust government policies" and "I trust the Parliament (Grand National Assembly of Turkey)". PPAT is composed of the items "I am satisfied with the services provided by the tax authorities" and "Tax revenues are used effectively

Political economy of compliance behavior 147

Table 7.18 Averages of TS and PPAT by city

Cities		PPAT	TS
Istanbul	Mean (M)	2.820	3.233
	N	676	676
	Std. Deviation (SD)	0.953	1.115
Şanlıurfa	Mean (M)	2.672	2.771
	N	338	338
	Std. Deviation (SD)	0.880	1.075
Diyarbakır	Mean (M)	2.257	2.450
	N	338	338
	Std. Deviation (SD)	0.908	1.125
Total	Mean (M)	2.642	2.922
	N	1352	1352
	Std. Deviation (SD)	0.952	1.156

and properly" statements. Cronbach's Alpha is 0.79 for TS and 0.77 for PPA, which shows a strong internal consistency.

Table 7.18 presents the averages and summary statistics of TS and PPAT by city. In the answers given to the items forming the factors, we determined that there was convergence in the cities of Istanbul (PPAT, $M = 2.820$, $SD = 0.955$; TS, $M = 3.233$, $SD = 1.115$) and Şanlıurfa (PPAT, $M = 2.672$, $SD = 0.879$; TS, $M = 2.771$, $SD = 1.075$). Although Diyarbakır is in the same region as Şanlıurfa, we concluded that taxpayers living in Diyarbakır (PPAT, $M = 2.257$, $SD = 0.908$; TS, $M = 2.445$, $SD = 1.125$) provided quite different answers to the items than the taxpayers living in Şanlıurfa.

We conducted a one-way ANOVA to determine if there is a difference in PPAT among cities (see Table 7.19). The first rule of ANOVA is the homogeneity of variance between groups. Since Levene's test was not significant ($p = 0.651$), this condition was fulfilled. The one-way ANOVA revealed a statistically significant difference among cities in terms of PPAT levels, $F(2,1351) = 60.501$; $p < 0.001$. The second part of the table shows the difference between groups. As can be seen, there are significant differences in perception concerning political authority and taxes (PPAT) between taxpayers from Istanbul and the other two cities.

As shown in Table 7.2, Şanlıurfa and Diyarbakır, which are in the same region, have very close welfare index values (*i.e.*, 0.354 and 0.349, respectively). Interestingly, taxpayers in these two cities gave different answers. What may be more interesting is that responses from taxpayers in Şanlıurfa are similar to those in Istanbul, despite the fact that Istanbul is located in a distant region and has a welfare index value of 0.649.

On the other hand, responses of taxpayers' from Diyarbakır are very different from those of taxpayers residing in the other two cities. In our view, this is mainly due to the taxpayers in Diyarbakır, who believe that they are victims of

Table 7.19 ANOVA – PPAT – by city

Homogeneity of Variance Test (PPAT)			
Levene Statistic	**df1**	**df2**	**Sig.**
0.429	2	1349	0.651

ANOVA					
	Sum of Squares	**Df**	**Mean Square**	**F**	**Sig.**
Between Groups	148.510	2	74.255	60.501	0.000
Total	1804.189	1351			

Multiple Comparison (PPAT Scheffe)				
(I) Your city	**(J) Your city**	**Mean Difference (I-J)**	**Std. Error**	**Sig.**
Istanbul	Şanlıurfa	0.46228*	0.07380	0.000
	Diyarbakır	0.78328*	0.07380	0.000

* The difference between the groups is statistically significant.

discrimination and that their citizenship rights are not respected enough. They find this situation unfair and, consequently, do not trust governing institutions much and tend to be less compliant with tax laws. According to GİB (2019), the tax collection rate of accrual revenues in Diyarbakır in 2018 was only 55.9%. The rate is higher in Istanbul and Şanlıurfa (*i.e.*, 83.2% and 61.3%, respectively).

The results of this study suggest that there is an important relationship between tax compliance and trust in the state when benefits and burdens are distributed fairly among members of society and tax revenues are used properly. Moreover, the level of education has an important effect on taxpayers' attitudes and behavior towards public authorities.

According to the multiple comparisons resulting from the one-way ANOVA (Table 7.20), there are significant differences between taxpayers' perceptions towards public authorities and taxes (PPAT) according to their education level. We found that PPAT of respondents with higher education levels are significantly different to those with secondary and tertiary education ($p < 0.001$).

Concluding remarks

We argued in this chapter that voluntary tax compliance depends primarily on the perceived fairness of the tax system, trust in governing institutions, and satisfaction with the collective goods and social amenities provided by the government. If taxpayers believe that their tax money is not spent well and corruption is high, they would feel cheated and their confidence in governing institutions would decrease significantly. In other words, voluntary tax compliance cannot be assumed as a social norm in countries where the tax system is not fair, trust in governing institutions is low, and corruption is widespread. This is mainly because an unfair tax system, a low level of institutional quality and a high level of perceived corruption in the public sector reduce citizens' trust in authorities and generate intense negative emotions regarding tax compliance. Therefore, to build up trust in public authorities, the enactment of fair practices should be a priority.

The basic expectation of taxpayers is that tax burdens be distributed fairly among members of society and that decent quality of public services and collective goods be provided by the government. Fairness requires a fair distribution of benefits and burdens. Responsible taxpayers do not approve of peers who breach this unwritten social contract and get away with it. It is the responsibility of governments to punish tax evaders in order to protect the rights of honest people who pay their fair share. If the government fails to deter tax evasion, responsible taxpayers will eventually adopt such behavior, and it would be unreasonable to expect them to meet tax duties in future interactions with authorities.

Empirical results from interviews with 1352 respondents in three cities (Istanbul, Şanlıurfa, and Diyarbakır) of two regions (Marmara and Southeastern Anatolian) support the conclusions above. According to our findings, tax compliance behavior in Turkey is closely related to taxpayers' fairness perception of

Table 7.20 ANOVA – PPAT – by education level

Homogeneity of Variance Test (PPAT)			
Levene Statistic	**df1**	**df2**	**Sig.**
1.916	4	1347	0.105

ANOVA					
	Sum of Squares	**df**	**Mean Square**	**F**	**Sig.**
Between Groups	66.152	4	16.538	12.817	0.000
Total	1804.189	1352			

Multiple Comparison (PPAT Scheffe)				
(I) Your education	**(J) Your education**	**Mean Difference (I–J)**	**Std. Error**	**Sig.**
Primary education	No primary education	−0.328	0.174	0.471
	Secondary education (including high school education)	−0.318*	0.091	0.017
	Tertiary education	−0.333	0.111	0.064
	Higher education and above	0.161	0.088	0.509
Higher education and above	No primary education	−0.490	0.167	0.073
	Primary education	−0.161	0.088	0.509
	Secondary education (including high school education)	−0.479*	0.077	0.000
	Tertiary education	−0.494*	0.100	0.000

* The difference between the groups is statistically significant.

Political economy of compliance behavior   151

their burdens, their trust in the government, their satisfaction from the public services, and the use of frequent tax amnesties. In the latter case, the frequent use of tax amnesties is probably one of the most serious problems impacting on voluntary tax compliance in Turkey. Results from Table 7.11 strongly support this claim. On average, 77% of respondents believe that the possibility of a tax amnesty leads to tax evasion. Tax amnesties undermine the idea that everyone in society is subject to the same laws and rules. This influences not only total tax revenue but also the sense of justice in society.

Our results reveal also other interrelated problems undermining tax compliance in Turkey. For example, the deterrence mechanism of tax non-compliance has serious shortcomings in Turkey. Even if tax evasion is detected, the necessary measures are not always taken or the sanctions imposed are not sufficiently harsh. Having a "lax" tax reconciliation institution within the judicial system creates other problems. Such an institution harms tax justice because it creates the perception that taxes are subject to negotiation. The manner in which the principle of confidentiality of fiscal information is applied constitutes another problem. Not only does it mask a considerable part of unregistered economic activity, but it also functions as an armor to protect tax evaders.

From the answers provided during interviews, it became clear that an overwhelming majority of respondents (79.6%) perceived the tax system in Turkey as unfair. They also considered that the benefits and burdens among members of society have not been distributed fairly. Only 19.8% of respondents believed that government efforts to secure taxpayers' rights were sufficient. Besides, most Turkish taxpayers were not pleased with the treatment they have been subjected to and considered the situation to be unfair.

Our results show that taxpayers' trust in the government is very low in Turkey. On average, only 36.4% of respondents declare that they trust authorities. This figure falls to 31.3% in Şanlıurfa and 22.4% in Diyarbakır. Taxpayers' trust in Parliament is not very different. On average, only 36.6% of respondents declare that they trust the Parliament. The level falls to 30.5% in Şanlıurfa and 26.3% in Diyarbakır. Moreover, 50.0% of respondents do not believe that tax administration transactions are accountable. On the other hand, 83.4% of respondents would like to be informed about the spending of tax revenue. These results imply that most respondents question the integrity of the tax administration. With such a low level of trust in government, Parliament, and the tax administration, high levels of voluntary tax compliance seem unlikely to be achieved.

Answers provided by respondents show that taxpayers seem quite hesitant to see taxes they have paid as the equivalent of public services. On average, 29.9% of respondents do not perceive a match between taxes paid and the quality of public services. Many respondents believe that public expenditures have not been optimally managed for citizens' benefit and that there is much room for improving public spending. Indeed, 33.2% of respondents in Şanlıurfa and 31.1% of respondents in Diyarbakır tend to see tax as a tribute. On average, only 53.4% of respondents believe that tax non-compliance harms the state. In our view, a possible explanation for these results is respondents' lack of trust in authorities' efforts to maximize social benefits in exchange for taxes collected. It could be the case that some respondents perceive that authorities have broken their promise on the unwritten social contract. Consequently, taxpayers do not feel obliged to honor their taxpaying duty.

The attitudes of Turkish taxpayers regarding taxes differ when compared to general ethical rules. Hence, they hardly consider taxpaying as a moral obligation towards society. On average, only 49.7% of respondents consider a non-compliant taxpayer to be dishonest and 28.2% of respondents see tax evasion as justifiable. Also, 71.1% of respondents think about how tax money is spent. Respondents question governing institutions about their competence to deliver decent quality and adequate public goods. Results may imply a high level of perceived corruption and a low level of trust in governing authorities regarding the management of tax revenues. As a result, the quality and quantity of public services provided are not considered sufficient to justify the existing tax burden.

All in all, our study suggests that there is a strong relationship between voluntary tax compliance and fair distribution of burdens and benefits among members of society. It is also extremely important to acknowledge that a strong and sustained fight against corruption would also mean a fight against tax evasion. Therefore, political leaders should eliminate corruption to improve voluntary tax compliance.

Acknowledgments

We would like to thank Savaş Çevik, Larissa Batrancea, Ebru Çağlayan Akay, and Hoşeng Bülbül for their very helpful comments and suggestions on this chapter. It goes without saying that all remaining errors are ours.

References

ActionAid (2013). *Annual Report 2013.* ActionAid International, Johannesburg, South Africa. Retrieved December 12, 2019 from https://actionaid.org/publications/2014/annual-report-2013-actionaid-international.

Ahrens, L. (2019). Theorizing the impact of fairness perceptions on the demand for redistribution. *Political Research Exchange, 1*(1), 1–17.

Alabede, O. J., Ariffin, Z. Z., & Kamil, M. I. (2011). Determinants of tax compliance behaviour: A proposed model for Nigeria. *International Research Journal of Finance and Economics, 78,* 121–136.

Allingham, M. G., & Sandmo, A. (1972). Income tax evasion: A theoretical analysis. *Journal of Public Economics, 1,* 323–338.

Alm, J., Kirchler, E., Muehlbacher, S., Gangl, K., Hofmann, E., Kogler, C., & Pollai, M. (2012). Rethinking the research paradigms for analysing tax compliance behaviour. *CESifo Forum, 13*(2), 33–40.

Alm, J., Martinez-Vazquez, J., & McClellan, C. (2016). Corruption and firm tax evasion. *Journal of Economic Behavior & Organization, 124,* 146–163.

Political economy of compliance behavior 153

Alt, J., Preston, I., & Sibieta, L. (2009). *The political economy of tax policy: Dimensions of tax design. The Mirrlees review*. Oxford: Oxford University Press.

Barone, G., & Mocetti, S. (2011). Tax morale and public spending inefficiency. *International Tax and Public Finance, 18*, 724–749.

Batrancea, L., Nichita, A., Batrancea, I., & Kirchler, E. (2016). Tax compliance behavior: An upshot of trust in and power of authorities across Europe and MENA. In: M. M. Erdoğdu & B. Christiansen (Eds.), *Handbook of research on public finance in Europe and the MENA region* (pp. 248–267). Hershey, PA: IGI Global.

Bellemare, C., Deversi, M., & Englmaier, F. (2019). Complexity and distributive fairness interact in affecting compliance behavior. CESifo Working Paper No. 7899.

Bird, R. (2007). Tax challenges facing developing countries: A perspective from outside the policy arena. Discussion draft available at: http://ssrn.com/abstract=1393991.

Bird, R. (2016). Transparency, technology and taxation. In: M. M. Erdoğdu & B. Christiansen (Eds.), *Handbook of research on public finance in Europe and the MENA region* (pp. 11–29). Hershey, PA: IGI Global.

Bird, R., Martínez-Vázquez, J., & Torgler, B. (2006). Societal institutions and tax effort in developing countries. In: J. Alm, J. Martinez-Vazquez, & M. Rider (Eds.), *The challenges of tax reform in the global economy* (pp. 283–338). New York: Springer.

Bobek, D. D., Hageman, A. M., & Kelliher, C. F. (2013). Analyzing the role of social norms in tax compliance behavior. *Journal of Business Ethics, 115*(3), 451–468.

Bradley, C. F. (1994). An empirical investigation of factors affecting corporate tax compliance behavior. Ph.D. dissertation, University of Alabama.

Braithwaite, V. (2003). A new approach to tax compliance. In: V. Braithwaite (Ed.), *Taxing democracy: Understanding tax avoidance and evasion* (pp. 1–11). Aldershot: Ashgate.

Castelfranchi, C., & Falcone, R. (2010). *Trust theory: A socio-cognitive and computational model*. Chichester, UK: Wiley.

Cummings, R. G., Martinez-Vazquez, J., McKee, M. & Torgler, B. (2009). Tax morale affects tax compliance: Evidence from surveys and an artefactual field experiment. *Journal of Economic Behavior & Organization, 70*, 447–457.

Çevik, S. (2016). Tax system, economic development, and good governance: A comparative analysis of the MENA countries. In: M. M. Erdoğdu & B. Christiansen (Eds.), *Handbook of research on public finance in Europe and the MENA region* (pp. 156–175). Hershey, PA: IGI Global.

Daude, C., Gutiérrez, H., & Melguizo, Á. (2014). The political economy of tax incentives for investment in the Dominican Republic: "Doctoring the Ball". OECD Development Centre Working Papers No. 322, OECD Publishing.

Dimitrakakis, C., Liu, Y., Parkes, D. C., & Radanovic, G. (2018). Bayesian fairness. Retrieved February 18, 2020 from https://arxiv.org/pdf/1706.00119.pdf.

Edlund, J., & Åberg, R. (2002). Social norms and tax compliance. *Swedish Economic Policy Review, 9*, 201–228.

Erdoğdu, M. M., Yılmaz, B. E., Aydın, M., & User, I. (2016). Political economy of tax evasion and tax loss in the real estate sector: A property tax reform proposal for Turkey. In: M. M. Erdoğdu & B. Christiansen (Eds.), *Handbook of research on public finance in Europe and the MENA region* (pp. 268–298). Hershey, PA: IGI Global.

Etzioni, A. (1986). Founding a new socioeconomics. *Challenge, 29*(5), 475–482.

Evans, C. C. (2008). Taxation compliance and administrative costs: An overview. In: M. Weninger, C. Lang, J. Obermair, C. Schuch, & P. Staringer (Ed.), *Tax compliance costs for companies in an enlarged European community* (pp. 447–468). Alphen aan den Rijn: Kluwer Law International.

Feld L. P., & Frey, B. S. (2007). Tax compliance as the result of a psychological tax contract: The role of incentives and responsive regulation. *Law & Policy, 29*(1), 102–120.

Fishbein, M., & Ajzen, I. (2010). *Predicting and changing behavior: The reasoned action approach.* New York: Taylor & Francis.

Gangl, K. Hofmann, E., Hartl, B., & Berkics, M. (2019). The impact of powerful authorities and trustful taxpayers: Evidence for the extended slippery slope framework from Austria, Finland, and Hungary. *Policy Studies, 41*(1), 98–111.

Gangl, K., Hofmann, E., & Kirchler, E. (2015). Tax authorities' interaction with taxpayers: A conception of compliance in social dilemmas by power and trust. *New Ideas in Psychology, 37*, 13–23.

GİB (2019). *Revenue Administration Presidency 2018 year activity report* [in Turkish]. Department of Strategy Development, Publication No. 314, 156–157.

Hanousek, J., & Palda, F. (2004). Quality of government services and the civic duty to pay taxes in the Czech and Slovak Republics, and other transition countries. *Kyklos, 57*(2), 237–252.

Head, J., Osberg, L., Green, L., Cassin, A., & Panitch, L. (1993). Tax-fairness principles: A conceptual, historical, and practical review. In: A. Maslove (Ed.), *Fairness in taxation* (pp. 3–62). Toronto: University of Toronto Press.

Ho, J. K., Loo, E. C., & Lim, K. P. (2006). Perspective of non-taxpayers' perception on issues of ethics and equity in tax compliance. *Malaysian Accounting Review, 5*(2), 47–59.

ICIJ (2018, January 15). A fair tax system will be lost to vested interests without public pressure: EU Tax Commissioner. International Consortium of Investigative Journalists. Retrieved on December 14, 2019 from www.icij.org/investigations/paradise-papers/fairer-transparent-tax-system-will-lost-vested-interests-without-public-pressure-warns-eu-tax-commissioner/.

Ilzetzkiy, E. (2018). Tax reform and the political economy of the tax base. *Journal of Public Economics, 164*, 197–210.

Imam, P. A., & Jacobs, D. F. (2007). Effect of corruption on tax revenues in the Middle East. IMF Working Paper WP/07/270. Retrieved December 12, 2019 from www.imf.org/external/pubs/ft/wp/2007/wp07270.pdf.

James, S., & Alley, C. (2002). Tax compliance, self-assessment and tax administration. *Journal of Finance and Management in Public Services, 2*(2), 27–42.

Kahneman, D. (2011). *Thinking, fast and slow.* New York: Farrar, Straus and Giroux.

Kallhoff, A. (2014). Why societies need public goods. *Critical Review of International Social and Political Philosophy, 17*(6), 635–651.

Katsimi, M., & Moutos, T. (2010). EMU and the Greek crisis: The political-economy perspective. *European Journal of Political Economy, 26*(4), 568–576.

Kiow, T. S., Salleh, M. F. M ,& Kassim, A. A. B. M. (2017). The determinants of individual taxpayers' tax compliance behaviour in Peninsular Malaysia. *International Business and Accounting Research Journal, 1*(1), 26–43.

Kirchler, E. (2007). *The economic psychology of tax behaviour.* Cambridge: Cambridge University Press.

Kirchler, E., Hoelzl, E., & Wahl, I. (2008). Enforced versus voluntary tax compliance: The "slippery slope" framework. *Journal of Economic Psychology, 29*(2), 210–225.

Kirchler, E., Hofmann, E., & Gangl, K. (2012). From mistrusting taxpayers to trusting citizens: Empirical evidence and further development of the slippery slope framework. In: A. N. Lebedev (Ed.), *Economic psychology in the modern world* (pp. 125–146). Moscow: Ekon-inform.

LaPorta, R., Lopez-de-Silanes, F., Shleifer, A., & Vishny, R. (1999). The quality of government. *Journal of Law, Economics and Organization, 15*(1), 222–279.

Mangoting, Y., Sukoharsono, E. G., Rosidi, & Nurkholis (2015). Developing a model of tax compliance from social contract perspective: Mitigating the tax evasion. *Procedia: Social and Behavioral Sciences, 211*, 966–971.

McGee, R.W., & Benk, S. (2016). Attitudes toward tax evasion in Turkey: An empirical study. In: M. M. Erdoğdu & B. Christiansen (Eds.), *Handbook of research on public finance in Europe and the MENA region* (pp. 299–318). Hershey, PA: IGI Global.

O'Connor, J. (2002). *The fiscal crisis of the state*. London: Transaction.

Raven, B. H., Schwarzwald, J., & Koslowsky, M. (1998). Conceptualizing and measuring a power/interaction model of interpersonal influence. *Journal of Applied Social Psychology, 28*, 307–332.

Rawls, J. (1971). *A theory of justice*. Cambridge, MA: Harvard University Press.

Robbins, S. P. (2001). *Organizational behavior* (9th ed.). New York: Prentice Hall.

Rosid, A., Evans, C., & Tran-Nam, B. (2018). Tax non-compliance and perceptions of corruption: Policy implications for developing countries. *Bulletin of Indonesian Economic Studies, 54*(1), 25–60.

SEC (2019). Presidential election and 27th term parliamentary election results. Supreme Election Council. Retrieved December 14, 2019 from www.ysk.gov.tr/tr/24-haziran-2018-secimleri/77536.

Siahaan, F. O. P. (2012). The influence of tax fairness and communication on voluntary compliance: Trust as an intervening variable. *International Journal of Business and Social Science, 3*(21), 191–198.

Sossin, L. (1992). Welfare state crime in Canada: The politics of tax evasion in the 1980s. *Windsor Yearbook of Access to Justice, 12*, 98–127.

Tankard, M. E., & Paluck, E. L. (2016). Norm perception as a vehicle for social change. *Social Issues and Policy Review, 10*(1), 181–211.

Thaler, R. H., & Sunstein, C. R. (2008). *Nudge: Improving decisions about health, wealth, and happiness*. New Haven, CT: Yale University Press.

Torgler, B. (2005). Tax morale and direct democracy. *European Journal of Political Economy, 21*, 525–531.

Torgler, B. (2007). *Tax compliance and tax morale: A theoretical and empirical analysis*. Cheltenham, UK: Edward Elgar.

Torgler, B. (2012). Tax morale, Eastern Europe and European enlargement. *Communist and Post-Communist Studies, 45*, 11–25.

Torgler, B., Schaffner, M., & Macintyre, A. (2007). Tax compliance, tax morale, and governance quality. CREMA Working Paper No. 2007–17.

Torgler, B., & Schneider, F. (2009). The impact of tax morale and institutional quality on the shadow economy. *Journal of Economic Psychology, 30*(2), 228–245.

TÜİK (2019a). Rankings and index values of well-being index for provinces. Turkish Statistical Institute. Retrieved December 14, 2019 from www.tuik.gov.tr/PreTablo.do?alt_id=1106.

TÜİK (2019b). The results of address based population registration system 2018. Turkish Statistical Institute. Retrieved December 14, 2019 from https://biruni.tuik.gov.tr/medas/?kn=95&locale=tr.

Tyler, T. R. (1997). The psychology of legitimacy: A relational perspective on voluntary deference to authorities. *Personality and Social Psychology Review, 1*(4), 323–345.

UNIDO (2008). *Public goods for economic development*. United Nations Industrial Development Organization, Vienna.

Uslaner, E. M. (2007). Tax evasion, corruption, and the social contract in transition. International Center for Public Policy Working Paper No. 0725, Andrew Young School of Policy Studies, Georgia State University.

Wenzel, M. (2003). Tax compliance and the psychology of justice: Mapping the field. In: V. Braithwaite (Ed.), *Taxing democracy: Understanding tax avoidance and evasion* (pp. 41–69). Aldershot: Ashgate.

8 Incidental emotions, integral emotions, and decisions to pay taxes

Janina Enachescu, Žiga Puklavec, Christian Martin Bauer, Jerome Olsen, Erich Kirchler, and James Alm

Introduction

Decisions to pay or to evade taxes are frequently seen as decisions under uncertainty. According to expected utility theory, taxpayers are motivated to maximize their own profit by rationally considering payoffs of compliance and non-compliance, balancing the gain from underreporting income against the loss from detection and non-punishment.

This perspective is formalized in the economics of crime paradigm by Becker (1962) and constitutes the basis for the standard model of tax evasion (Allingham & Sandmo, 1972; Srinivasan, 1973). In their analyses, the audit probability, the fine rate, the tax rate, and taxpayer's income along with attitude toward risk are the main determinants of compliance. They typically propose frequent audits and severe fines as the policy tools to enforce compliance. These seminal theoretical publications have fueled intense empirical work, and there are now many empirical studies on the impact of audits and fines on compliance. However, the emphasis on these financial factors is somewhat ironic, given Allingham and Sandmo's (1972, p. 326) explicit statement that their theory

> may perhaps be criticized for giving too little attention to nonpecuniary factors in the taxpayer's decision on whether or not to evade taxes. It need hardly be stressed that in addition to the income loss there may be other factors affecting utility if one's attempt at tax evasion is detected. These factors may perhaps be summarily characterized as affecting adversely one's reputation as a citizen of the community.

Indeed, numerous psychological studies show that in complex decision situations people do not behave according to expected utility theory. Instead, people are hardly likely to consider all potentially relevant aspects of a decision. Limited processing capabilities foster the use of heuristics, and an individual's risk behavior is affected by the framing of the decision situation (Kahneman, 2003).

In addition, there is increasing evidence that emotions affect judgments, decisions, and behavior (*e.g.*, Lerner, Li, Valdesolo, & Kassam, 2015). Despite

158 *Janina Enachescu et al.*

the existence of many studies that have examined various socio-psychological factors in tax compliance decisions (Kirchler, 2007), the impact of emotions on tax compliance decisions has been mostly neglected, with some notable exceptions (e.g., Coricelli, Joffily, Montmarquette, & Villeval, 2010; Murphy & Tyler, 2008).

We want to emphasize that the relative lack of research on emotions in tax compliance research can hardly be attributed to the origins of the rational choice paradigm. Elffers (2015) notes that many of the founding fathers of rational choice were well aware of the potential importance of emotions. He writes:

> Dirck Coornhert, Adam Smith, and Jeremy Bentham introduced in their original writings their perspectives in terms of norms, guilt, conscience, pity and other affects ... When considering Smith's work, even the title of his treatise, *The Theory of Moral Sentiments* (Smith 1759/1982), is an illustration of the point.
>
> (Elffers, 2015, p. 53)

Nonetheless, the importance of emotions in decision-making has been largely neglected in many empirical research fields for a long time (Elster, 1998).

In this chapter we present initial investigations of the role of emotions on tax compliance decisions. We first introduce selected emotion theories. We also present different paths by which emotions can possibly affect tax decisions, namely indirectly via mood and emotions unrelated to the tax decision itself (or "incidental emotions") and directly via emotions that are elicited in the taxation context itself (or "integral emotions"). We then discuss an experimental study investigating the first path suggested above, the influence of positive versus negative mood on tax compliance. Further, we also present and analyze a study exploring emotions elicited by the taxation context. Finally, we suggest that a fruitful path for future research is the integration of emotions into the slippery slope framework of tax compliance (Kirchler, 2007).

What are emotions?

Traditionally, cognitive processes and decision-making have been studied without considering affect, mood, and emotions (Loewenstein, 2000). Decisions were assumed to result from the individual evaluation of expected consequences of alternatives. Out of a set of alternatives, people should choose the alternative with the greatest and most likely positive consequences (Loewenstein & Lerner, 2003). In this tradition, emotions did not receive much attention. However, social psychologists have increasingly pointed to the importance of affect, positive and negative mood, and the quality of emotions in cognitive processes and decision-making (*e.g.*, Forgas, 1995; Lerner *et al.*, 2015; Schwarz, 2012). Here we discuss this research in order to lay the foundation for our subsequent discussion.

Most people have an instinctive understanding of what emotions are. However, in psychological theory, emotions are considered complex phenomena, and researchers are far from agreeing on a precise definition. Most generally, emotions are states of feelings accompanied by physical and psychological changes that affect behavior. Emotions are subjective and conscious experiences that are characterized by psycho-physiological reactions to biological states, mental states, and interpretations of the situation's experiences, or objects. Emotions are also connected to motivational and behavioral intentions. For theoretical clarity, we need to distinguish emotions that are acute, intense, and object-related (Zeelenberg & Pieters, 2006), from the more generic term "mood", which refers to less intense and more durable affective states that are not triggered by a specific event (Scherer, 2005).

Regarding the composition of emotions, Scherer (2005) distinguishes cognitive appraisal, bodily symptoms, action tendencies, expressions, and emotional experiences in his component process model. Cognitive appraisal refers to evaluations of events. Bodily symptoms indicate the psycho-physiological component of emotions. Action tendencies refer to the motivational aspects of emotions. Expressions are facial and vocal expressions that accompany emotions, and emotional experiences represent the subjective feelings of an individual.

Some researchers have proposed specific definitions of emotions. For example, Fehr and Russel (1984) asked people what comes readily to their mind when thinking about emotions, and they found that happiness, anger, sadness, love, fear, hate, and joy were the most often mentioned qualities of emotions. Izard (1977) defined a list of basic emotions including interest, joy, surprise, distress, anger, fear, shame, disgust, contempt, and guilt. These qualities of emotions are prototypical for categories of emotions. Indeed, the number of categories varies across research, and categories are generally fuzzy. Various scholars agree to organize emotion categories along one or more dimensions. For example, the Positive and Negative Affect Schedule (PANAS) is an instrument developed to assess affect, based on the assumption that emotions can be categorized along the valence dimension (Watson, Clark, & Tellegen, 1988). Other models organize distinct emotions along the dimensions valence and activation in a circumplex structure (Russell & Barrett, 1999). Turner and Stets (2005) distinguish between three basic dimensions of emotions: arousal indicates the intensity of emotions, valence indicates whether emotions are positive or negative, and potency expresses whether an individual feels strong or weak when experiencing a specific emotion.

Scherer (2005) developed the "Geneva Emotion Wheel", which distinguishes between 20 emotion qualities that vary from negative to positive valence and from low to high control or power (Figure 8.1). Sacharin, Schlegel, and Scherer (2012) write that the Geneva Emotion Wheel

> consists of discrete emotion terms corresponding to emotion families that are systematically aligned in a circle. Underlying the alignment of the emotion terms are the two dimensions valence (negative to positive) and

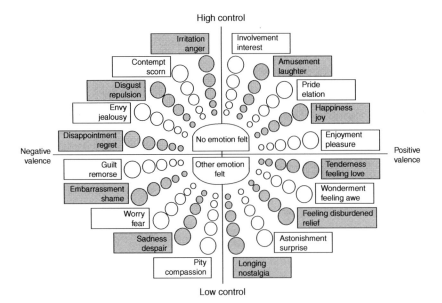

Figure 8.1 Geneva Emotion Wheel
Note: adapted from Sacharin, Schlegel, and Scherer (2012, p. 5) and Scherer, Shuman, Fontaine, and Soriano (2013, p. 289).

control (low to high), separating the emotions in four quadrants: Negative/low control, negative/high control, positive/low control, and positive/high control. Note that the control dimension is also called control/power … The response options are 'spikes' in the wheel that correspond to different levels of intensity for each emotion family from low intensity (towards the center of [the] wheel) to high intensity (toward the circumference of the wheel). Also, in the very center of the wheel, the response options 'no emotion' and 'other emotion' [are] offered.

In contrast to these dimensional approaches, other scholars emphasize the importance of looking at specific emotions when interested in behavioral consequences. Anger and fear, for instance, are two emotions of comparable negative valence that can have the same level of arousal but that are associated with different judgments and behavioral consequences (Lerner & Keltner, 2000). Anger is typically associated with fight, whereas fear tends to evoke flight. With regard to these behavioral consequences, it is therefore important to consider specific emotions rather than following a dimensional approach. Zeelenberg and Pieters (2006) propose the feeling-is-for-doing approach to emotions, emphasizing the need to investigate the role of specific emotions and to focus on the motivational component of emotions, an approach that they term "emotivation".

How do emotions influence decisions?

Loewenstein and Lerner (2003) developed a framework that illustrates the different paths by which emotions can influence decision-making processes. They distinguish between the influence of "anticipated" versus "immediate" emotions. For instance, taxpayers considering evading taxes may refrain from doing so because they anticipate regret in case of being caught and facing a severe fine or loss of reputation. Erard and Feinstein (1994) assume that shame and guilt are such "anticipated" moral costs of tax evasion when thinking about the possible consequences of honestly declaring income versus dishonestly cheating on one's declaration. The importance of such moral costs has been stressed by multiple authors (Blaufus, Bob, Otto, & Wolf, 2017; Bosco & Mittone, 1997; Grasmick & Bursik, 1990). People choose alternatives that are likely to elicit positive emotions, they try to avoid future regrets from not having chosen an alternative, and they avoid alternatives that are likely to cause negative feelings (van de Ven & Zeelenberg, 2011).

Besides anticipated emotions, emotions can be experienced immediately at the time of decision-making. An especially important distinction here is between "incidental" and "integral" emotions. Incidental emotions are not related to the decision context itself but arise from surrounding circumstances. For example, sunny weather can make one feel happy and this emotion can influence information processing as well as judgments and decision-making (Schwarz, 2012). On the other hand, integral emotions stem directly from the decision situation. For instance, consumer research shows that poor service quality can trigger anger, which in turn influences subsequent consumer decisions negatively (Bougie, Pieters, & Zeelenberg, 2003).

These distinctions suggest that a taxpayer's compliance decision might vary with emotions elicited during communications with tax authorities or with frustration triggered by complexity when filing a tax declaration. The different paths of emotional influences on decision-making are illustrated in Figure 8.2.

One example for research on incidental emotions is a study by Drouvelis and Grosskopf (2016), who investigated the impact of emotions on cooperation and sanctioning behavior in a laboratory contribution game. Anger and happiness were induced by presenting short video clips to participants before they had to make contribution decisions. They found that participants in the angry condition contributed significantly less than those in the happy condition, and that participants also tended to punish their counterparts more harshly than participants who were in a happy emotional state.

As for integral emotions, Coricelli et al. (2010) measured participants' arousal levels in a standard laboratory income-reporting game. Participants were endowed with a fixed income and they decided how much to report to the authorities. If caught underreporting, they had to pay a fine. However, in addition to the payment of the fine, participants who were detected cheating had their portrait publicly displayed. This experimental design therefore allowed Coricelli et al. (2010) to investigate the impact on compliance of the emotional

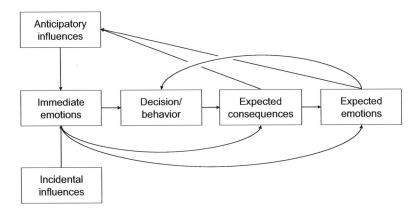

Figure 8.2 Determinants and consequences of immediate and expected emotions
Note: adapted from Loewenstein and Lerner (2003, p. 621).

costs of shaming people for tax evasion. Their results showed that the intensity of anticipated emotions before reporting income was positively related to tax evasion.

In another laboratory study, Dulleck *et al.* (2016) measured heart rate variability (or psychic stress), as an indicator for moral sentiments during a public goods game. Participants were either endowed with a fixed amount of income in each round or they earned money according to performance in a cognitive skills task. Dulleck *et al.* (2016) examined how the heart rate variability changed as participants made tax payment decisions. Contrary to Coricelli *et al.* (2010), Dulleck *et al.* (2016) found a positive relation between arousal and tax compliance. While the differentiated impact of specific emotions on tax compliance remains unclear, these two studies emphasize the importance of emotional experiences for taxation.

In yet another study, Olsen *et al.* (2018) conducted an experimental survey with real self-employed taxpayers in Turkey. They found that taxpayers reported different emotions in response to tax authorities' enforcement strategies. When tax authorities focus on harsh enforcement methods, such as audits and fines, negative emotions, which are related to increased readiness to evade taxes, are evoked. However, when tax authorities emphasize service that facilitates the payment of taxes, together with a trusting relationship between tax authorities and taxpayers, negative emotions are reduced and intentions to comply with the tax law are promoted.

Fochmann, Hechtner, Kirchler, and Mohr (2019) conducted two laboratory experiments testing the effect of incidental emotions on compliance behavior. They induced (or primed) both positive and negative emotions using pictures, which were intended to evoke either positive (*e.g.*, a mother with a baby) or negative (*e.g.*, a garbage dump) feelings. They found that individuals are less willing to comply after being primed with positive incidental emotions as compared to being primed with negative emotions. These results were especially true if individuals described themselves as sensitive to emotion-eliciting information. However, before concluding that positive incidental emotions lead to less compliance than negative emotions, the specific nature of the induced emotions should be considered. For example, while fun may affect behavior in one way, pride may have different effects. Similarly, anger and fear – both negative emotions – are likely to have different impacts on decisions.

These studies have made considerable contributions to our understanding of the potential role of emotions in taxpayer decisions. They all demonstrate that emotional experiences may affect taxpayer behavior. However, they also demonstrate that the impact of emotional experiences on taxpayer behavior is an unresolved issue. In the next sections, we discuss two studies of our own that attempt to advance our understanding of this issue.

Empirical study (1): incidental emotions and tax compliance

To further study the effect of incidental emotions on tax compliance, we conducted an incentivized laboratory tax experiment where mood was induced using background music. The experimental design comprised three between-subject conditions: a positive mood condition with background music by Wolfgang Amadeus Mozart, a negative mood condition with background music by Gustav Holst, and a control condition without any background music.

Emotions tend to guide our attention and to serve as indicators for pain or pleasure (Pfister & Böhm, 2008). According to the feelings-as-information theory, we rely on affective information when evaluating our environment and making judgments. While neutral or positive feelings are the status quo, negative feelings signal the presence of problems that require an explanation and elevated attention (Schwarz, 2012). Therefore, people tend to process information more thoroughly and systematically when they are in a negative mood as compared to a neutral mood. On the other hand, a positive mood is associated with heuristic information processing and the reliance on stereotypes. In line with the feelings-as-information theory background, we assumed that participants in the negative condition are likely to evade more taxes than those in the positive condition. Note that evading is assumed to be the rational strategy given the audit and fine parameters in our experiment.

Previous research suggests that background music is a promising method to induce positive or negative mood (Garlin & Owen, 2006; Kämpfe, Sedlmeier, & Renkewitz, 2011; Martin, 1990; White & Rickard, 2016). For instance, Thompson, Schellenberg, & Husain (2001) found that playing a piece by Wolfgang Amadeus Mozart induced high arousal and a positive mood in subjects, while subjects exhibited low arousal and a sad mood after listening to a piece composed by Tomaso Albinoni (Thompson *et al.*, 2001).

164 *Janina Enachescu et al.*

Table 8.1 Sample socio-demographic statistics

	Control condition	*Positive mood condition*	*Negative mood condition*	*Total*
N	41	41	41	123
Female (%)	26 (63.4%)	22 (53.7%)	23 (56.1%)	71 (57.7%)
Mean age (SD)	23.95 (4.34)	25.68 (6.08)	24.51 (4.87)	24.72 (5.16)
Student (%)	39 (94.3%)	38 (92.7%)	39 (95.1%)	116 (94.3%)
Employment status				
Unemployed (%)	20 (48.8%)	17 (41.5%)	16 (39.0%)	53 (43.1%)
Marginally employed (%)	12 (29.3%)	16 (39.0%)	13 (31.7%)	41 (33.3%)
Part-time employed (%)	7 (17.1%)	7 (17.1%)	6 (14.6%)	20 (16.3%)
Full-time employed (%)	2 (4.9%)	1 (2.4%)	6 (14.6%)	9 (7.3%)
Type of work				
No-employment (%)	21 (51.2%)	16 (39.0%)	19 (46.3%)	56 (45.5%)
Blue collar worker (%)	3 (7.3%)	3 (7.3%)	4 (9.8%)	10 (8.1%)
White collar worker (%)	16 (39.0%)	18 (43.9%)	14 (34.1%)	48 (39.0%)
Self-employed (%)	1 (2.4%)	4 (9.8%)	4 (9.8%)	9 (7.3%)

Method

Sample. Overall, 123 subjects participated in the experiment, of which 57.7% were female. Most participants were students of social sciences, with an average age of 24.7 years. Table 8.1 displays detailed socio-demographic information by experimental conditions.

Material and procedure. The experiment took place in the Social Science Research Lab at the Faculty of Psychology, University of Vienna. Participants were randomly assigned to one of three between-subject conditions, *i.e.*, positive mood, negative mood, and control. In the two mood conditions, a recording was played in the adjacent room. The wall between the two rooms was thin and noise-permeable. When participants arrived in the lab, the recording started with two people softly leading a discussion. The volume was adjusted so that participants would not hear what was being said, but would know that there were sounds in the adjacent room. After all participants were seated in one of the cubicles and the verbal instructions by the experimenter were finished, the recorded discussion ended and music started to play. The music was played loud enough so that it was very likely for everyone to hear. The nature of the music was not explained to participants in any way.

In the positive mood condition, Wolfgang Amadeus Mozart's "Sonata for Two Pianos in D Major, KV 448" was played. In the negative mood condition, Gustav Holt's "The Planets, Mars, The Bringer of War" was played (Baumgartner, Esslen, & Jäncke, 2006; Thompson *et al.*, 2001). In the control condition, the recording of the two-people discussion ended at the beginning of the experiment and no music was played.

Emotions and decisions to pay taxes 165

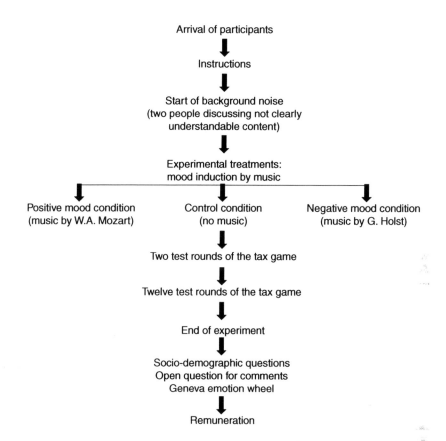

Figure 8.3 Experimental procedure

The actual experimental task consisted of an income-reporting tax game (Figure 8.3). The experiment started with two test rounds, followed by 12 actual decision rounds. In each round participants were endowed with a base income of 1000 ECU and could additionally earn up to 1000 ECU according to their performance in a real-effort slider task (Gill & Prowse, 2012). The effort task consisted of ten sliders per round, which participants had to move exactly to their center point. For each correctly solved slider, participants received 100 ECU additional income. Hence, a maximum income of 2000 ECU per round was possible.

After each round, participants had to declare the amount of taxes they wanted to pay. The tax rate was fixed at 40%, and there was an audit probability of 25%. To keep audit sequence effects constant across conditions, audits were pre-determined to occur in rounds 4, 6, and 11. In case of detected evasion, participants had to pay the evaded amount of taxes plus a fine of the same size. Participants were not informed about the number of rounds to be played. At the

166 *Janina Enachescu et al.*

Table 8.2 Positive and negative mood scores by condition

	Positive mood condition	Negative mood condition	Control condition
Positive mood Mean (SD)	5.34 (1.12)	5.33 (0.78)	5.20 (1.07)
Negative mood Mean (SD)	4.01 (1.23)	4.07 (1.06)	3.90 (1.31)

end of the experiment participants received remuneration according to their income in one randomly selected round (1 Euro = 300 ECU).

After playing the tax game, participants were asked to indicate their current affective state on the Geneva Emotion Wheel (Scherer, 2005), as presented in Figure 8.1. This measure served as a manipulation check to see whether exposure to different music or to no music lead to the expected changes in positive and negative mood. The experiment concluded with basic socio-demographic questions.

Results

We first report the results of the manipulation check of the mood induction, followed by results on the effects of mood on tax compliance. We also explore whether the audit outcome affected participants' moods.

Manipulation check. In order to check whether the manipulation of positive and negative mood was successful, we first aggregated the single emotion scores of all positive emotions to one positive mood score, and analogously all negative emotions to one negative mood score. See Table 8.2 for descriptive statistics.

We then ran two separate regression models with the positive and negative mood scores as the respective outcome variable. The condition variable was entered as predictor. The results revealed no significant effect of condition, neither for the positive mood score nor for the negative mood score. For detailed regression results, see Table 8.3.

Manipulation of mood by music also did not have a significant effect on specific emotion qualities. We conducted a linear mixed model with a random intercept for participants to account for the repeated measures structure of the data, predicting 20 specific emotion scores by condition. We found no significant overall effect of condition on the emotion scores when comparing the positive condition against the control condition ($b = 0.15, p = 0.524$). We also found no significant overall effect of condition on the emotion scores when comparing the negative condition against the control condition ($b = 0.19$, $p = 0.422$). The results did not change when we changed the reference category from the control condition to the positive condition.

Effect of mood on tax compliance. Irrespective of the failed manipulation, we conducted a linear mixed model with relative tax compliance in each round as

Emotions and decisions to pay taxes 167

Table 8.3 Manipulation check regression models for positive and negative mood scores

	Positive mood score			Negative mood score		
	B	SE	p	B	SE	p
Intercept	5.20	0.16	< .001	3.90	0.21	< .001
Positive condition	0.14	0.23	.541	0.12	0.30	.706
Negative condition	0.13	0.22	.560	0.17	0.29	.557
Intercept	5.34	0.16	< .001	4.01	0.22	< .001
Control condition	0.14	0.23	.541	0.12	0.30	.706
Negative condition	0.01	0.23	.971	0.06	0.30	.554

Note. N_{pos} = 118, N_{neg} = 98. The variable condition had three levels with *positive condition, negative condition*, and *control condition*. We ran each regression twice, changing the dummy coding to see all possible condition comparisons. In the top models, the *control condition* was set as the reference category; in the lower models, the *positive condition* served as reference group.

outcome variable (equal to paid tax/tax due) and condition as predictor. The predictor was dummy coded with the control condition as reference category. The model specified a random intercept for individuals, thereby controlling for the repeated measures data structure. The effect of the conditions on tax compliance across the 12 rounds of the tax game revealed a significant difference in tax compliance between the control condition and the positive mood condition ($b = 0.16, p = 0.018$). However, there was no significant difference between the control condition and the negative mood condition ($b = 0.07, p = 0.309$). Changing the reference category revealed no significant difference between the positive and negative mood condition ($b = 0.09, p = 0.170$). Figure 8.4 illustrates relative tax compliance for all 12 rounds by condition. Note that the sharp drops in compliance observable in each round directly following an audit can be explained by the bomb–crater effect (Mittone, 2006).

We conclude that playing different music pieces with the aim of inducing different moods did not translate into different tax compliance levels. We only observed that individuals exposed to the positive mood condition (or Mozart's "Sonata for Two Pianos in D Major, KV 448") paid more taxes than those in the control condition. We also ran another linear mixed model with the two mood scores as predictors and relative tax compliance as outcome variable. Neither the positive valence score ($b = -0.01, p = 0.793$) nor the negative valence score ($b = 0.01, p = 0.861$) was significantly related to tax compliance.

Discussion

Despite the success of using music to manipulate mood in previous studies, the intended manipulation was not successful in our study. One possibility is that the music manipulation might have been too subtle. By playing the music from the adjacent room and by not making it salient that the music was part

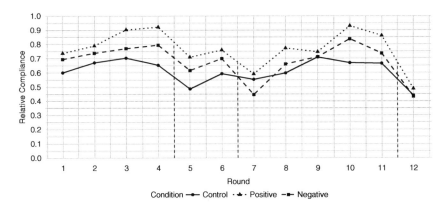

Figure 8.4 Tax compliance by conditions and experimental rounds

of the experiment, participants might have tried to ignore the music instead of actively listening to it. Furthermore, the experiment itself might have evoked stronger emotions than the ones elicited by the music. It is possible that the slider task itself evoked increased stress levels, thereby overshadowing the influence of music in the background.

Not surprisingly, we do not find the expected effects of positive versus negative mood on tax compliance. However, we do find that music intended for a positive mood leads to higher compliance levels than in a control condition. One must interpret this result cautiously, given the manipulation check was not successful. One potential interpretation could be that participants might have been less distracted in the control condition and therefore might have taken the risky but rational decision to evade taxes.

To successfully investigate the influence of incidental emotions on tax compliance, we conclude from the current study that emotion inductions should be more intense. One approach would be to use videos that evoke strong emotions instead of (or combined with) music. Visual stimuli might be better suited and less subtle than merely playing background music.

Empirical study (2): the role of integral emotions on tax compliance decisions

While incidental emotions can arise from all kinds of circumstances, emotions integral to the tax context are direct consequences of tax authorities' actions. This suggests that tax authorities could use emotions as a tool, aiming their actions to elicit positive emotions by, for example, focusing on the provision of professional, friendly, and helpful services, or by eliciting trust in the authorities. These actions could reduce taxpayers' fear or anger when they are trying to solve filing issues, making communications more pleasant and potentially more effective. For instance, the tax authority in many countries has taken steps to improve the website and the online tax filing system. By the same token, when these are poorly designed, there is anecdotal evidence that these features are prone to elicit stress, frustration, and anger. In the following sections we present an empirical study that investigates the aspects of the tax process that may elicit integral emotions, in an attempt to determine the relevance of emotions for tax compliance decisions.

Empirical investigation

Enachescu *et al.* (2019) conducted a comprehensive study consisting of a qualitative focus group study, followed by an independent quantitative survey, in a large sample of Austrian taxpayers. Their aim was to identify crucial tax-related situations and procedures that are susceptible to elicit emotions. They were interested both in creating instances in the process of taxation that elicit emotions and in identifying specific emotions that are evoked. The study also tested the association between these specific emotions and tax compliance intentions using an experimental online survey.

Part one: qualitative focus group study

In a first step, Enachescu *et al.* (2019) conducted a qualitative focus group study with employed taxpayers, self-employed taxpayers, and tax auditors, in order to identify tax-related situations and procedures that elicit emotions and to identify specific and relevant emotions. They conducted seven focus groups with a total of 24 participants. Self-employed and employed taxpayers discussed the bureaucratic procedures that are necessary to comply with tax obligations, along with their feelings when they go through the procedures of paying taxes. Tax auditors participated in separate focus groups to learn more about the auditing process and taxpayers' emotions during an audit from an outside perspective.

In Austria, self-employed and employed taxpayers go through different tax procedures. While self-employed taxpayers must declare income proactively, employees are subject to third-party reporting. These differences are reflected in the results: self-employed participants most frequently mentioned their tax advisors, whereas employed participants most often mentioned automatic tax withholding. General themes that emerged in both taxpayer groups were associating taxes with high work load, communicating with tax authorities over unresolved questions, and reflecting about tax audits. The most relevant emotions evoked by these events were stress and anger for self-employed participants, and fear for employed participants. Nervousness, uncertainty, feeling accused, guilt, anxiety, and frustration were mentioned in the range of negative emotions by both groups. Self-employed participants mentioned relief as the most prominent positive emotion, followed by feeling secure and happy. Employed participants most often mentioned surprise. Tax auditors reported

170 *Janina Enachescu et al.*

mostly emotions such as nervousness, anger, frustration, and fear during tax audits (Enachescu *et al.*, 2019).

Part two: quantitative survey study

Based on these qualitative results, Enachescu *et al.* (2019) developed an experimental survey to test the influence of emotions on intended tax behavior. First, they developed several tax scenarios meant to evoke emotions, and they also developed a comprehensive list of specific emotions. They hypothesized that participants experience different specific emotions depending on whether they have positive or negative experiences with tax authorities (*e.g.*, communications, audit procedures). In turn, these emotions were assumed to influence intended tax behavior.

A sample of 523 Austrian taxpayers (employed and self-employed; representative of the Austrian working population regarding gender and age) read a set of seven different tax-related scenarios that described either positive or negative situations encountered during different taxpaying procedures (between-subject). Scenarios were slightly adapted to match differences in filing procedures between employed and self-employed taxpayers. After reading each scenario, participants completed an emotion questionnaire, indicating how they would feel in such a situation. The emotion questionnaire comprised a list of 19 specific emotions: feeling accused, angry, annoyed, contented, dissatisfied, fearful, guilty, happy, helpless, hopeful, insecure, nervous, regretful, relieved, sad, secure, ashamed, stressed, and surprised.

The scenarios covered the following situations: (1) preparatory accounting tasks, (2) filing taxes, (3) contacting tax authorities with a question, (4) receiving feedback from tax authorities about a balance, (5) receiving an audit announcement, (6) experiencing an audit, and (7) evading taxes by claiming false deductions. Three of the seven scenarios (scenarios 3, 6, and 7) were additionally followed by a short questionnaire assessing tax compliance intentions, asking participants how likely they would make the following compliance decisions, after having experienced such a situation: paying taxes honestly, searching for loopholes to avoid taxes, evading taxes, or procrastinating in the decision. The 19 measured emotions for each scenario were clustered to four emotion groups using multidimensional scaling: emotions related to feelings of self-blame (*e.g.*, shame and guilt), anger-related emotions (*e.g.*, angry and annoyed), fear-related emotions (*e.g.*, fear and nervousness), and positive emotions (*e.g.*, happiness and relief).

For compliance intentions, Enachescu *et al.* (2019) found that tax compliance intentions are higher in the positive condition as compared to the negative condition in two of three scenarios (3 and 6). Most importantly, this relationship was mediated by self-blame and anger-related emotions in these two scenarios. This means that a negative experience with tax authorities elicits self-blame and anger, resulting in negative compliance consequences.

Discussion

The qualitative study of Enachescu *et al.* (2019) provided insights into which emotions are relevant in various tax-related situations. Their study allowed them to create research materials to systematically investigate the role of emotions in intended tax compliance decisions. Their results revealed that, even though taxes might not be associated with emotions in the very first instance, taxpayers recall numerous emotional episodes when given the opportunity to reflect on these matters. Also, tax auditors reported to have observed many emotional reactions in taxpayers during audits.

The survey study allowed further investigation of integral emotions. It revealed that these can best be described as self-blame, anger, fear, and general positive emotions. The key results were that experiencing anger-related emotions was associated with lower compliance intentions. Therefore, in order to promote compliance, it is of utmost importance to take emotional experiences of taxpayers into consideration when designing taxation procedures.

General discussion

A large body of research demonstrates that human rationality is bounded and that decisions are by no means exclusively influenced by purely financial incentives (*e.g.*, Kahneman, 2003). Emotional influences on judgment and decision-making have received growing interest from the research community in recent years (Lerner *et al.*, 2015). In the past, emotional influences have been viewed as a human fallacy hindering decision-making (Loewenstein, Baumeister, & Vohs, 2007). However, research shows that humans have ample difficulties in making "good" decisions once their emotional system is impaired, as exemplified by the famous case of Phineas Gage. Phineas Gage was an American railroad construction foreman who suffered from a frontal lobe lesion, a brain region associated with emotion processing, after a severe accident in which an iron rod was stuck through his skull. The accident caused dramatic changes in his personality, including the inability to experience emotions and to make rational decisions (Damasio *et al.*, 1994). Modern research presents evidence in both directions – emotional process as beneficial to (Bechara & Damasio, 2005) or hindering (Shiv *et al.*, 2005) decision-making. Emotions are now believed to have adaptive functions that guide our attention to important aspects of the environment, that inform us rapidly about whether different options are better or worse for our well-being, and that help us develop a commitment to social norms (Pfister & Böhm, 2008).

Research on emotions and decision-making can be differentiated by whether research investigates either incidental or integral emotions (Lerner *et al.*, 2015), two types of emotions that are relevant within different contexts. Incidental emotions are elicited by surrounding circumstances such as background music in a shopping center. This type of emotional influence is important to consider

172 *Janina Enachescu et al.*

when designing decision environments. Integral emotions are elicited by the decision situation itself, and it is important to consider this type of emotional influence when designing decision procedures.

The effect of incidental affect on decision-making was first shown by Johnson and Tversky (1983), by investigating risk taking-behavior under positive and negative moods. They found that participants perceive risks to be larger when induced with a bad mood as compared to a good mood. Fochmann *et al.* (2019) found similar effects in an experimental study investigating the impact of incidental emotions on tax compliance behavior, using affect-rich pictures to induce mood.

In this chapter we presented a study using background music for mood induction, a method that might have been too subtle to yield the desired effects. The influence of incidental emotions on tax compliance is therefore still an open question that needs further investigation. Based on previous findings on incidental emotions and risk taking, as well as theoretical concepts such as the feeling-as-information approach, we can argue for hypotheses that lead in different directions. On the one hand, a bad mood signaling a problematic situation could foster systematic information processing, which should lead to more rational decisions guided by expected values, namely more tax evasion. On the other hand, a good mood could make optimistic evaluations more accessible, fostering risk taking, also leading to more tax evasion. Moreover, focusing on good versus bad mood can only be a first step into investigating the role of incidental affect. Research on specific incidental emotions, such as anger and fear, is also needed, as different effects can be expected.

We also presented an additional study that investigated the effect of specific emotions elicited by the taxation context itself. As demonstrated by Enachescu *et al.* (2019), many emotions are elicited in various tax-related situations. The results on the relationship between integral emotions and intended tax compliance behavior suggest that anger-related emotions are associated with higher intentions to evade taxes, a finding in line with results from consumer research (Bougie *et al.*, 2003).

Tax compliance behavior has been investigated by economists, lawyers, and psychologists since the 1970s. How can these new findings on emotions and tax compliance be integrated in this well-established stream of research? Over a decade ago, psychological factors influencing tax compliance decisions were integrated into the existing research on economic factors, resulting in the "slippery slope framework" of Kirchler (2007) and Kirchler, Hoelzl, and Wahl (2008). We believe that that emotions can be usefully introduced into this framework.

The slippery slope framework is a two-dimensional framework that distinguishes between the "power" of authorities and taxpayers' "trust" in the authorities. Power encompasses economic determinants to enforce compliance, predominantly audit probability, audit efficiency, and severity of fines, and power is defined by taxpayers' perception of authorities' capacity to detect and punish tax evaders. Trust integrates socio-psychological determinants of tax

Emotions and decisions to pay taxes   173

compliance. Trust results from taxpayers' understanding of tax law, from attitudes towards taxation and taxes, from the belief that tax regulations are transparent, and from the belief that society accepts regulations and obeys the law (social norms). On the individual level, the framework differentiates between enforced compliance with tax law and voluntary compliance. Power of authorities is related to enforced compliance, while trust leads to voluntary compliance. On the aggregate level, the framework assumes that the exertion of strong power by the authorities fosters an antagonistic interaction climate, while trust yields a synergistic climate.

Empirical studies have generally confirmed the assumptions of the slippery slope framework (Kogler *et al.*, 2013; Muehlbacher, Kirchler, & Schwarzenberger, 2011). However, some studies come to inconclusive results regarding the effect of enforcement. While audit and fine rates are generally positively associated with tax compliance (Kirchler, Muehlbacher, Kastlunger, & Wahl, 2010), some studies also find backfiring effects of audits on tax compliance (Beer, Kasper, Kirchler, & Erard, 2015; Mendoza, Wielhouwer, & Kirchler, 2017). A possible explanation for the observed negative effects of strict enforcement measures on compliance is that voluntary compliance can be eroded when honest taxpayers who are audited may feel falsely accused as criminals. This assumption is supported by results from an experimental survey study with self-employed taxpayers in Turkey (Olsen *et al.*, 2018), who found that the exertion of power elevates the experience of negative as well as positive emotions. Olsen *et al.* (2018) interpreted these results by saying that the exertion of power can be perceived positively and so can elicit positive emotions when taxpayers feel that they are protected from free-riders by these measures; further, in the case of well-targeted coercive power towards tax evaders, honest taxpayers may feel protected from being exploited, which is not the case if coercive power is used undifferentiated. Olsen *et al.* (2018) also suggested that the non-targeted exertion of power can evoke strong negative emotions when honest taxpayers are subject to the same treatment as tax evaders. If honest taxpayers are audited and thereby treated as potential criminals, feelings of anger or fear are likely to be evoked. Anger has been shown to evoke retaliation behavior (*e.g.*, Bougie *et al.*, 2003) and will likely lead to deliberate decisions on whether it pays to evade or not. Tax avoidance and tax evasion are the likely reactions. In case of fear, taxpayers are likely to respond with avoidance measures, which can be legally justified. Taxpayers may also feel that they are forced to comply. Depending on whether coercive power is targeted or randomly wielded, taxpayers may therefore feel protected and generally positive, or they may instead become angry and react with fear.

In sum, the role of emotions in the slippery slope framework clearly needs further theoretical elaboration and empirical confirmation. Olsen *et al.* (2018) argue that the experience of negative emotions not only increases enforced tax compliance but also intentions to evade taxes. They also argue that the relationship between power and emotions is moderated by trust perceptions; that is,

174 *Janina Enachescu et al.*

when taxpayers perceive tax authorities to be trustworthy, the negative effects of power are moderated and even reversed.

Conclusions

Emotions have increasingly gained attention in the decision-making research community. While economists have traditionally focused on rational processes in predicting choice, it is now becoming clear that emotional processes must also be considered in understanding behavior, especially tax compliance decisions by individual taxpayers. In this chapter, we begin to dig into the sphere of emotions in taxation. We see that taxpayers are subject to emotional experiences that are evoked by taxation procedures, and we believe that similar effects can be observed for incidental emotions, as previous studies have suggested. However, more research is needed in order to better understand the power of emotions in this context.

Policy makers and tax authorities can profit from these insights by taking subjective experiences of taxpayers into account when designing taxation procedures. With our research we show that it is of ample importance to avoid causing frustration and anger when providing taxation services, and that it is worthwhile creating a confident atmosphere in which positive feelings can arise, in order to promote compliance.

Acknowledgment

We thank the students of the seminars on theory and empirical research in economic psychology at the Faculty of Psychology, University of Vienna, Austria, for their assistance in conducting the laboratory experiments.

References

Allingham, M. G., & Sandmo, A. (1972). Income tax evasion: A theoretical analysis. *Journal of Public Economics, 1,* 323–338.

Baumgartner, T., Esslen, M., & Jäncke, L. (2006). From emotion perception to emotion experience: Emotions evoked by pictures and classical music. *International Journal of Psychophysiology, 60,* 34–43.

Bechara, A., & Damasio, A. R. (2005). The somatic marker hypothesis: A neural theory of economic decision. *Games and Economic Behavior, 52,* 336–372.

Becker, G. S. (1962). Irrational behavior and economic theory. *The Journal of Political Economy, 70,* 1–13.

Beer, S., Kasper, M., Kirchler, E., & Erard, B. (2015). *Audit impact study: Taxpayer advocate service annual report to Congress.* Retrieved from www.taxpayeradvocate.irs.gov/Media/Default/Documents/2015ARC/ARC15_Volume2_3-AuditImpact.pdf.

Blaufus, K., Bob, J., Otto, P. E., & Wolf, N. (2017). The effect of tax privacy on tax compliance: An experimental investigation. *European Accounting Review, 26,* 561–580.

Bosco, L., & Mittone, L. (1997). Tax evasion and moral constraints: Some experimental evidence. *Kyklos, 50,* 297–324.

Bougie, R., Pieters, R., & Zeelenberg, M. (2003). Angry customers don't come back, they get back: The experience and behavioral implications of anger and dissatisfaction in services. *Journal of the Academy of Marketing Science, 31*, 377–393.

Coricelli, G., Joffily, M., Montmarquette, C., & Villeval, M. C. (2010). Cheating, emotions, and rationality: An experiment on tax evasion. *Experimental Economics, 13*, 226–247.

Damasio, H., Grabowski, T., Frank, R., Galaburda, A. M., & Damasio, A. R. (1994). The return of Phineas Gage: Clues about the brain from the skull of a famous patient. *Science, 264*, 1102–1105.

Drouvelis, M., & Grosskopf, B. (2016). The effects of induced emotions on pro-social behaviour. *Journal of Public Economics, 134*, 1–8.

Dulleck, U., Fooken, J., Newton, C., Ristl, A., Schaffner, M., & Torgler, B. (2016). Tax compliance and psychic costs: Behavioral experimental evidence using a physiological marker. *Journal of Public Economics, 134*, 9–18.

Elffers, H. (2015). Multiple interpretations of rationality in offender decision making. In: W. Bernasco, J.-L. van Gelder, & H. Elffers (Eds.), *The Oxford handbook of offender decision making* (pp. 52–66). Oxford: Oxford University Press.

Elster, J. (1998). Emotions and economic theory. *Journal of Economic Literature, 36*, 47–74.

Enachescu, J., Olsen, J., Kogler, C., Zeelenberg, M., Breugelmans, S. M., & Kirchler, E. (2019). The role of emotions in tax compliance behavior: A mixed-method approach. *Journal of Economic Psychology, 74*, 1–16.

Erard, B., & Feinstein, J. (1994). The role of moral sentiments in audit perceptions and tax compliance. *Public Finance, 49*, 70–89.

Fehr, B., & Russell, J. A. (1984). Concept of emotion viewed from a prototype perspective. *Journal of Experimental Psychology: General, 113*(3), 464–486.

Fochmann, M., Hechtner, F., Kirchler, E., & Mohr, P. (2019). When happy people make society unhappy: Incidental emotions affect compliance behavior (July 25, 2019). Available at SSRN: https://ssrn.com/abstract=3259071.

Forgas, J. P. (1995). Mood and judgment: The affect infusion model (AIM). *Psychological Bulletin, 117*, 39–66.

Garlin, F. V., & Owen, K. (2006). Setting the tone with the tune: A meta-analytic review of the effects of background music in retail settings. *Journal of Business Research, 59*, 755–764.

Gill, D., & Prowse, V. (2012). A structural analysis of disappointment aversion in a real effort competition. *American Economic Review, 102*, 469–503.

Grasmick, H. G., & Bursik, R. J. J. (1990). Conscience, significant others, and rational choice: Extending the deterrence model. *Law & Society Review, 24*, 837–862.

Izard, C. E. (1977). *Human emotions.* New York: Plenum Press.

Johnson, E. J., & Tversky, A. (1983). Affect, generalization, and the perception of risk. *Journal of Personality and Social Psychology, 45*, 20–31.

Kahneman, D. (2003). A perspective on judgment and choice: Mapping bounded rationality. *The American Psychologist, 58*, 697–720.

Kämpfe, J., Sedlmeier, P., & Renkewitz, F. (2011). The impact of background music on adult listeners: A meta-analysis. *Psychology of Music, 39*, 424–448.

Kirchler, E. (2007). *The economic psychology of tax behavior.* Cambridge: Cambridge University Press.

Kirchler, E., Hoelzl, E., & Wahl, I. (2008). Enforced versus voluntary tax compliance: The "slippery slope" framework. *Journal of Economic Psychology, 29*, 210–225.

176 *Janina Enachescu et al.*

Kirchler, E., Muehlbacher, S., Kastlunger, B., & Wahl, I. (2010). Why pay taxes? A review of tax compliance decisions. In: J. Alm, J. Martinez-Vazquez, & B. Torgler (Eds.), *Developing alternative frameworks for explaining tax compliance* (pp. 15–31). London: Routledge.

Kogler, C., Batrancea, L., Nichita, A., Pantya, J., Belianin, A., & Kirchler, E. (2013). Trust and power as determinants of tax compliance: Testing the assumptions of the slippery slope framework in Austria, Hungary, Romania and Russia. *Journal of Economic Psychology, 34,* 169–180.

Lerner, J. S., & Keltner, D. (2000). Beyond valence: Toward a model of emotion-specific influences on judgement and choice. *Cognition & Emotion, 14,* 473–493.

Lerner, J. S., Li, Y., Valdesolo, P., & Kassam, K. S. (2015). Emotion and decision making. *Annual Review of Psychology, 66,* 799–823.

Loewenstein, G. (2000). Emotions in economic theory and economic behavior. *American Economic Review, 90,* 256–260.

Loewenstein, G., Baumeister, R. F., & Vohs, K. D. (2007). *Do emotions help or hurt decision-making: A hedgefoxian perspective.* New York: Russell Sage Foundation.

Loewenstein, G., & Lerner, J. S. (2003). The role of affect in decision making. In: R. J. Davidson, H. H. Goldsmith, & K. R. Scherer (Eds.), *Handbook of affective science* (pp. 619–642). Oxford: Oxford University Press.

Martin, M. (1990). On the induction of mood. *Clinical Psychology Review, 10,* 669–697.

Mendoza, J. P., Wielhouwer, J. L., & Kirchler, E. (2017). The backfiring effect of auditing on tax compliance. *Journal of Economic Psychology, 62,* 284–294.

Mittone, L. (2006). Dynamic behaviour in tax evasion: An experimental approach. *Journal of Socio-Economics, 35,* 813–835.

Muehlbacher, S., Kirchler, E., & Schwarzenberger, H. (2011). Voluntary versus enforced tax compliance: Empirical evidence for the "slippery slope" framework. *European Journal of Law and Economics, 32,* 89–97.

Murphy, K., & Tyler, T. R. (2008). Procedural justice and compliance behaviour: The mediating role of emotions. *European Journal of Social Psychology, 38,* 652–668.

Olsen, J., Kasper, M., Enachescu, J., Benk, S., Budak, T., & Kirchler, E. (2018). Emotions and tax compliance among small business owners: An experimental survey. *International Review of Law & Economics, 56,* 42–52.

Pfister, H.-R., & Böhm, G. (2008). The multiplicity of emotions: A framework of emotional functions in decision making. *Judgment and Decision Making, 3,* 5–17.

Russell, J. A., & Barrett, L. F. (1999). Core affect, prototypical emotional episodes, and other things called emotion: Dissecting the elephant. *Journal of Personality and Social Psychology, 76,* 805–819.

Sacharin, V., Schlegel, K., & Scherer, K. R. (2012). *Geneva Emotion Wheel rating study* (Report). Geneva: University of Geneva, Swiss Center for Affective Sciences. Retrieved on January 15, 2019 from https://archive-ouverte.unige.ch/unige:97849.

Scherer, K. R. (2005). What are emotions? And how can they be measured? *Social Science Information, 44,* 695–729.

Scherer, K. R., Shuman, V., Fontaine, J. J. R., & Soriano, C. (2013). The GRID meets the wheel: Assessing emotional feeling via self-report. In: J. J. R. Fontaine, K. R., Scherer, & C. Soriano (Eds.), *Components of emotional meaning: A sourcebook* (pp. 281–298). Oxford: Oxford University Press.

Schwarz, N. (2012). Feelings-as-information theory. In: P. A. M. Van Lange, A. W. Kruglanski, & E. T. Higgins (Eds.), *Handbook of theories of social psychology: Volume 1* (pp. 289–308). Thousand Oaks, CA: Sage Publications.

Shiv, B., Loewenstein, G., Bechara, A., Damasio, H., & Damasio, A. R. (2005). Investment behavior and the negative side of emotion. *Psychological Science: A Journal of the American Psychological Society, 16*, 435–439.

Srinivasan, T. N. (1973). Tax evasion: A model. *Journal of Public Economics, 2*, 339–346.

Thompson, W. F., Schellenberg, E. G., & Husain, G. (2001). Arousal, mood, and the Mozart effect. *Psychological Science, 12*, 248–251.

Turner, J. H., & Stets, J. E. (2005). *The sociology of emotions.* Cambridge: Cambridge University Press.

van de Ven, N., & Zeelenberg, M. (2011). Regret aversion and the reluctance to exchange lottery tickets. *Journal of Economic Psychology, 32*, 194–200.

Watson, D., Clark, L. A., & Tellegen, A. (1988). Development and validation of brief measures of positive and negative affect: The PANAS scales. *Journal of Personality and Social Psychology, 54*, 1063–1070.

White, E. L., & Rickard, N. S. (2016). Emotion response and regulation to "happy" and "sad" music stimuli: Partial synchronization of subjective and physiological responses. *Musicae Scientiae, 20*, 11–25.

Zeelenberg, M., & Pieters, R. (2006). Feeling is for doing: A pragmatic approach to the study of emotions in economic behavior. In: D. De Cremer, M. Zeelenberg, & K. Murnighan (Eds.), *Social psychology and economics* (pp. 117–137). New York: Psychology Press.

9 Moral concerns and personal beliefs regarding tax evasion

Empirical results from Germany, Romania, Turkey, and the United Kingdom

Larissa Batrancea, Anca Nichita, Carla Startin,
Ioan Chirila, Ioan Batrancea, Robert W. McGee,
Serkan Benk, and Tamer Budak

Introduction

Oliver Wendell Holmes Jr., a US Supreme Court Justice, once famously said: "I like to pay taxes. With them, I buy civilization". In his book entitled *Stranger in a Strange Land* (1961, p. 358), author Robert A. Heinlein revealed the following dialogue between two characters: "'Is this Paradise?' / 'I can guarantee it ain't', Jubal assured him. 'My taxes are due'". As Heinlein suggested and Wendell Holmes Jr. asserted, taxpaying is a process that may elicit mixed emotions, beliefs and moral concerns among taxpayers (Enachescu *et al.*, 2019; Olsen *et al.*, 2018; Olsen, Kogler, Brandt, Dezső, & Kirchler, 2019; Sussman & Olivola, 2011), while it secures tax revenues for public budgets. A part of the general public may positively associate taxpaying with multiple benefits, including to the public goods system and civic duty, resulting in improvements to individuals' wellbeing and quality of life (Akay *et al.*, 2012; Helliwell, Layard, & Sachs, 2018) when paying their dues according to the law. Some well-paid taxpayers would even agree to be subject to higher tax rates.[1] Other taxpayers place a sign of equality between taxpaying and stress, red tape and stacks of paperwork, reporting deadlines, social shaming (Coricelli, Rusconi & Villeval, 2014), punishment (Murphy, 2008), or cheating (Coricelli, Joffily, Montmarquette, & Villeval, 2010).

According to the tax literature, tax attitudes and tax behavior are influenced by a complex of economic (Allingham & Sandmo, 1972; Slemrod, 2007; Slemrod & Yitzhaki, 2002; Srinivasan, 1973; Yitzhaki, 1974), psychological, political, or social factors (Batrancea, Nichita, & Batrancea, 2012; Batrancea *et al.*,

---

1 According to a survey conducted by *The Guardian* in 2017, many British taxpayers within the 1% top earners in the country would be willing to pay more taxes in order to finance public goods such as education, healthcare, or social services (www.theguardian.com/inequality/2017/may/17/voices-of-the-uk-i-should-be-taxed-more-maybe-other-well-paid-people-feel-same).

2019; Dunn, Farrar, & Hausserman, 2018; Kirchler, 2007; Kogler *et al.*, 2013; Pickhardt & Prinz, 2014). For the purpose of this chapter, we will focus on two psychological factors, which may ultimately drive taxpaying behavior, specifically moral concerns and personal beliefs regarding tax evasion.

The aim of this chapter is to explore insights into the moral concerns and personal beliefs surrounding tax evasion in four European countries, which experience various levels of regional integration, economic development, tax gaps, and distinct tax systems. The surveyed countries were selected in order to mirror the different stances of European nations regarding accession to the European Union (EU). Namely, at the time of the data collection process, two of the countries (Germany and the United Kingdom, UK) were among the old member states of the EU, one country (Romania) was listed among the new member states, and the fourth country (Turkey) was an aspiring member. The countries also differ in terms of their underlying tax systems. Hence, while Germany, Turkey, and the United Kingdom mainly favor progressive taxation when it comes to personal income, the Romanian tax system is centered on a flat rate, whether it is personal income or corporate income. Furthermore, differences arise from the level of economic development within the countries. Whereas Germany, Romania, and the UK are classified as developed economies, Turkey is considered a developing nation (United Nations, 2019, pp.169–170). Last but not least, the selected countries differed in their tax gap[2] when taking the year 2015 as a benchmark. Namely, according to estimations based on reported GDP (Murphy, 2019), Germany registered a tax gap of €125.1 billion, Romania €13.2 billion, and the UK €83 billion. As for Turkey, the country registered an estimated tax gap of €81.8 billion (Raczkowski & Mróz, 2018).

In our research, we chose to tackle moral concerns and personal beliefs regarding tax evasion because this phenomenon poses numerous problems for overall economies. Tax evasion mitigates tax revenues and thus deprives public goods systems of considerable financial resources, and worsens country credit ratings and raises lending costs, among many other problems (Markellos, Psychoyios, & Schneider, 2015). The crucial role of tax revenues for economies and citizens alike was emphasized by Adam Smith in his 1776 magnum opus *Wealth of Nations*, where he stated: "The subjects of every state ought to contribute towards the support of the government, as nearly as possible, in proportion to their respective abilities". As a general rule, taxpayers should acknowledge that taxes represent an important element of their social contract and that authorities are called upon to make people aware of this contract. Moreover, tax evasion acts should always be deemed unjustifiable by taxpayers, who would ideally have strong moral beliefs and resent those acting

---

2 The concept of *tax gap* quantifies the difference between the total amount of taxes that should be paid by taxpayers to national tax authorities and the amount of taxes that is actually paid by taxpayers. The tax gap can be expressed in cash terms or percentage.

180 Larissa Batrancea et al.

as free-riders against legal provisions. Nevertheless, despite the benefits entailed by honest taxpaying, tax evasion acts proliferate within modern societies on the basis that some taxpayers label the phenomenon as always justifiable or somewhat justifiable.

Our cross-cultural study adds to the existing literature by linking tax evasion with individual tax morale and beliefs about the tax morale of fellow countrymen. At the end of the day, individual decisions to pay or not to pay taxes stem also from how citizens position themselves relative to self-evident tax evasion acts and from how they believe other peers would react confronted with similar acts.

The structure of this chapter is the following. The second section includes a brief account on tax evasion-related acts. The third section describes the methodology behind data collection across countries. The fourth section reports the empirical results. The final section covers discussion points and brief concluding remarks.

Brief account on tax evasion-related acts

Empirical research on the topic of tax evasion (in general) and on taxpayers' stance toward the phenomenon (in particular) is engaging and challenging at the same time. On one hand, its engaging feature originates from the multitude of reasons for why some people evade taxes, whereas others decide to contribute honestly. Finding the "why" behind tax evasion acts is mainly important because such answers could assist authorities in designing efficient tax policies and allow them to better cater to their citizens. On the other hand, the challenge resides in the fact that, as noticed by Slemrod (2007, pp. 25–26) in a witty manner, estimating the "extent of evasion is not straightforward for obvious reasons. (Would you answer survey questions about tax evasion honestly?) Because tax evasion is both personally sensitive and potentially incriminating, self-reports are vulnerable to substantial underreporting". Nevertheless, surveys are mainly used to assess tax evasion levels and capture citizens' standing on evasion, since actual noncompliance behavior cannot be openly observed by researchers under real-world conditions (Gërxhani, 2007; Houston & Tran, 2001; Torgler, 2008). Surveys can be regarded as "snapshot views" (Cleary, 2013) into the minds of regular taxpayers and they may offer useful cues for improving the monitoring of tax systems.

Tax literature reports that contributors' decisions of eluding tax laws may be guided not only by their own moral concerns regarding tax evasion, but also by how they think other peers would act in a tax evasion context. In this regard, Slemrod (2007, p. 25) states that authorities cannot

> announce a tax system and then rely on taxpayers' sense of duty to remit what is owed. Some dutiful people will undoubtedly pay what they owe, but many others will not. Over time the ranks of the dutiful will shrink, as they see how they are being taken advantage of by the others.

Hence, the mitigation of the ratio of contributors to non-contributors is triggered by the fact that one believes many other peers deliberately free-ride on their taxes.

Tax systems around the world experience a variety of situations in which some taxpayers decide to free-ride on their obligation of supporting public goods systems. A first example is the fraudulent claiming of governmental benefits, which may come under the form of carer's allowance, income support, pension credit, jobseeker's allowance, disability benefits, housing tax benefit, home heating support schemes, child support, etc. in the participating countries. With the purpose of (at least) capping the ongoing rise of benefit fraud levels, authorities employ resourceful strategies and pass new laws. For instance, authorities in the UK use surveillance teams to investigate allegations reported by anonymous sources regarding taxpayers who possibly engage in benefit fraud acts.[3] The situations of these taxpayers in question (*e.g.*, the match between living conditions and income declared; number of dependents for whom a tax exemption is claimed; employment status; health condition) are closely investigated to determine whether they are rightfully entitled to claim certain benefits or are just attempting to scam the public goods system. In order to curb the practice commonly known as "benefit tourism", German authorities have enacted a law stating that citizens from other EU countries are entitled to receive child support only if they prove they are employed in Germany.

A second example comes from the practice of avoiding to pay fares on transport, which depletes local and national budgets of important revenues (*e.g.*, bus, underground, tram, or train tickets and subscriptions; road and bridge toll charges; compulsory vignettes). Provided all taxpayers incur the transport fares, collected resources could be reinvested into the transport system and existing infrastructure could be restored, modernized, and/or extended. Until the accomplishment of such a goal, some authorities go to great lengths to implement methods for preventing fare-dodging, which can turn out to be quite costly. Besides the traditional use of fare inspectors, electronic ticket gates, and strict access to stations based on tickets, some local authorities in the Netherlands attempt to turn fare evaders into paying customers.[4] That is, anyone who is detected as a first-time evader must purchase a "penalty package" priced below the penalty level, which gives access to multiple rides on the public transport system. Should noncompliance be detected a second time in the same person, the evader would be subject to penalty payment without the aforementioned travel benefits. We believe that the Dutch method entails a positive signal for the general public. If people notice that a higher number of previous fare-dodgers become active contributors and decide to rejoin the paying ranks, their own

3 www.theguardian.com/society/2011/feb/01/benefits-fraud-investigators (accessed February 12, 2020).
4 www.citylab.com/transportation/2019/01/fare-calculator-dutch-transit-enforcement-rail-bus-tickets/579715/ (accessed January 13, 2020).

182   *Larissa Batrancea et al.*

intentions of not paying transport fares on the account that others elude the system might be restrained.

A third situation stems from the fact that some taxpayers may decide to cheat on their tax returns if the opportunity arises. It goes without saying that noncompliance decisions are triggered when individuals think that tax evasion behavior is justifiable, let alone when individuals believe everybody else evades taxes on a daily basis. In such cases, opportunities might arise under various forms for both individual and corporate taxpayers, as follows: cash gifts and assets inherited from late relatives; lottery winnings and online gambling; buy-to-let rental income; income generated from self-employment, moonlighting,[5] or unreported work; personal expenses charged to the company; use of offshore bank accounts to protect assets.

A fourth example related to tax evading behavior is accepting a bribe in the course of public or legal duty, which generates in turn an increase in corruption level since bribery is one of many forms of corruption. Bribery can occur in both the public and private sectors, but for the purpose of this chapter we refer only to the public sector cases. In exchange for the bribe – be it cash payments, luxury goods, excessive corporate hospitality, gift–giving, favors, cronyism, nepotism, bribes disguised as charitable donations, political donations, or commissions (Muravska, Barrington, & Vitou, 2014) – recipients promise to facilitate access to certain public goods and services for the person/economic entity offering the "gift" directly or via intermediaries. Corruption and bribery are widespread practices in the business world. According to a Eurobarometer survey (TNS Political & Social, 2017), corruption is regarded as a problem of running everyday economic activities by 34% of EU businesses, while bribery represents one of the least complicated methods of securing a public service according to 60% of EU businesses. Having a specific benefit or contract in their minds, some taxpayers gamble with their public images, businesses, professional careers, and freedom, while taking the risk of being caught by authorities and prosecuted.

A fifth example consists of paying/charging only cash for goods or services in an attempt to evade taxation. At first glance and by applying short-term thinking, both the buyer and the seller/service provider gain some advantages: the buyer obtains the goods for a lower price (without VAT or sales tax) and the seller/service provider keeps the transaction off the books, avoids paying income tax, and uses the money for personal needs. In reality, when thinking long-term, everybody loses something: the buyer does not benefit from warranty, hence in the absence of a receipt/invoice proving the commercial transaction one cannot turn to the seller or authorities and claim a replacement/refund should the product be of low quality or damaged; by committing tax evasion, the seller jeopardizes the credibility and viability of the business,

---

5 *Moonlighting* is the term given to the practice of holding an additional job outside the regular working schedule with the purpose of gaining an extra income. It is also called "outside employment" and it often goes undeclared.

Morals and beliefs regarding tax evasion   183

starts operating in the shadow economy and risks detection by tax authorities; public budgets lose resources as the tax gap increases with the income tax and VAT/sales tax not paid or collected by the businessman. As a solution, various countries in the EU have imposed thresholds for daily cash payments to mitigate this type of tax evasion behavior.

Last but not least, another example arises when taxpayers engage in buying stolen goods. Their noncompliance behavior is motivated by the fact that the price at which such properties are traded is well below the market price, which includes value added, indirect taxation (VAT/sales tax, excise), besides the manufacturing costs. Nevertheless, such illegal behavior finances the underground economy and substantially mitigates public budgets.

Method

Participants

The aggregated sample consisted of 1593 subjects from Germany, Romania, Turkey, and the UK. Participants were recruited mainly from the undergraduate, graduate, and faculty populations at the following higher education institutions: University of Hamburg (Hamburg, Germany), Babes-Bolyai University (Cluj-Napoca, Romania), Zonguldak Bülent Ecevit University (Zonguldak, Turkey), and University of Exeter (Exeter, UK). The majority were undergraduate students, studying business, economics, and accounting, followed by graduate students and a few faculty members. Taking account of the country subsamples, participants had the following characteristics: *252 subjects* were surveyed in Germany (56.0% males; 81.3% aged 15–29 years; 47.2% Christian; 83.3% never been married); *356 subjects* were surveyed in Romania (43.3% males; 83.7% aged 15–29 years; 93.8% Christian; 70.5% never been married); *397 subjects* were surveyed in Turkey (33.2% males; 98.0% aged 15–29 years; 100.0% Muslim; 97.2% never been married); *588 subjects* were surveyed in the UK (52.6% males; 75.5% aged 15–29 years; 51.0% Agnostic/Atheist; 59.2% never been married).

Materials

The 1593 participants were asked to complete a survey that included several items used in multiple waves of the World Values Survey,[6] specifically: "claiming government benefits to which you are not entitled"; "avoiding a fare on public transport"; "cheating on taxes if you have a chance"; "someone accepting a bribe in the course of their duties"; "buying stolen goods". An item included in various rounds of the European Values Study[7] was also presented to our participants, *i.e.*, "paying cash for services to avoid taxes". Moreover, several

6 www.worldvaluessurvey.org.
7 www.europeanvaluesstudy.eu/.

184 *Larissa Batrancea et al.*

items with similar wordings were also used by the Irish tax authority (Cleary, 2013, p. 20) in a section comprising moral questions in order to assess the acceptability degree of noncompliance behaviors (*i.e.*, "deliberately claim social benefits from the Dept. of Social and Family Affairs that you are not entitled to"; "claim credits or reliefs from Revenue that you are not entitled to"; "use public transport (for example, buses, trains, LUAS, DART) without a valid ticket"; "deliberately not pay the taxes you are supposed to pay"; "knowingly buy stolen goods").

Overall, our survey consisted of two main parts and a demographics section. For Part 1 of the survey, participants were asked to rate on a scale from 1 to 10 how justifiable they thought a series of six actions were, with 1 being never justifiable and 10 being always justifiable. Therefore, the six items we used were the following (listed as in the survey): (1) "Claiming government benefits to which you are not entitled"; (2) "Avoiding a fare on public transport"; (3) "Cheating on taxes if you have a chance"; (4) "Someone accepting a bribe in the course of their duties"; (5) "Paying cash for services to avoid taxes"; (6) "Buying stolen goods".

For Part 2 of the survey, participants were asked how many of their compatriots they thought took a series of five tax evasion-related actions. The items were the following: (1) "How many of your compatriots do you think claim government benefits to which they are not entitled?"; (2) "How many of your compatriots do you think cheat on taxes if they have the chance?"; (3) "How many of your compatriots do you think pay cash for services to avoid taxes?"; (4) "How many of your compatriots do you think avoid paying a fare on public transport?"; (5) "How many of your compatriots do you think accept a bribe in the course of their duties?". They had to select from the following answer options: 1 = "almost all"; 2 = "many", 3 = "some", 4 = "almost none"; 5 = "don't know".

At the end of the survey, participants had to provide brief demographic data on their *academic status* ("undergraduate student"; "graduate student"; "faculty member"; "other"), *major* ("Accounting"; "Business/Economics"; "Theology/ Religious studies"; "Philosophy"; "Law"; "Engineering"; "other"), *sex, age* ("15–29"; "30–49"; "50 or more"), *religious preference* ("Christian"; "Hindu"; "Jewish"; "Muslim"; "Agnostic/Atheist"; "other") and *marital status* ("married or in a committed relationship"; "divorced or separated"; "never been married"; "other").

The rationale for structuring the survey into two main parts was the following. The items included in the first part were chosen because they capture participants' moral concerns regarding tax evasion. In addition, we deemed it was important to inquire about participants' beliefs on how their fellow countrymen may position themselves with regard to several tax evasion-related actions. As the literature puts forward, country levels of tax evasion are determined not only by individual moral concerns (*e.g.*, OECD, 2019; Torgler, 2007), but also by how we think our peers (might) act in certain situations entailing illegal tax behavior (Kahan, 1997; Wakolbinger & Haigner, 2009; Wartick & Rupert,

2010). Therefore, one could say that tax evasion is linked to both one's own tax morale and one's beliefs about others' tax morale.

Procedure

Data were collected during several rounds (Turkey 2010; Germany 2012; Romania 2013; United Kingdom 2014) based on a standard research protocol, which was uniformly applied in each country. Part of the data was previously reported in the literature (James, McGee, Benk, & Budak, 2019; McGee, Benk, Ross, & Kılıçaslan, 2012). Participants were recruited on a voluntary basis, with no incentives being provided to them (*e.g.*, course credit, money).

The original English survey was rendered into German, Romanian, and Turkish following the standard translation–back translation procedure in order to control for possible inconsistencies and to ensure the accuracy of the translated material. The survey was distributed in a paper and pencil format. Participants took approximately five minutes to answer all items. The anonymity of participants was fully ensured.

Results

Moral concerns regarding tax evasion

Of the 1593 participants, 11 participants had missing sex or age data and so were excluded from further analyses. From the remaining 1582 participants, nine of them had missing data for at least one question of Part 1, leaving 1573 individuals with complete data for this first part. Furthermore, 537 participants had missing data or had answered "don't know" to at least one question, leaving 1045 individuals with complete data for Part 2.

Considering this, in the following paragraphs we will presents results for each of the two main parts of the survey.

The mean response for the items included in Part 1 was first calculated. Responses to all items and the mean response for Part 1 showed significant positive skew, indicating that non-parametric analysis should be used. Sample comparisons for the four countries indicated there were differences in age and sex between the groups. As these variables may independently be associated with moral concerns, we therefore calculated the residuals for each item and for the mean response of Part 1, adjusting for age and sex. Non-parametric Kruskal-Wallis tests and post-hoc Mann-Whitney U tests were then used to compare these score residuals between countries.

Demographics and responses for Part 1 of the survey can be seen in Table 9.1. Age significantly differed between the samples, with participants from Turkey having a younger age profile and those from the UK having an older age profile. Sex also differed between the samples, with slightly more than half of the participants in the groups from Germany and the UK being male, and the opposite occurring for the groups from Romania and Turkey.

Table 9.1 Demographics and statistical results by country for participants included in the analyses of Part 1

PART 1	Germany	Romania	Turkey	United Kingdom (UK)	Group comparison statistics
N = 1573	**248**	**352**	**391**	**582**	**Kruskal–Wallis test**
Age (years)	203 (81.9%) age 15–29, 42 (16.9%) age 30–49, 3 (1.2%) age 50+	297 (84.4%) age 15–29, 49 (13.9%) age 30–49, 6 (1.7%) age 50+	383 (98.0%) age 15–29, 8 (2.0%) age 30–49, 0 (0.0%) age 50+	440 (75.6%) age 15–29, 90 (15.5%) age 30–49, 52 (8.9%) age 50+	$\chi^2(6) = 120.62$, p < 0.001
Sex	108 (43.5%) female, 140 (56.5%) male	200 (56.8%) female, 152 (43.2%) male	261 (66.8%) female, 130 (33.2%) male	273 (46.9%) female, 309 (53.1%) male	$\chi^2(3) = 49.20$, p < 0.001
	Median score and interquartile range for country subsamples				**Kruskal–Wallis and post-hoc Mann–Whitney U tests**
Claiming government benefits to which you are not entitled	2.00 (3.00)	1.00 (2.00)	1.00 (1.00)	1.00 (1.00)	Overall p < 0.001, Germany *vs* Romania p = 0.002, Germany *vs* Turkey p < 0.001, Germany *vs* UK p < 0.001, Romania *vs* Turkey p < 0.001, Romania *vs* UK p = 0.085, Turkey *vs* UK p = 0.007
Avoiding a fare on public transport	4.00 (4.00)	2.00 (4.00)	1.00 (1.00)	3.00 (3.00)	Overall p < 0.001, Germany *vs* Romania p < 0.001, Germany *vs* Turkey p < 0.001, Germany *vs* UK p = 0.075, Romania *vs* Turkey p < 0.001, Romania *vs* UK p < 0.001, Turkey *vs* UK p < 0.001

Cheating on taxes if you have a chance	2.00 (3.00)	1.00 (1.00)	1.00 (0.00)	2.00 (2.00)	Overall p < 0.001, Germany *vs* Romania p < 0.001, Germany *vs* Turkey p < 0.001, Germany *vs* UK p = 1.000, Romania *vs* Turkey p = 0.009, Romania *vs* UK p < 0.001, Turkey *vs* UK p < 0.001
Someone accepting a bribe in the course of their duties	1.00 (1.00)	1.00 (1.00)	1.00 (0.00)	1.00 (1.00)	Overall p < 0.001, Germany *vs* Romania p = 0.939, Germany *vs* Turkey p = 0.010, Germany *vs* UK p = 0.088, Romania *vs* Turkey p < 0.001, Romania *vs* UK p = 1.000, Turkey *vs* UK p < 0.001
Paying cash for services to avoid taxes	3.00 (4.00)	2.00 (4.00)	2.00 (4.00)	3.00 (3.00)	Overall p < 0.001, Germany *vs* Romania p = 0.023, Germany *vs* Turkey p = 0.001, Germany *vs* UK p = 1.000, Romania *vs* Turkey p = 1.000, Romania *vs* UK p = 0.039, Turkey *vs* UK p = 0.001
Buying stolen goods	1.00 (2.00)	1.00 (2.00)	1.00 (0.00)	1.00 (2.00)	Overall p < 0.001, Germany *vs* Romania p = 1.000, Germany *vs* Turkey p < 0.001, Germany *vs* UK p = 0.820, Romania *vs* Turkey p < 0.001, Romania *vs* UK p = 0.989, Turkey *vs* UK p < 0.001
Mean response	2.67 (1.96)	2.17 (2.33)	1.50 (1.17)	2.33 (1.50)	Overall p < 0.001, Germany *vs* Romania p = 0.001, Germany *vs* Turkey p < 0.001, Germany *vs* UK p = 0.008, Romania *vs* Turkey p < 0.001, Romania *vs* UK p = 1.000, Turkey *vs* UK p < 0.001

Note: Number and percentage (in parentheses) are shown for the variables *age* and *sex*. Median score and interquartile range (in parentheses) are shown for whether or not certain actions are ever justifiable.

188 *Larissa Batrancea et al.*

Significant differences were also identified between participants from the four countries in how justifiable they thought the different actions related to tax evasion to be, and their mean rating for these actions. Overall, individuals from Turkey considered the actions to be less justifiable compared to participants from the other countries, with the exception of whether it is ever justifiable to pay cash for services in order to avoid taxes. For this particular action there was no significant difference in the response of participants from Romania and Turkey.

The mean score of participants from Germany was significantly higher than that of scores from the other three countries, though the results of pairwise comparisons between Germany and both Romania and the UK differed depending on the specific action. Regarding the claiming of undeserving benefits, accepting a bribe, or buying stolen merchandise, British and Romanian participants did not show significantly different moral concerns. The only significant difference was registered for avoiding a fare on public transport and cheating on taxes, where participants from the UK perceived the actions as more justifiable than participants from Romania.

Personal beliefs regarding tax evasion

For Part 2 of the survey, again sample comparisons for the four countries indicated there were differences in age and sex between the groups. Therefore, we calculated the residuals for each item, adjusting for age and sex. We used the same non-parametric Kruskal–Wallis tests and post-hoc Mann–Whitney U tests to compare the score residuals between countries as for Part 1.

Demographics and responses for Part 2 of the survey can be seen in Table 9.2. Again, both age and sex significantly differed between the samples, with the same patterns observed as reported for Part 1 of the survey.

Significant differences were also identified in the number of compatriots participants thought took each action. Overall, participants from the UK believed fewer compatriots took each action compared to participants from the other countries, with the exception of avoiding to pay fares on public transport. For this action no significant differences were found between participants from the UK and Germany.

The results of pairwise comparisons between Germany, Romania, and Turkey depended upon the specific action. Of particular note, participants from Turkey considered more of their compatriots claimed government benefits to which they were not entitled, while participants from Germany considered a smaller proportion of their compatriots took this action. German, Romanian, and Turkish subjects reported similar answers on how many compatriots would avoid taxes by using cash payments. Moreover, in the matter of cheating on taxes if the opportunity arises, participants from Germany and Romania shared similar beliefs about others' actions. In contrast, Turkish subjects shared different opinions as compared to German and Romanian subjects. Finally, participants from Germany thought fewer of their compatriots accepted bribes in the

Table 9.2 Demographics and statistical results by country corresponding to the survey items included in Part 2

PART 2	Germany	Romania	Turkey	United Kingdom (UK)	Group comparison
N = 1045	**196**	**184**	**313**	**352**	**Kruskal–Wallis test**
Age	158 (80.6%) age 15–29, 35 (17.9%) age 30–49, 3 (1.5%) age 50+	159 (86.4%) age 15–29, 23 (12.5%) age 30–49, 2 (1.1%) age 50+	307 (98.1%) age 15–29, 6 (1.9%) age 30–49, 0 (0.0%) age 50+	263 (74.7%) age 15–29, 59 (16.8%) age 30–49, 30 (8.5%) age 50+	$\chi^2(6) = 94.06$, p < 0.001
Sex	85 (43.4%) female, 111 (56.6%) male	110 (59.8%) female, 74 (40.2%) male	206 (65.8%) female, 107 (34.2%) male	161 (45.7%) female, 191 (54.3%) male	$\chi^2(3) = 38.61$, p < 0.001
How many of your compatriots do you think …	**Median score and interquartile range for country subsamples**				**Kruskal–Wallis and post-hoc Mann–Whitney U tests**
… claim government benefits to which they are not entitled?	3.00 (1.00)	2.50 (1.00)	2.00 (1.00)	4.00 (1.00)	Overall p < 0.001, Germany *vs* Romania p = 0.050, Germany *vs* Turkey p < 0.001, Germany *vs* UK p < 0.001, Romania *vs* Turkey p < 0.001, Romania *vs* UK p < 0.001, Turkey *vs* UK p < 0.001
… cheat on taxes if they have the chance?	2.00 (1.00)	2.00 (1.00)	2.00 (0.00)	3.00 (1.00)	Overall p < 0.001, Germany *vs* Romania p = 0.828, Germany *vs* Turkey p < 0.001, Germany *vs* UK p < 0.001, Romania *vs* Turkey p < 0.001, Romania *vs* UK p = 0.005, Turkey *vs* UK p < 0.001

(continued)

Table 9.2 (Cont.)

PART 2	Germany	Romania	Turkey	United Kingdom (UK)	Group comparison
... pay cash for services to avoid taxes	2.00 (1.00)	2.00 (1.00)	2.00 (1.00)	3.00 (1.00)	Overall p < 0.001, Germany *vs* Romania p = 1.000, Germany *vs* Turkey p = 0.277, Germany *vs* UK p < 0.001, Romania *vs* Turkey p = 0.240, Romania *vs* UK p = 0.001, Turkey *vs* UK p < 0.001
... avoid paying a fare on public transport?	3.00 (1.00)	2.00 (1.00)	3.00 (0.00)	3.00 (2.00)	Overall p < 0.001, Germany *vs* Romania p = 0.001, Germany *vs* Turkey p < 0.001, Germany *vs* UK p = 0.152, Romania *vs* Turkey p < 0.001, Romania *vs* UK p < 0.001, Turkey *vs* UK p = 0.011
... accept a bribe in the course of their duties?	3.00 (1.00)	2.00 (1.00)	2.00 (1.00)	4.00 (1.00)	Overall p < 0.001, Germany *vs* Romania p < 0.001, Germany *vs* Turkey p < 0.001, Germany *vs* UK p = 0.001, Romania *vs* Turkey p = 1.000, Romania *vs* UK p < 0.001, Turkey *vs* UK p < 0.001

Note: Number and percentage (in parentheses) are shown for the variables *age* and *sex*. Median score and interquartile range (in parentheses) are shown for how many compatriots the surveyed participants thought took each of the five tax evasion-related actions.

Morals and beliefs regarding tax evasion 191

course of their duties compared to participants from both Romania and Turkey. For the latter, we identified similar opinions regarding the behavior of their countrymen.

Discussion and concluding remarks

The present chapter brings forward insights into the moral concerns and personal beliefs surrounding tax evasion of participants surveyed in Germany, Romania, Turkey, and the UK.

First, we investigated how justifiable a set of six actions appeared to be in the minds of our participants. Participants from Turkey rated five of the six actions as less justifiable compared to participants from all the other countries. Only in the case of avoiding taxes via cash payments did Romanian subjects express similar concerns as their Turkish counterparts.

Another interesting result was the fact that participants from Germany reported significantly higher means than the rest of the subjects, thus indicating that sometimes it was justifiable to perform such actions. These less harsh opinions on tax evasion matters are not very surprising. Even for developed economies like Germany (or the UK) it is not as uncommon to number taxpayers who consider tax evasion to be defensible in some cases. Moreover, all countries register a certain level of shadow economy (Batrancea, Nichita, Batrancea, & Gaban, 2018; Kelmanson, Kirabaeva, Medina, Mircheva, & Weiss, 2019; Medina & Schneider, 2018; OECD, 2017), which comprises – among other elements – tax evasion acts that afflict legal economic activities and illegal activities such as trading stolen merchandise (Lippert & Walker, 1997, p. 5). Even in this day and age, tax evasion could be considered justifiable by a growing number of German contributors since German authorities disagree on the public release of tax information belonging to multinational corporations via country-by-country reporting.[8]

For the action of claiming government benefits by providing false information, participants from Romania and the UK reported uniform moral concerns, namely that obtaining such advantages under false pretenses was never justifiable. The same pattern was observed for the actions of accepting a bribe while on duty and buying stolen goods. However, participants from the UK thought that avoiding public transport fares and cheating on taxes when possible were more justifiable than did Romanian participants.

---

8 Under the Base Erosion and Profit Shifting (BEPS) Action Plan 13 developed by the OECD, country-by-country reporting (CbCR) entails that all multinational corporations registering at least 750 million euros in total should produce annually a report containing detailed information about their financial statements for each jurisdiction in which the corporation operates (Deloitte, 2016). Under these provisions, tax authorities aim to mitigate cross-border tax avoidance and tax evasion. www.theconversation.com/tax-avoidance-might-be-legal-but-its-time-we-seriously-questioned-its-ethics-87133 (accessed January 12, 2020); www.mnetax.com/german-finance-minister-endorses-public-country-by-country-reporting-of-mne-tax-information-35799 (accessed January 21, 2020).

192 *Larissa Batrancea et al.*

Across country subsamples, participants' beliefs about their compatriots' benefit fraud actions registered different values. Participants from Germany, Romania, and Turkey believed that at least some compatriots were fraudulently claiming government benefits in cash and/or kind. At least half of the UK participants thought almost no compatriots committed such actions. The issue of benefit fraud has been raising concerns among European governments for many years now (*e.g.*, Blauberger & Schmidt, 2014; Jorens, Gillis, & De Coninck, 2015). For instance, according to the UK Department for Work and Pensions (2015), the value of benefit fraud and error (claimant or official) estimated by British authorities in 2013–2014 was 3.4 billion GBP, *i.e.*, 2.1% of total benefit outlays.

The action about cheating on taxes when opportunities arise seemed to have placed participants from Germany and Romania on the same side. Our results showed that British participants believed that a lower number of their fellow countrymen would use cash payments to avoid taxes than did participants from Germany, Romania, and Turkey.

In terms of how many compatriots participants thought to be avoiding transport fares, both British and German subjects reported more positive beliefs about their countrymen than Romanian and Turkish participants. One possible explanation for the significant results could be the differences in bus fares and purchasing power parities (PPP) registered by these countries.[9] For instance, in 2014, the UK had a PPP value of 0.699, followed by Germany with 0.769, Turkey with 1.105 and Romania with 1.628. Another possible explanation could refer to the approaches implemented by public authorities for clamping down on fare-dodging. While public authorities in Germany and the UK seem to have found a balance between honesty-backed systems and coercion (*e.g.*, unannounced inspectors; boarding by the front door only systems; turnstiles; corroborating travel card data with street surveillance imagery to identify free-riders), public authorities in Romania and Turkey are more likely to favor the use of deterrence (*e.g.*, ticket controllers, fines). Nevertheless, irrespective of the country, fare-dodging takes its toll by creating black holes in public budgets.[10] A case in point, the Transport for London public company estimates yearly losses of at least 100 million GBP due to fare-dodging.[11] For authorities in Berlin, the losses caused by free-riding on public transport are estimated at approximately 20 million euros each year.[12]

---

9 www.data.oecd.org/conversion/purchasing-power-parities-ppp.htm (accessed January 20, 2020).

10 Ironically, the German word for traveling without a ticket on public transport is *schwarzfahren*, which literally translates into "black riding" (*i.e.*, fare-dodging).

11 www.standard.co.uk/stayingin/tvfilm/fare-dodgers-is-a-compelling-but-depressing-look-behind-the-scenes-a4267041.html (accessed January 13, 2020).

12 www.trainsfare.eu/germany-considers-decriminalising-fare-dodging-public-transport/ (accessed January 14, 2020).

Our results on participants' opinions regarding the number of compatriots who would accept bribes while being on duty go in line with the estimates of the 2014 Corruption Perceptions Index (CPI) (Transparency International, 2013). The index has been released annually since 1995 by the Transparency International organization and it ranks countries and territories worldwide through capturing citizens' perceptions on the corruption level in the public sector. Country scores range on a scale from 0 ("highly corrupt") to 100 ("very clean"). Hence, a high CPI score registered by a country translates into a low corruption level perceived by the inquired citizens with respect to their civil servants. According to this index, Germany (12th) and the United Kingdom (14th) were ranked higher than Turkey (64th) and Romania (69th), with the corresponding CPI country scores of 79, 78, 45, and 43, respectively. Hence, the beliefs expressed by our participants follow the 2014 CPI estimates for the most part, with German and British countrymen being perceived as more ethical than their Romanian and Turkish counterparts.

As with the majority of studies, our research has some potential limitations. The first limitation stems from the fact that subsamples are not representative of the populations residing in the surveyed countries, because they include mainly undergraduate and graduate students in addition to faculty members. Therefore, future research studies could focus on broadening the sample pool by constructing it using standard sampling techniques (*e.g.*, random; stratified; systematic). The second limitation is that items describe only a few instances of tax evasion acts. To further develop our endeavor, other studies might consider expanding the item list with other straightforward examples of tax evasion concerning undeclared income from self-employment, salary, or wage (Lippert & Walker, 1997, p. 5), lottery prizes, inherited assets, etc. Moreover, demographics such as income level, employment status, work experience, or political affiliation could also be considered.

The results reported in this chapter may inform tax authorities interested to decrease or at least control tax compliance costs in the long run. As the tax behavior literature points out, our moral concerns and beliefs about other people's involvement in tax evasion acts may influence tax compliance levels. The more a large number of citizens believe that tax evasion is always unjustifiable and that taxpaying should be the norm for everybody, the more compliance levels might increase, which in turn would benefit individuals and society as a whole. If citizens consider that they are entitled to evade taxes (based on various grounds) and that most of their compatriots free-ride on this civic duty, tax noncompliance levels will eventually rise and authorities will have to spend significant amounts of financial resources on monitoring tax systems. In countries where the vast majority of taxpayers favor compliance, authorities are called to support this category of contributors by providing high-quality public goods (*e.g.*, strong social security and benefits systems; a secure and reliable public transportation system; an effective tax system; incorruptible civil servants) and to elicit such positive compliance behaviors among the taxpayers who do the opposite.

194 *Larissa Batrancea et al.*

References

Akay, A., Bargain, O., Dolls, M., Neumann, D., Peichl, A., & Siegloch, S. (2012). Happy taxpayers? Income taxation and well-being. *SOEP – The German Socio-Economic Panel Study at DIW Berlin* No. 526–2012.

Allingham, M., & Sandmo, A. (1972). Income tax evasion: A theoretical analysis. *Journal of Public Economics*, *1*(3-4), 323-338.

Batrancea, L. M., Nichita, R. A., & Batrancea, I. (2012). Understanding the determinants of tax compliance behavior as a prerequisite for increasing public levies. *The USV Annals of Economics and Public Administration*, *12*(15), 201–210.

Batrancea, L., Nichita, A., Batrancea, I., & Gaban, L. (2018). The strength of the relationship between shadow economy and corruption: Evidence from a worldwide country-sample. *Social Indicators Research*, *138*(3), 1119–1143.

Batrancea, L., Nichita, A., Olsen, J., Kogler, C., Kirchler, E., Hoelzl, E. … & Zukauskas, S. (2019). Trust and power as determinants of tax compliance across 44 nations. *Journal of Economic Psychology*, *74*, 102191.

Blauberger, M., & Schmidt, S. K. (2014). Welfare migration? Free movement of EU citizens and access to social benefits. *Research & Politics*, 1–7.

Cleary, D. (2013). A survey on attitudes and behaviour towards tax and compliance: A population assessment for Ireland in 2008/2009. Research & Analytics Branch, Irish Tax and Customs.

Coricelli, G., Joffily, M., Montmarquette, C., & Villeval, M. C. (2010). Cheating, emotions, and rationality: An experiment on tax evasion. *Experimental Economics*, *13*(2), 226-247.

Coricelli, G., Rusconi, E., & Villeval, M. C. (2014). Tax evasion and emotions: An empirical test of re-integrative shaming theory. *Journal of Economic Psychology*, *40*, 49-61.

Deloitte (2016). Country-by-country reporting. The FAQs.

Department for Work and Pensions (2015). Fraud and error in the benefit system 2013/14 estimates (biannual). Retrieved December 12, 2019 from: www.gov.uk/government/statistics/fraud-and-error-in-the-benefit-system-2013-to-2014-estimates.

Dunn, P., Farrar, J., & Hausserman, C. (2018). The influence of guilt cognitions on taxpayers' voluntary disclosures. *Journal of Business Ethics*, *148*, 689–701.

Enachescu, J., Olsen, J., Kogler, C., Zeelenberg, M., Breugelmans, S. M., & Kirchler, E. (2019). The role of emotions in tax compliance behavior: A mixed-methods approach. *Journal of Economic Psychology*, *74*, 102194.

Gërxhani, K. (2007). "Did you pay your taxes?" How (not) to conduct tax evasion surveys in transition countries. *Social Indicators Research*, *80*, 555–581.

Heinlein, R. A. (1961). *Stranger in a strange land*. New York: Ace Books.

Helliwell, J., Layard, R., & Sachs, J. (2018). *World happiness report 2018*. New York: Sustainable Development Solutions Network.

Houston, J., & Tran, A. (2001). A survey of tax evasion using the randomized response technique. In: *Advances in taxation*, Vol. 13 (pp. 69–94). Bingley: Emerald.

James, S., McGee, R. W., Benk, S., & Budak, T. (2019). How seriously do taxpayers regard tax evasion? A survey of opinion in England. *Journal of Money Laundering Control*, *22*(3), 563–575.

Jorens, Y., Gillis, D., & De Coninck, J. (2015). *Fraud and error in the field of social security coordination*. Directorate-General for European Union.

Kahan, D. M. (1997). Social influence, social meaning, and deterrence. *Virginia Law Review*, *83*, 349–395.

Kelmanson, B., Kirabaeva, K., Medina, L., Mircheva, B., & Weiss, J. (2019). Explaining the shadow economy in Europe: Sizes, causes and policy options. IMF Working Paper WP/19/278.

Kirchler, E. (2007). *The economic psychology of tax behaviour.* Cambridge: Cambridge University Press.

Kogler, C., Batrancea, L., Nichita, A., Pantya, J., Belianin, A., & Kirchler, E. (2013). Trust and power as determinants of tax compliance: Testing the assumptions of the slippery slope framework in Austria, Hungary, Romanian and Russia. *Journal of Economic Psychology, 34,* 169-180.

Lippert, O., & Walker, M. (Eds.) (1997). *The underground economy: Global evidences of its size and impact.* Vancouver: The Frazer Institute.

Markellos, R. N., Psychoyios, D., & Schneider, F. (2015). Sovereign debt markets in light of the shadow economy. *European Journal of Operational Research, 252*(1), 220-231.

McGee, R. W., Benk, S., Ross, A. M., & Kılıçaslan, H. (2012). Cheating on taxes if you have a chance: A comparative study of tax evasion opinion in Turkey and Germany. In: R. W. McGee (Ed.), *The ethics of tax evasion: Perspectives in theory and practice* (pp. 357–369). New York: Springer.

Medina, L., & Schneider, F. (2018). Shadow economies around the world: What did we learn over the last 20 years? IMF Working Paper WP/18/17.

Muravska, J., Barrington, R., & Vitou, B. (2014). *How to bribe: A typology of bribe-paying and how to stop it.* Transparency International UK.

Murphy, K. (2008). Enforcing tax compliance: To punish or persuade? *Economic Analysis and Policy, 38*(1), 113-135.

Murphy, R. (2019). The European tax gap. A report for the socialists and democrats group in the European Parliament. Retrieved February 20, 2020, from www.taxresearch.org.uk/Documents/EUTaxGapJan19.pdf.

OECD (2017). *Shining light on the shadow economy: Opportunities and threats.* Paris: OECD.

OECD (2019). *Tax morale: What drives people and businesses to pay tax?* Paris: OECD.

Olsen, J., Kasper, M., Enachescu, J., Benk, S., Budak, T., & Kirchler, E. (2018). Emotions and tax compliance among small business owners: An experimental study. *International Review of Law and Economics, 56,* 42-52.

Olsen, J., Kogler, C., Brandt, M. J., Dezső, L., & Kirchler, E. (2019). Are consumption taxes really disliked more than equivalent costs? Inconclusive results in the USA and no effect in the UK. *Journal of Economic Psychology, 75,* 102145.

Pickhardt, M., & Prinz, A. (2014). Behavioral dynamics of tax evasion: A survey. *Journal of Economic Psychology, 40,* 1–19.

Raczkowski, K., & Mróz, B. (2018). Tax gap in the global economy. *Journal of Money Laundering Control, 21*(4), 545-554.

Slemrod, J. (2007). Cheating ourselves: The economics of tax evasion. *Journal of Economic Perspectives, 1,* 25-48.

Slemrod, J., & Yitzhaki, S. (2002). Tax avoidance, evasion, and administration. In: A. J. Auerbach and M. S. Feldstein (Eds.), *Handbook of public economics,* Vol. 3 (pp. 1423–1470). Amsterdam: Elsevier.

Srinivasan, T. (1973). Tax evasion: A model. *Journal of Public Economics, 2*(4), 339-346.

Sussman, A. B., & Olivola, C. Y. (2011). Axe the tax: Taxes are disliked more than equivalent costs. *Journal of Marketing Research, 48,* 91-101.

TNS Political & Social (2017). *Businesses' attitudes towards corruption in the EU.* European Commission, Directorate-General for Communication.

Torgler, B. (2007). *Tax compliance and tax morale: A theoretical and empirical analysis.* Cheltenham: Edward Elgar.

Torgler, B. (2008). What do we know about tax fraud? An overview of recent developments. *Social Research: An International Quarterly, 74*(4), 1239–1270.

Transparency International (2013). Corruption Perceptions Index 2014. Retrieved January 20, 2020 from: www.transparency.org/cpi2014/results.

United Nations (2019). *World economic situation and prospects 2019 (WESP).* New York: United Nations.

Wakolbinger, F., & Haigner, S. D. (2009). Peer advice in a tax-evasion experiment. *Economics Bulletin, 29*(3), 1653–1669.

Wartick, M. L., & Rupert, T. J. (2010). The effects of observing a peer's likelihood of reporting income on tax reporting decisions. In: T. Stock (Ed.), *Advances in taxation,* Vol. 19 (pp. 65–94). Bingley: Emerald.

Yitzhaki, S. (1974). A note on "Income tax evasion: A theoretical analysis". *Journal of Public Economics, 3*(2), 201–202.

10 Paying is caring?

Prosociality and gender in fiscal compliance

John D'Attoma, Clara Volintiru, and Antoine Malézieux

Introduction

Countries face a number of challenges that have consequently led to controversial budget cuts. As Steinmo (1993, p. 1) puts it, "Governments need money. Modern governments need lots of money". It is, thus, essential that governments can increase revenue without necessarily increasing tax rates. One way governments can increase revenue without raising taxes is through better tax compliance. Governments lose a considerable amount of money due to tax avoidance and evasion – for example, the Tax Justice Network estimates that the world economy loses approximately $3.1 trillion from tax evasion (Werdigier, 2011). It is thus useful to understand both when, why, and which people would choose to pay their taxes honestly and how to elicit voluntary compliance. In this chapter, we explore tax behavior employing a large tax compliance experiment conducted in five countries. We ask the following research questions: First, are prosocial individuals more tax compliant? Secondly, are women more tax compliant than men? Finally, does Social Value Orientation (SVO) mediate the effect of gender on tax compliance?

This chapter[1] brings an important empirical contribution to the academic literature by examining whether gender differences in tax compliance are due to higher prosociality among women. We conducted a large cross-national tax compliance experiment carried out in different countries – Italy, UK, USA, Sweden, and Romania. We uncover that women declare a significantly higher percentage of their income than men in all five countries. While some scholars have argued that differences in honesty between men and women are mediated by prosociality, we find that women are not more prosocial than men in all countries and we do not find a mediating effect of prosocial behavior on tax compliance. Though tax evasion is a form of dishonesty, the tax compliance experiment is quite different from an honesty experiment, which is certainly one explanation for the different results. We conclude that although differences

---

1 This book chapter has been previously published in a slightly modified version as D'Attoma, J., Volintiru, C., & Malézieux, A. (2018). Gender, social value orientation, and tax compliance. CESifo Working Paper No. 7372.

in prosociality between men and women seem to be context-dependent, differences in tax compliance are indeed much more consistent.

A recent study by Grosch and Rau (2017) suggests women are more honest than men. They not only show that *women are more honest than men, but that higher levels of prosociality among women mediate the effects of gender on honesty*. Our contribution extends upon these results by examining a specific policy domain: tax compliance.

Social Value Orientation (SVO) can inform the decision to share or give away some of your profits. Much like tax compliance, it involves a rationalization of resources between oneself and peers, or society in general. However, in the case of paying one's taxes, the choice involves risk and monetary incentives that the SVO decision does not.

Tax compliance, thus, is not necessarily the same as honesty. Tax evasion is always illegal, whereas many forms of dishonesty are not. There is also an enormous amount of moral and ethical gray area in the tax compliance decision that might not be the same as in some other forms of dishonest behavior. For example, in our experiment, the audit rate is 5%, which brings forth the risk of being caught – that is not present in a die experiment (Fischbacher & Föllmi-Heusi, 2013), on top of any ethical concerns subjects might have with regard to paying taxes. Nevertheless, we know that most tax compliance experiments display larger compliance rates than what would normally be attributable to audit rates or fear of being exposed (Andreoni, Erard, & Feinstein, 1998; Calvet & Alm, 2014). Because tax fraud is essentially a type of dishonest behavior, we argue that gender differences with regard to tax compliance are comparable to findings related to honesty in general. As such, while prosocial attitudes may have an impact on honesty as shown by Grosch and Rau (2017), we show that this is not necessarily the case when looking at tax compliance.

Although there is a large body of experimental literature on gender, tax compliance, and SVO, we have yet to come across a study that links these three variables. We, therefore, add a theoretical and methodological contribution to the tax compliance literature by examining whether gender differences in tax compliance are due to higher prosociality among women.

Theoretically, we suggest that individual behavior is embedded with a large set of psychological motivations informed by the set of norms and beliefs. We argue that institutions frame the tenets and the weights that individuals assign to the different motivations involved in tax compliance decisions. Let us say, for example, that the tax compliance decision is made up of three primary motivations: self-interest, norms, and social values. Institutions help individuals assign a weight to each of these motivations. The weight assigned to social values might be different in Italy than in Sweden, for instance, where the effectiveness and efficiency of institutions varies significantly. It is thus important to test behavior in different contexts. Methodologically, we use data that we collected from five different countries in Europe and America. We are able to control for behavioral variations that might be context-dependent and ascertain more clearly the relationship between prosocial attitudes and honesty.

To preview our results: we find that SVO is an important aspect of the tax compliance decision, and women are also more tax compliant than men (in all countries) – supporting a large body of tax compliance literature. However, differences in SVO vary by gender only in some countries, meaning that women are not more prosocial than men in all countries. As such, we suggest that prosocial values might be context-dependent, while gender differences in tax compliance are much more consistent across countries.

Literature review

Social Value Orientation and tax compliance

The SVO scale has been a frequently employed metric in experimental studies. It is an expressive metric of how much people care for others' wellbeing. We used for the present study the continuous version developed by Murphy and his colleagues (Murphy, Ackermann, & Handgraaf, 2011). Murphy and Ackermann regard SVO as the "predominant conceptualization of social preferences in psychology" (2014, p. 13). As opposed to previous categorical versions of the SVO, this newer version allows us to have a more detailed assessment of individual differences. Prosocial subjects tend to be more reactive to social norms of cooperation than self-interest maximization. As audit rates and penalties have been proven to be insufficient in deterring tax evasion (Graetz & Wilde, 1985; Feld & Frey, 2002), our goal in using SVO measurement is to assess the extent to which a person's SVO can help explain their fiscal compliance (or lack of).

SVO has also been analyzed in relation to trust and reciprocity (Kanagaretnam, Mestelman, Nainar, & Shehata, 2009), cooperation (see meta-analysis from Balliet, Parks, & Joireman, 2009), and expectations (Pletzer et al., 2018). This entices us to look for the effects of prosociality on cooperative behavior in a fiscal setting. A series of studies have applied a similar methodological framework in contextualizing fiscal behavior in cross-cultural circumstances (Alm & Torgler, 2006; Kogler et al., 2013, Alm et al., 2017). Large comparative studies are not the norm in experimental studies, and yet the insights they provide are very valuable indeed: they show the extent to which social norms vary (or not) with respect to paying taxes.

Moreover, location matters when we look at the drivers of tax compliance. While economic incentives account for a certain level of compliance, Richardson (2006, 2008) also points out the role of non-economic factors (e.g., tax morale, institutional complexity) in the decision to evade taxes. Similarly, Kogler et al. (2013) test the role of the slippery slope framework (i.e., cumulative effect of trust in authorities and power of authorities in tax compliance) in a cross-cultural design in Austria, Hungary, Romania, and Russia, and find a strong association between evasion and low trust/low power. Such studies suggest that there is a notable cross-country variation in fiscal behavior that is driven by individuals' expectations, not just incentives.

200 *John D'Attoma et al.*

We focused our present assessment on countries in Europe and North America that share many similarities in terms of the structure of their economies and the institutional context (*e.g.*, taxation system, enforcement capacity). Yet even within this sample of cases, we can still see significant variation in their actual collection levels. Despite member states' efforts to achieve better fiscal and institutional alignment, in the European Union tax gaps vary from 7.98% in Luxembourg to 29.51% in Romania (Murphy, 2019). This points to persistent differences in behavior that are harder to change through (relatively) recent institutional reforms. Previous studies revealed cross-national variation in tax compliance behavior driven by (perceived) legitimacy of the state and quality of government, or individuals' expectations and obligations towards society (Alm & Torgler, 2006; Cummings, Martinez-Vazquez, McKee, & Torgler, 2009; Kogler *et al.*, 2013; D'Attoma, 2017, 2020; Zhang *et al.*, 2016, Andreoni, Erard, & Feinstein, 1998; Pampel, Andrighetto, & Steinmo, 2018; D'Attoma, Volintiru, & Steinmo, 2017). Building on these findings, we also expect differences in SVO and compliance (and their interaction) across countries.

While there are notable studies regarding the effects of tax morale on tax compliance (Alm & Torgler, 2006; Torgler, 2007), much fewer have concerned the impact of SVO. Brizi, Giacomantonio, Schumpe, and Mannetti (2015), however, suggest that SVO is a strong predictor of tax compliance. If SVO influences cooperation and public goods contributions, we would also expect SVO to impact an individual's willingness to pay taxes. But, we have yet to come across a study that examines SVO as it relates to tax compliance.

Gender

There is quite a large catalog of literature that examines the effects of gender on honesty. Studies are at odds, however, on this issue. The majority of honesty games suggest that women are more prone to honest behavior (Erat & Gneezy, 2012; Capraro, 2018). Still, there are also those that challenge gender differences. Biziou-van-Pol, Haenen, Novaro, Liberman, and Capraro (2015) have questioned this assumption, suggesting that the debate on gender differences in lying is not settled. Most recently, however, Grosch and Rau (2017) have confirmed gender differences, as they find men are less honest than women in a deception game (*i.e.*, cheat significantly more), and they link these gender differences to SVO (*i.e.*, consideration of others).

According to Byrnes, Miller, and Schafer (1999) risk taking means accepting the possibility of a negative outcome as a result of the option made. Women seem less inclined to accept such negative outcome despite the upside of potentially higher returns. Several studies indicate that women are more risk averse than men (Byrnes *et al.*, 1999; Croson & Gneezy, 2009; Charness & Gneezy, 2012). Charness and Gneezy (2012) show through a cross-country investment experiment that women make less financially risky decisions. Furthermore, much more visible gender differences are recorded in affluent countries (Falk & Hermle, 2018), and the relationship between gender and tax compliance is strongest in Europe and North America (Hofmann, Voracek, Bock, & Kirchler, 2017). That said, a recent large meta-analysis emphasizes that an overwhelming majority of published papers – more than 90% – do not find any gender differences in their experiments (Filippin & Crosetto, 2016, p. 12).

Tax compliance experiments overwhelmingly demonstrate gender differences (Hasseldine & Hite, 2003; Chung & Trivedi, 2003; Gërxhani, 2007; Gylfason, Arnardottir, & Kristinsson, 2013; Bruner, D'Attoma, & Steinmo, 2017; D'Attoma, Volintiru, & Steinmo, 2017). These studies all find that women are more tax compliant than men in most countries in laboratory environments, as did a meta-analysis on this topic by Alm and Malézieux (2018). For example, D'Attoma, Volintiru, and Steinmo (2017), examining differences between men and women in the US, Sweden, UK, and Italy, assert that women are less likely than men to cheat on taxes, across countries and across cultures. However, in another study using the same data, Bruner *et al.* (2017) uncover that although women are more compliant than men, men are more responsive to an increase in the payoff from a public good.

Hypotheses

Tax compliance is a decision that is embedded with a host of personal and psychological motivations as well as consideration for institutional constraints and context, such as the payoff from the public good, risk, or tax rates. More than a calculation of perceived risks, tax compliance is an inherently prosocial decision (Alm *et al.*, 2012; Brizi *et al.*, 2015; Drus, 2016): when paying taxes, taxpayers contribute some of their earnings to a government, who then takes that money to provide public goods. Being prosocial and acting prosocial (*i.e.*, paying one's taxes) adds to perceived individual benefit. Therefore, people who derive higher utility by making others better off should also be more likely to contribute their earnings in the form of tax payments (Erard & Feinstein 1994; Dunn, Aknin, & Norton, 2014). Similarly, a more individualistic person who is more concerned with maximizing their own payoff will more likely evade their fiscal obligations.

If participants acted purely rational in our experiments, proportional to the stated audited risk, the optimal decision would always be to report zero income. We therefore posit the following hypothesis:

Hypothesis 1: Individuals with higher SVOs will report significantly more of their earnings in all countries.

Gilligan (1982) suggests that men's and women's divergent behavior can be compartmentalized into two theoretical constructs. Masculine behavior is more instrumental as it stresses the role of hierarchical relationships, individual rights, competition, and equates morality with justice. Females behave in a manner that is more reactive to context, by emphasizing communal relationships, cooperation, and avoidance of harm to others.

202 *John D'Attoma et al.*

There is an extensive body of experimental literature addressing behavioral differences between men and women in altruistic preferences and willingness to contribute to the public good. Eckel and Grossman for example have consistently demonstrated that women are the fairer sex and more altruistic. In an ultimatum game, Eckel and Grossman (2001) showed that women are not only more cooperative, but in addition, offers from women are significantly more likely to be accepted. Because women are more cooperative, they were more willing to accept unequal splits. In a similar line of research in which one partner is the sender and the other is the receiver, men tend to send more money, especially when women are on the receiving end of the partnership, but women return more money to the sender (Buchan, Croson, & Solnick, 2008). This again speaks to the contextual/instrumental behaviors of men and women. According to Buchan *et al.* (2008, p. 7), "the only possible motivation to be trustworthy is a communal one (an empathetic response, perhaps the need to live up to expectations)".

Building on our comparative research design, our expectation is that on average women are more prosocial than men in all countries (H2a). Since prosociality relates to a higher preoccupation with the wellbeing of others and a number of studies have demonstrated that women are more cooperative, we assume that on average women will report more income than men (H2b).

> *Hypothesis 2: (a) On average women are more prosocial than men in all countries. (b) On average women will report more income than men.*

Extending upon Grosch and Rau (2017), we suggest that this relationship between SVO, gender, and honesty should be applicable to tax compliance as well. If it is the case that women are more prosocial than men, this prosocial preference could be a mediating variable between gender and tax compliance.

> *Hypothesis 3: The individual SVO mediates the effect of gender on dishonest behavior.*

Experimental design

Our experiments were conducted over the course of two years (2015–2017) in different sites across Europe and America.[2] We chose experimental locations to

---

2 The experimental sites included Bologna Laboratory for Experiments in Social Sciences, Centro d'Economia Sperimentale A Roma Est, and Experimental Economics Lab of the University of Milano Bicocca in Italy, Oxford Experimental Laboratory, Experimental Economics Laboratory-Royal Holloway in London, Finance and Economics Experimental Laboratory at Exeter, and ESSEXLab at Essex in Britain, Learning & Experimental Economics Projects at University of California-Santa Cruz, Social Science Experiments Lab at the University of Colorado-Boulder, Appalachian Experimental Economics Laboratory in Boone, North Carolina, Center for Behavioral Political Economy in Stony Brook, New York, and University of Hawaii Laboratory for Computer-Mediated Experiments and the Study of Culture in Honolulu, Hawaii, in the

best represent regional variation within countries, and the significant variation between Western democratic countries. One of the researchers working on the "Willing to Pay" project was always present during the experiments for quality assurance and to make sure the experiments were conducted in the same way in all locations. Our *within*-subjects experimental design follows the basic elements of most tax compliance experiments. First, subjects earn money and we ask them to report their income for tax purposes. We specifically framed our experiment as a tax game to make the experiment resemble a real-world tax paying scenario. Only at the end of the experiment does the computer reveal the results of taxpayers selected for an independent audit and the fine subjects pay for underreporting. For our experiments, there was a 5% audit probability and a fine equal to twice the taxes owed. Throughout the experiment there was a 30% tax rate.

On the day of the experiment, we invited subjects to a computer lab; most sessions had between 20 and 28 subjects with a minimum of eight and a mean of 18. We asked participants (mostly students) to take a seat and we began to read them the instructions, which they could also read on their screens. We first asked subjects to perform a simple clerical task for which they copied a row of fictitious names from a sheet of paper to the computer (see Figure 10.1). For each row copied correctly they received ten currency units, which would be exchanged at the rate of 0.01 for real money. We then showed participants their earnings for the round and asked them to declare their income for tax purposes. They could declare any amount that they wanted, but if they declared less than what they earned, there was a 5% probability of being caught, and if caught, there was a penalty of twice the taxes owed for underreporting. Final income was equal to the earned income plus the redistributed revenues from collective choices of contribution, less taxes levied and fines.[3]

The experimental design consisted of a total of six reporting rounds separated in two stages.[4] In the first stage of the experiment we manipulate the payoff to the public good, while in the second round we vary the public institution to which subjects contribute. Before each round they were given examples of the payoff mechanism.

In stage one, we investigated how redistribution affected willingness to pay taxes. Therefore, after one five-minute clerical task, we gave subjects the parameters, and we asked subjects to report their income. Figure 10.2 is a screen capture of the reporting screen. The rationale behind the six rounds, instead of

US, and the Behavioural lab in Stockholm and Behavioural and Experimental Economics in Gothenburg in Sweden, Bucharest University of Economic Studies (ASE) and National School of Political Science and Public Administration (SNSPA) in Bucharest, and Babes-Bolyai University in Cluj-Napoca, Romania.

3 Another paper from this study using the same design can be found in D'Attoma (2020).

4 For this article we have chosen to only study the effects of gender and SVO on tax compliance overall, instead of looking at the individual treatment effects. We, therefore, limit our discussion of each individual treatment. For more details, see D'Attoma (2020).

204 *John D'Attoma et al.*

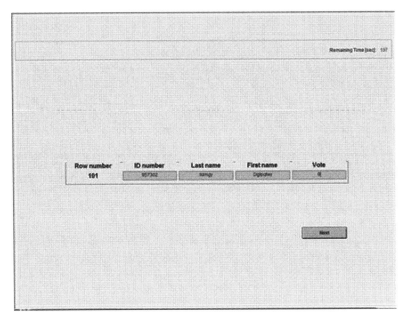

Figure 10.1 Screen capture of the clerical task

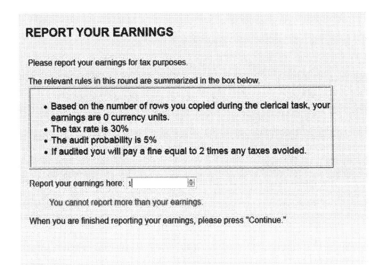

Figure 10.2 Screen capture of the reporting screen

Paying is caring? 205

Table 10.1 Description of experimental treatments

Task	Description
Clerical 1: 5 minutes	Earn income that is reported in Rounds 1–3.
Round 1: No Pot	Flat 30% tax rate on all reported income; No redistribution.
Round 2: Redistribution	Flat 30% tax rate on all reported income; Tax revenues are put into a general fund and redistributed equally to all subjects.
Round 3: Progressive Redistribution	Flat 30% tax rate on all reported income; General fund is portioned into two funds; One part (80%) will be allocated to portion A, and a second part (20%) will be allocated to portion B. All of the money in portion A will be distributed in equal parts to all of the participants, regardless of how much each participant earned, and how much he or she put into the fund. The money in portion B will be distributed in equal parts to the lowest 20% of income earners, regardless of how much each person in this group put into the fund.
Clerical 2: 4 minutes	Earn income that is reported in Round 4.
Round 4: Public Institution (National Government, randomized)	Flat tax rate of 30% on all reported income; Tax revenues are collected and sent to the National Government (Department of Treasury).
Clerical 3: 4 minutes	Earn income that is reported in Round 5.
Round 5: Public Institution (Pension Fund, randomized)	Flat tax rate of 30% on all reported income; Tax revenues are collected and sent to the National Pension Scheme.
Clerical 4: 4 minutes	Earn income that is reported in Round 6.
Round 6: Public Institution (Fire Department, randomized)	Flat tax rate of 30% on all reported income; Tax revenues are collected and sent to the Fire and Rescue Department.

using only the last three rounds, was that we wanted to test how participants behave when given an abstract public good that we could hold constant in all countries compared to using their real-world institutions which vary significantly by country.

In round 1 (our baseline), there was no payoff from the public good (see Table 10.1). Essentially the money was burned. In round 2, we collected their money, summed, and put it into a general fund which was then redistributed equally to all participants. Here there was no multiplier, and thus, the utility maximizing strategy would be to always report 0. Finally, in round 3, the money was collected into a general fund divided into two portions: one part (80%) was allocated to portion A, and a second part (20%) was allocated to portion B. All of the money in portion A was distributed in equal parts to all of the participants, regardless of how much each participant earned, and how much they put into the fund. The money in portion B was distributed in equal parts

206 John D'Attoma et al.

Table 10.2 Social Value Orientation allocation decisions (example)

Decision	1	2	3	4	5	6
1	(85, 85)	(85, 76)	(85, 68)	(85, 59)	(85, 50)	(85, 41)
2	(85, 15)	(87, 19)	(89, 24)	(91, 28)	(93, 33)	(94, 37)
3	(50, 100)	(54, 98)	(59, 96)	(63, 94)	(68, 93)	(72, 91)
4	(50, 100)	(54, 89)	(59, 79)	(63, 68)	(68, 58)	(72, 47)
5	(100, 50)	(94, 56)	(88, 63)	(81, 69)	(75, 75)	(69, 81)
6	(100, 50)	(98, 54)	(96, 59)	(94, 63)	(93, 68)	(91, 72)

Notes: In each allocation, the first value is the number of tokens the decision-maker keeps for herself and the second value is the number of tokens the other person receives.

to the lowest 20% of income earners, regardless of how much each person in this group put into the fund.

In stage two, we examined how perceptions of participants' real-world institutions influenced tax compliance. In this stage, we asked subjects to perform a four-minute clerical task before each reporting round, for which they would earn money and pay taxes directly to their real-world institutions (national government, pension fund, and fire department). Therefore, there was not an abstract public good, but instead, there was an actual public good attached to this stage, since we did send all revenues to the specified public institutions of the country in which they live at the end of the experiment. We randomized the rounds in stage two.

After the income reporting rounds, subjects were tasked with six allocation decisions to elicit their "social value orientation" (Murphy *et al.*, 2011). The decision was a simple allocation task. Individuals were required to choose a proportion of coins to be shared between them and a randomly chosen anonymous partner (see Table 10.2 for an example of the first six decisions). These decisions are created to gauge the extent to which a subject cares about other subjects' earnings relative to their own.[5]

We construct the SVO angle as such: first, we calculate the average number of tokens a participant keeps to herself, y_1, and the average number of tokens she gives to the other participant, y_2. Then we subtract 50 from each in order to shift the coordinates. Finally, we take the arctangent of the ratio of the corrected allocation to the other participant relative to oneself to calculate the SVO angle,

$$SVO° = arctan \frac{(y2 - 50)}{(y1 - 50)}.$$

---

5 The last nine decisions determined whether prosocial behavior was driven by inequality aversion or joint gain maximization. Since the motivation for prosocial behavior is not relevant for this research question, these decisions are omitted from Table 10.3 and the subsequent analysis.

Murphy *et al.* (2011, p. 772) argue that this approach of measuring social preferences is superior to other methods, such as a SVO index or a categorical variable representing prosocials and individualists, because other measures do not provide consistent results, lack sensitivity to individual differences, and require a great deal of time from participants. At the end of the experimental rounds, subjects were asked to take a short ten-minute survey that collected demographic information, as well as information regarding trust attitudes towards taxation, and levels of risk tolerance.

Subjects were recruited through a common recruitment system called Online Recruitment System for Experimental Economics (ORSEE) (Greiner, 2015), and the experiments were programmed in Behavery. Sessions lasted approximately 60 minutes. Payment structure was based on 1.5 times the country's minimum wage. In total we had 1124 subjects of which 55% were men and 45% were women. Session size varied between 8 and 28 participants. The average age was 22, and 61% of our sample had previously partaken in behavioral experiments. Finally, the average earnings were approximately $13 dollars with a $5 (or equivalent) show up fee.

To maximize the extent of our study, including the number of participants, the number of countries and locations in which we conducted the experiment, and the consistency of our experiment, we did make some methodological sacrifices. For example, we did not reorder treatments. We did randomize the last three rounds, but we did not reorder the treatments to control for order effects. However, in our previous experiment, with a similar design, we did control for ordering in the tax compliance experiment and the order did not affect the overall results (citation anonymized for peer review). Another limitation of our study is that there could be post-treatment bias in our SVO task and survey instrument since they were conducted after the tax experiment. Our primary concern was running a large tax compliance experiment, and we, thus, chose to run the SVO and survey after the tax compliance experiment so as to not affect subject's behavior in the tax experiment. It would have been too costly to reorder, randomize treatments, and run the SVO task before and after the tax treatment. Table 10.3 displays our descriptive statistics.

Results

Result 1: SVO is positively correlated with the average compliance rate overall.

Here we test the effects of SVO on tax compliance. From Figure 10.3, we can observe a bimodal distribution, which is typical of a tax compliance experiment. This means that we get a large number of respondents either reporting 0 income or all income. Interestingly, the number of people who report 100% of their income far surpasses the number of individuals who report 0, although reporting 0 is the optimal decision in each round.

Now we move on to examine the relationship between SVO and reporting behavior. We do this first by using our pooled data set, followed by investigating

208 John D'Attoma et al.

Table 10.3 Descriptive statistics

	WOMEN (N = 3720)		MEN (N = 3024)		SIGN. DIFF.	FULL SAMPLE (N = 6744)	
	Mean	STD. DEV.	Mean	STD. DEV.	T-test	Mean	STD. DEV.
Average compliance rate	0.73	0.38	0.48	0.45	★★★	0.62	0.43
Compliance rate Round 1	0.68	0.40	0.38	0.43	★★★	0.55	0.44
Compliance rate Round 2	0.74	0.36	0.50	0.44	★★★	0.63	0.42
Compliance rate Round 3	0.73	0.37	0.55	0.44	★★★	0.65	0.41
Compliance rate Round 4	0.70	0.38	0.43	0.45	★★★	0.58	0.43
Compliance rate Round 5	0.74	0.37	0.48	0.45	★★★	0.62	0.43
Compliance rate Round 6	0.79	0.34	0.53	0.46	★★★	0.68	0.42
Risk	5.79	2.31	6.38	2.34	★★★	6.06	2.34
Econ major (%)	0.28	0.45	0.40	0.49	★★★	0.33	0.47
Trust in government	-0.03	0.61	-0.03	0.64	★★★	0	0.61
Past participation	0.61	0.49	0.61	0.49	n.s.	0.61	0.49
SVO	21.02	14.60	18.08	15.76	★★★	19.70	15.20
Age	21.85	5.57	22.27	5.54	★★★	22.04	5.56
# observations: Italy	714	--	906	--	--	1620	--
# observations: UK	504	--	336	--	--	960	--
# observations: US	1464	--	1080	--	--	2544	--
# observations: Sweden	282	--	366	--	--	648	--
# observations: Romania	756	--	336	--	--	1092	--

Notes: n.s. means non-significant.
★ p < 0.1; ★★ p < 0.05; ★★★ p < 0.01.

the relationship in each individual country. The scatter plot in Figure 10.4 demonstrates that there is strong positive correlation between SVO angle and the average compliance rate. A Spearman's Rho of Þ = 0.30 ($p < 0.001$) demonstrates a strong statistically significant relationship between the two variables. Specifically, individuals with higher SVO angles report a significantly higher proportion of their income than individuals with lower SVOs.[6]

This supports previous literature on the effects of SVO on honest behavior. However, we are also interested in whether this relationship holds up when testing it in a number of countries.

To do this, we run Spearman's correlation coefficient in each individual country. We confirm that SVO is significantly and positively correlated with tax compliance in each country.[7]

---

6 This result also holds when considering each different round of the experiment: SVO is positively correlated with tax compliance in each round.
7 Italy: Þ = 0.24 ($p < 0.001$), the UK: Þ = 0.26 ($p < 0.001$), the US: Þ = 0.33 ($p < 0.001$), Sweden: Þ = 0.25 ($p < 0.001$), and Romania: Þ = 0.15 ($p < 0.001$).

Paying is caring? 209

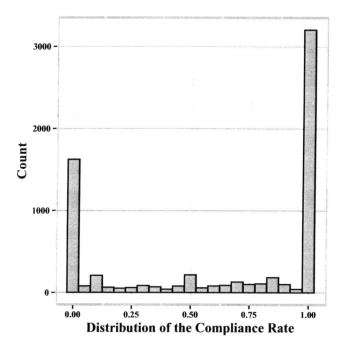

Figure 10.3 Distribution of tax compliance

Result 2: Women are significantly more tax compliant than men overall and in each individual country; however, whether women are more prosocial depends on the country in which the experiment was conducted.

In this section, we test whether women are more tax compliant and prosocial than men. From the bar graph in Figure 10.5, we can clearly see that women are more tax compliant than men in each country. On average women report an astounding 73% of their income across countries, while men report approximately 48% of their income. We also perform a Mann-Whitney test for our pooled sample and within countries. Our test confirms the figure demonstrating that women are significantly more compliant than men across (Mann-Whitney test: $p < 0.001$) and within countries.[8]

We also explore the relationship between gender, SVO, and tax compliance. As such, we examine differences in the SVO angle between men and women overall and within countries. Figure 10.6 illustrates Cumulative Distribution Functions (CDF) for men and women for each individual country.

---

8 Mann-Whitney test: Italy: ($p < 0.001$), the UK: ($p < 0.001$), the US: ($p < 0.001$), Sweden: ($p < 0.001$), and Romania: ($p < 0.001$).

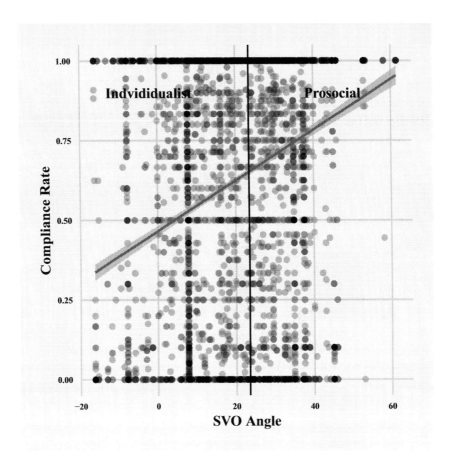

Figure 10.4 Effects of SVO on tax compliance

We find that overall there seem to be significant differences between men and women regarding SVO (Mann-Whitney: $p < 0.001$). Indeed, women have an average SVO angle of 21, whereas men have an average SVO angle of 18. However, somewhat surprisingly, our data suggest that women are only more prosocial than men in Italy and the United States, as the Mann-Whitney test shows (Italy: $p < 0.001$, UK: $p = 0.20$, US: $p < 0.001$, Sweden: $p = 0.19$, and Romania: $p = 0.71$).

Though we cannot begin to speculate as to why women are more prosocial in some countries but not others, this result would suggest that differences between men and women with regard to prosociality are largely context-dependent.

Individual level models

In this section, we test our individual level models. In the first model (seen in column 1 of Table 10.4), we examine the effects of gender on the average

Paying is caring? 211

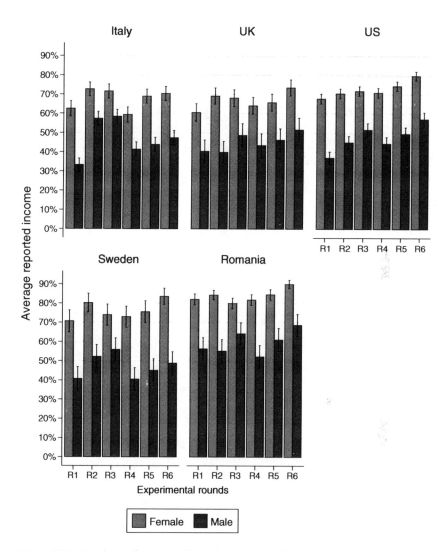

Figure 10.5 Bar chart of tax compliance by gender and country

tax compliance rate across all six rounds and each individual decision, controlling for a number of variables, with standard errors clustered at the subject level. Female is a dummy variable with 0 representing men and 1 representing women. We measure risk attitudes from a question in our post-experimental survey in which we asked participants how willing they are to take risks – 0 meaning completely unwilling to take risks and 10 meaning completely willing to take risks. Age is a continuous measure of age; Economics majors represent those who study economics; Past-participation measures whether participants have participated in laboratory experiments before. Trust in government is a

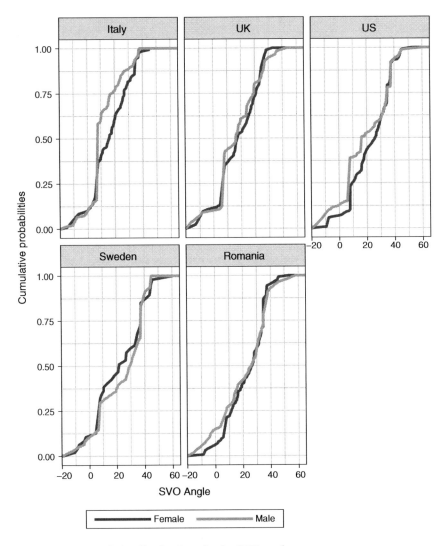

Figure 10.6 Cumulative distributions for the SVO angle

factor index of four variables: trust in national government, trust in the pension system, trust in the fire department, and trust in city. Finally, we control for country and round fixed effects.

First, the coefficient on the female variable is highly significant with a very large substantive effect. Being female increases compliance by 21% all else being equal. SVO angle is also highly significant and positive. These first two results confirm our results above. Moreover, as individuals become more risk tolerant compliance decreases. We expected this since there is some amount

Table 10.4 Individual level models and mediation analysis

	Compliance	Compliance	Compliance	Compliance	SVO	Compliance	SVO
	OLS (1)	Extensive Margin (2)	Intensive Margin (3)	SEM (4)	SEM (5)	SEM (6)	SEM (7)
Female	0.208★★★ (0.023)	−0.156★★★ (0.023)	0.173★★★ (0.024)	0.208★★★ (−0.023)	1.746★ (−1.043)	0.229★★★ (−0.019)	3.004★★★ (−0.916)
SVO	0.007★★★ (0.001)	−0.007★★★ (0.001)	0.003★★★ (0.001)	0.007★★★ (−0.001)		0.007★★★ (−0.001)	
Risk	−0.021★★★ (0.005)	0.021★★★ (0.005)	−0.011★★ (0.005)	−0.021★★★ (−0.005)	-0.786★★★ (−0.238)		
Age	0.002 (0.003)	−0.004 (0.003)	−0.002 (0.003)	0.002 (−0.003)	0.177 (−0.132)		
Econ major	−0.059★★ (0.025)	0.074★★★ (0.027)	−0.006 (0.025)	−0.059★★ (−0.025)	−4.243★★★ (−1.114)		
Trust in gov.	0.051★★ (0.020)	−0.048★★ (0.022)	0.035★ (0.021)	0.051★★ (−0.020)	2.629★★★ (−0.994)		
Past participation	−0.114★★★ (0.024)	0.124★★★ (0.026)	−0.063★★ (0.026)	−0.114★★★ (−0.024)	−3.099★★★ (−1.135)		
UK	−0.047 (0.047)	0.001 (0.052)	−0.075★ (0.041)	−0.047 (−0.047)	0.371 (−2.024)		
US	−0.073★★ (0.030)	0.070★★ (0.033)	−0.040 (0.028)	−0.073★★ (−0.030)	4.861★★★ (−1.334)		
Sweden	−0.167★★★ (0.048)	0.155★★★ (0.049)	−0.088★★ (0.043)	−0.167★★★ (−0.048)	2.579 (−2.291)		
Romania	0.062 (0.041)	−0.112★★ (0.049)	−0.019 (0.052)	0.062 (−0.041)	6.761★★★ (−2.041)		

(continued)

Table 10.4 (Cont.)

	Compliance	Compliance	Compliance	Compliance	SVO	Compliance	SVO
	OLS *(1)*	Extensive Margin *(2)*	Intensive Margin *(3)*	SEM *(4)*	SEM *(5)*	SEM *(6)*	SEM *(7)*
Constant	0.531★★★ (0.084)		0.344★★★ (0.078)	0.531★★★ (−0.084)	19.063★★★ (−3.679)	0.354★★★ (−0.019)	18.021★★★ (−0.702)
Var (Compliance)				0.153★★★		0.159★★★	
R^2	0.2		0.128				
Obs.	5005	5034	2645	5005	5005	6712	6712
Round fixed effect	YES	YES	YES	YES	YES	NO	NO

Notes: Robust standard errors between parentheses. Standard errors are clustered at the individual level. Italy has been omitted to avoid multicollinearity bias.
★ p < 0.1; ★★ p < 0.05; ★★★ p < 0.01.

Paying is caring? 215

of risk in the compliance decision, although the chance of being caught cheating in our experiment is quite small. Importantly, the coefficient on the female variable is very large even controlling for the fact that women are significantly more risk averse. Studying economics and participating in previous experiments also significantly reduces tax compliance, ceteris paribus. Finally, trust in government is positive and has a significant influence on tax compliance.[9]

In column 2, we examine the extensive margin of tax compliance. There are two steps in the tax compliance decision. First, participants make the decision to evade, then among those who make the decision to evade, the second decision is how much they evade. The extensive margin estimates the effects of the independent variables on the decision to evade; we code those who decide to evade as 1 and those who comply as 0. Each cell represents marginal effects with standard errors in parentheses. Again, we observe that being female reduces the probability of being an evader by 16% compared to men. Consistent with the other results, SVO angle, risk, economics majors, past participation, and trust in government are all statistically significant and in the expected direction.

In column 3, we report the second part of the compliance decision: the intensive margin. Here the intensive margin is continuous as the dependent variable represents the amount of evasion engaged in by evaders. We detect that among the subsample of evaders, women report more income. Overall, this result tells us that being a woman both decreases the probability of being an evader, and women who evade report more income than men who evade. SVO angle, risk, trust in government, and past participation are all significant and in the expected direction. However, among the subsample of evaders, compliance behavior between economics majors and non-economics majors is no longer significantly different. In the following sections, we further examine the role of gender on tax compliance. Specifically, we look at whether SVO might be a mediator between gender and tax compliance.

Interestingly, we find that Americans and Swedes are significantly more likely to make the decision to evade than Italians, but among those who evade, the Swedes evade less than Italians. There is not a significant difference between Italians and Americans on the intensive margin. Romanians are less likely to evade than Italians, but there is no difference between those who evade. Finally, the Brits do not demonstrate any differences when compared to Italians. Though this is an experiment on university students, these results do challenge the culturalist argument that Italians and Romanians are more dishonest than other Western countries (see, *e.g.*, Guerra & Harrington 2018 on this topic).

---

9 These results come from an OLS model. Substituting a Tobit regression for the OLS does not change any of the conclusions on the significance of being a female on compliance – see Table 10.5 (column 1).

216   *John D'Attoma et al.*

Table 10.5 Mediation analysis with Structural Equation Modeling

	Compliance	Compliance	Risk	Compliance	Risk
	Tobit (1)	SEM (2)	SEM (3)	SEM (4)	SEM (5)
Risk	−0.071★★★ (0.017)	−0.021★★★ (0.005)		−0.022★★★ (0.004)	
SVO	0.023★★★ (0.003)	0.007★★★ (0.001)	−0.018★★★ (0.005)		
Female	0.694★★★ (0.080)	0.208★★★ (0.023)	−0.651★★★ (0.157)	0.237★★★ (0.020)	−0.586★★★ (0.139)
Age	0.007 (0.012)	0.002 (0.003)	−0.045★ (0.025)		
Econ major	−0.226★★★ (0.082)	−0.059★★ (0.025)	−0.154 (0.171)		
Trust in gov.	0.158★★ (0.069)	0.051★★ (0.020)	−0.474★★★ (0.142)		
Past participation	−0.421★★★ (0.083)	−0.114★★★ (0.024)	−0.228 (0.170)		
Constant	0.614★★ (0.298)	0.531★★★ (0.084)	7.414★★★ (0.611)	0.623★★★ (0.031)	6.380★★★ (0.104)
Var (Compliance)		0.153★★★ (0.004)		0.169★★★ (0.003)	
Country fixed effect	YES	YES	YES	NO	NO
Round fixed effect	YES	YES	YES	NO	NO

Notes. Robust standard errors between parentheses. Tobit model is censored at 0 and 1.
★ $p < 0.1$; ★★ $p < 0.05$; ★★★ $p < 0.01$.

Mediation analysis

We now examine whether SVO mediates the effect of gender on tax compliance. First from Table 10.5, we can see that there are significant differences between men and women in their levels of self-reported risk aversion, along with men being much more likely to study economics.

We compute possible mediating effects of SVO in columns 4, 5, 6, and 7 of Table 10.4. We also include control variables such as the self-declared risk tolerance, subject's age, economics majors, trust in government, number of past participations, and the different country dummies for the countries in which the experiment was run, along with the round dummies.

Figure 10.7 demonstrates the Structural Equation Model. Including the potential mediator (SVO angle) in the path model (in black), we observe almost no changes to the effect of being a female on tax compliance. The coefficient on the SVO variable means that being female increases tax compliance by 23%, all else being equal. Even so, computing the proportion of total

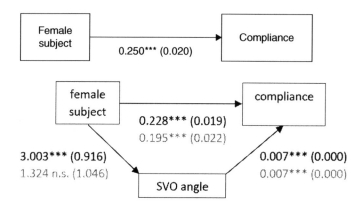

Figure 10.7 Schematic diagram of mediation analysis results
Notes: Path values are reported coefficients with standard errors in parentheses. Data in gray represent results when covariates (risk tolerance, age, economics background, trust in government, country) are considered. Significance levels: ★ $p < 0.1$; ★★ $p < 0.05$; ★★★ $p < 0.01$.

effect mediated, we observe that only 8.66% of the effect of being a female on compliance is mediated by scores at the SVO. Moreover, the impact of being female on SVO disappears ($p = 0.094$) when control variables are considered (in gray).[10]

To sum up, contrary to our expectations based on Grosch and Rau (2017), we can hardly claim that the impact of gender on tax compliance is mediated by subjects' SVO. Instead, females are more tax compliant than men in every round and every country, even while controlling for several variables.

> Result 3: *SVO does not mediate the effect of gender on tax compliance. Indeed, our mediation analysis demonstrates that the effect of gender on tax compliance barely budges when introducing the mediator.*

Concluding remarks

In this chapter, we tested if SVO mediates the effect of gender on tax compliance. We provide evidence suggesting that women are more tax compliant than men across a large sample of countries and institutional contexts. Though many studies have examined the role of SVO on social dilemma games, few have examined its effect on tax compliance. Our data supports

---

10 Investigating the role of subjective risk attitude, we observe in Table 10.5 that risk aversion is not a better mediator than SVO scores. Computing the proportion of total effect mediated, only 5.11% of the effect of being a female on compliance is mediated by self-perceived risk attitude.

218   John D'Attoma et al.

the idea that prosocial individuals are more tax compliant, and that levels of prosociality vary by gender in some countries but not all countries. Finally, we examine whether SVO mediates the effect of gender on tax compliance and conclude that women are more tax compliant despite being more prosocial.

This chapter makes three important contributions to the existing literature. First, we further explore and provide evidence which supports gender-based behavioral differences regarding tax compliance across a wide number of countries, regions, and institutional settings. Moreover, we extend previous literature by controlling for social values, determining that *despite* differences in SVO overall, there are still large gender differences in tax compliance. Secondly, we extend upon the SVO literature by demonstrating that though SVO varies by gender in some countries, it does not vary by gender in all countries. Prosociality is an important feature of most decisions that require cooperation, and thus scholars should explore what determines SVO and why it varies between genders in some countries, but not others. Finally, the extent and scope of our study make it one of the largest and most comprehensive tax compliance and SVO experiments to date.

One could also argue that SVO allocation and tax compliance decisions are just two sides of the same phenomenon. Even though both have been found to be significantly positively correlated together here, the magnitude of this correlation remains rather weak (Spearman's Þ = 0.30, Pearson's r = 0.28).

To conclude, our findings make three important contributions to the literature; however, our study still does not provide a definitive answer or shut the door on this important debate with regard to gender differences in tax compliance. From our research, along with many other studies mentioned in the literature review, it seems clear that there are large gender differences in the willingness to pay taxes. But, unfortunately, the literature does not seem to provide an answer to why this may be. Grosch and Rau (2017) suggest that gender differences in honesty are at least somewhat due to higher levels of prosociality in women. Though tax compliance is related to honesty, it encompasses several other motivations as well, such as cooperation, and therefore, it is not exactly the same. Indeed, we find that prosociality has very little mediating influence on the effect of gender on tax compliance. Therefore, further research should explore this interesting puzzle: why are women so tax compliant?

Acknowledgments

This project was funded by the European Research Council under the European Union's Seventh Framework Programme (FP7/2007–2013) / ERC Grant Agreement n. [295675]. [Anonymous] acknowledges an ESRC grant from Tax Administration Research Centre (TARC) for this research (ESCR Grant ES/S00713X/1).

References

Alm, J., Bernasconi, M., Laury, S., Lee, D. J., & Wallace, S. (2017). Culture, compliance, and confidentiality: Taxpayer behavior in the United States and Italy. *Journal of Economic Behavior & Organization, 140*, 176–196.

Alm, J., Kirchler, E., Muehlbacher, S., Gangl, K., Hofmann, E., Kogler, C., & Pollai, M. (2012). Rethinking the research paradigms for analysing tax compliance behaviour. *CESifo forum, 13*(2), 33–40.

Alm, J., & Malézieux, A. (2018). 40 years of tax evasion games: A meta-analysis. Working paper.

Alm, J., & Torgler, B. (2006). Culture differences and tax morale in the United States and in Europe. *Journal of Economic Psychology, 27*(2), 224–246.

Andreoni, J., Erard, B., & Feinstein, J. (1998). Tax compliance. *Journal of Economic Literature, 36*(2), 818–860.

Balliet, D., Parks, C., & Joireman, J. (2009). Social value orientation and cooperation in social dilemmas: A meta-analysis. *Group Processes & Intergroup Relations, 12*(4), 533–547.

Biziou-van-Pol, L., Haenen, J., Novaro, A., Liberman, A.O. & Capraro, V. (2015). Does telling white lies signal pro-social preferences? *Judgment and Decision Making, 10,* 538–548.

Brizi, A., Giacomantonio, M., Schumpe, B. M., & Mannetti, L. (2015). Intention to pay taxes or to avoid them: The impact of social value orientation. *Journal of Economic Psychology, 50*, 22–31.

Bruner, D. M., D'Attoma, J., & Steinmo, S. (2017). The role of gender in the provision of public goods through tax compliance. *Journal of Behavioral and Experimental Economics, 71*, 45–55.

Buchan, N. R., Croson, R. T., & Solnick, S. (2008). Trust and gender: An examination of behavior and beliefs in the Investment Game. *Journal of Economic Behavior & Organization, 68*(3–4), 466–476.

Byrnes, J. P., Miller, D. C., & Schafer, W. D. (1999). Gender differences in risk taking: A meta-analysis. *Psychological Bulletin, 125*(3), 367–383.

Calvet, R., & Alm, J. (2014). Empathy, sympathy, and tax compliance. *Journal of Economic Psychology, 40*, 62–82.

Capraro, V. (2018). Gender differences in lying in sender-receiver games: A meta-analysis. *Judgement and Decision Making, 13*(4), 345–355.

Charness, G., & Gneezy, U. (2012). Strong evidence for gender differences in risk taking. *Journal of Economic Behavior & Organization, 83*(1), 50–58.

Chung, J., & Trivedi, V. U. (2003). The effect of friendly persuasion and gender on tax compliance behavior. *Journal of Business Ethics, 47*(2), 133–145.

Croson, R., & Gneezy, U. (2009). Gender differences in preferences. *Journal of Economic Literature, 47*(2), 448–474.

Cummings, R. G., Martinez-Vazquez, J., McKee, M., & Torgler, B. (2009). Tax morale affects tax compliance: Evidence from surveys and an artefactual field experiment. *Journal of Economic Behavior & Organization, 70*(3), 447–457.

D'Attoma, J. (2017). Divided nation: The north–south cleavage in Italian tax compliance. *Polity, 49*(1), 69–99.

D'Attoma, J. (2020). More bang for your buck: Tax compliance in the United States and Italy. *Journal of Public Policy*, 1–24.

220 *John D'Attoma et al.*

D'Attoma, J., Volintiru, C., & Malézieux, A. (2018). Gender, social value orientation, and tax compliance. CESifo Working Paper No. 7372. Retrieved from https://papers.ssrn.com/sol3/papers.cfm?abstract_id=3338701.

D'Attoma, J., Volintiru, C., & Steinmo, S. (2017). Willing to share? Tax compliance and gender in Europe and America. *Research & Politics, 4*(2), 1–10.

Drus, M. (2016). *Happy taxpayers: How paying taxes can make people happy* (Unpublished doctoral thesis). University of Kansas, United States.

Dunn, E. W., Aknin, L. B., & Norton, M. I. (2014). Prosocial spending and happiness: Using money to benefit others pays off. *Current Directions in Psychological Science, 23*(1), 41–47.

Eckel, C. C., & Grossman, P. J. (2001). Chivalry and solidarity in ultimatum games. *Economic Inquiry, 39*(2), 171–188.

Erard, B., & Feinstein, J. (1994). The role of moral sentiments and audit perceptions in tax compliance. *Foundation Journal of Public Finance, 49*, 70–89.

Erat, S., & Gneezy, U. (2012). White lies. *Management Science, 58*(4), 723–733.

Falk, A., & Hermle, J. (2018). Relationship of gender differences in preferences to economic development and gender equality. *Science, 362*(6412), 1–6.

Feld, L. P., & Frey, B. S. (2002). Trust breeds trust: How taxpayers are treated. *Economics of Governance, 3*(2), 87–99.

Filippin, A., & Crosetto, P. (2016). A reconsideration of gender differences in risk attitudes. *Management Science, 62*(11), 3138–3160.

Fischbacher, U., & Föllmi-Heusi, F. (2013). Lies in disguise: An experimental study on cheating. *Journal of the European Economic Association, 11*(3), 525–547.

Gërxhani, K. (2007). Explaining gender differences in tax evasion: The case of Tirana, Albania. *Feminist Economics, 13*(2), 119–155.

Gilligan, C. (1982). *In a different voice.* Cambridge, MA: Harvard University Press.

Graetz, M. J., & Wilde, L. L. (1985). The economics of tax compliance: Fact and fantasy. *National Tax Journal, 38*(3), 355–363.

Greiner, B. (2015). Subject pool recruitment procedures: Organizing experiments with ORSEE. *Journal of the Economic Science Association, 1*(1), 114–125.

Grosch, K., & Rau, H. A. (2017). Gender differences in honesty: The role of social value orientation. *Journal of Economic Psychology, 62*, 258–267.

Guerra, A., & Harrington, B. (2018). Attitude–behavior consistency in tax compliance: A cross-national comparison. *Journal of Economic Behavior & Organization, 156*, 184–205.

Gylfason, H. F., Arnardottir, A. A., & Kristinsson, K. (2013). More on gender differences in lying. *Economics Letters, 119*(1), 94–96.

Hasseldine, J., & Hite, P. A. (2003). Framing, gender and tax compliance. *Journal of Economic Psychology, 24*(4), 517–533.

Hofmann, E., Voracek, M., Bock, C., & Kirchler, E. (2017). Tax compliance across sociodemographic categories: Meta-analyses of survey studies in 111 countries. *Journal of Economic Psychology, 62*, 63–71.

Kanagaretnam, K., Mestelman, S., Nainar, K., & Shehata, M. (2009). The impact of social value orientation and risk attitudes on trust and reciprocity. *Journal of Economic Psychology, 30*(3), 368–380.

Kogler, C., Batrancea, L., Nichita, A., Pantya, J., Belianin, A., & Kirchler, E. (2013). Trust and power as determinants of tax compliance: Testing the assumptions of the slippery slope framework in Austria, Hungary, Romania and Russia. *Journal of Economic Psychology, 34*, 169–180.

Murphy, R. (2019). *The European tax gap*. A report for the Socialists and Democrats Group in the European Parliament. Tax Research UK. Retrieved from www.socialistsanddemocrats.eu/sites/default/files/2019-01/the_european_tax_gap_en_190123.pdf.

Murphy, R. O., & Ackermann, K. A. (2014). Social value orientation: Theoretical and measurement issues in the study of social preferences. *Personality and Social Psychology Review, 18*(1), 13–41.

Murphy, R. O., Ackermann, K. A., & Handgraaf, M. J. (2011). Measuring social value orientation. *Judgment & Decision Making, 6*(8), 771–781.

Pampel, F., Andrighetto, G., & Steinmo, S. (2018). How institutions and attitudes shape tax compliance: A cross-national experiment and survey. *Social Forces, 97*(3), 1337–1364.

Pletzer, J. L., Balliet, D., Joireman, J., Kuhlman, D. M., Voelpel, S. C., & Van Lange, P. A. (2018). Social value orientation, expectations, and cooperation in social dilemmas: A meta-analysis. *European Journal of Personality, 32*(1), 62–83.

Richardson, G. (2006). Determinants of tax evasion: A cross-country investigation. *Journal of International Accounting, Auditing and Taxation, 15*(2), 150–169.

Richardson, G. (2008). The relationship between culture and tax evasion across countries: Additional evidence and extensions. *Journal of International Accounting, Auditing and Taxation, 17*(2), 67–78.

Steinmo, S. (1993). *Taxation and democracy: Swedish, British, and American approaches to financing the modern state*. New Haven, CT: Yale University Press.

Torgler, B. (2007). *Tax compliance and tax morale: A theoretical and empirical analysis*. Cheltenham: Edward Elgar Publishing.

Werdigier, J. (2011). Tax evasion costs governments $3.1 trillion annually, report says. *The New York Times*. Retrieved August 1, 2018, from www.nytimes.com/2011/11/26/business/global/26iht-tax26.html.

Zhang, N., Andrighetto, G., Ottone, S., Ponzano, F., & Steinmo, S. (2016). "Willing to pay?" Tax compliance in Britain and Italy: An experimental analysis. *PloS One, 11*(2), e0150277.

11 Tax compliance theories and fiduciary taxes

Do the shoes fit?

Elaine Doyle, Brian Keegan, and Eoin Reeves

Introduction

Theories focused on tax compliance fall broadly into two distinct categories; those emphasising rational economic behaviour by assuming that tax compliance decisions are taken to maximise outcomes for the taxpayer, and those which also recognise the moral, psychological, and social factors influencing tax compliance (Kornhauser, 2007; McKerchar & Evans, 2009). The link between both sets of theories is a focus on individual taxpayers and their relationship with the relevant revenue authority (James, 2012). That relationship is usually framed either in terms of the taxpayer's assessment of the capacity of the revenue authority to detect and penalise tax default, or in terms of respect for the revenue authority and the fairness of their approach along with social norms and trust in how the authorities deal with people and how the system is run (Likhovski, 2007; Rawlings, 2004). While undoubtedly shedding light on how some compliance decisions are made, this focus may obscure other important factors within tax systems of modern economies where fiduciary taxes paid on behalf of individual taxpayers make up a significant majority of the tax take. The two main taxes paid by individuals – income tax and value added tax (VAT) (or goods and services tax, depending on the jurisdiction) – are typically incurred by individual taxpayers as workers or consumers without necessarily having any direct contact with the revenue authority. For example, the employing organisation is an intermediary between the taxpayer and the revenue authority in the case of income tax. The organisation selling goods or services is an intermediary between the taxpayer and the revenue authority in the case of value added tax. In both cases, the organisation computes and remits the tax owing by the taxpayer to the revenue authority. Public attention is often drawn to the high-profile tax default of well-known individuals such as the Argentinian soccer star Lionel Messi (Aarons, 2016) or the actor Wesley Snipes (Glaister, 2008). Yet the tax collection consequences of a default by one individual taxpayer are minor in comparison to a default by an organisation of their fiduciary tax obligations.

Major failures in fiduciary tax compliance by organisations during the 1990s in Ireland led to a parliamentary enquiry into the banking sector. It

Tax compliance and fiduciary taxes 223

established that there was significant noncompliance in fiduciary tax obligations by organisations across the entire industry. The relevant organisations failed to withhold Deposit Interest Retention Tax or DIRT (which is a fiduciary tax) on the deposit interest paid on their customers' deposit accounts. This ultimately led to material exposures to tax, interest, and penalties for the banking organisations. The value of the settlements totalled IR£173.3m (€220m) or almost 2% of the entire income tax collected in Ireland during 2000 (Department of Finance, 2000). Furthermore, the correct operation of DIRT results in financial institutions reporting the existence of deposits held by individual taxpayers to the revenue authority. It transpired that 12,175 such depositors uncovered by the DIRT enquiry had used tax evasion techniques (Revenue Commissioners, 2016a). An additional €649m in underpaid tax, interest, and penalties was subsequently recovered from these depositors. The failure to operate DIRT by just 25 financial institutions prejudiced the tax compliance of 12,175 taxpayers.

As the DIRT enquiry illustrates, if the fiduciary system of computation and remittance breaks down, the consequences for tax yields are significant. Firstly, there is a multiplier effect associated with fiduciary taxes. A single default by an employer on payroll taxes can result in an income tax payment shortfall for however many employees are on the payroll. Second, there is potential damage to the normative effect of maintaining high levels of fiduciary tax compliance.

Extant research on taxpayer behaviour is almost entirely based on consideration of, or experimentation on, self-assessed income tax cases (Alm, Liu, & Zhang, 2019; Sapiei & Kasipillai, 2013), largely ignoring organisations and fiduciary taxes. This diminishes the capacity of the literature to explain or predict overall tax yields (Alm, 2011). Could the primary tax compliance theories have assisted in predicting the systemic failure within the Irish banking sector or be useful in shedding light on exactly what went wrong? In this chapter, we explore conceptually whether the existing tax compliance theories are appropriate in the context of tax compliance within developed countries relying heavily on fiduciary tax collection mechanisms.

Tax compliance theories

James and Alley (2002) describe the two dominant tax compliance theories. They identify the "Economic Approach", characterised by Expected Utility concepts but distinguish this from the "Behavioural Approach" involving issues of equity and fairness, and a desire on the part of the taxpayer to be a good citizen. Riahi-Belkaoui (2004) refers to the latter as fiscal psychology theories. Others have combined both ideas, for example, the slippery-slope model (Alm et al., 2012; Batrancea et al., 2019; Kirchler, Hoelzl, & Wahl, 2008). A brief description of the dominant tax compliance theories follows.

Expected Utility Theory (Allingham & Sandmo, 1972) states that decisions about risky or uncertain prospects are made by comparing their "expected utility" values – the values of outcomes multiplied by their respective probabilities. For the past half-decade, the theory has underpinned many theoretical and

224   *Elaine Doyle et al.*

research-based approaches to understanding tax compliance (Alm & Jacobson, 2007; Hashimzade, Myles, & Tran-Nam, 2013). Heinemann and Kocher (2010, p. 231) summarise Allingham and Sandmo's construct of Expected Utility Theory for tax compliance as follows:

> Investment into tax cheating will be the larger, the lower the risk of detection (determined by the audit system and the audit probability), the lower the potential loss (determined by the construction and the size of the fine), the higher the potential return (determined by the tax rate) and the lower the individual risk aversion (which is usually negatively correlated to income).

The four key influences in decision-making under Expected Utility Theory are therefore: (1) Risk of Detection; (2) Penalty; (3) Potential Return; and (4) Risk Aversion. As a predictive construct, the theory has problems (Frey, 2003; Horowitz & Horowitz, 2000; Kleven, Knudsen, Kreiner, Pedersen, & Saez, 2011; Sandmo, 2005; Torgler, 2007). It deviates from the real world in numerous respects. For example, it fails to recognise that advanced economies typically make extensive use of third party information reporting whereby employers, banks, investment funds, and pension funds report the taxable income of individuals directly to the revenue authority (Kleven *et al.*, 2011). It also leads to predicted compliance levels not compatible with empirical observations (the model predicts too much tax evasion). Expected Utility Theory is entirely predicated on the taxpayer being an independent agent, capable of taking a decision about whether to comply, and personally suffering the consequences of their decision (Alm *et al.*, 2012).

Prospect Theory involves framing and is an extension of Expected Utility Theory (Kahneman, 2011). Guthrie (2003) identifies four elements of Prospect Theory which differentiate it from standard utility theory. Firstly, individuals evaluate choices relative to some reference point – often the status quo. In assessing possible outcomes, gains or losses are evaluated in relative rather than absolute terms. Second, individuals will take decisions that tend to guard against losses, but will be willing to wager at the prospect of a gain. Third, individuals suffer losses more than they enjoy gains, even if the absolute amounts are the same. Finally, Prospect Theory suggests biases in people's minds in assessing the likelihood of an event.

Earlier the articulation of tax decisions within Expected Utility Theory by Heinemann and Kocher (2010) was cited. Using the same construct to articulate tax decisions within Prospect Theory would read as follows (Prospect Theory concepts in bold):

> Investment into tax cheating will be the larger, the lower the risk of detection (determined by the audit system and the perception of audit probability shaped by the taxpayer's own experience), the lower the potential loss (determined by the taxpayer's relative circumstances before and

Tax compliance and fiduciary taxes 225

after the decision), the higher the potential return (also determined by the taxpayer's relative circumstances before and after the decision) and the lower the individual risk aversion (which is greater in contemplation of a loss than in expectation of a gain).

There is conflicting evidence about the applicability of Prospect Theory in a tax compliance context (Choo, Fonseca, & Myles, 2016; Kahneman, 2011). One feature of Expected Utility models (including Prospect Theory) is that they assume an individual pays taxes only because of the economic consequences of noncompliance (Alm, 2011). They disregard the possibility of the rational economic actor taking decisions for moral or ethical reasons. The significance of a sense of fairness and a moral imperative to comply underpins theories of taxpayer behaviour known collectively as tax morale (Kornhauser, 2007). Kornhauser observes that within the construct of tax morale, correct conduct in tax compliance is in itself its own reward. Torgler (2008) has described tax morale as the intrinsic motivation to pay taxes.

Factors of importance when looking at tax morale include: the taxpayer's belief that it is morally or ethically wrong to evade tax due; his/her perception of the fairness of the tax system; his/her perception of normal tax compliance behaviour within the trade; his/her degree of respect for the revenue authority and; his/her appreciation of the broader social contract which recognises that taxes must be paid if social services are to be maintained (McKerchar, Bloomquist, & Pope, 2013).

In an attempt to combine the main tax compliance theories, Kirchler *et al.* (2008) propose a "slippery-slope" model. This model considers the relationship between authorities and citizens, and the climate of interaction: antagonistic vs. synergistic. The authors suggest that if a tax system is seen by taxpayers to be legitimate, it will be complied with. The key elements of the slippery-slope model are, first, an awareness of the power of the tax authorities – their perceived potential in the minds of taxpayers to detect and to punish evasion and, second, trust in the tax authorities – taxpayers' perception of tax authorities as benevolent and working for the common good. According to this model, tax compliance will be maximised where both power and trust are in abundant supply. Conversely, where the taxpayer is indifferent to the power of the tax authority, and/or where the taxpayer does not trust that the tax authority is working towards the common good, tax compliance rates will fall. The contribution of Kirchler and his colleagues is their attempt to unify Expected Utility concepts with tax morale concepts. The "power" axis of Kirchler's "slippery-slope framework" encompasses the risk of detection and the application of penalties intrinsic to Expected Utility Theory and Prospect Theory. The "trust" axis encompasses tax morale values such as trust in the revenue authority and an appreciation of the fairness of the tax system.

All these tax compliance theories and the slippery-slope model are predicated on a simplified model involving a taxpayer at personal financial risk interacting with a revenue authority capable of detecting and penalising wrongdoing. They

226 *Elaine Doyle et al.*

also include the impact of moral, psychological, and social factors in influencing compliance decisions. The drawback of these approaches is that they fail to acknowledge that most taxes are collected by organisations using fiduciary methods.

Fiduciary taxes

Most taxpayers pay tax at source, for instance through the application of VAT or GST on their purchases or on their income through the operation of "pay as you earn" (PAYE) on payroll. In such instances, tax compliance is a matter entirely outside their control. Organisations act as fiduciaries when withholding taxes from their customers, employees, or other stakeholders. The organisation collects tax "in trust". To put this into context, between them, income tax and VAT, which are largely collected as fiduciary taxes, make up 66% of the tax take in Ireland (2017) and 51% in the UK for (2017/18) (HM Revenue & Customs, 2018; HM Revenue & Customs KAI Indirect Taxes Customs & Coordination, 2018; Revenue Commissioners, 2018). Drilling down into the Irish figures reveals that 73% of the tax yield for the financial year 2017 consisted of fiduciary taxes (Revenue Commissioners, 2018). In the tax year 2017/18, income tax collected by fiduciary methods represented approximately 58% of income tax collected in the UK (HM Revenue & Customs KAI Indirect Taxes Customs & Coordination, 2018).

Furthermore, it appears that the most serious forms of tax default involve failures in observing fiduciary tax obligations. There were 388 cases of tax default in Ireland published by the Irish revenue authority (hereafter Irish Revenue) in 2015. In 85% of cases, the tax default listed involved a failure by an organisation to operate correctly fiduciary taxes. Irish Revenue secured court prosecutions in 16 cases of serious tax evasion during 2015 with 28 convictions. Of these cases all except one concerned fiduciary tax default (Revenue Commissioners, 2016b). It is clear from the published outcomes that the instances of tax default in Ireland most susceptible to public prosecution are usually defaults in fiduciary tax compliance.

Comparable figures for the UK are not published to the same degree of granularity, but a 2015 report from the UK National Audit Office suggests that the majority of prosecutions for tax fraud concern fiduciary taxes. Sixty-nine percent of the cases prosecuted in the UK in the tax year 2014/15 concerned VAT and Excise Duties, both fiduciary taxes. A further 22% concerned an aggregate category of Income Tax, National Insurance Contributions, Capital Gains Tax, and Inheritance Taxes, some element of which would have involved fiduciary tax (National Audit Office, 2015).

This suggests that when considering tax compliance, a nuanced understanding of the different types of taxes and collection methodologies is required. The discussion must recognise the role of fiduciary tax collection and the organisations accountable for it. This form of organisational compliance behaviour is not well understood. Joulfaian (2009) describes the scant availability of empirical research on business tax evasion as being in sharp contrast to the "voluminous" literature on individual compliance behaviour. Others have lamented the scarcity of empirical research regarding large organisations' tax behaviour in the context of the importance of corporate tax compliance (Siglé, Goslinga, Speklé, van der Hel, & Veldhuizen, 2018). We begin below to explore this area by examining the existing tax theories in the context of organisations.

Tax compliance theories and organisations

Nur-tegin (2008) suggests that the approach to studying organisational compliance behaviours should be different to that taken for individuals. Cullis, Jones, and Lewis (2006) note that Expected Utility Theory is founded on the concept of rational economic man. The caricature involves a rational individual actor egoistic in terms of economic self-interest. In an organisational context, it is necessary to consider if there are differences in how organisations measure value. Studies examining the impact of economic factors on the tax compliance behaviour of organisations have found some similarities between organisations and individual taxpayers (Hoopes, Mescall, & Pittman, 2012; Joulfaian, 2000; Kamdar, 1997). However, additional issues arise because of the separation of ownership and control (Chen & Chu, 2005; Crocker & Slemrod, 2005; Hanlon & Heitzman, 2010). Do organisations start from a different position in assessing tax risk and measuring tax compliance utility than individual taxpayers – in short, are they likely to take different types of tax compliance decisions than individual taxpayers? The impact of imposing penalties on tax managers if tax evasion is discovered was theoretically examined by Crocker and Slemrod (2005). They found that penalties imposed on tax managers are more effective in reducing evasion than those imposed on shareholders. Chen and Chu (2005) explored theoretically the link between internal control and the external evasion decisions of businesses, concluding that tax evasion increases organisational profit. However this is subject to the risk of being detected and also at the cost of loss of internal control efficiency. Empirical research suggests that audits act as an effective deterrent to corporate tax noncompliance but find that an increase in penalties does not increase compliance (Kamdar, 1997).

Kahneman (2011) observes that the impact of Prospect Theory heuristics may be less pronounced in organisational decision-making. Describing them as factories that manufacture judgements and decisions, he asserts that organisations are better than individuals are when it comes to avoiding errors, in part because they have the power to impose orderly procedures upon themselves.

Turning to tax morale, are organisations, or the compliance decision makers working within them, influenced by moral, psychological, and social factors? There is evidence that tax professionals believing strongly in the importance of ethical and socially responsible behaviour are more committed to ensuring their clients are tax compliant (Shafer & Simmons, 2008). Tax professionals who believe corporate ethics and social responsibility to be important are also significantly less likely to express intentions to facilitate tax fraud by a

228 *Elaine Doyle et al.*

client (Shafer, Simmons, & Yip, 2016). However, both these studies examine tax practitioners in private practice advising clients, thereby shedding limited light on the issue of tax morale in an organisational context. Moral persuasion approaches failed to enhance the tax reporting behaviour of corporations in a study in Israel (Ariel, 2012). The author points to the importance of groups of actors holding various degrees of responsibility, distinguishing corporate tax compliance from individual compliance. Employees acting on behalf of organisations experience different incentives than individual taxpayers who bear the tax burden personally. They are also able to hire professional advisors to manage tax planning and compliance activities, placing them in a stronger position to contest tax laws (Siglé *et al.*, 2018). Alm and McClellan (2012) blame the absence of firm-level information, that would allow a firm's tax morale to be measured, for firm-level tax morale being largely ignored. They found that enforcement efforts had little impact on tax reporting at firm level. However, reducing obstacles to compliance, especially corruption and complexity, had a positive impact.

Corporate tax risk management has been historically described as "a bit of a black art, not necessarily understood even by those in the tax function" (PricewaterhouseCoopers, 2004, p. 2; cited by Wunder, 2009, p. 15). Hanlon and Heitzman (2010, p. 139) describe the literature on corporate tax compliance as "relatively young" and call for research examining the role of executives on the tax compliance behaviour of corporates. Siglé *et al.* (2018, p. 5) observe that a more nuanced understanding of the real world factors that determine tax compliance decisions of large organisations will contribute to improved regulatory strategies for such organisations, which will benefit tax authorities in their fight against corporate tax evasion. The dominant tax compliance theories have seldom been examined within an organisational context to explain the linkage between tax compliance stimulus and tax compliance outcomes, either for direct or for fiduciary taxes. As we can see from the above, the studies that have been conducted at an organisation level tend to focus on a limited number of variables to examine corporate tax compliance in a quantitative manner (Alm & McClellan, 2012; Joulfaian, 2000; Kamdar, 1997; Siglé *et al.*, 2018). Their findings have yielded mixed results.

In order to move the existing theoretical models forward, we first need to understand their applicability in an organisational context. This will give us a stronger base from which to test empirically the relevant variables and models in subsequent research studies. When considering organisations, we must recognise that they do not think, feel, make decisions, or have observable behaviour. Ultimately, organisational decisions are made by individuals employed by the organisation. Taking this agency perspective to its logical extreme, it is the behaviour of the individuals working on the organisation's tax affairs that may shed light on corporate tax compliance behaviour (Killian, 2006). As such, it is necessary to understand the practical experience of those who are responsible, at least in part, for the tax compliance decisions taken by organisations.

Conclusions

The dominant theories of tax compliance and research into taxpayer behaviour derive from Expected Utility Theory, Prospect Theory, and theories of tax morale – the "intrinsic motivation" to pay taxes (Frey, 2003). These theories are most often considered in the literature in the context of tax compliance decisions made by self-assessed taxpayers who are in a direct relationship with the revenue authority and who will bear, in full, the consequences of their compliance decision. The prevailing theories of tax compliance behaviour have their advantages and disadvantages, but none seem able to describe or predict empirically established compliance levels. It is unclear as to the extent to which theories of tax compliance apply equally to individuals and organisations, as most of the theoretical and experimental work has involved tax compliance decisions by individuals and there is some evidence to suggest that there is a different context for organisational compliance behaviour.

In monetary terms, fiduciary tax compliance by organisations yields far more tax than direct tax compliance by individuals. The more serious forms of tax default often involve failure to operate fiduciary taxes. However, despite their role in operating fiduciary taxes, the contribution of organisations to overall tax compliance appears neglected.

This chapter aimed to explore this area by questioning whether the primary tax compliance theories can explain tax compliance behaviour within an organisation discharging its fiduciary tax obligations. Our objective is to bring the role of the organisation in tax compliance and particularly the contribution of fiduciary taxes to the overall tax yield into sharper focus. Alm (2011) commented that the puzzle of tax compliance behaviour may well be why people pay taxes, not why they evade them. We would argue that one of the reasons is that tax is withheld by organisations with an obligation to collect fiduciary taxes. As a result, at no point is there an actual tax compliance decision taken by the individual in relation to those taxes. Instead, the decision makers within organisations are key actors in modern tax systems, and while they have been largely ignored in the tax compliance literature to date, their tax decision-making behaviour is likely to shape the success or otherwise of the tax system as a whole. We suggest here that a focus on the individual taxpayer's compliance decision in the context of his or her direct engagement with a revenue authority needs to be broadened out to encompass this reality.

References

Aarons, E. (2016). Lionel Messi handed 21-month tax fraud sentence but is unlikely to serve time. *The Guardian*, 6 July. Retrieved on 15 December 2019 from www.theguardian.com/football/2016/jul/06/lionel-messi-barcelona-prison-21-months-tax-fraud.

Allingham, M. G., & Sandmo, A. (1972). Income tax evasion: A theoretical analysis. *Journal of Public Economics*, 1, 323–338.

230   *Elaine Doyle et al.*

Alm, J. (2011). Measuring, explaining, and controlling tax evasion: Lessons from theory, experiments, and field studies. *International Tax and Public Finance, 19*(1), 54–77.

Alm, J., & Jacobson, S. (2007). Using laboratory experiments in public economics. *National Tax Journal, 60*(1), 129–152.

Alm, J., Kirchler, E., Muehlbacher, S., Gangl, K., Hofmann, E., Kogler, C., & Pollai, M. (2012). Rethinking the research paradigms for analysing tax compliance behaviour. *CESifo Forum, 13*(2), 33–40.

Alm, J., Liu, Y., & Zhang, K. (2019). Financial constraints and firm tax evasion. *International Tax and Public Finance, 26*(1), 71–102.

Alm, J., & McClellan, C. (2012). Tax morale and tax compliance from the firm's perspective. *Kyklos, 65*(1), 1–17.

Ariel, B. (2012). Deterrence and moral persuasion effects on corporate tax compliance: Findings from a randomized controlled trial. *Criminology, 50*(1), 27–69.

Batrancea, L., Nichita, A., Olsen, J., Kogler, C., Kirchler, E., Hoelzl, E. … & Zukauskas, S. (2019). Trust and power as determinants of tax compliance across 44 nations. *Journal of Economic Psychology, 74*, 102191.

Chen, K. P., & Chu, C. Y. C. (2005). Internal control versus external manipulation: A model of corporate income tax evasion. *RAND Journal of Economics, 36*(1), 151–164.

Choo, C. Y. L., Fonseca, M. A., & Myles, G. D. (2016). Do students behave like real taxpayers in the lab? Evidence from a real effort tax compliance experiment. *Journal of Economic Behavior & Organization, 124*, 102–114.

Crocker, K. J., & Slemrod, J. (2005). Corporate tax evasion with agency costs. *Journal of Public Economics, 89*(9), 1593–1610.

Cullis, J., Jones, P., & Lewis, A. (2006). Tax framing, instrumentality and individual differences: Are there two different cultures? *Journal of Economic Psychology, 27*(2), 304–320.

Department of Finance (2000). *Budget statistics and tables 2001*. Dublin. Retrieved on 15 December 2019 from www.budget.gov.ie/Budgets/2001/Tables.aspx.

Frey, B. S. (2003). Deterrence and tax morale in the European Union. *European Review, 11*(3), 385–406.

Glaister, D. (2008). Snipes jailed for three years for tax evasion. *The Guardian*, 25 April. Retrieved on 15 December 2019 from www.theguardian.com/film/news/story/0,,2276261,00.html.

Guthrie, C. (2003). Prospect theory, risk preference, and the law. *Northwestern University Law Review, 97*(3), 1115–1163.

Hanlon, M., & Heitzman, S. (2010). A review of tax research. *Journal of Accounting and Economics, 50*(2), 127–178.

Hashimzade, N., Myles, G. D., & Tran-Nam, B. (2013). Applications of behavioural economics to tax evasion. *Journal of Economic Surveys, 27*(5), 941–977.

Heinemann, F., & Kocher, M. (2010). Tax compliance under tax regime changes. Munich Discussion Paper No. 2010–17. Retrieved from https://epub.ub.uni-muenchen.de/11443/1/Heinemann_Kocher_20100320.pdf.

HM Revenue & Customs (2018). *Income tax receipts statistics*.

HM Revenue & Customs KAI Indirect Taxes Customs & Coordination (2018). *HMRC Tax & NIC Receipts*.

Hoopes, J. L., Mescall, D., & Pittman, J. A. (2012). Do IRS audits deter corporate tax avoidance? *The Accounting Review, 87*(5), 1603–1639.

Horowitz, I., & Horowitz, A. R. (2000). Tax audit uncertainty and the work-versus-leisure decision. *Public Finance Review, 28*(6), 491–510.

James, S. (2012). Behavioural economics and the risks of tax administration. *eJournal of Tax Research, 10*(2), 345–363.

James, S., & Alley, C. (2002). Tax compliance, self-assessment and tax administration. Munich Personal RePEc Archive.

Joulfaian, D. (2000). Corporate income tax evasion and managerial preferences. *The Review of Economics and Statistics, 82*(4), 698–701.

Joulfaian, D. (2009). Bribes and business tax evasion. *European Journal of Comparative Economics, 6*(2), 227–244.

Kahneman, D. (2011). *Thinking, fast and slow.* New York: Macmillan.

Kamdar, N. (1997). Corporate income tax compliance: A time series analysis. *Atlantic Economic Journal, 25*(1), 37–49.

Killian, S. (2006). Where's the harm in tax competition? Lessons from US multinationals in Ireland. *Critical Perspectives on Accounting, 17*(8), 1067–1087.

Kirchler, E., Hoelzl, E., & Wahl, I. (2008). Enforced versus voluntary tax compliance: The "slippery slope" framework. *Journal of Economic Psychology, 29*(2), 210–225.

Kleven, H. J., Knudsen, M. B., Kreiner, C. T., Pedersen, S., & Saez, E. (2011). Unwilling or unable to cheat? Evidence from a tax audit experiment in Denmark. *Econometrica, 79*(3), 651–692.

Kornhauser, M. E. (2007). A tax morale approach to compliance. *Florida Tax Review, 8*(6), 599–640.

Likhovski, A. (2007). "Training in citizenship": Tax compliance and modernity. *Law & Social Enquiry, 32*(3), 665–700.

McKerchar, M., Bloomquist, K., & Pope, J. (2013). Indicators of tax morale: An exploratory study. *eJournal of Tax Research, 11*(1), 5–22.

McKerchar, M., & Evans, C. (2009). Sustaining growth in developing economies through improved taxpayer compliance: Challenges for policy makers and revenue authorities. *eJournal of Tax Research, 7*(2), 171–201.

National Audit Office (2015). *Tackling tax fraud: How HMRC responds to tax evasion, the hidden economy and criminal attacks.* Retrieved on 15 December 2019 from www.nao. org.uk/wp-content/uploads/2015/12/Tackling-tax-fraud-how-HMRC-responds-to-tax-evasion-the-hidden-economy-and-criminal-attacks.pdf.

Nur-tegin, K. D. (2008). Determinants of business tax compliance. *B. E. Journal of Economic Analysis and Policy: Topics in Economic Analysis and Policy, 8*(1), 1–28.

PricewaterhouseCoopers (2004). *Tax risk management.* London: PwC.

Rawlings, G. (2004). Cultural narratives of taxation and citizenship: Fairness, groups and globalisation. Centre for Tax System Integrity, Research School of Social Sciences, Australian National University No. 52.

Revenue Commissioners (2016a). Annual report 2015. Dublin.

Revenue Commissioners (2016b). Prosecutions archive – 2015. Dublin. Retrieved on 15 December 2019 from www.revenue.ie/en/press/prosecutions/archive/index. html.

Revenue Commissioners (2018). Annual report 2017. Dublin.

Riahi-Belkaoui, A. (2004). Relationship between tax compliance internationally and selected determinants of tax morale. *Journal of International Accounting, Auditing and Taxation, 13*(2), 135–143.

Sandmo, A. (2005). The theory of tax evasion: A retrospective view. *National Tax Journal, 58*(4), 643–663.

Sapiei, N. S., & Kasipillai, J. (2013). External tax professionals' views on compliance behaviour of corporation. *American Journal of Economics, 3*(2), 82–89.

232 *Elaine Doyle et al.*

Shafer, W. E., & Simmons, R. S. (2008). Social responsibility, Machiavellianism and tax avoidance: A study of Hong Kong tax professionals. *Accounting, Auditing & Accountability Journal, 21*(5), 695–720.

Shafer, W. E., Simmons, R. S., & Yip, R. W. Y. (2016). Social responsibility, professional commitment and tax fraud. *Accounting, Auditing & Accountability Journal, 29*(1), 111–134.

Siglé, M., Goslinga, S., Speklé, R., van der Hel, L., & Veldhuizen, R. (2018). Corporate tax compliance: Is a change towards trust-based tax strategies justified? *Journal of International Accounting, Auditing and Taxation, 32*, 3–16.

Torgler, B. (2007). *Tax compliance and tax morale: A theoretical and empirical analysis.* Cheltenham: Edward Elgar.

Torgler, B. (2008). What do we know about tax fraud? An overview of recent developments. *Social Research, 75*(4), 1239–1270.

Wunder, H. F. (2009). Tax risk management and the multinational enterprise. *Journal of International Accounting, Auditing and Taxation, 18*(1), 14–28.

12 How to tax the powerful and the sophisticated?

Paul Frijters, Katharina Gangl, and Benno Torgler

Introduction

Taxes are the fuel that makes civilisation work (Adams, 1993). It is said that the history of civilisation is the history of taxation: in order to build the palaces[1] and fund the scribes, rulers have relied on taxing their populations. No taxes means no palaces and no records of what humans were up to.

Thus, the role of taxation was as critical 6000 years ago as it is today for modern nation-state bureaucracies. As the inscription over the entrance to the Internal Revenue Service building in Washington, DC states, "taxes are what we pay for a civilized society". In his magnum opus *The History of Government*, Finer (1999, p. 81) stated that as a general rule "the more differentiated the polity, the more it needs to levy taxation".

By implementing effective taxation, kings and bureaucracies have funded education, armies, public goods, and the indoctrination activities needed to self-replicate into the next generation. Whether one views taxation as organised theft or as the "quid" in a "quid pro quo" social contract between rulers and ruled, taxation provides the lifeblood of kingdoms and nations.

Throughout the history of civilisation, it is rare to find a tax system in which the powerful and rich did not distort it to their advantage (for a discussion, see Finer, 1999). For example, during the Roman Empire, fiscal privileges were given to a small but enormously wealthy Senatorial Order, which additionally enriched itself at state expense by making illicit profits from monopolised offices. After the Empire became officially Christian, priests and other clergy enjoyed tax immunity on their increasing endowed estates despite being paid better than civil servants. In late-medieval Europe, for example, the extensive nobility secured exemption from the direct land tax *taille*, a model that inspired many imitators in late-medieval Europe. At the end of the T'Ang dynasty

---

1 Structures such as the Egyptian pyramids or the Great Wall of China were built by an intensive mobilisation of forced labour, which in China was also often partly integrated into the fiscal system as the population was subject to tax contributions and forced labour. When the Han dynasty set to build their new capital in 192 BC, nearly 150,000 male and female conscripts were recruited (Finer, 1999).

234 *Paul Frijters et al.*

(874–907) and in the Roman Republic individuals paid large bribes to become provincial governors. Finer (1999, p. 797), for instance, refers to a T'Ang official who paid 2 million strings of cash in ready money. Obviously, most borrowed the money as the bribe was estimated to be recouped three times over the course of a single provincial tenure.

In recent decades, Western bureaucracies have failed to tax the most sophisticated and wealthiest of its citizens and organisations (Frijters & Foster, 2015; Murray & Frijters, 2017). Via a myriad of accounting tricks, the "plutocrats" have been increasingly successful in avoiding taxation. Whether it is via nominally transferring all ownership to a barren rock in the Pacific Ocean, or by declaring oneself a charitable organisation with unusually high expense accounts, the plutocrats have beaten the tax system (Zucman, 2013, 2014).

Unchecked, the plutocrats would end up controlling all major areas of organised production without contributing to the public good, which would mean a collapse in the tax system as a whole. That would be socially destructive and lead to a break-up of the nation-state or a revolt by its citizens. There is a way out for the most able of the middle classes unwilling to pay for the plutocrats: they can migrate to other countries to sell their human capital where their tax burden is lower (Epstein, Hillman, & Ursprung, 1999). Due to an increasing uniformity in culture and languages, those with human capital to sell have more and more alternative marketplaces to which they can migrate.

The tax evasion of the plutocrats also erodes the belief in a joint national identity with shared responsibility. Plutocrats in a sense are then no longer part of the population but have taken over the role of rulers, without taking on the role of custodians that real rulers have. This weakening ultimately would make the nation an easy prey for other nations and other cohesive groups.

Thus, the tax authorities will have to find a counter-move to the tax avoidance of the plutocrats. It can be delayed by the plutocrats: for example, they have so far managed to disband investigative units in Western tax offices that have gone after them, but the needs of the nation trump even the games of capture played by its elites. External threats or internal revival will force the issue.

In this chapter we therefore present a brief and stylised history of taxation, followed by a plan for how to tax the plutocrats based on tributes. A spin-doctor might label the proposal "market-determined contributory taxation". A more apt name would be "blackmail taxation".

A very brief history of taxation

Recurrent taxation

Recurrent taxation started some 5000–10,000 years ago with overlords putting levies on farmers: under the threat of kicking them off their land, brutal violence, and denying them access to water, local warlords were able to demand regular levies from farmers (Carlson, 2005; Pennisi, 2012). The demands could be based on the weather, the amount of cultivated land, and the skill of the farmer and his extended family. If the local warlord knew less about the circumstances of the farmers and lacked the capacity of finding out what was going on, levies would be more crude and constant: so many bushels per family, every year, and a bit more when the local warlord went to war. The local warlord himself would be taxed by a king: the warlord of warlords. The lower warlords would owe the king taxes, whether in the form of wheat, help in times of war against another king or upstart warlord, or labour when he wanted something constructed (Carmona & Ezzamel, 2007). Hence early recurrent taxation was primarily about getting something from the majority that was unable to resist (farmers), and for the warlords to fight it out amongst themselves as to who could tax the other warlords (Bonney, 1999). Apart from the king and his retinue, everybody of means paid taxes.

One could go further back in time than the advent of the early agricultural kingdoms with organised levies on farmers, but it gets less clear what is meant by recurrent taxation. Activities of roaming gangs of bandits terrorising independent simple farming communities, the hierarchical relations between men and women or the intergenerational systems in which youngsters were used by elders to get things done could all be seen as "recurrent taxation". But these were not organised systems with dedicated institutions to collect and calculate taxes.

Recurrent taxation is institutionalised resource extraction, which is regular in its timing. It is distinct from own production, but related to a production hierarchy in which the top gets a slice of the output of the whole. Getting a slice from the proceeds of a hierarchical organisation, such as when a king has his own vassals or runs a brothel (a very normal means of generating revenue for a long time (McGinn, 2013)), is a form of recurrent taxation because the slice comes off the production generated by others and is institutionalised. Particularly if the slice comes about via an internal levy-getting unit and is recurrent, such as when the prostitutes have to cough up a certain amount every month, the gains from hierarchy are virtually identical to that of a tax office.

These early forms of recurrent taxation were crude and had inherent disadvantages: if farmers could not pay due to accidental circumstances (such as the weather), a warlord had to mete out punishment to keep his authority, but this was costly, since a killed farmer represented a loss of investment and a disgruntled extended family or village. There was also no inherent mechanism for the warlord to maximise the ultimate resource under his control (land or water): he did not necessarily have the most productive farmers on his land, nor did his farmers have much incentive to work harder than taxation and their own needs required.

Over time, other forms of taxation arose, centred around different types of economic activity and war, as well as around innovations in bureaucratic control such as incidental taxation or seigniorage tax (Cooper, 1982). Taxation became less crude.

Incidental taxation

Incidental taxation probably originated with trade. Trade probably preceded agriculture, but we have little knowledge of whether there was meaningful taxation on that early trade. We imagine the Fertile Crescent – the region where agriculture and hierarchical kingdoms first arose – as having dense groups of hunter-gatherers before the advent of agriculture around 10,000 years ago. We currently think there were semi-permanent villages and bands that were constrained by others in their ability to move around. It is hard to know whether groups occupying a territory demanded some kind of payment for passing their territory, or whether they had a system of hospitality and information sharing with strangers (which is another kind of taxation-on-information), since written records of cultures were not made during the first several thousands of years of agriculture. But the subsistence bases of all the earliest major states of antiquity in Mesopotamia, Egypt, Indus Valley, and Yellow River were grain states; thus units of grain served as standards of measurement and value for trade and tribute against which the value of other commodities (including labour) was calculated. The Roman Empire, for example, did not extend much beyond the grain line (Scott, 2017). In addition, above-ground grains had the advantage of being assessable by state tax collectors who also classified fields in terms of soil quality. Where the grain stopped, state power also began to degrade, which explains (for example) why the power of early Chinese states was confined to the arable drainage basin of the Yellow and Yangzi Rivers (see also Scott, 2017, p. 134). Thus, fixed capital – usually land – is taxable in a way that is virtually impossible with movables (Finer, 1999). Hunters and gatherers, maritime foragers, mobile pastoralists, or shifting cultivators who actually traded and exchanged vigorously with the "grain people" were too dispersed, variable in community size, and mobile to be tracked. For example, the Ottoman Empire was founded by pastoralists, and found it very difficult to tax herders at the one moment of the year when they stopped for lambing and shearing (Scott, 2017). But tax-avoidance practices such as harvesting some of the grains before they were fully ripe led Archaic states to mandate a planting time for a given district (Scott, 2017). In ancient Egypt elaborate surveys called cadastre were used to assess the income the land brought in. But price changes, yield changes, and owner changes made it difficult to keep the cadastre up to date. This led to situations such as that in Ming China that the assessment became more and more outdated. Moreover, large landowners had various extra-legal modes of tax evasion (Finer, 1999).

When more hierarchical groups emerged that had significant and permanent violent potential at their disposal (soldiers fed off agricultural surplus), trade became more intense and subject to taxation. The obvious ways to tax trade were to control the passages over rivers, seas, and mountains that traders would have to negotiate (Pennisi, 2012). Demanding a proportion of the value of the traded goods (or a flat fee) was thereby a different early form of taxation. We would now call them import duties, which are usually proportional to value, or tolls, which are usually flat fees. Import duties and tolls are incidental because they are not necessarily recurrent. Yet, of course, when trade becomes more regular and subject to seasons, the distinction between taxing farmers and traders starts to blur.

The specialisation and concentration of production that became possible with trade and with permanent cities allowed for another form of incidental taxation: the organisation of trade itself and access to that trade. Physical markets where goods are traded are prime examples of club goods provided by authorities who hold the monopoly of violence, to which access fees could be levied from both traders and customers. Those could have been one-off fees, or based on a particular period. In a way, this is the logical next step after taxing existing trade routes: building a platform where trade is easier, and then taxing access to that platform. The early markets in Sumeria and Babylon were thus the ancient forerunners of eBay and Jobseek. In those days, the fees would have probably included access fees, and nowadays the fees come in the form of advertising space (a tax on concentration and time).

The right to sell specific agricultural goods with access to urban markets and monopoly rights to provide luxury clothing, jewellery, boats, and other items of high value would have been worth a lot. Rulers could charge for granting that right, promising to leave the trader alone who had obtained the monopoly and promising to kill any competitors that violated the monopoly.

This type of access fee continues to exist to this day, with particular countries or cities charging fees for particular firms to be the monopoly supplier of cable television, radio waves, or coffee on the beach. One of the main reasons this type of taxation can be seen a lot in less developed countries today, and why it was one of the main sources of taxation in most Western countries until a few centuries ago, is that this form of taxation is particularly easy to collect (Adams, 1993). In order to collect the monopoly-granting fee, the taxing authority does not need to observe all the buyers, all the sellers, or have a continuous presence on roads or rivers. The taxing authority in essence only needs to be able to credibly grant immunity to one trader should the taxing authorities or their representatives meet him, while being able to kill any competitor should they come across one of those. In addition, the monopoly trader is highly motivated and able in assisting to sustain this access arrangement (*e.g.*, by spying on the rest) which further increases the ease of policing.

Seigniorage tax

When the circulation of money with less innate value than the mandated (face) value became accepted, another form of taxation on trade arose, similar in spirit to charging access to a physical market place. Brass coins or paper money had a higher mandated value (*i.e.*, the conversion rate with gold and other precious metals) than intrinsic value (*i.e.*, the cost of making it). This allowed authorities to cheat on the combined stock of money in a whole economy by simply producing more of the money and spending it, something called seigniorage tax.

238   *Paul Frijters et al.*

Unlike taxing steady streams of production or trade, seigniorage tax is more effective if it is done one-off and unexpectedly: the less expected the printing of more money, the greater the purchasing value of the additional money because traders and consumers will not initially know there is now more money for the same amount of goods, and will hence not immediately increase their prices. If consumers and traders do anticipate increased printing of money, they will increase their prices and also move their own money holdings into goods or foreign forms of money so as to avoid the tax.

Seigniorage tax is thereby a form of robbery, as it works much like a raid on physical goods, which also works best if the raid is unexpected. The distortions of such a tax are enormous, with individuals and communities trying to avoid the raids or defend against them, such as by moving money holdings or using different types of money.

Tribute tax

The monopoly of violence of past kingdoms also allowed a form of indirect taxation – the tribute – which involved having the actual taxation of production and trade carried out by another entity. A tribute is a regular payment made by one ruler or region to another in order to avoid being killed or punished (Adams, 1993). The canonical example is the tribute in grain from Egypt to Rome, an arrangement that continued for centuries, allowing the Roman rulers to hand out grain to their population and maintain an empire. On the other side of the Eurasian continent, the Chinese rulers paid tributes of valuables and women to the Mongolian warlords in order to secure their safety. And of course, the protection rackets of the mafia and other criminal groups also belong to this form of taxation.

A key characteristic of tribute is that it is not grounded on a rules-based measurement of the profits or costs of the contributor. The taxing authority simply makes a guess of how much it can demand, possibly based on what could be demanded of others in similar situations, but in principle does not need sophisticated measurement. Tribute is a payment that is demanded under some threat of harm and merely needs the demander to credibly threaten harm to the contributor. It is a form of blackmail with no right to appeal or judicial oversight.

While there is regular tribute, there is also irregular tribute, *i.e.*, appropriation. Throughout the ages, kings have been tempted to just grab the possessions of others as a means of increasing their own coffers. The more unexpected, the more could be grabbed and thus, as with seigniorage, taxation becomes highly distortionary.

There are plenty of historical examples of appropriation. Henry VIII of England famously raided the monasteries in northern Britain in the 16th century, while the Roman emperors had no qualms about dispossessing wealthy families that had fallen out of political favour. The Fugger banking family from Germany that rose to wealth in the 15th century similarly was stripped of much of its immense wealth around 1600 by the Spanish kings who defaulted on their loans, essentially because they could (Drelichman & Voth, 2011).

Accounting-based taxes

A new method of taxation became possible when production was organised in and by large companies during the Industrial Revolution. These companies needed to keep detailed records of their purchases and their labourers because they had payrolls, divisions, and delayed payments (Steinmo, 2003). Their accounting methods had developed over centuries, greatly helped by the inventions of the Italian city states in the 13th to 16th century, perfected in the Netherlands, the UK, and elsewhere: double-entry book-keeping, limited liability companies, traded shares, future options, bonds, and other accounting inventions that were the administrative backbone of industrial organisation.

The detailed records kept by major companies allowed tax authorities to introduce taxation on the income of labourers and the profits of enterprises. Tax authorities could insist they got a slice of the payroll before any income was handed out to labourers (the "payroll tax"): companies could not hide the workers they employed because they were so big and their workers would go there so regularly (Steinmo, 2003). Hence the recurrent nature and organised book-keeping of industrial firms made it possible for tax authorities to tax the entities closely associated with those companies (workers). What started as something to improve the efficiency of the organisations (book-keeping) over time simply became mandatory and a means for tax authorities to measure and tax surplus.

The crucial difference between previous taxes and these "accounting-based" taxes is that the latter require the cooperation of the taxed in record-keeping. Neither the recurrent taxation on farmers, nor the incidental taxation on traders, nor seigniorage taxation required this active cooperation. The key problem is immediately evident: why would the taxed cooperate to this degree? Why not cheat as much as possible?

Income tax and profit taxes are sophisticated taxes because they make subtle distinctions between the taxation of inputs and an after-cost notion of profits. To work well, they need good measures of the costs of all inputs, including investments made years ago into capital goods still used in production. Their sophistication is only possible because of the emergence of large production entities that are too big to hide: large factories with expensive buildings and machines – supplied by visible lorries and airplanes – simply cannot hide many of their activities from the eyes of the tax authorities. The idea, for example, that taxation should be progressive is not more than 100 years old in Western countries such as England (Webber & Wildavsky, 1986).

In contrast, smaller production and consumption entities are still able to avoid income taxation and profit taxation. Household production is the prime example of a large sector of the economy that tax authorities have given up trying to tax, because it is just too easy to hide the level of income truly generated

240   *Paul Frijters et al.*

within households. If a tax authority decides to tax households on the basis of how much home production they engage in, households can easily cheat on the reports. Thus, accounting-based taxation cannot tax home production.

The activities of self-employed small traders and producers are similarly notoriously hard to tax, and internet entities with unknown ownership and employee structures can also hide from tax authorities for a long time. Hence, accounting-based taxation is only viable as long as there is not too much production taking place in households or via small bilateral trades.

Much of modern taxation is thereby predicated on the simple rule of thumb that you can tax that which is too big to hide, which in turn requires there to be a real productive advantage of being big and/or of having sophisticated visible book-keeping. Hence, taxation in modern economies involves a tricky balance between distorting markets (*e.g.*, through creating exclusive markets for innovators, trade rules) sufficiently to have big enough entities on which taxation can be based, without these big entities becoming so sophisticated and powerful that they can avoid taxation altogether.

Over time, the extensive book-keeping also allowed Value Added Tax to be gathered on the goods and services flowing in and out of organisations (James, 2011). Value Added Tax is a taxation that relies on the inability of whole chains of production and consumption to hide. Value Added Tax works on the principle that every sale involves a tax liability, but that the next chink in the chain from initial producer to final customer can get a tax break on anything they sell on due to the costs of what they had to purchase. Only the final consumer really pays the Value Added Tax because s/he does not pass the tax on to anyone else, but every part of the chain before the final consumer is mandated to ensure they collect sales data. Because the whole chain involved in Value Added Tax will comply only if there is some part that cannot escape and thus allows to be traced back, value added taxation also relies on "too big to hide" entities. They help enforce taxation on all the entities involved in the same chain, from small suppliers to customers. Accounting-based taxation is thereby entirely reliant on large organisations and the market imperfections under which they become so big.

If we fast-forward to the present day, we see many different forms of taxation by different taxing authorities inside Western countries. There are taxes on highly visible sales pretty much everywhere, like the sale of houses or land, because such sales are easy to tax and difficult to hide, and of high value. There are taxes on wages, on profits, on various markets, on the usage of various goods (think of tolls!), on transactions, on wealth, on inheritances, etc.

How were plutocrats taxed in the past?

With some idea in mind of what was taxed and how over the ages, we can discern some patterns as to what kind of circumstances call for different types of institutionalised taxation in general and for the plutocrats in particular. In all cases, there must be some real economic surplus for institutionalised taxation to

How to tax the powerful and sophisticated? 241

make sense or to be sustainable. Just as one cannot squeeze blood out of a stone, so too can one not tax individuals and households more than what would drive them to die, rebel, or leave entirely.

When the ultimate resource that produces the surplus cannot be removed, such as land or water, then charging access to those resources emerges as the dominant form of taxation. When the resource that produces the surplus can itself be produced but is then contained in a physical place, such as irrigation works (*e.g.*, the Nile Delta), there is the option of state production, taxation of the key element, or to charge for the ownership of that resource. However, if one gets the access prices wrong and charges too much, a peasant rebellion or mass migration provides feedback that the charge was excessive. One needs to maintain some violence potential and a register for who has rented what patch of land, but access prices do not require a very sophisticated system of population records or economic transactions. One then has optimal incentives to provide public goods that increase the surplus of the land, recuperating the costs from the increased land rates.

When the surplus is created within a network of productive relations, such as when surplus comes from combinations of knowledge and other factors (where there is no pivotal observable factor that can be taxed itself), taxation is hard because the key resource cannot be observed and the surplus could be created elsewhere, out of sight (Olbert & Spengel, 2017). In such a case, Value Added Tax is only possible if visible goods have some link in to the production chain that is too big to hide. However, when the surplus is created in a network of productive relations and involves a fairly large visible entity that has significant productive facilities that cannot avoid detection and where the entity is not big or sophisticated enough to control the information reaching the tax authority, then quite sophisticated accounting-based taxation is possible on all elements in the production chain. One can optimally tax inputs, workers, outputs, creative works, trade, capital goods, and access in such a way so as to minimise the distortion subject to the taxed amount. Nonetheless, accounting systems do not work for small entities such as home production, YouTube videos, or friends bartering services.

For about 100 years, this has been the dominant situation in the West, with largish companies coerced into cooperation with payrolls, capital gains taxation, profit taxes, value added taxes, etc. These taxes were based on bureaucratic rules about the definition of labour, capital, profits, goods, etc. Companies, individuals, and financial entities were obliged to report their activities in a certain way, to declare their tax liabilities and pay them. Because the system is predetermined, all actors can plan their investments and activities, safe from major tax surprises, allowing them to optimally strategise.

Accounting-based taxation has hence been surprisingly successful for over a century, but it contains the seeds of its own demise: it relies on strong market imperfections, which means there is an automatic tendency for concentrations of profits, which in turn provide the means to capture the regulator and outwit the accounting structures. An overly large reliance on accounting-based taxation

242   *Paul Frijters et al.*

thereby creates a group of competitors to the tax authorities of the nation-state: the entities that are too big to hide become too sophisticated to tax.

Historically speaking, when the surplus was created by visible big entities who were sophisticated, tributes have been the preferred option. In exchange for not deploying the potential of violence of the whole realm upon these big entities, the plutocrats had to pay a tribute that was intermittently set by the tax authority, usually in some form of negotiation so as to prevent wars from breaking out.

The tribute is an obvious solution to the case where the tax authorities cannot fracture the activities and productive entities they want to tax, but the local plutocrats can, such as when they have an independent set of controls and information on productive relations. As long as the tax authority can credibly threaten the plutocrat or a large part of his productive assets/relations, then the tax authority can successfully demand tribute without needing to duplicate the information and control available to the plutocrat. So, if the plutocrat is too sophisticated to capture in bureaucratic rules enforceable by the tax authority, the tribute is one of the few alternative avenues remaining.

In the last thousand years or so, banking conglomerates and overseas trading companies are key examples of international corporations that became major political powers independent of the countries from which they came. Let us take two examples that emerged in the late Middle Ages in Europe: the Fugger conglomerate of German bankers and the British East India Company of London-based traders. These two are amongst the biggest corporations the world has ever seen. Today's major corporations are small compared to the British East India Company at its height around 1850, when it occupied a territory bigger than the whole of Europe.

How did these companies pay tax? The Fuggers tried to play kings and regions off against each other, accepting mines and other monopoly rights as repayments for loans when kings could not pay their debts (Graulau, 2008). Yet, they were not in charge of a major country and hence could not raise armies loyal to them personally. Instead, they ended up allying themselves to others who could generate mass loyalty: they allied with the Habsburgs, loaning them vast amounts of money and helping them in their rise in the middle of Europe. These loans were a kind of tribute, as if the Fuggers were barons looking for a king to ally themselves with to protect them from other kings. While the Fuggers are still incredibly wealthy to this day, over 600 years since their rise, they lost a lot of their wealth when the Spanish king defaulted on them around 1600.

Historically, it proved difficult to impose sales taxes until the 17th century in Europe. The British East India Company paid custom taxes to the British Crown on the goods it brought into Britain or exported from Britain, a classic form of tax that is proportional to the value (Robin, 2012). This tax was possible because trade came via a couple of major ports and was hence highly visible, unlike, for instance, international services delivered by the internet today. For example, in England the government could tax wool exports easily at the

How to tax the powerful and sophisticated? 243

ports due to its being an island (Finer, 1999). The East India Company also gave large loans to the British Crown and did the bidding of the British Crown in colonial disputes.

In return, the British Crown took up the interests of the British East India Company where necessary, such as by destroying the Chinese court's forces when they refused to allow the opium of the East India Company onto the Chinese market. One can see these large loans and the symbiotic relation between the Crown and the Company as a tribute system. Eventually, the East India Company overextended itself by fighting too many wars for which it used soldiers hired from the Crown and others, and the company was nationalised. A similar story held for the (Dutch) East India Company, which ran as a private company for about two centuries (1600 to 1800). It was nationalised during the Napoleonic Wars. Until then, it paid customs duties to the ports in Amsterdam and would extend loans to the local authorities.

Yet, because there was no powerful centralised authority in the Netherlands in that period, the East India Company in effect was a major political player. In some periods, the company was effectively in control of policy in Amsterdam and surroundings.

So, one can argue that the historical examples of cross-national companies suggest that visible activities also led to taxation based on a tribute system when the relevant tax authority was in need of funds. The tributes often took the form of loans that were not paid back, or paid back on terms advantageous to the party holding the guns.

As an aside, these three examples also contain a warning note to tax authorities: in all three cases, the tax authority has ended up paying tribute to these companies rather than the other way around. When the British East India Company first arrived in India, it paid taxes to the local princedoms, but ended up extracting tributes from them! This was also the case for the Dutch East India Company in Indonesia, and the Fuggers who ended up taxing owners of the County of Kirchberg and Weissenhorn. There is hence ample precedence for tax authorities at some point being taken over by the companies they taxed! A more recent example is the agreed compensation payment of possibly almost a billion Euro to the energy supply companies Vattenfall and RWE in Germany due to the 2011 agreed nuclear power phase-out.[2]

A reflection on today's plutocrats

The story of the modern nation is not merely the story of how tax came to be accepted; the story of many of our institutions is also the story of tax revolts (Adams, 1993). As we can see from this very brief tour of the history of taxation, a recurrent issue in taxation is how to tax the big and powerful entities.

2 See, e.g., www.dw.com/de/bundestag-billigt-atomkonzern-entsch%C3%A4digung/a-44451 536 (accessed 10 July 2019).

244   *Paul Frijters et al.*

One might say that countries are defined by the borders of what a royal court managed to tax, with some of those royals previously being mere nobles in the taxation systems of others. One can even argue that democracy itself arose from the wish of the plutocrats to avoid taxation, including appropriation, by a king. The whole point of parliaments was often to constrain the taxation on the plutocrats, and new countries arose from tax revolts. Remember that Tea Party!

In the present day, the plutocrats are at it again, but not in the way they used to operate. In the early days of agricultural kingdoms, plutocrats who did not pay taxes formed their own country and founded new monarchies. Nowadays they have managed to avoid the taxes of the big countries, without occupying their home countries or physically threatening its leaders. This novelty is due to the unusual form of taxation that has become dominant: accounting-based taxation that involves the active cooperation of the taxpayers, and that requires the emergence of profit-intensive large entities that are too big to hide.

Let us explain the somewhat unusual situation we find ourselves in today wherein the most powerful entities (nation-states) are unable to tax much weaker and highly visible entities (large multinational corporations) operating within their borders. This situation is so clearly not sustainable in any long-run sense that future generations are bound to think it strange that this situation has lasted for so long, wondering why tax authorities did not hit upon a counter-move much sooner.

The essence of modern tax evasion arises from the complexity of the modern economy and the need of tax authorities to tax economic activities while not undermining that economic activity too much. Goods, people, and services now travel across regional and internal boundaries as a matter of course, some-times in the space of years and sometimes in the space of micro-seconds. Large corporations combine goods and services produced in dozens of countries, involving labourers from pretty much all countries in the world, selling produce almost everywhere. Tax authorities wishing to get their fair share in principle want to tax the value added portion that occurs during production and from trade, partly by taxing the "surplus" as it is created (labour, profits, rents, con-sumption) and when it becomes accumulated in wealth.

The problem arises that allowing for production and consumption across boundaries simultaneously comes with the problem of how to ascertain just how much value added a company has created or accumulated in any particular place. A whole myriad of exemptions and dependencies were deemed politic-ally expedient or economically efficient. Bureaucracies did what bureaucracies do in such cases: write vast amounts of tax regulation that attempted to define such things as labour income, capital gains, sources of production, etc.

Of course, politicians and bureaucrats were partly co-opted by those with a lot of tax liabilities, getting them to write favourable regulations, reduce enforcement of unfavourable rules, etc. And, of course, those with tax liabilities tried to play countries, governments, and regions off each other, throwing their support and production facilities behind those doing their bidding.

How to tax the powerful and sophisticated? 245

Just as the barons of England in the 13th century coordinated and schemed behind the back of the king (and the king schemed against them!), so too do wealthy individuals and organisations now play the current political landscape to their advantage. Naturally, they all claim it is just and right in a moral and economic sense that they get their way. Previously this self-moralising gave us the Magna Carta (Baumol, 2004; Radin, 1947). Nowadays we have privately funded think tanks producing books.

How does modern tax avoidance work?

One trick is for wealthy individuals to have their wealth nominally parked in a tax haven, such that their financial and physical assets are supposedly owned by a company in, say, the Cayman Islands even though the physical and network assets are in the UK, the US, China, or elsewhere (Zucman, 2013). This often takes advantage of legislation that was designed to lure foreign capital into a country by promising lower taxes on purchases by overseas companies. This can then be used by people who have never been abroad to move their assets nominally abroad. Tax treaties that respect ownership by foreigners to allay fears of appropriation then work to indeed make it hard to tax the foreign-based wealth. Profitable multinational corporations take advantage of ample opportunities offered by the international tax regime. For example, the double taxation rule not only protects taxpayers from the threat of double taxation, but also offers a lot of chances to avoid taxes through, for example, tax arbitrage, which means exploiting inconsistencies among national tax rules (Elkins, 2017).

A similar trick is for companies with different branches to inflate the prices a branch in, say, the US has to pay for the goods imported from another branch in, say, Korea. That way, the Korean branch of the company ends up with a supposedly higher profit than the US branch, which is handy if profit taxes in the US are higher than in Korea. A company can also have branches paying rents to other branches in order to use technologies, such as paying for the use of patents or formulas. By strategically parking those patents and formulas, international companies can pretty much arbitrarily increase their profits in one country and decrease them in another (Crivelli, De Mooij, & Keen, 2016). At the moment, this latter trick is almost impossible for tax authorities to stop, because stopping it would require authorities to raise barriers to the transfer of patent rights across countries, which is essentially a barrier on transferring ownership across countries.

Yet another trick is to re-label things. Taxation on labour can be circumvented by renting the services of an overseas-registered consulting firm consisting of a single individual. Taxation on headquarters can be circumvented by promoting a small or even virtual office in an appropriate place as headquarters. Inheritances can be repacked as loans or income or profit. Tax deductions for investments are particularly easy to use to write-off almost anything.

These are but the best well-known and debated tricks. In reality, there are thousands upon thousands of tricks, involving multiple countries and a myriad

246　*Paul Frijters et al.*

of fake companies and institutions (Harrington, 2012). Whole armies of tax consultants are poring over legislations (and writing new favourable legislation!) to see whether there is something there they can use for their clients.

At the moment, the legal institutions around taxation are of an enormous volume and complexity. The Australian income tax code alone is over 6000 pages.[3] And that is just income tax in a single country, so one can imagine the volumes on profit taxes, stamp duties, import levies, infrastructure tolls, superannuation, banking, etc. No person will be totally on top of all of that legislation, and efforts to simplify tax laws in different countries often failed (James & Edwards, 2008).

The complexity of the tax law raises the question: who has the strongest incentive to know the relevant legislation and to know how to avoid taxation: individual taxation officers who will be paid a fixed salary anyway, or the entities being taxed? The entities that have hundreds of billions of dollars to hide each year also have hundreds of billions of dollars at their disposal each year to effectuate that hiding, lobbying for favourable tax environments, and having the best brains working for them. Let us give here also an historical example of such a resource asymmetry: in medieval Europe and Asia, for instance, local notables in the agrarian polities had great followings of dependants and clients while governments' local tax officials "were small fry". This made it easy for the notables to pay proportionately less, while smallholders and fee peasantry therefore had to pay more (Finer, 1999, p. 84).

It is crucial to realise the advantages that the large international corporations have in terms of dominating the tax agenda: they are in the room and at the table when most trade negotiations occur, most financial regulation processes get decided, and where major analyses from outsiders are discussed and presented. They fund think tanks, universities, career open days, internet sites, and political parties. Their combined resources rival that of large nation-states.

It is also crucial to realise where they are truly weak. The plutocrats of today, unlike those of centuries ago, do not have armies of their own. They do not run whole education streams, propagate stories of the uniqueness of their population, nor do they actively invent new religions based around themselves. In short, they do not create mass loyalty and cannot create that because they do not control whole lives from cradle to grave within a territory.

So, in truth, though their resources are as immense as that of the plutocrats of old times, modern international corporations are powerless against the machinery of the nation-state, as soon as that machinery has a united approach towards them. The tax evaders rely on disunity in the actions of nation-states and encourage it.

This is of course largely why tax evasion and tax avoidance currently have produced a race to the bottom between countries as to how much they tax the plutocrats. Some countries have specialised in harbouring large international

---

3 For an historical overview on the number of pages of income tax legislation, see www.aphref. aph.gov.au/house/committee/jcpaa/taxation06/report/chap3.htm (accessed 12 July 2019).

corporations and protecting their sources of information in order to obtain some of the corporations' surpluses. This is why, throughout the 20th century, the Swiss have had their banking secrecy laws. This is why today, the Dutch still have their post-code companies, the Cayman Islands have particular rules about ownership disclosure, and Ireland has such a low corporation tax combined with a very unusual definition of "corporation tax". There are and there always will be countries willing to help companies take advantage of any rules they can find to reduce their "normal" tax payments and thus, to frustrate any international agreement that requires most of the countries in the world to cooperate. It is the game as a whole that matters, which is not dependent on specific definitions or tricks.

These latter points have so far not been accepted in the public arena, and tax authorities have hence so far been reduced to fighting tax evasion with their hands behind their backs: they have tried to come up with ever increasing rules on the information they must be provided with and with rules on how to interpret key terms. They have tried to foster international consensus on how to tax major companies and wealthy individuals. They have written whole libraries on optimal taxation in worlds that have never existed, where they as tax authorities have perfect information and publicly minded politicians and have befriended countries to do their bidding. Their favourite solutions involve things that will never be, such as universally accepted and enforced simple tax codes, or perfect measurement of all activities. They need a change of perspective.

Back to tributes?

So, what are tax authorities to do with the largest Western companies of the age, such as Facebook, Apple, Google, Starbucks, Microsoft, Amazon, BHP, BP, the biggest banks, and hundreds of others? These companies facilitate taxation on labour, but many of their senior executives and workers are not classified as such. They pay Value Added Tax, insofar as there is any nominal value added in the country of final sale (which is not much if the input is "expensive" and comes from another country). They pay profit tax in the countries where they nominally make profits, which is usually a country with close to zero profit tax. Their sophisticated strategies of profit shifting have been widely discussed and publicised (see, *e.g.*, Campbell & Helleloid, 2016; Elkins, 2017). Starbucks, for example, operated in the UK for a number of years but was able to avoid paying tax through the following contortions: coffee beans were purchased through a subsidiary corporation in Switzerland, which were roasted in the Netherlands, so as to resell at a much higher price to its UK affiliation, while they paid royalty to a related corporation in the Netherlands, that then paid royalties to another one in Switzerland. Diverting income in this way, paying royalties, and covering the high cost of beans reduced the taxable income to zero. Google, on the other hand, used the "Double Irish Dutch Sandwich" roundabout manoeuvre to avoid withholding taxes, moving royalties between corporations who reside in countries that are exempt from withholding. Google's overseas operation

248   *Paul Frijters et al.*

profits were earned by an Irish subsidiary, which paid a royalty to a Dutch subsidiary, which in turn paid royalty to another subsidiary registered in Ireland but headquartered in Bermuda, and the Irish/Bermudian subsidiary paid a royalty to a subsidiary registered and headquartered in Bermuda (Elkins, 2017, pp. 156–157).

The plutocrats that control these large organisations derive many benefits that are not treated as income or consumption, but are rather called business expenses and field trips. Estimates differ as to how much tax they should pay versus what they pay, but it is fair to guess that they pay much less than half in total of the surplus made.

We have learned above that it is futile to expect to bring them to heel via international cooperation, because several countries have a strong incentive to derail such agreements. As Elkins (2017) points out, "many of the world's wealthiest and most powerful countries themselves would be classified as tax havens or as engaging in harmful tax competition" (p. 163). It is futile to think one can find the perfect definitions, transparency rules, data sharing rules, and basic tax principles that will "solve" the problem.

One must look at the system with four constraints in mind to the solution: it must be based on enforcement; it cannot be based on any system that allows for a court of appeal that judges the application of complex rules; it cannot be based purely on international cooperation (as suggested, for example, by the OECD/G20 BEPS Project that lists actions to address tax avoidance[4]); and it cannot require perfect measurement.

The obvious solution is to go back to tributes: to send large corporations and wealthy individuals an unspecified tax bill that they have to cough up or else face criminal charges for refusing to abide by the demanded tribute. A country as a sovereign entity is allowed under customary international law to impose tax on foreigners who are economically active within its territory (Elkins, 2017, p. 179).

How could this work in a way that is credible and avoids some of the historical problems of tributes, primarily the difficulty in determining how much to tax, and how to address circumstances where political interference in the level of the tribute becomes a game in itself?

One way to overcome the problem of unsustainable tribute is to base the tribute on an estimate of the surplus created in the relevant region: taxing a proportion of the surplus is by definition sustainable. It might be argued that workers could migrate, companies could take their capital elsewhere, and intellectual property can be moved, but this is no more the case under a system of tributes than it is under a system that only manages to tax a bit of consumption and labour (the current situation).

Tributes should attract more high-skilled labour and consumers to a region, because the tributes would allow the tax authority to reduce the taxes on them,

4 See www.oecd.org/ctp/beps-actions.htm (accessed 12 July 2019).

How to tax the powerful and sophisticated? 249

in turn attracting more activities of large multinational corporations. Similarly, wealthy individuals cannot truly run because they cannot take their physical assets with them (land, buildings), nor can they escape international police forces that would enforce the tax dicta of their country of origin.

One way to overcome the problem of arbitrary levels of tribute that are politically gamed is to have tributes market-based, *i.e.*, based on market signals about the amount of surplus created by the entity to be taxed, within the region controlled by the tax authorities.

The basic logic of the tribute is that the party with superior punishment abilities (the nation-state) can demand a bribe from the party that cannot run away and that has less punishment abilities (individuals and international corporations). There are four crucial elements to a new system of tributes:

1. It would make sense to restrict a system of tributes to large entities because it will require more administration and political hassles to impose a tribute than "normal" taxation.
2. Rights of appeal must not be allowed anywhere in the system, because that returns to the current situation. For better or worse, once the tribute is set, it has to be paid. If it is not paid, criminal law can be applied to the owners and controllers of an organisation.
3. The system of tributes and tribute-level determination must be institutionalised so as to insulate it from short-run political factors: the amount of money and know-how available to disrupt the process on the side of the large entities is phenomenal. Hence, the bureaucratic component must be rule based and recurrent so as to make political interference as hard as possible.
4. The part of the system that has discretion (those who set the level of the tribute) must have the right incentives, *i.e.*, must have the incentive to produce an unbiased estimate of the surplus.

Now, requirement 4 forces us to consider the setting of the tribute outside of the state bureaucracy: inside the state bureaucracy, the incentives are to follow rules and not make mistakes, which would mean estimates of surplus that are very conservative and that pander to the political interference. While it would not be desirable for the overall system to be an institutionalised one, such as when it is mandated that 75% of the estimated surplus is paid in tribute, the actual estimate of the surplus cannot be rules based. If it were rules based, we would be back where we are now: based on statistics that would be gamed.

What would a non-rules-based, non-bureaucratic system of estimating the surplus of major corporations look like? One can think of many ways, but a market-led approach seems sensible, whereby the estimator gets a proportion of the whole stream of taxation coming from the company that has to pay the tribute. By having a stake in the stream of taxation, the estimating entity has an inherent interest in getting it right and in avoiding "killing the goose that lays the golden eggs".

250   *Paul Frijters et al.*

There are many ways that a private tribute-estimating company can be given a portion of the stream of taxation. It can be allocated the contract to estimate the surplus for a long time, or it could be paid a proportional fee of taxation now, subject to future penalties if the taxed entities were taxed too much and went away.

However, it would not be optimal for a single private entity to estimate the surplus. So the business of surplus estimation would itself become an international industry, involving specialists for different activities (*e.g.*, internet-based versus property-based) and contract types (*e.g.*, short-run and long-run tributes), much like the companies that currently specialise in providing credit ratings of companies.

Various aspects would need to be thought through to get a precise system of contracts between the tax authorities and the surplus-estimating private entities. There is the issue of who gets provided what information from whom. There is the issue of national security surrounding military firms. Allowances would have to be made for movements in the whole economy as they impact the results of individual companies.

A new system of tributes that simply mandates major corporations and super-wealthy individuals to pay a proportion of what they are worth seems the logical reaction to the problems we have today. It is highly likely that within two decades, sophisticated systems of tribute will have emerged to deal with the biggest corporations and the wealthiest individuals.

There are of course obvious alternatives to tributes. It is possible to increase land taxes and other taxes on big consumer goods that cannot hide. Nationalisation is an option when an activity requires large returns to scale and the technology involved is settled. This is particularly attractive in the case of platform-based intermediation (*e.g.*, Uber and Airbnb), where nationalisation would come with the advantage of measuring the micro-trades that take place via the platform, thus allowing the taxation of the micro-trades. There is also the option of returning to taxation of individuals in the form of time. However, both nationalisation and time-taxation come with potential loss of the advantages of dynamic international specialisation and the profit motive.

Conclusions

In this brief historical story of taxers and taxed, we paid attention to the problem of taxing the biggest non-state organisations and the wealthiest individuals in a time when the state bureaucracy is less informed and less organised. We argued that coordination between states is unlikely to provide solace, and that the historically "normal" form of taxation of big and sophisticated entities was to simply demand tribute. We described how a modern form of tribute could be administrated.

Our current mindset for handling big entities is wrong, as it is stuck in the logic of rules willingly followed by gullible entities. Plutocrats are not sheep and are actively playing all parts of the system, so we should let go of the idea that

How to tax the powerful and sophisticated? 251

we know better. We cannot know exactly how much to tax them and cannot afford to give them a right to appeal. We should simply send them bills that they have to pay, based on market signals of what they could pay, which is the surplus their activities generate in our country.

Taxation has always been a game of cat and mouse, with the cat being the one with the claws and the mouse trying to run away. At the moment, some of the big mice have managed to bind the paws of the cat and escape her attentions entirely, which is bad for the other mice and eventually for the cat, too. It is time for the cat to realise that even big mice are, after all, just mice.

References

Adams, C. (1993). *For good and evil: The impact of taxes on the course of civilization*. London: Madison Books.

Baumol, W. (2004). Red-queen games: Arms races, rule of law and market economies. *Journal of Evolutionary Economics, 14*(2), 237–247.

Bonney, R. (1999). *The rise of the fiscal state in Europe, c.1200–1815*. Oxford: Oxford University Press.

Campbell, K., & Helleloid, D. (2016). Starbucks: Social responsibility and tax avoidance. *Journal of Accounting Education, 37*, 38–60.

Carlson, R. H. (2005). A brief history of property tax. *Fair and Equitable, 3*(2), 3–9.

Carmona, S., & Ezzamel, M. (2007). Accounting and accountability in ancient civilizations: Mesopotamia and Ancient Egypt. *Accounting, Auditing & Accountability Journal, 20*(2), 177–209.

Cooper, R. (1982). William Pitt, taxation, and the needs of war. *Journal of British Studies, 22*(1), 94–103.

Crivelli, E., De Mooij, R., & Keen, M. (2016). Base erosion, profit shifting and developing countries. *Public Finance Analysis, 72*(3), 268–301.

Drelichman, M., & Voth, H. J. (2011). Lending to the borrower from hell: Debt and default in the age of Philipp II. *Economic Journal, 121*, 1205–1227.

Elkins, D. (2017). The case against income taxation of multinational enterprises. *Virginia Tax Review, 36*, 143–204.

Epstein, G. S., Hillman, A. L., & Ursprung, H. W. (1999). The king never emigrates. *Review of Development Economics, 3*(2), 107–121.

Finer, S. E. (1999). *The history of government*, Vols. 1–3. Oxford: Oxford University Press.

Frijters, P., & Foster, G. (2015). Rising inequality: A benign outgrowth of markets or a symptom of cancerous political favours? *Australian Economic Review, 48*(1), 67–75.

Graulau, J. (2008). Finance, industry and globalisation in the early modern period: The example of the metallic business of the House of Fugger. *Rivista di studi politici internazionali – Nuova serie, 75*(4), 554–598.

Harrington, B. (2012). Trust and estate planning: The emergence of a profession and its contribution to socioeconomic inequality. *Sociological Forum, 27*(4), 825–846.

James, K. (2011). Exploring the origins of global rise of VAT. In: *The VAT reader: What a federal consumption tax would mean for America* (pp.15–22). Washington, DC: Tax Analysts.

James, S., & Edwards, A. (2008). Developing tax policy in a complex and changing world. *Economic Analysis and Policy, 38*(1), 35–53.

252 *Paul Frijters et al.*

McGinn, T. A. J. (2013). *Prostitution. The Encyclopedia of Ancient History*, 5590–5592.

Murray, C., & Frijters, P. (2017). *Game of mates: How favours bleed the nation*. Retrieved from https://gameofmates.com/.

Olbert, M., & Spengel, C. (2017). International taxation in the digital economy: Challenge accepted? *World Tax Journal, 9*(1), 3–45.

Pennisi, E. (2012). Our egalitarian Eden. *Science, 344*(6186), 824–825.

Radin, M. (1947). The myth of Magna Carta. *Harvard Law Review, 60*(7), 1060–1091.

Robin, N. (2012). *The corporation that changed the world*. New York: Pluto Press.

Scott, J. C. (2017). *Against the grain: A deep history of the earliest states*. New Haven, CT: Yale University Press.

Steinmo, S. (2003). The evolution of policy ideas: Tax policy in the 20th century. *British Journal of Politics & International Relations, 5*(2), 206–236.

Webber, C., & Wildavsky, A. B. (1986). *A history of taxation and expenditure in the Western world*. New York: Simon & Schuster.

Zucman, G. (2013). The missing wealth of nations: Are Europe and the U.S. net debtors or net creditors? *Quarterly Journal of Economics, 128*(3), 1321–1364.

Zucman, G. (2014). Taxing across borders: Tracking personal wealth and corporate profits. *Journal of Economic Perspectives, 28*(4), 121–148.

13 Starbucks and media allegations of tax avoidance

An examination of reputational loss

Yingyue Ding, Jane Frecknall-Hughes, and Ja Ryong Kim

Introduction

Different from tax evasion, which is an illegal act, tax avoidance is not unlawful, but is increasingly perceived as unethical (see, Prebble & Prebble, 2010): it deprives governments of the revenue required to provide public services and help for the needy in society, and is not seen as socially responsible – and much has now been written about this (see, *e.g.*, Christensen & Murphy, 2004; Dowling, 2014; Hoi, Wu & Zhang, 2013; Lanis & Richardson, 2015; Sikka, 2010).[1] Although legislation cannot prevent corporations from implementing practices for paying less or even zero corporate tax, there is now considerable pressure upon corporations to move away from their traditional "shareholder-first" philosophy. In 2019, the Business Roundtable, one of America's largest business groups, abandoned a shareholder-first philosophy and urged companies to consider other stakeholders and the environment as well (Henderson & Temple-West, 2019). Similar action has been called for by the Institute of Directors in the UK to raise public trust in business (Thomas, 2019). In this chapter, we investigate how a firm's tax avoidance practices attracted media attention and caused a reputational loss to shareholders and other stakeholders.

We focus on reputational loss based on Graham, Hanlon, Shevlin, and Shroff's (2014) finding that one of the most pervasive motives for executives not taking part in aggressive tax schemes is reputation. Therefore, it might be expected that media attention on a firm's tax avoidance will cause a reputational loss for the firm, and could potentially change the firm's tax reporting practice (Wartick, 1992). We have focused in this chapter on Starbucks, as one of the

---

1 There are many different ways in which multinationals may implement tax avoidance measures, for example, by transfer pricing/profit shifting methods, tax arbitrage (essentially "playing off" the tax rules of one jurisdiction against another, which expensively advised multinationals have been perceived as doing), etc. It is not the purpose of this chapter to delve into specific avoidance methods but to highlight the role played by media in influencing opinion and behaviour. The tax avoidance practices that multinationals were perceived as implementing ultimately led to both national and international initiatives to combat tax avoidance, such as the Base Erosion and Profit Shifting (BEPS) measures under the aegis of the Organisation for Economic Cooperation and Development (OECD).

254   *Yingyue Ding et al.*

first multinationals to attract media attention for alleged tax avoidance practices. On 15 October 2012, Reuters issued a special report, "How Starbucks Avoids UK Taxes", detailing how the multinational coffee chain made £1.2 billion of sales yet appeared to make no profits on which corporate tax was paid in the preceding three years (Bergin, 2012). This was in comparison, for instance, with Kentucky Fried Chicken (KFC), a similar multinational restaurant chain, which paid £36 million in tax on £1.1 billion in UK sales.[2] The report caused repercussions in the UK: Starbucks occupied the headline news of mainstream media (see later); customers boycotted Starbucks for its perceived aggressive taxation practices; and the company became the target of public protest and demonstrations by UK Uncut with banners such as "They're our bucks not Starbucks – Close tax loopholes" (McVeigh, Stewart, & Bowers, 2012; *The Guardian*, 2012), leading to the concept of "tax shaming" being used in the press (Barford & Holt, 2013), with the UK Public Accounts Committee also moved to investigate (Frecknall-Hughes, Moizer, Doyle, & Summers, 2017, p. 729). Under pressure from the public and the reputational loss brought about by the media reports, Starbucks agreed to pay £20 million to the British government over the two-year period 2013 and 2014 (Starbucks, *The Times*, 8 December, 2012). In addition, the corporation modified its accounting practices, and started to report positive profits and has paid corporation tax since 2015 (Ram, 2015). The case illustrates that media attention can exert a certain influence on a firm's tax avoidance practices.

In this chapter, we use stakeholder theory and aim to provide a holistic perspective of the case. This is in contrast to an event study method that would investigate a narrow perspective of a specific event across multiple cases. Prior literature on tax avoidance and reputational loss found mixed results. On the one hand, tax avoidance is beneficial to firms as it increases cash reserves and value (Gallemore, Maydew, & Thornock, 2014); but on the other hand, tax avoidance creates a reputational loss to firms, creating a negative net effect (Austin & Wilson, 2017). The mixed findings could have been caused by the use of different perspectives and measures for reputational loss, hence we use a mixed method covering multiple perspectives for different stakeholders. Specifically, we use a quantitative method to measure the reputational loss for

---

2   Media reports commonly refer to multinationals paying no corporate taxes, despite making very large amounts of sales. This is, per se, misleading. Corporate (or corporate income) tax is not payable on sales, but on corporate profits, and it is quite possible to have a high sales figure and make losses without any particular avoidance practices being implemented to engineer tax losses (or low profits) artificially. It should also be stressed that commentators do not agree on issues of tax avoidance and planning: "One man's idea of acceptable tax planning is undoubtedly another man's idea of criminally subversive activity" (Gillett, 1999, p. 1), whereas others think no problem exists, and that "tax avoidance is a conceptual anomaly that exists in the mind of those whose sense of morality is violated by certain effective tax practices" (Orow, 2004, p. 415). It occurs "where legislative intention and policy miscarried and failed to anticipate and reach the transaction under consideration" (Orow, 2004, p. 415). See also Hasseldine and Morris (2013) and Sikka (2013).

shareholders, while we use a qualitative method to measure the reputational loss for customers, rivals, and governments.

We found that, after the initial report by Reuters in the UK, Starbucks had lost 7.7% of share returns over the next four days, equivalent to a \$2.7 billion loss in market value. The decrease in market value makes the £20 million tax payment that was eventually promised to Her Majesty's Revenue and Customs (HMRC) seem almost negligible – and indicates a net negative effect of tax avoidance for shareholders. In addition, by examining media articles about public reaction, we found that Starbucks suffered a reputational loss in terms of criticism from governmental sectors, was listed with other tax avoiders, experienced a loss of customers, protests from the public, and thus felt an obligation to pay taxes to restore its reputation. Our chapter contributes to the literature on tax avoidance and reputational loss by examining the role of the media in a specific case. The rest of the chapter is structured as follows. The following section discusses the prior literature and develops our hypothesis; the chapter then outlines the choice of research methods used and gives details of the data collection; the next section then discusses the empirical results; and the final section offers our conclusions.

Review of prior literature and development of our hypothesis

Starbucks – the background

As previously mentioned, on 15 October 2012, Reuters (London) published an article entitled "Special Report: How Starbucks Avoids UK Taxes", on Starbucks' alleged tax avoidance practices (Bergin, 2012). The article detailed how Starbucks had paid no tax, making no profits on its sales of £1.2 billion in the UK in the previous three years. Put simply, it reported three main elements to the company's tax strategy. First, Starbucks deducted intellectual property fees – a cost charged by its Dutch office allowing Starbucks to use its own brand for its British operation (see also MoneyWeek, 2012). Six per cent of UK revenue was absorbed by this charge (Bergin, 2012). However, a prerequisite for this deduction was to show that a licence for which the royalty was paid was essential for the subsidiary to make profit – and Starbucks showed no UK profits, despite its officials saying that it was profitable (Bergin, 2012). Secondly, Starbucks minimised its tax bills using complex transfer pricing arrangements involving The Netherlands and Switzerland in respect of buying and roasting coffee beans, determining where profit might be located. The third element was The issuing of inter-company loans so that interest payments (an allowable deduction for tax purposes) could be used to reduce specific subsidiaries' profit. The interest rate was set by the corporation itself, agreed with the local government. Starbucks' UK unit was entirely funded by debt (Bergin, 2012), which meant it needed to pay a substantial amount of interest to its Dutch headquarters. It charged its UK unit 4% interest – higher than KFC's 2% in comparison.

256　*Yingyue Ding et al.*

On the same day, *The Guardian* newspaper cited the Reuters article and highlighted the contradiction between profits reported to investors and losses reported to HMRC (Neville, 2012). The next day, the *BBC News* and *Channel 4 News* also reported the alleged tax avoidance practices of Starbucks (Gompertz, 2012; Ritchie, 2012). In the US, the Bureau of Investigative Journalism reported the news on 17 October 2012 (Serle, 2012).

Reputational loss

Reputation means "a level of one's belief regarding another person or an organization" and reputational loss is simply "a degradation of the level of beliefs among the stakeholders regarding the company and its attributes" (Zardasti, Yahaya, Valipour, Rashid, & Noor, 2017, p. 72). According to Bennett and Kottasz (2000, p. 234), corporate reputation is defined as:

> an amalgamation of all expectations, perceptions and opinions of an organization developed over time by customers, employees, suppliers, investors and the public at large in relation to the organization's qualities, characteristics and behaviour, based on personal experience, hearsay or organization's observed past actions.

Reputation is a broad concept and several studies have identified the indicators of reputational loss (Gatzert, 2015). Chen, Wu, Chen, Kang, He, & Miao (2019), for instance, explain that reputational loss consists of investor, customer, employee, and public factors. According to Hokstad and Steiro (2006), reputational loss involves factors such as human beings, the environment, material, production, data/information/knowledge, and the market. In a loan contract case, Deng, Willis, and Xu (2014) found that shareholder litigation caused a reputational loss to a firm in terms of increased borrowing costs, increases in collateral requirement, and higher up-front charges.

From an accounting perspective, reputation can be an intangible asset measured by goodwill (Clardy, 2012). However, reputation is not like other assets fully controlled by a company. Booth (2000) argues that reputation emerges from a combination of organisational and individual dimensions: a company's reputation is a characteristic acknowledged by the key interest groups. Fombrun and Shanley (1990, p. 92) define reputation in terms of capital: "a company's reputational capital is the excess market value of its shares – the amount by which the company's market value exceeds the liquidation value of its assets". This gives an overall framework for reputational loss. Based on this definition, Booth (2000) gives reputation five elements: legitimacy, liability, credibility, confidence, and trust. Specifically, measured on a historical foundation, reputation is a mixture of competence, consistency, truthfulness, message, communication, and competition power compared to other organisations. Hence, poor performance in/by any of these elements may cause a reputational loss.

Starbucks and allegations of tax avoidance 257

The literature shows that customers move to another substitute seller or expect lower prices from the same seller in response to negative news, resulting in a loss of expected cash flows to the firm (Engelen, 2012). For example, after the exposure of the Sanlu milk powder scandal in 2008,[3] the company experienced a considerable decline in its reputation. The loss was so great that the company could not turn the situation around and eventually went into liquidation.

Reputational loss is not measurable like other accounting losses presented in the financial statements, but is a penalty imposed on a company in various ways (Engelen, 2012). The penalty influences the company through different aspects: customers, suppliers, creditors, or even through its labour force. As mentioned, the penalty includes the loss of regular customers. It can also lead to stricter conditions being imposed by suppliers because socially conscious suppliers prefer companies they can rely on (Engelen, 2012). They may demand higher prices, offer a reduced credit period, or even end a contract. Giving credit is based on trust between creditors and debtors. Normally, creditors are more willing to give credit if the two parties have stable and recurrent transactions. However, a steady business is not enough to obtain credit. The debtor needs a decent reputation to maintain the creditor's trust. In other words, a company can hardly obtain credit if it is in disrepute (Graham, Li, & Qiu, 2008). As regards the work force, socially conscious labour tends to join a respected company – and once a company's reputation has been damaged, the existing employees may perform poorly, or absenteeism may increase (Vitell & Davis, 1990). A similar impact can be seen for equity holders (Hribar & Jenkins, 2004): investors will require a higher rate of return from the stock market. Owing to the increase in a required return, the company's value will decrease after reputational damage.

The relationship between reputational loss and tax avoidance

Companies have a dilemma: on one hand, they need to build a reputation, but on the other hand, decreasing their tax payment will increase their profits (Lavermicocca & Buchan, 2015). There is also an argument that companies should not only pay tax in the country where they are registered but also contribute to the tax revenue in the countries where they operate, since the governments offer the infrastructure necessary to support the company doing

---

3 This Chinese milk power scandal was a widespread food safety issue occurring in China in 2008. The scandal did not attract public attention until the media reported on 10 September 2008 that 14 babies had fallen ill, although the milk issue itself was discovered in 2007. The crisis started when Sanlu – the oldest milk powder company in China – was found adding melamine into its milk powder to increase the protein content. This toxic chemical caused illness in over 50,000 babies and the death of at least four. Although the situation had been known about for some years, it was only treated seriously after the media intervened. Sanlu had a high reputation before the event but went out of business within three months of the media report (in December 2008).

258 *Yingyue Ding et al.*

business (Hoi, Wu, & Zhang, 2013; Lanis & Richardson, 2015; Sikka, 2010). The existing literature, however, provides mixed evidence of the relationship between reputation and tax avoidance. Some authors claim that companies suffer reputational loss if they engage in aggressive tax avoidance activities, while others think that there is no relationship between tax avoidance and reputation.

Austin and Wilson (2017) find a positive and significant association between effective tax rate and consumer-based brand equity (CBBE). *The Times* also comments that the result of avoiding tax is the loss of trust as, while the public may still trust a particular industry, they will probably not trust a specific company any more (Lea, 2013). Graham, Hanlon, Shevlin, and Shroff, (2014, p. 34) conducted a survey, which showed that 69% of executives believed that "potential harm to firm reputation" is a reason for not using aggressive tax planning activities. These results suggest that managers may modify the tax planning activities to avoid potential reputational loss. However, there are other views about reputational losses and tax avoidance. Gallemore, Maydew, and Thornock (2014) point out that after a series of tests, they failed to find evidence in support of senior executives needing to deal with a reputational loss even though they used aggressive tax avoidance transactions. Empirical evidence suggests that, while Amazon used Luxembourg as a tax shelter for years, its share price actually climbed significantly. In addition, Google was accused of avoiding paying £1.5 billion in tax, which is the equivalent of one year's salary for 60,000 nurses or the cost of building 75 new schools (Hiscott, 2019). However, Google's stock performed well over a long period: a $1,000 investment in Google in 2007 would have been worth $2,922 in 2017 (Carter, 2018).

Stakeholder theory

Stakeholder theory is an alternative theory to the shareholder theory proposed by Milton Friedman in 1970 (Friedman, 1970). According to shareholder theory, a company should set the interests of shareholders as its priority because they are the ultimate owners of the organisation and, therefore, the goal of the company should be to maximise its profits and returns to the shareholders. Freeman (1984), on the other hand, suggests the company should take other stakeholders into consideration – defining stakeholders (p. 52) as the "groups and individuals who can affect, or are affected by, the achievement of an organisation's mission" and identifying them as owners, the financial community, activist groups, customers, consumer advocate groups, unions, employees, trade associations, competitors, suppliers, government, and political groups. Hence there is a wide variety of different interests which need to be considered in addition to shareholders, including government.

Stakeholder theory thus provides a holistic approach to considering the problems and challenges that a company faces (Freeman, 1994). The goal of the organisation thus becomes the maximisation of all stakeholders' interests, which will drive the company forward, but the firm must hence take more responsibility in terms of providing timely and relevant information to the stakeholders, to help them make better decisions (Freeman, 1994). Moreover, focusing on all stakeholders' interests enables the organisation to create more and different kinds of values (Jensen, 2002). The value of a company should not be considered as dependent only on its financial returns. Stakeholder theory provides a new perspective of measuring the overall corporate value, and assessing performance from the perspective of different stakeholders contributes to a company's economic longevity and sustainability (Harrison & Wicks, 2013). In other words, if a company only cares about making a large profit for shareholders but is unconcerned about other stakeholders' interests, it might achieve its goal in the short term but cannot be sustainable in the long run. Stakeholder theory provides a more ethical and versatile framework for assessing a company's value.

Based on stakeholder theory, companies should take all the stakeholders' interests into consideration when it comes to making business decisions, including tax planning. The loss of tax revenue will negatively affect HMRC and the UK government in funding essential public services. Customers will also be negatively affected by the decrease in the perceived value of the products or services provided by the firm. Customers' negative reaction will reduce the expected cash flows for the firm, reducing the value of the firm and shareholders' wealth. The business community in general will also be negatively affected by a firm's tax avoidance as the public will lose trust in the business. In the short term, however, direct rival firms might benefit, owing to customers moving away and looking for alternative products or services from companies other than the tax-avoiding firm.

Taking into account all of the above, we would therefore expect that the (alleged) tax avoidance behaviour of Starbucks would affect its shareholders and other stakeholders negatively, following the media report, hence:

> *H1: Starbucks will suffer a reputational loss after the report of Reuters on its tax avoidance practice.*

Research method and data collection

Choice of methods

In order to develop an in-depth structure and give a better understanding of the phenomenon and the theory (Saunders, Lewis, & Thornhill, 2019), the research was based on a single case study. This chapter uses a mixed research method to measure the reputational loss in terms of both quantitative and qualitative aspects. The reason why a mixed method approach was chosen is that a single research method could possibly lead to a biased result. It is apparent from prior literature that there is a debate about the influence of media on tax avoidance and the mixed results on tax avoidance might have come from using different research methods. For example, a serious customer protest may break out after a media report, which can be categorised as a sign of damage to reputation, yet the stock price may remain stable at that time. Conversely, there might be a

260 *Yingyue Ding et al.*

large fall in stock price, which might be a strong indicator of damage to reputation, although a company might seem not to be influenced by the crisis if it has loyal suppliers and customers and the public does not care about the activities that have attracted criticism. Hence the company need not put any effort into restoring its reputation. We set out below the approach adopted.

Share return analysis

Following Chen, Wu, Chen, Kang, He, & Miao's (2019) reputational loss indicators, we use share returns to measure the investor factor of reputational loss, while investigating newspaper articles to measure the customer, employee, and public factors of reputational loss. We chose share returns, instead of accounting information, to measure the impact of media coverage on reputational loss owing to the time sensitivity of share returns. While share prices are available on a daily basis, enabling a daily analysis of the impact of media coverage, accounting information is only available periodically. Given that Starbucks' financial year runs from 1 October to 30 September, the impact of a media report on 15 October 2012 on accounting information would only be reported in the annual statements for the year ended 30 September 2013, leaving an almost year-long time gap between the event and information announcement. Market capitalisation can also be used to measure the impact on investors as an aggregate measure. However, because Starbucks' number of shares outstanding did not change over the event period, we used share returns that provide the same result as market capitalisation.

Since the media coverage on Starbucks' alleged tax avoidance practices occurred at a discrete point in time, we used an event study method to measure the impact of media coverage on the company's share returns. We used an estimation period of 250 days (-260, -11), followed by an event period of 21 days (-10, 10). Given that the event day, t, 0, was 15 October 2012, when Reuters published its special report on Starbucks' tax avoidance, we therefore collected data on share returns and value-weighted market returns from the Center for Research in Securities and Prices (CRSP) database between 4 October 2011 and 31 October 2012. Other studies have also used an event study method to examine the impact of discrete events, such as new hotel openings (Nicolau, 2002), celebrity endorsement (Agrawal & Kamakura, 1995), major channel expansion (Homburg, Vollmayr, & Hahn, 2014), and charges of deceptive advertising (Jeong & Yoo, 2011). By using share returns, we rely on the Efficient Market Hypothesis (EMH). According to the EMH, the share price reflects all publicly available information that has an impact on a firm's expected cash flows (Fama, 1970). Therefore, if media coverage has any impact on Starbucks' expected cash flows, thereby causing a reputational loss to investors, we will observe a share price decrease around the event day. We measured three types of share returns: Starbucks' share returns, abnormal returns over the market index, and abnormal returns based on the Market model. All returns include dividend distributions and are calculated using daily information at t as:

$$Return_t = \frac{\left(Price_t + Dividend_t - Price_{t-1}\right)}{Price_{t-1}} \tag{1}$$

For the abnormal returns over the market index, we used the CRSP value-weighted market index, which consists of all investable equity shares in the USA.[4] The abnormal return over the market index measures the share return of Starbucks compared to that of the market ($\beta = 1$). The abnormal return based on the Market model, however, employs Starbucks' own beta when calculating abnormal returns. Following Agrawal and Kamakura (1995), we estimated the Market model based on 250 daily observations in the estimation period ($t - 260$ to $t - 11$ days relative to the event day, $t = 0$) as below:

$$Return_t = \alpha + \beta MarketReturn_t + \varepsilon_t \tag{2}$$

The abnormal returns for the event period ($t - 10$ to $t + 10$ days) are calculated as:

$$\varepsilon_t = Return_t - \hat{\alpha} - \hat{\beta}MarketReturn_t \tag{3}$$

The cumulative returns over different time windows were also calculated to present the cumulative effect of media coverage on Starbucks' alleged tax avoidance. Although typical event studies employ multiple cases of the event and examine the statistical significance of the event cross-sectionally, this chapter only uses the case of Starbucks. Therefore, we checked the statistical significances of the returns based on Starbucks' past returns during the estimation period.

Thematic analysis

A thematic research method was used for analysing qualitative data. In order to find the themes across the data set, we first coded the data into several groups by labelling each piece of news or image with a code that represented its meaning (Saunders, Lewis, & Thornhill, 2019). After retrieving and rearranging all the data under relevant codes, we categorised them into different themes, in accordance with stakeholder theory. Based on the existing literature (Claeys, Cauberghe, & Vyncke, 2010; Coombs, 2007; Gaultier-Gaillard, Louisot, & Rayner, 2009), we found themes relating to the loss of customers, protest from

---

4 We also used the CRSP equal-weighted market index for the benchmark, but the results are essentially the same.

Figure 13.1 Process of thematic analysis

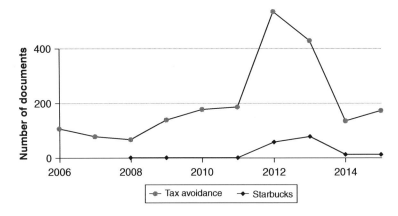

Figure 13.2 Frequency of the terms "tax avoidance" and "Starbucks", 2006–2015

the public, and obligation to restore the company's reputation. In addition, we were also open to finding new themes emerging from the codes that could enrich the indicators of reputational loss, and found themes relating also to HMRC and various aspects of tax payment, government/MPs' reactions, the EU, benefits to rivals, etc. (see later Tables 13.2 and 13.3). The thematic analysis followed the procedure outlined in Figure 13.1.

For the thematic analysis, we investigated newspaper articles from 2012 to 2015 as the issue might continue to influence reports for several years. As media source materials, we used primarily British Library Newspapers, The Economist Historical Archive, The Telegraph Historical Archive, Picture Post Historical Archive, and The Times Digital Archive, which are searchable media databases, available via Gale Primary Sources. Gale obtains news from 13 sources, but in order to narrow the search field, we chose only the five sources identified above, because they are business-related newspapers or periodicals. Graphing the frequencies of terms "tax avoidance" and "Starbucks" from the year 2006 to the year 2015, we found the highest frequencies in 2012, gradually decreasing to approximately the same amount as before by 2015. In addition, the fact that "tax avoidance" and "Starbucks" show similar levels of frequency indicates that the case of Starbucks is a suitable example for researching the effect of a media report on alleged tax avoidance. Figure 13.2 shows the frequency of the terms.

Starbucks and allegations of tax avoidance 263

We also carried out further searches, using keywords/phrases such as "Starbucks tax", "boycott Starbucks", "consumers Starbucks", "protest Starbucks", "Starbucks profit", and "Starbucks sales", looking especially for news and images focusing on the nexus of tax avoidance and the consequences. The initial research returned 236 newspaper/periodical articles. We required them to be written in English, resulting in a decrease in the number to 191. We did not add "the UK" in the keywords because some of the reports used "Britain" instead, while others did not mention either the UK or Britain because they were British-based and, therefore, a UK context was implied.

Empirical results

Starbucks' share returns

The share returns, abnormal returns over the market index, and abnormal returns based on the Market model of Starbucks over the event period are reported in Table 13.1 and shown in Figure 13.3. Surprisingly, the effect of media coverage on Starbucks' tax avoidance came two days after the event day. We suspect that this is because Starbucks was trading in the USA while news on its tax avoidance was reported in the UK, creating a time lag. As the timeline above indicates, the news was only reported in the US media on 17 October 2012, two days after the event, through the Bureau of Investigative Journalism. The cumulative returns of Starbucks' shares from $t + 2$ day to $t + 5$ day are −7.7%, indicating a significant loss to shareholders in those four trading days. Given that Starbucks' market capitalisation on $t - 1$ day was \$35.2 billion, this cumulative loss over four days represents \$2.7 billion loss for investors (untabulated). Similar results are obtained when abnormal returns over the market index and abnormal returns based on the Market model are used. The cumulative abnormal returns over the four-day period were −6.4% and −6.8%, respectively, representing economically significant losses of \$2.2 billion and \$2.4 billion respectively for investors. We examined the statistical significance of the returns for the period from $t + 2$ to $t + 5$ days. All daily returns (and abnormal returns) during that period were significantly different from the mean returns (and mean abnormal returns) over the estimation period (−260, −11) at the 1% level, indicating that investors suffered an economically and statistically significant reputational loss as a result of reaction to the media coverage of Starbucks' tax avoidance. Table 13.1 and Figure 13.3 show the returns and abnormal returns, and Figure 13.4 the cumulative abnormal returns, over the event period.

Over the period from $t + 2$ to $t + 5$, Starbucks suffered a significant decrease in share returns from −4.6% to −11.1%. Similar results are shown when cumulative abnormal returns are used, indicating that Starbucks' reputational loss is prevalent across different abnormal return measures. Our results show that Starbucks suffered from a reputational loss in terms of the investor factor after the media coverage of its tax avoidance. The economic impact was severe, representing −7.7% return and \$2.7 billion loss over four days.

264 Yingyue Ding et al.

Table 13.1 Returns and abnormal returns

Event day	Daily return	Abnormal return over the market index	Abnormal return based on the Market model
–10	–0.011	–0.014	–0.014
–9	–0.017	–0.018	–0.018
–8	0.004	0.001	0.001
–7	0.008	0.016	0.015
–6	–0.007	–0.007	–0.008
–5	0	0.004	0.003
–4	–0.029	–0.019	–0.021
–3	–0.008	–0.003	–0.004
–2	0.004	0.003	0.002
–1	0	0.004	0.003
0	0.010	0.003	0.002
1	0.027	0.017	0.018
2	–0.012	–0.017	–0.017
3	–0.020	–0.018	–0.018
4	–0.036	–0.021	–0.023
5	–0.008	–0.009	–0.009
6	–0.007	0.006	0.003
7	0.006	0.009	0.008
8	0.022	0.019	0.018
9	–0.008	–0.007	–0.008
10	0.001	–0.002	–0.002

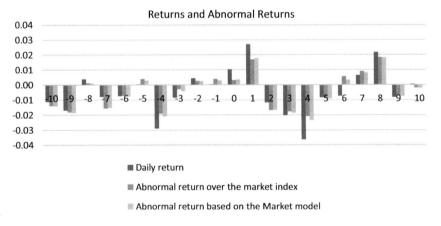

Figure 13.3 Returns and abnormal returns

Thematic analysis

Both the public and media reacted to the Reuters report, and the responses gave rise to a variety of pressures. Other media propagated the news and drew more attention to it. Finally, the company faced a situation where consumers

Starbucks and allegations of tax avoidance 265

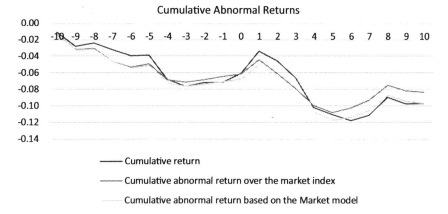

Figure 13.4 Cumulative abnormal returns

took radical measures to force Starbucks to make a change, notably in the form of a boycott of Starbucks' products and a public protest outside its coffee shops.

In order to give a clear outline of the reputational loss that Starbucks experienced, we coded the social reactions based on the definition of reputational loss in relation to stakeholder theory. Table 13.2 shows the reactions.

It can be seen from the table that not only was Starbucks itself influenced by the report but there was an impact also on other stakeholders, including the British government, HMRC, customers, rivals, shareholders, and even the EU. This impact is discussed in more detail below.

The government and the politicians were among the first groups to react. The Prime Minister (PM) and Members of Parliament (MPs) started to criticise Starbucks for its affairs which resulted in negligible tax amounts being payable. MPs (via the Public Accounts Committee) and Margaret Hodge, its Chair, questioned the legality of Starbucks' tax schemes. They also called for HMRC to be more careful in dealing with Starbucks. Although the media also reported that the tax schemes were not illegal, reports produced anger and resentment among consumers. HMRC were also reported as considering penalties for Starbucks. Moreover, EU commentators were of the opinion that the Starbucks' tax issue was not only a UK issue: it was a problem within the EU more widely – and Starbucks' actions also might not accord with the laws of the EU, even if legal in the UK. There was also a call for legislation specifically aimed at tax avoiders. It was clear that the Starbucks "scandal" attracted a lot of government attention.

Buyers were also affected – with the risk that they chose substitute products or services. Starbucks had attracted its customer loyalty by issuing membership cards and stylish products. However, customers started to leave because of perceiving that its dealings in its tax affairs were unethical. For example, as reported above in *The Times* in 2012, a regular Starbucks customer said she destroyed the membership card and would find new coffee shops. She also appealed to more

266   *Yingyue Ding et al.*

Table 13.2 Public reactions after the Reuters report

Relevant stakeholder	Description by the media	Source (author, year, media)
HMRC	"… has made the coffee retailer the latest US company to come under the spotlight for its negligible contribution to Her Majesty's Revenue & Customs".	(Ebrahimi, 2012a) *The Daily Telegraph*
	"Cameron calls for HMRC inquiry as large corporations avoid payments".	(Armitstead, 2012) *The Daily Telegraph*
	"HMRC criticised as firm accused of using accounting strategies to 'play the system'".	(Ebrahimi, 2012b) *The Daily Telegraph*
	"STARBUCKS' tax bills have come to further scrutiny".	(Peacock & Blackden, 2012) *The Daily Telegraph*
	"… calling Starbucks' tax bill 'legal and probably negligible'".	(Samuel, 2012) *The Times*
European Union (EU)	"The tax avoidance by multinational companies is not a purely British issue. It is common to most of the EU".	(Lyons & Mallalieu, 2012) *The Times*
	"Starbucks' deal with the Dutch may be illegal state aid, says EU".	(Roland, 2014) *The Daily Telegraph*
	"In Europe, the anger has focused on big firms. Amazon and Starbucks have faced consumer boycott for using clever accounting tricks".	(*The Economist*, 2013)
Government, MPs	"Margaret Hodge, chairman of the Public Accounts Committee, called for HMRC to look at the company's tax affairs".	(Ebrahimi & Armitstead, 2012) *The Daily Telegraph*
	"Lin Homer, the head of the Revenue, prepared to be questioned by MPs on Monday".	(Schlesinger, 2012) *The Times*
	"Starbucks, Google and Amazon will give evidence to MPs on how they used legal tax schemes to avoid paying millions of pounds to the UK".	(Wilson, 2012) *The Daily Telegraph*
	"We are not accusing you of being illegal: we are accusing you of being immoral".	(Schlesinger, 2012) *The Times*
	"Alexander, the Chief Secretary to the Treasury. 'I just want to make sure that taxpayers' money isn't funding tax dodgers'".	(Savage, 2012) *The Times*
	"Lords call for tough penalties to crack down on tax avoiders".	(Osborne, 2013) *The Daily Telegraph*
	"Cameron tells tax avoiders: wake up and smell the coffee".	(Armitstead, 2013) *The Daily Telegraph*
	"Don't tell tax-avoiding corporations to 'do the right thing'. Tell them what to pay and make them pay it".	(Rifkind, 2012) *The Times*
The more neutral public	"It may be legal but it is not moral".	(Ebrahimi, 2012b) *The Daily Telegraph*

Starbucks and allegations of tax avoidance 267

Table 13.2 (Cont.)

Relevant stakeholder	Description by the media	Source (author, year, media)
	"We have a roasting plant there – and they have an attractive tax rule".	(Schlesinger, 2012) *The Times*
	"Starbucks is not a tax avoider. It's obeying the law of the land".	(Worstall, 2012) *The Times*
Customers/ general public	"There is a growing anger among ordinary people".	(Ebrahimi, 2012b) *The Daily Telegraph*
	"For years, Google, Starbucks, Amazon suckered us with their groovy logos, funky corporate HQs full of think-pods and juice bar".	(Turner, 2012) *The Times*
	"The coffee chain was facing the prospect of a customer boycott after being accused by MPs of 'immorally' avoiding tax".	(MacLean, 2012) *The Times*
	"Faced with a boycott of its coffee shops and serious damage to its brand".	(*The Daily Telegraph*, 2012a)
	"Uncut staged protests at dozens of British Starbucks stores".	(*The Economist*, 2012)
	"My love affair with Starbucks is over".	(Treneman, 2012) *The Times*
	"I have felt that I should boycott ever since the original Reuter report on this came out".	(Treneman, 2012) *The Times*
	"I have cut up my loyalty card, I find new beans. I will change my routine to work. I do hope I'm not the only one".	(Treneman, 2012) *The Times*
	"A recent consumer boycott of Starbucks over its tax affairs in the UK is expected to have given Costa coffee owner Whitbread a lift in the last few days".	(*The Daily Telegraph*, 2012b)
Rivals	"… would not look to mimic the practice of its rival Costa Coffee".	(Ebrahimi & Armitstead, 2012) *The Daily Telegraph*
	"Independent outlets are thriving as consumers seek brands with 'clean slate'".	(Milner, 2013) *The Times*
	"Costa Coffee is the 'taxman's favourite coffee shop', the chief executive of parent company Whitbread has declared, after the public furore about the lack of UK tax paid by rival Starbucks helped to drive sales for Costa".	(Ruddick, 2012) *The Daily Telegraph*
	"People's interest is piqued, in time they start to seek out better coffee".	(Middleton, 2014) *The Daily Telegraph*
	"Meanwhile, rival Caffè Nero reports revenue bubbling ever upwards".	(Middleton, 2014) *The Daily Telegraph*
	"We encourage people to buy Costa coffee because it tastes better and makes a bigger contribution to the economy".	(Walsh, 2012) *The Times*

(continued)

268 *Yingyue Ding et al.*

Table 13.2 (Cont.)

Relevant stakeholder	Description by the media	Source (author, year, media)
Other (alleged) tax avoiders	"Facebook UK generated revenues of £20.4m last year and paid just £238,000 in tax to the revenue".	(Ebrahimi & Armitstead, 2012) *The Daily Telegraph*
Shareholders	"Starbucks' shareholders may not agree that paying more tax voluntarily is 'doing the right thing' by them".	(Reece, 2012) *The Daily Telegraph*
	"Starbucks has suffered its first-ever drop in UK sales, during a period when the company came in for criticism over its tax practices".	(Campbell, 2014) *The Daily Telegraph*

people to boycott Starbucks. This was not a single instance. *The Times* and *The Daily Telegraph* both mentioned that customers were seeking new coffee shops and the boycott from customers caused damage to the Starbucks brand. This, however, created opportunities for its rivals. In 2012, Whitbread announced that the boycott of Starbucks brought Costa an increase in sales. In 2014, Starbucks' sales decreased for the first time since it had established its operation in the UK, but Caffè Nero reported a sales rise at the same time. This finding is in line with the definition of reputational loss: customers choose their substitute stores once they realise that their current one is suffering from reputational loss. After the media exposure, Starbucks' regular customers turned to other coffee shops that had a better reputation. In addition, people gathered in front of Starbucks' stores waving banners, protesting against Starbucks. People claimed that the tax avoided by Starbucks could have been used in other public sectors. The protest had so significant an impact on Starbucks' reputation that it eventually forced the company to make changes (see later). The company was also associated with other alleged tax avoiders, such as Google and Amazon (Google giving its name to a tax on profit shifting activities – the "Google tax" (Neate, 2014)). Being listed with other corporations with a bad reputation is another sign of reputational loss – but at least the proposed tax was not referred to as the "Starbucks tax". A theme subsumed within others was that of unethical behaviour. Also, certain themes overlapped, for example, customers boycotting stores had a beneficial effect on rivals' business.

Starbucks' response to the crisis

After the boycott and the protest, Starbucks occupied the headline news for a few more weeks before it realised that it needed to take measures to rebuild public trust. This section examines what Starbucks did after the crisis. Table 13.3 shows relevant information about Starbucks' response to the media.

Starbucks and allegations of tax avoidance 269

Table 13.3 Starbucks' response to the crisis

Reaction	Description by the media	Source (author, year, media)
Changed its practices	"After talks with Revenue & Customs, royalties were lowered to 4.7 per cent".	(Schlesinger, 2012) *The Times*
	"The company is looking to declare larger profits in Britain and thus pay more tax".	(Hurley, 2012) *The Daily Telegraph*
	"We have listened to feedback from customers and employees, and understand that to maintain and further rebuild public trust we need to do more".	
	"Starbucks to pay corporation tax after HO moved to Britain".	(Titcomb, 2014) *The Daily Telegraph*
	"We listened to our customers in December and so decided to forgo certain deductions which would make us liable to pay £10m in corporation tax this year and a further £10m in 2014".	(Rowley, 2013) *The Daily Telegraph*
	"STARBUCKS recorded a profit of £1.1m in the year to September 2014".	(Anderson, 2015) *The Daily Telegraph*
Paid/will pay tax	"The company has rationalized a payment of £10 million a year to Her Majesty's Revenue & Customers on the ground that it will keep customers happy".	(Reece, 2012) *The Daily Telegraph*
	"Coffee giant gives £5m corporation tax to HMRC".	(Ahmed, 2013) *The Sunday Telegraph*
	"Starbucks will commit to paying a significant amount of tax during 2013 and 2014 regardless of whether the company is profitable during these years".	(Starbucks, 2012) *The Times*
	"We have now paid £5m and will pay the remaining £5m later this year".	(Rowley, 2013) *The Daily Telegraph*

Starbucks decided to pay HMRC £20 million over the two-year period 2013 and 2014 (Rowley, 2013). The money for the voluntary payment would be derived from cutting the royalties paid to its Dutch HQ. In addition, it moved its HQ from Amsterdam to London, resulting in the payment of intellectual property fees to Britain. Although there is no explicit evidence that the motive behind Starbucks' HQ move was to eliminate public anger, Starbucks started to be profitable after the relocation. As a result, it started to pay tax to the UK government, commencing with a voluntary payment of £10m in 2013. Starbucks was profitable in 2014 as well and paid corporation tax. Starbucks had to maintain or rebuild its reputation in the market. Our result is consistent with

270 *Yingyue Ding et al.*

the definition of reputational loss in that the company felt obliged to address such consequences. The "voluntary" payment of a tax also attracted attention. Most of the general public would perceive tax due as being calculated according to strict legal rules, so labelling a payment "voluntary" raises a question about what exactly a tax is.

Summary

After analysing both quantitative and qualitative data, the results show that Starbucks indeed suffered reputational losses in terms of both stock market and stakeholder opinion after the Reuters report. Starbucks suffered a significant loss in its market value equivalent to $2.7 billion within four days of the report. In addition, criticism by politicians, loss of customers, public protests, and being listed with other tax avoiders are the reasons that Starbucks made changes in its accounting practices to restore its reputation. There is no evidence showing that Starbucks has stopped all tax-avoiding schemes. However, it certainly made compromises to public opinion after the media exposure. Without the Reuters report, perhaps the public would not have boycotted Starbucks and Starbucks might still be implementing the same accounting/tax practices and would not be paying corporation tax in the UK. Therefore, media played an essential role in this case, bringing public attention to Starbucks and compelling the company to change its alleged tax avoidance behaviour.

Conclusion

This study investigates the influence of media on tax avoidance in the UK assessed by reputational loss using Starbucks as a case study. In order to distinguish this study from prior literature, we used both quantitative and qualitative research methods to evaluate the influence of media reports. Using information from the stock market and newspaper archives, this research gives an overview of both financial and social/public opinion perspectives.

Our findings indicate that Starbucks had suffered a reputational loss after the media report on its alleged tax avoidance. We found that most of Starbucks' stakeholders, including shareholders, were the victims of the reputational loss. Shareholders suffered a significant decrease in their wealth after the report. The UK government and the EU lost tax revenues that could have been used for the provision of public services. Customers felt ashamed of consuming Starbucks coffee and moved to other coffee chains. Public trust in the business was diminished. The only parties that benefited from the scandal in the short term were its rivals, such as Costa and Caffè Nero, which experienced an increase in customers and sales.

In our thematic analysis, we identified five areas that suffered effects as a result of the reputational loss Starbucks experienced: (i) customers were lost; (ii) public protest arose; (iii) the company felt an obligation to restore its reputation; (iv) criticism from governmental sectors was rife; and (v) the company was listed with other tax avoiders. Although the first three areas were identified in the existing literature as reputational loss (Coombs, 2007; Claeys, Cauberghe, & Vyncke, 2010; Gaultier-Gaillard, Louisot, & Rayner, 2009), to the best of our knowledge, the last two themes have not previously been considered as part of reputational loss.

Our findings are also important to tax authorities dealing with tax avoidance. Based on the tax rules, tax authorities were unable to investigate tax avoidance of Starbucks as it was, strictly, operating within the rule of law. However, the media "played the moral card", which proved to have the power to influence the firm to change its tax practices and reduce avoidance. With the growth of the internet and social media, to supplement the role of traditional media, this all provides a degree of assistance to tax authorities' efforts to reduce corporate tax avoidance that might not have been expected.

The criticism against Starbucks did not stop until at least 2015. Although we cannot find evidence that Starbucks desisted from all its alleged tax avoidance practices, it at least modified its practices and started to pay corporation tax to HMRC. Although the media cannot eliminate tax avoidance, we believe its influence can bring corporations to compromise with public sentiment. In essence, the media shine a spotlight on a problem and provoke a reaction.

References

Agrawal, J., & Kamakura, W. A. (1995). The economic worth of celebrity endorsers: An event study analysis. *Journal of Marketing*, *59*(3), 56–62.

Ahmed, K. (2013, June 23). Starbucks pays first tax since 2008. *The Sunday Telegraph*, p. B1. Retrieved August 20, 2019, available via subscription from Thomson-Gale.

Anderson, E. (2015, February 5). First profit for Starbucks since arriving in Britain. *The Daily Telegraph*, p. B3. Retrieved August 21, 2019, available via subscription from Thomson-Gale.

Armitstead, L. (2012, October 25). Crackdown looms for foreign "tax avoiders". *The Daily Telegraph*, p. B1. Retrieved August 20, 2019, available via subscription from Thomson-Gale.

Armitstead, L. (2013, January 25). Cameron tells tax avoiders: Wake up and smell the coffee. *The Daily Telegraph*, p. B3. Retrieved August 20, 2019, available via subscription from Thomson-Gale.

Austin, C. R. R., & Wilson, R. J. J. (2017). An examination of reputational costs and tax avoidance: Evidence from firms with valuable consumer brands. *Journal of the American Taxation Association*, *39*(1), 67–93.

Barford, V., & Holt, G. (2013, May 21). Google, Amazon, Starbucks: The rise of "tax shaming". *BBC News*. Retrieved March 26, 2019, from www.bbc.co.uk/news/magazine-20560359.

Bennett, R., & Kottasz, R. (2000). Practitioner perceptions of corporate reputation: An empirical investigation. *Corporate Communications: An International Journal*, *5*(3), 224–234.

Bergin, T. (2012). Special report: How Starbucks avoids UK taxes. *Reuters*. Retrieved August 12, 2019, from https://uk.reuters.com/article/us-britain-starbucks-tax/special-report-how-starbucks-avoids-uk-taxes-idUKBRE89E0EX20121015.

272   *Yingyue Ding et al.*

Booth, A. (2000). How can organisations prepare for reputational crises? *Journal of Contingencies and Crisis Management, 8*(4), 197–207.

Campbell, S. (2014, April 25). Starbucks reports sales drop in UK for first time. *The Daily Telegraph*, p. B3. Retrieved August 20, 2019, available via subscription from Thomson-Gale.

Carter, S. (2018, January 11). If you invested $1,000 in Google 10 years ago, here's how much you'd have now. *CNBC*. Retrieved August 17, 2019, from www.cnbc.com/2018/01/11/if-you-put-1000-in-google-10-years-ago-heres-what-youd-have-now.html?fbclid=IwAR2jLurRnpOZ1t2TS4Uiaq3e0CeJudj4eLIhJRPv1TWhQMAzhpUOsFxGrTs.

Chen, X., Wu, Z., Chen, W., Kang, R., He, X., & Miao, Y. (2019). Selection of key indicators for reputation loss in oil and gas pipeline failure event. *Engineering Failure Analysis, 99*, 69–84.

Christensen, J., & Murphy, R. (2004). The social irresponsibility of corporate tax avoidance: Taking CSR to the bottom line. *Development, 47*(3), 37–44.

Claeys, A., Cauberghe, V., & Vyncke, P. (2010). Restoring reputations in times of crisis: An experimental study of the situational crisis communication theory and the moderating effects of locus of control. *Public Relations Review, 36*(3), 256–262.

Clardy, A. (2012). Organizational reputation: Issues in conceptualization and measurement. *Corporate Reputation Review, 15*(4), 285–303.

Coombs, W. (2007). Protecting organization reputations during a crisis: The development and application of situational crisis communication theory. *Corporate Reputation Review, 10*(3), 163–176.

Deng, S., Willis, R. H., & Xu, L. (2014), Shareholder litigation, reputational loss, and bank loan contracting. *Journal of Financial and Quantitative Analysis, 49*(4), 1101–1132.

Dowling, G. (2014). The curious case of corporate tax avoidance: Is it socially irresponsible? *Journal of Business Ethics, 124*(1), 173–184.

Ebrahimi, H. (2012a, October 16). Starbucks pays no UK tax after £398m sales. *The Daily Telegraph*, p. B1. Retrieved August 20, 2019, available via subscription from Thomson-Gale.

Ebrahimi, H. (2012b, November 3). £11bn tax bill "owed" by foreign companies. *The Daily Telegraph*, p. 37. Retrieved August 20, 2019, available via subscription from Thomson-Gale.

Ebrahimi, H., & Armitstead, L. (2012, October 18). Dismal record to blame for UK tax, says Starbucks. *The Daily Telegraph*, p. B3. Retrieved August 20, 2019, available via subscription from Thomson-Gale.

Engelen, P. (2012). What is the reputational cost of a dishonest CEO? Evidence from US illegal insider trading. *CESifo Economic Studies, 58*(1), 140–163.

Fama, E. F. (1970). Efficient capital markets: A review of theory and empirical work. *Journal of Finance, 25*(2), 383–417.

Fombrun, C., & Shanley, M. (1990). What's in a name? Reputation building and corporate strategy. *Academy of Management Journal, 33*(2), 233–258.

Frecknall-Hughes, J., Moizer, P., Doyle, E., & Summers, B. (2017). An examination of ethical influences on the work of tax practitioners. *Journal of Business Ethics, 146*(4), 729–745.

Freeman, R. E. (1984). *Strategic management: A stakeholder approach*. Boston, MA: Pitman.

Freeman, R. E. (1994). The politics of stakeholder theory: Some future directions. *Business Ethics Quarterly, 4*(4), 409–421.

Friedman, M. (1970). The social responsibility of business is to increase its profits. *The New York Times Magazine*. Retrieved November 26, 2019, from https://web. archive.org/web/20060207060807/https://www.colorado.edu/studentgroups/ libertarians/issues/friedman-soc-resp-business.html.

Gallemore, J., Maydew, E., & Thornock, J. (2014). The reputational costs of tax avoidance. *Contemporary Accounting Research, 31*(4), 1103–1133.

Gatzert, N. (2015). The impact of corporate reputation and reputation damaging events on financial performance: Empirical evidence from the literature. *European Management Journal, 33*(6), 485–499.

Gaultier-Gaillard, S., Louisot, J.-P., & Rayner, J. (2009). Managing reputational risk: From theory to practice. In: J. Klewes & R. Wreschniok (Eds.), *Reputation capital* (pp. 161–178). Berlin: Springer.

Gillett, P. (1999). The consultative document on a general anti avoidance rule for direct taxes: A view from business. *British Tax Review, 1*, 1–5.

Gompertz, S. (2012). Starbucks "paid just £8.6m UK tax in 14 years". *BBC News*. Retrieved November 14, 2019, from www.bbc.co.uk/news/business-19967397.

Graham, J., Hanlon, M., Shevlin, T., & Shroff, N. (2014). Incentives for tax planning and avoidance: Evidence from the field. *Accounting Review, 89*(3), 991–1023.

Graham, J., Li, S., & Qiu, J. (2008). Corporate misreporting and bank loan contracting. *Journal of Financial Economics, 89*(1), 44–61.

Harrison, J. S., & Wicks, A. C. (2013). Stakeholder theory, value, and firm performance. *Business Ethics Quarterly, 23*(1), 97–124.

Hasseldine, J., & Morris, G. (2013). Corporate social responsibility and tax avoidance: A comment and reflection. *Accounting Forum, 37*(1), 1–14.

Henderson, R., & Temple-West, P. (2019). Group of US corporate leaders ditches shareholder-first mantra. *The Financial Times*. Retrieved November 2019, from www. ft.com/content/e21a9fac-c1f5-11e9-a8e9-296ca66511c925.

Hiscott, G. (2019, April 7). Google "avoided paying £1.5bn in tax" that could have paid for 60,000 nurses. *Mirror*. Retrieved July 15, 2019, from www.mirror.co.uk/news/ uk-news/google-avoided-paying-15bn-tax-14250344.

Hoi, C., Wu, Q., & Zhang, H. (2013). Is corporate social responsibility (CSR) associated with tax avoidance? Evidence from irresponsible CSR activities. *Accounting Review, 88*(6), 2025–2060.

Hokstad, P., & Steiro, T. (2006). Overall strategy for risk evaluation and priority setting of risk regulations. *Reliability Engineering & System Safety, 91*(1), 100–111.

Homburg, C., Vollmayr, J., & Hahn, A. (2014). Firm value creation through major channel expansions: Evidence from an event study in the United States, Germany, and China. *Journal of Marketing, 78*(3), 38–61.

Hribar, P., & Jenkins, N. (2004). The effect of accounting restatements on earnings revisions and the estimated cost of capital. *Review of Accounting Studies, 9*(2–3), 337–356.

Hurley, J. (2012, December 3). Starbucks first to cave in over tax backlash. *The Daily Telegraph*, p. B1. Retrieved August 20, 2019, available via subscription from Thomson-Gale.

Jensen, M. (2002). Value maximization, stakeholder theory, and the corporate objective function. *Business Ethics Quarterly, 12*(2), 235–256.

Jeong, J., & Yoo, C. Y. (2011). Deceptive advertising and abnormal stock returns. *International Journal of Advertising, 30*(3), 509–535.

274 *Yingyue Ding et al.*

Lanis, R., & Richardson, G. (2015). Is corporate social responsibility performance associated with tax avoidance? *Journal of Business Ethics, 127*(2), 439–457.

Lavermicocca, C., & Buchan, J. (2015). Role of reputational risk in tax decision making by large companies. *eJournal of Tax Research, 13*(1), 5–50.

Lea, R. (2013, November 5). The price of tax avoidance is loss of trust, warns King. *The Times*. Retrieved July 15, 2019, available via subscription from Thomson-Gale.

Lyons, T., & Mallalieu, H. (2012, November 21). Starbucks, Amazon and public boycotts. *The Times*, p. 33. Retrieved August 21, 2019, available via subscription from Thomson-Gale.

MacLean, R. (2012, December 7). Starbucks agrees to pay £20m in tax after customer backlash. *The Times*, p. 8. Retrieved August 20, 2019, available via subscription from Thomson-Gale.

McVeigh, T., Stewart, H., & Bowers, S. (2012, December 9). UK Uncut protesters shut down Starbucks shops. *The Guardian*. Retrieved March 26, 2019, from www. theguardian.com/business/2012/dec/09/starbucks-stores-uk-uncut-protest.

Middleton, C. (2014, May 3). Coffee wars – and the caffeine fix the country just can't ditch. *The Daily Telegraph*, p. 28. Retrieved August 20, 2019, available via subscription from Thomson-Gale.

Milner, L. (2013, July 22). Coffee shops begin stirring fightback against the mighty Starbucks and Co. *The Times*, p. 39. Retrieved August 20, 2019, available via subscription from Thomson-Gale.

MoneyWeek (2012). *Why does Starbucks pay so Little tax?* [Video File]. Retrieved August 12, 2019, from https://youtube/Th4fxMFRIt0.

Neate, R. (2014, September 29). What is the "Google tax"? *The Guardian*. Retrieved August 23, 2019, from www.theguardian.com/politics/2014/sep/29/what-is-google-tax-george-osborne.

Neville, S. (2012). Starbucks "pays £8.6m tax on £3bn sales". *The Guardian*. Retrieved November 14, 2019, from www.theguardian.com/business/2012/oct/15/starbucks-tax-uk-sales.

Nicolau, J. L. (2002). Assessing new hotel openings through an event study. *Tourism Management, 23*(1), 47–54.

Orow, N. (2004). Structured finance and the operation of general anti-avoidance rules. *British Tax Review, 4*, 410–435.

Osborne, A. (2013, July 31). Lords call for tough penalties to crack down on tax avoiders. *The Daily Telegraph*, p. B1. Retrieved August 20, 2019, available via subscription from Thomson-Gale.

Peacock, L., & Blackden, R. (2012, November 2). Starbucks under scrutiny for its short-sized European tax bills. *The Daily Telegraph*, p. B3. Retrieved August 20, 2019, available via subscription from Thomson-Gale.

Prebble, Z., & Prebble, J. (2010). The morality of tax avoidance. *Creighton Law Review, 43*(3), 693–746.

Ram, A. (2015, December 15). Starbucks pays £8.1m corporation tax as profits rise. *The Financial Times*. Retrieved August 28, 2019, from www.ft.com/content/96a707cc-a327-11e5-bc70-7ff6d4fd203a.

Reece, D. (2012, December 7). Starbucks' overblown and odd tax gesture will not solve anything. *The Daily Telegraph*, p. B2. Retrieved August 20, 2019, available via subscription from Thomson-Gale.

Rifkind, H. (2012, December 4). You and I can't fix the Starbucks problem. *The Times*, p. 29. Retrieved August 21, 2019, available via subscription from Thomson-Gale.

Ritchie, M. (2012). Starbucks "paid no UK income tax" since 2009. *Channel 4 News*. Retrieved November 14, 2019, from www.channel4.com/news/starbucks-coffee-income-tax-uk.

Roland, D. (2014, November 15). Starbucks' deal with the Dutch may be illegal state aid, says EU. *The Daily Telegraph*, p. 35. Retrieved August 20, 2019, available via subscription from Thomson-Gale.

Rowley, E. (2013, June 24). Starbucks wakes up to £5m UK corporation tax. *The Daily Telegraph*, p. B3. Retrieved August 20, 2019, available via subscription from Thomson-Gale.

Ruddick, G. (2012, December 12). Record sales at "taxman's favourite" Costa boosts Whitbread. *The Daily Telegraph*, p. B1. Retrieved August 20, 2019, available via subscription from Thomson-Gale.

Samuel, J. (2012, December 4). Wake up and smell the … . *The Times*, p. 48. Retrieved August 20, 2019, available via subscription from Thomson-Gale.

Saunders, M., Lewis, P., & Thornhill, A. (2019). *Research methods for business students* (8th ed.). Harlow: Pearson.

Savage, M. (2012, December 8). No hiding place as crackdown on tax havens includes Isle of Man. *The Times*, p. 11. Retrieved August 21, 2019, available via subscription from Thomson-Gale.

Schlesinger, F. (2012, November 13). Starbucks brews secret tax deal in Netherlands. *The Times*, p. 14. Retrieved September 1, 2019, available via subscription from Thomson-Gale.

Serle, J. (2012). Starbucks: Another company avoiding UK tax on a huge scale. *The Bureau of Investigative Journalism*. Retrieved November 14, 2019, from www.thebureauinvestigates.com/stories/2012-10-17/starbucks-another-company-avoiding-uk-tax-on-a-huge-scale.

Sikka, P. (2010). Smoke and mirrors: Corporate social responsibility and tax avoidance. *Accounting Forum*, *34*(3–4), 153–168.

Sikka, P. (2013). Smoke and mirrors: Corporate social responsibility and tax avoidance: A reply to Hasseldine and Morris. *Accounting Forum*, *37*(1), 15–28.

Starbucks (2012, December 8). *The Times*, p. 31. Retrieved August 20, 2019, available via subscription from Thomson-Gale.

The Daily Telegraph (2012a, December 8). A lot of froth over Starbucks and tax, p. 31. Retrieved August 20, 2019, available via subscription from Thomson-Gale.

The Daily Telegraph (2012b, December 10). Whitbread likely to benefit from Starbucks' boycott with boost in sales, p. B7. Retrieved August 21, 2019, available via subscription from Thomson-Gale.

The Economist (2012, December 15). Wake up and smell the coffee, p. 64. Retrieved August 20, 2019, available via subscription from Thomson-Gale.

The Economist (2013, February 16). The missing $20 trillion, p. 11. Retrieved August 21, 2019, available via subscription from Thomson-Gale.

The Guardian (2012, December 8). UK Uncut v Starbucks – in pictures. Retrieved March 26, 2019, from www.theguardian.com/uk/gallery/2012/dec/08/uk-uncut-starbucks-in-pictures.

Thomas, D. (2019). IoD calls for new ethical code of boardroom conduct. *The Financial Times*. Retrieved November 25, 2019, from www.ft.com/content/e11d8788-0ac8-11ea-bb52-34c8d9dc6d84.

Titcomb, J. (2014, April 17). Starbucks to pay corporation tax after HQ moves to Britain. *The Daily Telegraph*, p. B5. Retrieved September 1, 2019, available via subscription from Thomson-Gale.

Treneman, A. (2012, November 16). My love affair with Starbucks is over: The boycott is on. *The Times*, p. 34. Retrieved August 27, 2019, available via subscription from Thomson-Gale.

Turner, J. (2012, November 17). There's nothing hip about avoiding your taxes. *The Times*, p. 29. Retrieved August 20, 2019, available via subscription from Thomson-Gale.

Vitell, S., & Davis, J. (1990). The relationship between ethics and job satisfaction: An empirical investigation. *Journal of Business Ethics, 9*(6), 489–494.

Walsh, D. (2012, October 24). How coffee can help to cut the deficit. *The Times*, p. 43. Retrieved August 21, 2019, available via subscription from Thomson-Gale.

Wartick, S. (1992). The relationship between intense media exposure and change in corporate reputation. *Business & Society, 31*(1), 33–49.

Wilson, H. (2012, November 12). High-profit water companies reduce tax bills to a trickle. *The Daily Telegraph*, p. B1. Retrieved September 1, 2019, available via subscription from Thomson-Gale.

Worstall, T. (2012, November 20). Starbucks is no tax avoider: It's obeying the law of the land. *The Times*, p. 28. Retrieved August 20, 2019, available via subscription from Thomson-Gale.

Zardasti, L., Yahaya, N., Valipour, A., Rashid, A. S. A., & Noor, N. M. (2017). Review on the identification of reputation loss indicators in an onshore pipeline explosion event. *Journal of Loss Prevention in the Process Industries, 48*, 71–86.

14 The effect of media on tax compliance

Hypothetical scenarios study

N. Tolga Saruç, Çiğdem Börke Tunalı, Hakan Yavuz, and Tunç İnce

Introduction

It is well known that people do not always behave as predicted by the rational choice theory, this applies especially in the case of tax compliance. Tax compliance in general is higher than the classic economic model predicts. Behavioural tax compliance models are useful in explaining tax behaviour and improving predictions of classic economics models. This study aims to analyse a media effect, especially the news in the newspaper about taxes on tax compliance decisions of people. In order to analyse the effect of different news on people's behaviour, five different scenarios are randomly presented to a total of 820 students. In the first section, the basic model of tax evasion is explained briefly and behavioural models and some nudges are discussed. The second section presents the methodology and the model of the study. Results are discussed in the final section.

Tax Compliance Models

Tax evasion is a risky and illegal activity. In economic terms, taking risks in a legitimate activity is not very different from taking risks in an illegal activity. Therefore, it seems reasonable to employ methods used in other fields of public economics to tax evasion. So, the standard economic model of tax evasion uses expected utility maximisation.

Expected utility models assume a particular form of deterrence theory, in which the probability of audit and the severity of fine act as evasion control policy. Different alternatives are assessed by considering the likely consequences or outcomes. The utility of each outcome is evaluated and probabilities are attached to uncertain outcomes, leading to the expected utility of the alternatives. The individual chooses the alternative with the highest expected utility.

Allingham and Sandmo's (1972) model is quite simple. They assume that behaviour is affected by factors such as the tax rate, the penalties for tax evasion, and the probability of detection. In each time period, an individual has to decide how much income to declare to the tax authority. They derived results

278   *N. Tolga Saruç et al.*

about the influence of tax rates, penalties, and detection rates on tax evasion (Allingham & Sandmo, 1972).

The basic models consider the individual's decision to evade as a simple gamble that is affected mainly by the probability of expected fine and the tax rate. However, most empirical studies point out that there are some other factors such as perception, attitudes and moral judgements, and demographic variables. Alm, McClelland, and Schulze (1992) state that in most countries the audit rate and the penalty for tax evasion are very small. Therefore, according to the basic economic model, everybody should evade taxes and the amount of tax evasion should be much more than it is. Then, the question that researchers should try to answer is not "Why do people evade taxes?" but "Why do people pay taxes?" Dean, Keenan, and Kenney (1980) were highly critical of the way economic theory tries to explain tax evasion. They argued that the assumptions of analytical models "are naive and far-removed from reality" (Dean, Keenan, & Kenney, 1980, p. 29). The authors claimed that although there may be a relationship between the expected fine and evasion, criminological and social studies found more important factors influencing criminal acts such as moral beliefs and lack of peer involvement of an individual, etc. (Dean, Keenan, & Kenney, 1980). Frey (1992, 1997) indicates that a higher enforcement by tax authorities may actually result in lower tax compliance by individuals, when the increased enforcement crowds out the intrinsic motivation that causes people to pay their taxes. Dean, Keenan, and Kenney (1980, p. 29) indicated that these types of studies "have long abandoned the primitive sanctions/ deterrence model". They claimed that "how taxpayers might act if they were condemned to being entirely rational, utility maximising automatons can only serve to postpone the emergence of realistic tax theories and useful policy insights" (Dean, Keenan, & Kenney, 1980, p. 44).

Some limitations of the basic economic models are that they ignore the roles of tax practitioners, cost of compliance, ongoing interaction between taxpayers and tax authority and different sources of income, the effect of media on tax behaviour, etc. Now there is considerable amount of empirical work on the subject of income tax evasion, which finds these and many other variables to be relevant to income tax evasion. The Internal Revenue Service (IRS) in the USA has detailed 64 potential compliance factors (Jackson & Milliron, 1986) ranging from "income" and "age" to "mental health".

The criticisms of the expected utility model lead to development of an alternative model: prospect theory model. The theory was developed by Kahneman and Tversky (1979) and it is reviewed and discussed by several authors such as Lattimore and Witte (1985), Jackson and Milliron (1986), Roth, Scholz, and Witte (1989), Tversky and Wakker (1995) amongst others. Prospect theory explores how decisions are made and it is developed in order to overcome some problems associated with expected standard utility theory.

Kahneman and Tversky (1979, 1984) suggested that there is a two-phase assessment process when an individual chooses between risky alternatives. First, the editing phase, and second, the evaluation phase (in which the edited

The relevance of prospect theory for tax compliance is indicated by authors such as Jackson and Milliron (1986), Loftus (1985), Spicer (1986), Smith and Kinsey (1987), Chang, Nichols, and Schultz (1987), Roth, Scholz, and Witte (1989), Carroll (1987, 1989, 1992), Webley *et al.* (1991), Elffers and Hessing (1997), Robben *et al.* (1990), and Yaniv (1999). These studies indicate that framing is very important in tax decisions. For example, an analysis of focus-group discussion indicates that taxes which have to be paid with tax returns at the end of the year, as well as tax amounts owed in general, especially those due on income from secondary sources, have greater utility than taxes that are withheld, especially from the primary salary (Ekstrand, 1980). Accordingly, the overwhelming majority of taxpayers in the USA (75%) prefer to have more withheld than is necessary (Smith & Kinsey, 1987) and there was a storm of protest in the USA against the 1986 tax reform because the act intended to lower advance tax payments for many, thus lowering their tax refunds (Elffers & Hessing, 1997). Loftus (1985) noted that withholdings lead to a shift of the reference point and higher withholdings thus decrease the motivation to reduce taxes at the time of filings both by legal and illegal means. However, as Carroll (1989) pointed out, increases in withholdings reduce tax evasion only if: (i) the reference point is zero taxes owed at filing time; and (ii) the reference point on withheld income sources also shifts to new reduced levels. A taxpayer who has paid £5,000 in taxes and owes another £200 at the filing time can take his/her reference point as a £200 loss, a £5,200 loss, or, say, £500 gain if s/he paid a total of £5,700 in taxes last year. The taxpayer could also take the reference point as what his/her colleagues, neighbours, or other people similar to him/her in some aspects (*e.g.*, income sources, amount of income, spending level, etc.) have paid. Thus, the reference point can be almost anything, and it is arbitrary.

Carroll (1989) indicates that a discontinuity in the decision weight function at the reference point in prospect theory causes a difficulty to base policy on its existence, since the exact location of the discontinuity is unknown. Accordingly, if the probability of audit has been doubled and taxpayers have been told about it, there may have been four different outcomes: (i) it might have no effect, if taxpayers consider the probability was too low anyway; (ii) it might have a small effect, if the probabilities were in the shallow part of the curve; (iii) it might have an important effect, if the probabilities were in the steep part of the curve; (iv) it might have a very significant effect, if the increase in probabilities resulted in a shift in decision weight from certainty of no risk to uncertainty of risk. The author noted that an annual 1% probability of getting caught at tax evading can be thought of as a 50% chance when continued over a working lifetime of 37 years. If a taxpayer coded the probability of audit as in the second case, it would produce a much greater deterrence effect. Moreover, a taxpayer who perceives 2% probability of an audit and 50% probability of being fined (if audited), tends to weight the second stage probability more strongly than the first stage (Carroll, 1989). This indicates that decisions depending separately on the probability of audit and the probability of fine can lead to more compliance than would be expected from the joint probability of being fined. Furthermore, it implies that more deterrence effect could be obtained from the same policy by advertising a highly probable conditional probability (fine rate) rather than a low probability event (audit rate). The basic effect was named as the pseudo certainty effect by Tversky and Kahneman (1981). Johnson and Payne (1985) gave another example to demonstrate this: (i) for every event of serious tax evasion, 1 in 500 evaders is sent to jail to spend some time; (ii) over the average life time of paying taxes (50 years), evaders who continue to evade taxes seriously faces a 1 in 10 chance of being detected and convicted, and when convicted s/he is certain to spend time in jail. Of course, the second way of explaining the outcomes would have a much higher deterrence effect.

If a taxpayer frames taxes as government waste, a loss to the individual and to the society as a whole, then the taxpayer may have strategies for identifying loopholes and the various ways to evade. On the other hand, if the taxpayer frames taxes as contribution and sharing, s/he may have strategies for identifying legal obligations and fulfilling them. Although prospect theory indicates the importance of editing and framing, there is not a theory about how the editing processes work exactly (Carroll, 1989).

Elffers and Hessing (1997) suggested that the incentive for tax evasion could be eliminated by the tax authority's deliberately setting taxpayers' advance tax payments slightly higher than their true tax liabilities. However, using prospect theory and assuming the reference point is income after the payment of tax advance (as it was assumed by Elffers and Hessing, 1997), Yaniv (1999) showed that although increases in advance tax payments would encourage more compliance, they would not completely eliminate the incentive for tax evasion. This would only be possible if taxpayers significantly overestimate the low probability of audit, which is prevalent in many countries. Empirical findings by Chang, Nichols, and Schultz (1987), Carroll (1992), and Varma and Doob (1998) also indicated that taxpayers are mainly concerned about out-of-pocket gains and losses at the time of filing.

Alm and Beck (1990) pointed out that an individual is unlikely to participate in an amnesty if his/her reference point is the initial level of previously unreported income. Tax evasion for this individual is a norm and paying taxes in the amnesty is a loss. The individual in this case is a risk-seeker rather than a risk-averter. However, if the individual takes the reference point as "the level of amnesty income less full amnesty taxes", then s/he will be much more likely to declare any unpaid taxes from previous years. In this case, the individual regards paying taxes as a norm and considers participating to the amnesty as a gain. So, it is very important to change the individual's reference point by indicating that paying taxes is the normal and accepted form of behaviour (*e.g.*, indicating tax evasion is a very serious crime, honest taxpayers are victimised

The effect of media on tax compliance   281

by such behaviour and stress that tax authorities intend to catch and punish tax evaders). Thus, an amnesty increases compliance only if the amnesty makes the individual recognise that paying taxes is the norm.

Tversky and Kahneman (1973) suggested that events are judged to be more probable if they come more readily to mind. In the literature this is named as "availability" heuristic. Availability identifies the subjective sense of the probability of an event's occurrence. Thus, easily imaginable or recallable events are in general thought to have high likelihood of occurrence. People depend heavily on salient information, which is easily retrievable from memory. Spicer and Hero (1985), Benjamini and Maital (1985), and Webley (1987) found that tax compliance was higher among individuals who had been previously audited. Moreover, information about friends and family members of being audited should affect the perceived risk of evasion positively. Accordingly, recent news on the media about a tax evasion case might temporarily increase the perceived probability of punishment, especially when there are similarities between the taxpayers and the convicted evaders (such as occupation, income, living in the same city, etc.). Carroll (1989) noted that "the IRS seems to save some juicy fraud convictions for late March to take advantage of the availability heuristics just before taxes are due" (Carroll, 1989, p. 244). However, it is also possible that the news of a convicted evader may have the opposite effect; the taxpayer might think that the IRS is busy with more important tax frauds, which involve large amounts, and therefore an average evader might feel safer. The taxpayer may also consider the audit resources are fixed, so every known case of evasion decreases his/her risk of audit, or else the taxpayer might be concerned about the probabilities, in which situation every known case of tax evasion increases the perceived risk. People usually interpret information in terms of their prior understanding to support their views. It might also be possible that an audited person might reduce the perceived audit rate, thinking the low rate of occurrence of an audit has just happened for him/her, and it will take at least a while for another to happen.

Scholz and Pinney (1995) noted that in real life taxpayers do not have precise information about the probability of audit and the fine for evasion. They indicate that duty heuristics provide both a direct and indirect effect to tax compliance. According to this, taxpayers subconsciously observe the performance of the government relative to the amount of taxes they pay. The taxpayers summarise their observations in a judgement, which authors call "tax duty", and take decisions about compliance depending on this core of previous experience. So, apart from the direct effect of tax duty in providing a motivation to comply, it also indirectly biases self-interest beliefs in the same direction. Thus, the duty heuristics inadvertently reduce the conflict between self-interest and collective rationality by diminishing the conflict between duty and fear for compliance decisions. Accordingly, taxpayers' sense of duty to pay taxes significantly affects the perceived probability of the expected fine for tax evasion. Taxpayers with duty heuristics will therefore perceive the expected fine for evasion as high, whereas taxpayers with little duty will perceive a low risk of expected fine.

282   *N. Tolga Saruç et al.*

These hypotheses are confirmed in the empirical studies carried out by Scholz and Pinney (1995) and Scholz and Lubell (1998a, 1998b). Moreover, they found that duty heuristics have more effect on perceived expected fine than the objective probabilities of risk. This was the case even for taxpayers who are facing the greatest temptation to evade because of the high potential gains from tax evasion.

Scholz and Lubell (1998a, 1998b) note the importance of trust as a heuristic in tax compliance. According to this, when trustworthy democratic institutions succeed in issuing socially beneficial laws that are willingly followed by trusting citizens, the trusting relationship between citizens and state benefits society in two ways: (i) trust between citizen and government (vertical trust) can expand the range of collective problems that legal authorities are able to tackle. Trusted government institutions will be able to extend the benefits of social cooperation to collective problems, which are too costly to resolve in the absence of trust. In order to achieve this, legal authorities use law to define "focal points" for cooperative solutions; (ii) trust among citizens (horizontal trust) diminishes the enforcement cost of maintaining collective solutions. The higher the trust, the less the need for monitoring and punishment mechanisms, which are costly. So, trust increases social capital by decreasing the enforcement cost involved in maintaining collective solutions.

In the absence of trust, the potential benefits of collective action rely either on altruism or on expected punishments. The effect of trust in large-scale collectives, however, will not necessarily provide compliance, unlike small-scale collectives. A club member who avoids his/her obligations is very likely to be found out and to lose the benefits of membership. On the other hand, since the cost of monitoring and punishment are much higher in large-scale collectives, a taxpayer who evades taxes is less likely to be found out or lose benefits even if caught. Nevertheless, Scholz and Lubell (1998a, 1998b) point out that the relationship between trust and trustworthiness can be developed in large-scale collectives, even though there is no credible institutional foundation. Authors indicate that individuals learn different heuristics for assessing trust in small-scale collectives, in which the relationship between trust and trustworthiness is strengthened through potential punishments.

Positive experiences of obtaining benefits from a collective increase in trust, and so increase the probability of complying with obligations to that collective, while negative experiences decrease both trust and compliance. Therefore "attitudes of trust serve as an action related summary measure of the benefits of a given collective that enables citizens to cooperate in the most beneficial collectives while avoiding exploitation in less beneficial ones" (Scholz & Lubell, 1998a, p. 401). It is possible that taxpayers generalise this heuristic, use of trust, to large-scale societies. In this case, there will be a positive relationship between trust and tax compliance, even though the probability of potential punishments will be much lower in a large-scale collective. The empirical study by Scholz and Lubell (1998a, 1998b) indicated that trust changes according to changes

The effect of media on tax compliance   283

in net benefit (taxes paid *minus* public goods obtained). So, trust increases significantly when the amount of taxes paid decreases, and it reduces when taxes increase. Moreover, both vertical and horizontal trust positively and significantly affect the probability of compliance. However, in contradiction to the compliance heuristics explained above, a study by Steenbergen, McGraw, and Scholz (1992) did not find a significant effect of tax changes on attitudes.

Kirchler (2007) explained the slippery slope framework of tax compliance. According to this, trust in tax authorities and power of tax authorities are two interacting dimensions that explain tax compliance. Kasper, Kogler, and Kirchler (2015) carried out a questionnaire-based experiment with 487 employees which found that media coverage affected both indicated trust in tax authorities and the perceived power of governmental institutions. Therefore, media coverage has an important effect on intended tax compliance.

Nevertheless, media news can be used as a nudge for the people to behave as they are expected to behave. This chapter investigates how newspaper affects the intended decision to declare taxes.

Methodology

A scenario-based study was carried out in order to analyse the effect of news about taxes on students' hypothetical decision to evade. There were five experimental groups in which 820 students were randomly assigned. After they were presented with reading material, each student had to assume that they were working as self-employed business owners such as accountants. It was indicated that after a financial year they had earned a certain amount of taxable income. Then, students were asked if they would declare the whole income to the tax authorities. Students' perceived audit, perceived fine rates, risk aversion, and tax ethics are measured also considering gender and age variables.

Scenario 1

A text is given to one group of students about the importance of tax week organisations that have been carried out in Turkey since 1990. In this respect many events are carried out to increase voluntary compliance rates, tax awareness, and tax ethics of citizens. The text explains that honour plaques and gift sets are given to taxpayers who paid the highest amount of taxes. Tax officials visit taxpayers for a week to listen and record their suggestions, complaints, and expectations. Panels are carried out about taxes. Moreover, informative programmes run on TVs, radios, and newspapers. Slogans like "Taxes are our bright future", "Taxable income is blessed", "Taxes are the foundation of development", "Better life, better Turkey with taxed income" are advertised everywhere. This experimental group's purpose is to analyse the effect of the knowledge of events that is carried out to increase voluntary compliance in Turkey during tax week.

Scenario 2

Scenario 2 is created as a control group, a neutral text about tax legislation is presented to students. After students read the text, they answered the same questionnaires.

Scenario 3

IRS statistics of Turkey indicate that tax evasion is widespread in the country and newspapers use these statistics and run stories about how some taxpayers with certain occupations declare really low income with headlines such as "Businessmen, doctors, lawyers, architects, engineers, restaurant owners, and jewellers are poor (!)", "Some doctors and lawyers are under the hunger threshold", "Turkish people are expert at evading taxes". The text given to students comprises all these headlines and some additional news about how widespread tax evasion in Turkey is. We aimed to measure the effect of media news on tax evasion in Turkey.

Scenario 4

The Ministry of Finance makes some declarations in the media, one of the aims being to increase tax compliance by giving important messages to taxpayers. The text for this group includes headlines and news such as "The fine for tax evasion is really heavy, we will catch all evaders", "You are warned, do not evade taxes otherwise the consequences will be heavy", "If you do not document your VAT and pocket the money, it is a theft and you will get caught", "Tax evasion is very risky, evading tax is taking a high risk unnecessarily", "Fighting against the underground economy is as important as fighting terrorism". This experimental group was used to measure the effect of "warning headlines" on intended tax declaration behaviour.

Scenario 5

There has been a tax amnesty almost every couple of years since 1960 in Turkey. Some perceived that tax amnesties penalise honest taxpayers who carry out their duty in a timely manner. The topic of tax amnesties was often analysed in newspapers with headlines such as "Payers are suckers", "Tax festival", "You will regret it if you miss the opportunity". In this experimental group, the effect of news about the frequent tax amnesties on hypothetical tax declaration is investigated.

After different students read each scenario, they were asked if they would declare all of their income to the tax authority. Participants responded with "yes", "most probably", "maybe", "I doubt it", or "no". The number of students who responded with "no" was small. So, we assumed that participants who responded with "yes" and "most probably" would declare their income and

The effect of media on tax compliance   285

those who responded with "maybe", "I doubt it", and "no" would not declare. So, the first two answers were coded with 1 and the other three were coded with 0.

In addition to asking participants if they would declare all of their income to the tax authority, participants were asked to what extent they agreed with the following statements: "The auditing rate of the independent accountant you assume is in place is low", "I think tax penalties are a deterrent", "I can take risks in order to succeed at my job", and "Since it is unethical, I never evade taxes". Participants responded to these statements with "I completely agree", "I agree", "I am undecided", "I do not agree", and "I completely do not agree". Similar to the question of whether respondents would declare all of their income to the tax authority, responses "I completely agree" and "I agree" were coded with 1 and responses "I am undecided", "I do not agree", and "I completely do not agree" were coded with 0. Together with all these questions, participants' age and gender were added to the model. In terms of gender, "male" was coded with 1 and "female" was coded with 0.

The estimated model is given below:

$$\begin{aligned} Declaration\ decision =\ & scenario\,1 + scenario\,3 + scenario\,4 + scenario\,5 \\ & + perceived\ audit + perceived\ fine + risk + ethics \\ & + gender + age + \varepsilon \end{aligned}$$

In the above model, the declaration decision represents whether respondents would declare all of their income to the tax authority. Scenario 1, scenario 3, scenario 4, and scenario 5 are the dummy variables which show the scenarios presented to the participants. Perceived audit represents the dummy variable showing whether the respondent agrees with the statement "The auditing rate of the independent accountant you assume is in place is low". Perceived fine represents the dummy variable showing whether the respondent agrees with the statement "I think tax penalties are a deterrent". Risk represents the dummy variable indicating whether the respondent agrees with the statement "I can take risks in order to succeed at my job". Ethics represents the dummy variable indicating whether the respondent agrees with the statement "Since it is unethical, I never evade tax" and ε is the error term. Scenario 2 is taken as the reference category in the model. The estimated model is run as a logit regression since the dependent variable takes the values of 0 and 1.

Results

Table 14.1 indicates the results of the analyses. As can be seen, the variable ethics is significant at 1%, scenario 3, risk and gender variables are significant at 5%, while scenario 5 at 10%. Therefore, one can state that these variables affect the probability of declaring income. Analysing the coefficients of these variables, it can be stated that participants reading scenario 3 (*i.e.*, have read that the

286 N. Tolga Saruç et al.

Table 14.1 Predicted results of the model

Variables	Marginal effects
Scenario 1	−0.06074
	(0.03753)
Scenario 3	−0.08305**
	(0.03938)
Scenario 4	0.00125
	(0.03655)
Scenario 5	−0.07602*
	(0.03952)
Perceived audited	0.02078
	(0.02563)
Perceived fine	0.00318
	(0.02889)
Risk	−0.05490**
	(0.02716)
Ethics	0.35661***
	(0.02456)
Gender	−0.06328**
	(0.02562)
Age	−0.00616
	(0.00653)

Notes: ***, **, * indicate $p < 0.01$, $p < 0.05$ and $p < 0.10$, respectively. Standards errors are given in parentheses. The model was estimated using the Stata 13 software.

underground economy and tax evasion are widespread in Turkey) are 0.083 more likely not to declare their whole income compared to the control group (scenario 2; have read a neutral text about tax issues). Similarly, participants reading scenario 5 (*i.e.*, tax amnesties are often carried out) are more likely not to declare their income by 0.076 compared to the control group.

Participants willing to incur high risks have a higher probability of not declaring their income than those with low risk. The variable ethics, also significant at 10%, indicated that people with high ethics have a higher propensity to declare their whole income than those with low ethics (*i.e.*, 0.3566). Finally, the variable gender showed that male participants' propensity not to declare all income is higher than females' propensity.

Conclusion

Our results indicate that media news have a significant effect on tax compliance. More specifically, news about frequent tax amnesties and a large amount of tax evasion have a negative effect on tax compliance. On the other hand, the study did not find any significant effect of reading about different efforts to increase tax compliance made by tax authorities in order to increase voluntary compliance rates. It seems that various slogans used to increase tax awareness did not increase participants' compliance rates. Similarly, the statement regarding the

The effect of media on tax compliance 287

Ministry of Finance on how hard the institution tackled evaders did not significantly affect compliance. Results concerning ethics, risk, and gender were in line with the tax compliance literature.

The results indicate that the news about "huge tax evasion in Turkey" and "tax amnesties that have been carried out too often" had very important negative effects on tax declaration behaviour. Trust increases social capital by decreasing the enforcement cost involved in maintaining collective solutions. It is likely that these kinds of news reduce both vertical and horizontal trust. The lesser the trust, there is more need for monitoring and punishment mechanisms, which are costly. "The widespread tax evasion" and "too often tax amnesties" and the news about them change the individual reference point by indicating that not paying taxes is the normal and accepted form of behaviour. Thus, too many tax amnesties decrease compliance and make the individual recognise that tax evasion is the norm. It is probable that when taxpayers are aware of a large amount of tax evasion and tax amnesties that are carried out too often the effect of tax admiration efforts to increase voluntary compliance rates, tax awareness, and tax ethics of citizens are limited. In the absence of trust, the potential benefits of collective action rely either on altruism or on expected punishments. Similarly, it may be possible that the Ministry of Finance declarations in the media to increase tax compliance by giving important messages to taxpayers do not yield a significant effect because of tax amnesties and perceived tax evasion. It is difficult to change the individual's reference point by indicating that paying taxes is the normal and accepted form of behaviour when there are so many tax amnesties.

There may be some policy implications of the results of the study; news about large amounts of non-compliance increase the probability of one not declaring his/her income. Similarly, news about the high frequency of tax amnesties affects compliance negatively. It is not possible to control the news in democratic countries with established democratic institutions. Therefore, the underlying reason for these kinds of news should be eliminated. When considering a new tax amnesty, its potential effect on trust and tax duty amongst taxpayers should be considered. Government and relative authorities can publicly declare that under no circumstances will there be a general tax amnesty in the future. It may be declared that there will be one tax amnesty in one generation at maximum. Several other policies to increase trust in tax administrations should be employed. Strengthening the democratic accountability for the highly perceived tax evasion, the main root for the perception should be investigated, and it should be tackled accordingly. For example, relatively high-earning self-employed income groups with the opportunities to evade should be monitored more closely in respect to their tax declaration behaviours.

References

Allingham, M. G., & Sandmo, A. (1972). Income tax evasion: A theoretical analysis. *Journal of Public Economics, 1*, 323–338.

288 *N. Tolga Saruç et al.*

Alm, J., & Beck, W. (1990). Tax amnesties and tax revenues. *Public Finance Quarterly*, *18*(4), 433–453.

Alm, J., McClelland, G. H., & Schulze, W. D. (1992). Why do people pay taxes? Journal *of Public Economics*, *48*, 21–38.

Benjamini, Y., & Maital, S. (1985). Optimal tax evasion and optimal tax evasion policy: Behavioral aspects. In: W. Gaertner & A. Wenig (Eds.), *The economics of the shadow economy: Proceedings of the international conference on the economics of the shadow economy held at the University of Bielefeld West Germany, October 10–14, 1983* (pp. 245–264). Berlin: Springer.

Carroll, J. S. (1987). Compliance with the law: A decision-making approach to taxpaying. *Law and Human Behaviour*, *11*, 319–335.

Carroll, J. S. (1989). A cognitive-process analysis of taxpayer compliance. In: J. A. Roth & J. T. Scholz (Eds.), *Taxpayer compliance: Social science perspectives* (pp. 228–272). Philadelphia, PA: University of Pennsylvania Press.

Carroll, J. S. (1992). How taxpayers think about their taxes: Frames and values. In: J. Slemrod (Ed.), *Why people pay taxes: Tax compliance and enforcement* (pp. 43–63). Ann Arbor, MI: University of Michigan Press.

Chang, O. H., Nichols, D. R., & Schultz, J. J. (1987). Taxpayer attitudes toward tax audit risk. *Journal of Economic Psychology*, *8*, 299–309.

Dean, P., Keenan, T., & Kenney, F. (1980). Taxpayers' attitudes to income tax evasion: An empirical survey. *British Tax Review*, *1*, 28–44.

Ekstrand, L. E. (1980). Factors affecting compliance: Focus group and survey results. In: S. J. Bower (Ed.), *Proceedings of the 73 Annual Conference on Taxation Held under the Auspices of the National Tax Association-Tax Institute of America*, 73, 253–262.

Elffers, H., & Hessing, D. J. (1997). Influencing the prospects of tax evasion. *Journal of Economic Psychology*, *18*, 289–304.

Frey, B. S. (1992). Tertium datum: Pricing, regulating, and intrinsic motivation. *Kyklos*, *45*, 161–184.

Frey, B. S. (1997). *Not just for the money: An economic theory of personal motivation.* Cheltenham: Edward Elgar Publishers.

Jackson, B. R., & Milliron, V. C. (1986). Tax compliance research: Findings, problems, and prospects. *Journal of Accounting Literature*, *5*, 125–165.

Johnson, E., & Payne, J. (1985). The decision to commit a crime: An information-processing analysis. In: D. B. Cornish & R. V. Clarke (Eds.), *The reasoning criminal: Rational choice perspectives on offending* (pp. 170–185). New York: Springer.

Kahneman, D., & Tversky, A. (1979). Prospect theory: An analysis of decision under risk. *Econometrica*, *47*(2), 263–291.

Kahneman, D., & Tversky, A. (1984). Choices, values and frames. *American Psychologist*, *39*, 341–350.

Kasper, M., Kogler, C., & Kirchler, E. (2015). Tax policy and the news: An empirical analysis of taxpayers' perception of tax related media coverage and its impact on tax compliance. *Journal of Behavioral and Experimental Economics*, *54*, 58–63.

Kirchler, E. (2007). *The economics of psychology of tax behavior.* Cambridge: Cambridge University Press.

Lattimore, P. K., & Witte, A. D. (1985). Models of decision making under uncertainty: The criminal choice. In: D. B. Cornish & R. V. Clarke (Eds.), *The reasoning criminal: Rational choice perspectives on offending* (pp. 129–155). New York: Springer.

Loftus, E. F. (1985). To file, perchance to cheat. *Psychology Today*, April, 35–39.

The effect of media on tax compliance 289

Robben, H. S. J., Webley, P., Weigel, R. H., Warneryd, K., Kinsey, K. A., Hessing, D. J., & Scholz, J. T. (1990). Decision frame and opportunity as determinants of tax cheating: An international experimental study. *Journal of Economic Psychology, 11,* 341–364.

Roth, J., Scholz, J., & Witte, A. (1989). *Taxpayer compliance: An agenda for research,* Vol. 1. Philadelphia, PA: University of Pennsylvania Press.

Scholz, J.T., & Lubell, M. (1998a). Trust and taxpaying: Testing the heuristic approach to collective action. *American Journal of Political Science, 42*(2), 398–417.

Scholz, J. T., & Lubell, M. (1998b). Adaptive political attitudes: Duty, trust, and fear as monitors of tax policy. *American Journal of Political Science, 42*(3), 903–920.

Scholz, J.T., & Pinney, N. (1995). Duty, fear, and tax compliance: The heuristic basis of citizenship behavior. *American Journal of Political Science, 39*(2), 490–512.

Smith, K.W., & Kinsey, K.A. (1987). Understanding taxpaying behavior: A conceptual framework with implications for research. *Law and Society Review, 21*(4), 639–663.

Spicer, M.W. (1986). Civilization at a discount: The problem of tax evasion. *National Tax Journal, 39,* 13–20.

Spicer, M.W., & Hero, R. E. (1985). Tax evasion and heuristics: A research note. *Journal of Public Economics, 26,* 263–267.

Steenbergen, M. R., McGraw, K. M., & Scholz, J.T. (1992). Taxpayer adaptation to the 1986 tax reform act: Do new tax laws affect the way taxpayers think about taxes? In: J. Slemrod (Ed.), *Why people pay taxes: Tax compliance and enforcement* (pp. 9–37). Ann Arbor, MI: University of Michigan Press.

Tversky, A., & Kahneman, D. (1973). Availability: A heuristic for judging frequency and probability. *Cognitive Psychology, 5,* 207–232.

Tversky, A., & Kahneman, D. (1981). The framing of decisions and the psychology of choice. *Science, 211,* 453–458.

Tversky, A., & Wakker, P. (1995). Risk attitudes and decision weights. *Econometrica, 63,* 1255–1280.

Varma, K. N., & Doob, A. N. (1998). Deterring economic crimes: The case of tax evasion. *Canadian Journal of Criminology, 40*(2), 165–184.

Webley, P. (1987). Audit probabilities and tax evasion in a business simulation. *Economics Letters, 25,* 267–270.

Webley, P., Robben, H. S. J., Elffers, H., & Hessing, D. J. (1991). *Tax evasion: An experimental approach.* Cambridge: Cambridge University Press.

Yaniv, G. (1999). Tax compliance and advance tax payments: A prospect theory analysis. *National Tax Journal, 52*(4), 753–764.

Names index

Aarons, E. 222, 229
Åberg, R. 130, 153
Ackermann, K. A. 199, 221
Adams, C. 233, 237, 238, 243, 251
Agrawal, J. 260, 261, 271
Ahmed, K. 269, 271
Ahn, J. J. E. 86, 91
Ahrens, L. 131, 152
Ajzen, I. 130, 154
Akay, A. 178, 194
Akay, E. Ç. 152
Akerlof, G. A. 7, 14, 18, 25, 35
Aknin, L. B. 201, 220
Alabede, O. J. 129, 134, 152
Albright, M. 12–14
Aliber, R. 6, 14
Alley, C. 129, 154, 223, 231
Allingham, M. G. xx, xxv, 125, 152, 157, 174, 178, 194, 223–224, 229, 277–278, 287
Alm, J. xx, xxv, 21, 35, 125, 133, 152–3, 175, 198–201, 219, 223–225, 228–230, 278, 280, 288
Altman, M. 16, 19–20, 25–26, 29
Anderson, E. 269, 271
Ando, A. 38, 49
Andreoni, J. 198, 200, 219
Andrighetto, G. 200, 221
Ariel, B. 228, 230
Ariely, D. 5, 7, 14, 41–42, 49
Ariffin, Z. Z. 129, 134, 152
Armitstead, L. 266–268, 271–272
Arnardottir, A. A. 201, 220
Arrow, K. J. 3, 14
Atkinson, A. 116, 120
Austin, C. R. R. 254, 258, 271
Avi-Yonah, R. S. 86–88, 91
Aydın, M. 153

Baker-Goering, M. M. 44, 49
Balliet, D. 199, 219, 221

Barford, V. 254, 271
Bargain, O. 194
Barone, G. 134, 153
Barrett, L. F. 159, 176
Barrington, R. 182, 195
Barros, G. xix, xxv
Bator, F. M. 7, 14
Batrancea, I. 153, 178, 191, 194
Batrancea, L. 130, 152–153, 176, 178, 191, 194–195, 220, 223, 230
Baumeister, R. F. 171, 176
Baumgartner, T. 164, 174
Baumol, W. 245, 251
Bechara, A. 171, 174, 177
Beck, W. 280, 288
Becker, G. S. xx, xxv, 157, 174
Beer, S. 173–174
Belianin, A. 176, 195, 220
Bellemare, C. 130, 153
Benartzi, S. 38, 49
Benjamini, Y. 281, 288
Benk, S. 134, 155, 176, 185, 194–195
Bennett, R. 256, 271
Berg, N. 19, 35
Bergin, T. 254–255, 271
Berkics, M. 154
Bernasconi, M. 219
Bhandari, M. 105, 121
Bhargava, S. 43, 49
Bird, R. xvii, 126, 130, 133–135, 153
Biziou-van-Pol, L. 200, 219
Blackden, R. 266, 274
Blanchflower, D. G. 30, 35
Blauberger, M. 192, 194
Blaufus, K. 161, 174
Bloemer, J. 60, 78
Bloomquist, K. 225, 231
Bob, J. 161, 174
Bobek, D. D. 130, 153
Bock, C. 201, 220

Names index 291

Böhm, G. 163, 171, 176
Böhmelt, T. 80, 91
Bolgár, V. 103, 120
Bonney, R. 235, 251
Booth, A. 256, 272
Bosco, L. 161, 174
Bougie, R. 161, 172–173, 175
Bowers, S. 254, 274
Bowles, S. 54, 77
Bradley, C. F. 130, 153
Braithwaite, V. A. xx, xxv, 132–133, 153, 156
Brandt, M. J. 178, 195
Brizi, A. 200–201, 219
Bruner, D. M. 201, 219
Buchan, J. 257, 274
Buchan, N. R. 202, 219
Buchanan, J. M. 10, 12, 14
Budak, T. 176, 185, 194–195
Bülbül, H. 152
Bursik, R. J. J. 161, 175
Byrnes, J. P. 200, 219

Calvet, R. 198, 219
Camerer, C. 59, 77
Campbell, K. 247, 251
Campbell, S. 268, 272
Capraro, V. 200, 219
Card, D. 29, 35
Carlson, R. H. 234, 251
Carmona, S. 235, 251
Carroll, J. S. 279–281, 288
Carter, S. 258, 272
Cassin, A. 154
Castelfranchi, C. 133, 153
Castleman, B. 47, 49
Cauberghe, V. 261, 272
Cawley, J. H. 44, 49
Çevik, S. 127, 152–153
Chan, H. F. 61, 78
Chang, O. H. 279–280, 288
Charness, G. 200, 219
Chen, K. P. 227, 230
Chen, S. H. 35
Chen, W. 272
Chen, X. 256, 260, 272
Chetty, R. 39, 49
Choo, C. Y. L. 225, 230
Christensen, J. 253, 272
Christiansen, B. 153, 155
Chu, C. Y. C. 227, 230
Chun, R. 21, 35
Chung, J. 201, 219
Churchill, W. xvi
Claeys, A. 261, 271–272

Clardy, A. 256, 272
Clark, L. A. 159, 177
Cleary, D. 180, 184, 194
Coase, R. 26, 36
Cohen, M. 53, 77
Colm, G. xvi
Congdon, W. J. xx, xxv, 8, 14
Coombs, W. 261, 271–272
Cooper, G. 118, 120
Cooper, R. 235, 251
Coricelli, G. 158, 161–162, 175, 178, 194
Crivelli, E. 245, 251
Crocker, K. J. 227, 230
Crosetto, P. 201, 220
Croson, R. 200, 202, 219
Crowe, K. 82, 91
Cullis, J. 227, 230
Cummings, R. G. 130, 134, 153, 200, 219
Cyert, R. 26, 36

D'Attoma, J. 197, 200–201, 203, 219–220
Dalton, H. 9, 14
Damasio, A. R. 171, 174–175, 177
Damasio, H. 171, 175, 177
Darby, M. R. 61, 77
Darity, W. Jr. 32, 36
Datta, S. 8, 14
Daude, C. 127, 153
Davidson, R. J. 176
Davis, J. 257, 276
Dean, P. 278, 288
De Coninck, J. 192, 194
De Mooij, R. 245, 251
Deng, S. 256, 272
Deversi, M. 130, 153
Dezső, L. 178, 195
Dimitrakakis, C. 129, 153
Dobreva, J. 126
Dolls, M. 194
Doob, A. N. 280, 289
Dopfer, K. 35
Dowling, G. 253, 272
Downs, A. 3, 14
Doyle, E. 126, 254, 272
Drelichman, M. 239, 251
Driessen, P. H. 60, 78
Drinkhall, J. 82, 91
Drouvelis, M. 161, 175
Drus, M. 201, 220
Duflo, E. xvi
Dulleck, U. 60–61, 77–78, 162, 175
Dunn, E. W. 201, 220
Dunn, P. 179, 194

292   Names index

Eatwell, J. 36
Ebrahimi, H. 266–268, 272
Eckel, C. C. 202, 220
Edlund, J. 130, 153
Edwards, A. 9, 14, 246, 251
Eitel, A. 61, 78
Ekstrand, L. E. 279, 288
Elffers, H. 158, 175, 279–280, 288–289
Elkins, D. 245, 247–248, 251
Elster, J. 158, 175
Enachescu, J. 131, 169–172, 175–176, 178, 194–195
Engelen, P. 257, 272
Englmaier, F. 130, 153
Epley, N. 41–42, 49
Epstein, G. S. 234, 251
Erard, B. 161, 173–175, 198, 200–201, 219–220
Erat, S. 200, 220
Erdoğdu, M. M. 128, 134, 153, 155
Esslen, M. 164, 174
Etzioni, A. 130, 153
Evans, C. 130, 132, 153, 155, 231, 222, 231
Ezrow, L. 80, 91
Ezzamel, M. 235, 251

Falcone, R. 133, 153
Falk, A. 200, 220
Fama, E. F. 5–7, 14, 260, 272
Farrar, J. 179, 194
Fasiani, M. 11, 14
Fehr, B. 159, 175
Feinstein, J. 161, 175, 198, 200–201, 219–220
Feld, L. P. xxi, xxv, 21, 36, 129, 131–132, 134, 154, 199, 220
Filippin, A. 201, 220
Finer, S. E. 233–234, 236, 243, 246, 251
Fischbacher, U. 198, 220
Fishbein, M. 130, 154
Fochmann, M. 162, 172, 175
Föllmi-Heusi, F. 198, 220
Fombrun, C. 256, 272
Fonseca, M. A. 225, 230
Fontaine, J. J. R. 160, 176
Fooken, J. 175
Forgas, J. P. 158, 175
Foster, G. 234, 251
Frank, R. 175
Frankel, S. 105
Franklin, E. H. 53, 77
Frantz, R. 26–27, 35–36
Frecknall-Hughes, J. 254, 272
Freeman, R. B. 29, 36

Freeman, R. E. 258–259, 272
French, K. R. 5, 14
Frey, B. S. xxi, xxv, 21, 36, 129, 131–132, 134, 154, 199, 220, 224, 229–230, 278, 288
Friedman, D. 64, 77
Friedman, M. 5, 258, 273
Frijters, P. 127, 128, 234, 251–252
Fry, E. H. 82, 91

Gaban, L. 191, 194
Gaertner, W. 288
Gagliardi, A. 53, 78
Galaburda, A. M. 175
Galdieri, E. 103, 120
Gallemore, J. 254, 258, 273
Gangl, K. 126–128, 131, 133, 152, 154, 219, 230
García Prats, A. 120
Garlin, F. V. 163, 175
Gatzert, N. 256, 273
Gaultier-Gaillard, S. 261, 271, 273
Gërxhani, K. 180, 194, 201, 220
Giacomantonio, M. 200, 219
Gianni, L. 120
Gigerenzer, G. 18–19, 35, 36, 37
Gilboa, I. 55, 58, 77
Gill, D. 165, 175
Gillett, P. 254, 273
Gilligan, C. 201, 220
Gillis, D. 192, 194
Glaister, D. 222, 230
Glennerster, R. 67, 77
Gneezy, U. 200, 219–220
Goldsmith, A. H. 32, 36
Goldsmith, H. H. 176
Goldstein, D. 40, 49
Gompertz, S. 256, 273
Goslinga, S. 227, 232
Grabowski, T. 175
Graetz, M. J. 199, 220
Graham, J. 253, 257–258, 273
Grasmick, H. G. 161, 175
Graulau, J. 242, 251
Green, J. R. 54, 78
Green, L. 154
Greenspan, A. 6, 14
Greifeneder, R. 53, 78
Greiner, B. 207, 220
Grosch, K. 198, 202, 217–218, 220
Grosskopf, B. 161, 175
Grossman, P. J. 202, 220
Groves, H. M. 11–12, 14
Guerra, A. 215, 220

Names index 293

Guthrie, C. 224, 230
Gutiérrez, H. 127, 153
Guyon, J. 82, 91
Gylfason, H. F. 201, 220

Haenen, J. 200, 219
Hageman, A. M. 130, 153
Hahn, A. 260, 273
Hallsworth, M. 9, 14
Handgraaf, M. J. 199, 221
Hanlon, M. 227–228, 230, 253, 258, 273
Hanousek, J. 134, 154
Harrington, B. 215, 220, 246, 251
Harrison, G. W. 60, 67, 77
Harrison, J. S. 259, 273
Hartl, B. 154
Hashimzade, N. 224, 230
Haslehner, W. 104, 120
Hasseldine, J. 201, 220, 254, 273
Hausserman, C. 179, 194
He, X. 272
Head, J. 127, 154
Hechtner, F. 162, 175
Heinemann, F. 224, 230
Heinlein, R. A. 178, 194
Heitzman, S. 227–228, 230
Helleloid, D. 247, 251
Helliwell, J. 178, 194
Henderson, R. 253, 273
Hermle, J. 200, 220
Hero, R. E. 281, 289
Hertwig, R. 64, 77
Hessing, D. J. 279, 280, 288–289
Heukelom, F. 35
Heydt, V. 120
Higgins, E. T. 176
Hillman, A. L. 234, 251
Hirschman, A. O. 26, 36
Hiscott, G. 258, 273
Hite, P. A. 201, 220
Ho, J. K. 131, 154
Hoelzl, E. xxi, xxv, 21, 36, 125, 154, 172, 175, 194, 223, 230–231
Hofmann, E. 131, 133, 152, 154, 201, 219, 220, 230
Hoi, C. 253, 258, 273
Hokstad, P. 256, 273
Holt, G. 164, 254, 271
Homburg, C. 260, 273
Hoopes, J. L. 227, 230
Horowitz, A. R. 224, 230
Horowitz, I. 224, 230
Houston, J. 180, 194
Hribar, P. 257, 273

Huber, J. 40, 49
Huberman, G. 38, 49
Hurley, J. 269, 273
Husain, G. 163, 177

Idson, D. 41, 49
Ilzetzkiy, E. 127, 154
Imam, P. A. 133, 154
Issacharoff, S. 59, 77
Iyengar, S. S. 38, 49
Izard, C. E. 159, 175

Jackson, B. R. 278–279, 288
Jacobs, D. F. 133, 154
Jacobson, S. 224, 230
Jadad, A. R. 53, 78
James, K. 240, 251
James, S. 9, 14, 21, 36, 129, 154, 185, 194, 222–223, 231, 246, 251
Jäncke, L. 164, 174
Jenkins, N. 257, 273
Jensen, M. 259, 273
Jeong, J. 260, 273
Jiang, W. 38, 49
Joffily, M. 158, 175, 194
John, P. 8, 14
Johnson, E. J. 40, 49, 172, 175, 280, 288
Joireman, J. 199, 219, 221
Jolls, C. 42, 49, 55, 78
Jones, P. 227, 230
Jorens, Y. 192, 194
Joulfaian, D. 226–228, 231

Kagel, J. H. 60, 78
Kahan, D. M. 184, 194
Kahneman, D. xv, xix, xxv, xxvi, 4–7, 14–15, 19–20, 36, 41–42, 49, 54, 78, 80, 92, 125, 154, 157, 171, 175, 224–225, 227, 231, 2782–81, 288–289
Kallhoff, A. 129, 154
Kamakura, W. A. 260–261, 271
Kamdar, N. 227–228, 231
Kamil, M. I. 129, 134, 152
Kämpfe, J. 163, 175
Kanagaretnam, K. 199, 220
Kang, R. 272
Kaplan, R. L. 82–4, 91
Karni, E. 61, 77
Kasipillai, J. 223, 231
Kasper, H. 60, 78
Kasper, M. 173–174, 176, 195, 283, 288
Kassam, K. S. 157, 176
Kassim, A. A. B. M. 134, 154
Kastlunger, B. 173, 175

294 Names index

Katona, G. 4, 14
Katsimi, M. 133, 154
Katz, J. L. 83, 91
Keegan, B. 126
Keen, M. 245, 251
Keenan, T. 278, 288
Kelliher, C. F. 130, 153
Kelmanson, B. 191, 195
Keltner, D. 160, 176
Kemmeren, E. 120
Kenney, F. 278, 288
Kerschbamer, R. 61, 77
Kılıçaslan, H. 185, 195
Killian, S. 228, 231
Kindleberger, C. P. 6, 14
Kingdon, J. W. 81, 91
Kinsey, K. A. 279, 289
Kiow, T. S. 134, 154
Kirabaeva, K. 191, 195
Kirchler, E. xxi, xxv, 21, 36, 125, 131,
    133, 152–154, 158, 172–176, 178–179,
    194–195, 201, 219, 220, 223, 225, 230,
    231, 283, 288
Klein, L. R. 7, 14
Kleven, H. J. 224, 231
Klewes, J. 273
Kling, J. R. xx, xxv, 8, 14
Knudsen, M. B. 224, 231
Kocher, M. 224, 230
Koessler, A.- K. 60, 77
Kofler, G. 120
Kogler, C. 152, 173, 175–176, 178–179,
    194–195, 199–200, 219–220, 230, 283,
    288
Kopp, R. J. 64, 78
Kornhauser, M. E. 222, 225, 231
Koslowsky, M. 134, 155
Koszegi, B. 42, 49
Kottasz, R. 256, 271
Krawietz, W. 106, 120
Kreiner, C. T. 224, 231
Krier, J. E. 81, 91
Kristinsson, K. 201, 220
Kropp, S. 80, 91
Krueger, A. B. 29, 35
Kruglanski, A. W. 176
Kuhlman, D. M. 221

Lang, C. 153
Lang, M. 120
Lanis, R. 253, 258, 274
LaPorta, R. 128, 134, 155
Lattimore, P. K. 278, 288
Laury, S. 219

Laver, M. 80, 91
Lavermicocca, C. 257, 274
Layard, R. 178, 194
Lea, R. 258, 274
Lebedev, A. N. 154
Lee, B. K. 53, 78
Lee, D. J. 219
Lee, W. N. 53, 78
Lehrer, R. 80, 91
Leibenstein, H. 26–27, 36
Leicester, A. xxi, xxv, 8, 14
Lenzner, R. 86, 91
Lerner, J. S. 157–158, 160–162, 171, 176
Levell, P. xxi, xxv, 8, 14
Lewis, A. xxv, 227, 230
Lewis, M. 6–8, 14
Lewis, P. 259, 261, 275
Li, S. 257, 273
Li, Y. 157, 176
Liberman, A. O. 200, 219
Likhovski, A. 222, 231
Lim, K. P. 131, 154
Liotine, V. G. 120
Lippert, O. 191, 193, 195
List, J. A. 5, 9, 14–15, 60, 67, 77
Littlewood, M. 115, 120
Liu, Y. 153, 223
Loewenstein, G. 41, 43, 49, 59, 77, 158,
    161–162, 171, 176–177
Loftus, E. F. 279, 288
Loo, E. C. 131, 154
Lopez–de–Silanes, F. 155
Louisot, J.- P. 261, 271, 273
Lubell, M. 282, 289
Lubin, P. C. 67, 78
Lucas, R. 20, 24–26, 30, 32–34, 36
Lyons, T. 266, 274

McCaffrey, E. xxv, 4, 8, 15
McClellan, C. 133, 152, 228, 230
McClelland, G. H. xx, xxv, 21, 35, 278, 288
MacCormick, N. 106, 120
McGee, R. W. 134, 155, 185, 194–195
McGinn, T. A. J. 235, 252
McGraw, K. M. 283, 289
Maciejovsky, B. 21, 36
Macintyre, A. 132, 155
McKee, M. 153, 200, 219
McKerchar, M. 222, 225, 231
MacLean, R. 267, 274
McVeigh, T. 254, 274
Maital, S. 281, 288
Mak, L. C. 49
Malézieux, A. 197, 201, 219, 220

Names index   295

Mallalieu, H. 266, 274
Mangoting,Y. 129, 131, 134, 155
Mannetti, L. 200, 219
Mao, P. 86, 91
March, J. G. 18, 26, 36
Markellos, R. N. 179, 195
Marshall, A. xv, 24
Martin, M. 163, 176
Martinez-Vazquez, J. 133–135, 152–153, 175, 200, 219
Mas-Colell, A. 54, 78
Maslove, A. 154
Maslow, A. H. 32, 36
Matjasko, J. L. 44, 49
May, P. J. 58, 78
Maydew, E. 254, 258, 273
Mazar, N. 42, 49
Medina, L. 191, 195
Medoff, J. L. 29, 36
Melguizo, Á. 127, 153
Meltzer, A. 36
Mendoza, J. P. 173, 176
Mescall, D. 227, 230
Messi, L. 222, 229
Mestelman, S. 199, 220
Metcalfe, R. D. 9, 14
Meurers, D. 61, 78
Miao, Y. 272
Middleton, C. 267, 274
Miller, B. P. 61, 78
Miller, D. C. 200, 219
Miller, D. S. 87, 91
Millgate, M. 36
Milliron, V. C. 278–279, 288
Milner, L. 267, 274
Mircheva, B. 191, 195
Mittone, L. 161, 167, 174, 176
Mocetti, S. 134, 153
Modigliani, F. 38, 49
Mohr, P. N. C. 162, 175
Moizer, P. 254, 272
Montmarquette, C. 158, 175, 178, 194
Morris, G. 254, 273
Mousavi, S. 35
Moutos, T. 133, 154
Moy, N. 61, 78
Mróz, B. 179, 195
Muehlbacher, S. 152, 173, 175–176, 219, 230
Mueller, D. C. 10, 15
Mullainathan, S. xx, xxv, 8, 14
Muravska, J. 182, 195
Murphy, K. 158, 176, 178, 195
Murphy, R. 179, 195, 200, 221, 253, 272

Murphy, R. O. 199, 206–207, 221
Murray, C. 234, 252
Musgrave, R. 3–4, 11–12, 15
Myles, G. D. 224–225, 230

Nainar, K. 199, 220
Neate, R. 268, 274
Neumann, D. 194
Neville, S. 256, 274
Newman, P. 36
Newton, C. 175
Nichita, A. 153, 176, 178, 191, 194–195, 220, 230
Nichols, D. R. 279–280, 288
Nicolau, J. L. 260, 274
Nisbett, R. E. 47, 49
Noll, R. G. 81, 91
Noor, N. M. 256, 276
Norton, M. I. 201, 220
Novaro, A. 200, 219
Nur- tegin, K. D. 227, 231

O'Connor, J. 131, 155
O'Donoghue, T. 59, 77
Obermair, J. 153
Olbert, M. 241, 252
Olivola, C. Y. 178, 196
Olsen, J. 162, 173, 175–176, 178, 194–195, 230
Orow, N. 254, 274
Ortiz-Ospina, E. 21, 36
Ortmann, A. 64, 77
Osberg, L. 154
Osborne, A. 266, 274
Osterloh-Konrad, C. 95, 120
Oswald, A. J. 30, 35
Otto, P. E. 161, 174
Ottone, S. 221
Owen, K. 163, 175

Palda, F. 134, 154
Paluck, E. L. 130, 155
Pampel, F. 200, 221
Panitch, L. 154
Pantya, J. 176, 195, 220
Parkes, D. C. 153
Parks, C. 199, 219
Paul, R. 82, 92
Payne, J. 280, 288
Payne, J. W. 40, 49
Peacock, L. 266, 274
Pedersen, S. 224, 231
Peichl, A. 194
Pennisi, E. 234, 236, 252

296 Names index

Pfister, H.- R. 163, 171, 176
Piccinni, R. 120
Pickhardt, M. 179, 195
Pieters, R. 159, 160–161, 175, 177
Piketty, T. 116, 120
Pinney, N. 281–282, 289
Pittman, J. A. 227, 230
Plantamura, P. M. 120
Pletzer, J. L. 199, 221
Pluto, C. 40, 49
Pollai, M. 152, 219, 230
Pommerehne, W. W. 64, 78
Ponzano, F. 221
Pope, J. 225, 231
Prebble, J. 96–97, 105–106, 118, 120–121, 253, 274
Prebble, R. 96, 105, 118, 121
Prebble, Z. 253, 274
Preston, I. 127, 153
Prinz, A. 179, 195
Prowse, V. 165, 175
Psychoyios, D. 179, 195
Puri, M. 60, 78
Puviani, A. 11, 13, 15

Qiu, J. 257, 273

Rabin, M. 59, 77
Raczkowski, K. 179, 195
Radanovic, G. 153
Radin, M. 245, 252
Ram, A. 254, 274
Rashid, A. S. A. 256, 276
Rasul, I. xxi, xxv, 8, 14
Rau, H. A. 220
Raven, B. H. 133, 155
Rawlings, G. 222, 231
Rawls, J. 129, 155
Rayner, J. 261, 271, 273
Reece, D. 268–269, 274
Reeves, E. 126
Renkewitz, F. 163, 175
Riahi-Belkaoui, A. 223, 231
Richardson, G. 199, 221, 253, 258, 274
Rickard, N. S. 163, 177
Rider, M. 153
Rifkind, H. 266, 274
Ristl, A. 175
Ritchie, M. 256, 275
Robben, H. S. J. 279, 289
Robbins, S. P. 132, 155
Robin, N. 242, 252
Rocholl, J. 60, 78
Roland, D. 266, 275

Rosenblat, P. 111–114, 121
Roser, M. 21, 36
Rosid, A. 130, 132, 155
Rosidi 155
Ross, A. M. 185, 195
Roth, A. E. 60, 78
Roth, J. A. 278–279, 288–289
Rowley, E. 269, 275
Rubin, H. 82, 92
Ruddick, G. 267, 275
Rupert, T. J. 184, 196
Rusconi, E. 178, 194
Russell, J. A. 159, 175

Sabia, R. 120
Sacharin, V. 159–160, 176
Sachs, J. 178, 194
Saez, E. 224, 231
Salleh, M. F. M. 134, 154
Samuel, J. 266, 275
Samuelson, J. 82, 92
Sandmo, A. xx, xxv, 125, 152, 157, 174, 178, 194, 223–224, 229, 231, 277–278, 287
Sapiei, N. S. 223, 231
Saunders, M. 259, 261, 275
Savage, M. 266, 275
Sawyer, A. 21, 36
Schafer, W. D. 200, 219
Schaffner, M. 60, 77, 132, 155, 175
Scheibehenne, B. 53, 78
Scheiter, K. 61, 78
Schellenberg, E. G. 163, 177
Schelling, T. C. 4, 15
Scherer, K. R. 159–160, 166, 176
Scheve, K. 116, 121
Schlegel, K. 159–160, 176
Schlesinger, F. 266–267, 269, 275
Schmidt, S. K. 192, 194
Schneider, F. 21, 36, 132–133, 155, 179, 191, 195
Scholz, J. T. 278–279, 281–283, 288–289
Schuch, C. 153
Schultz, J. J. 279 280, 288
Schulze, W. D. xx, xxv, 21, 35, 278, 288
Schumpe, B. M. 200, 219
Schwartz, J. 87, 91
Schwarz, N. 64, 78, 158, 161, 163, 176
Schwarzenberger, H. 173, 176
Schwarzwald, J. 133, 155
Scott, J. C. 236, 252
Sedlmeier, P. 163, 175
Sergenti, E. 80, 91
Serle, J. 256, 275
Shafer, W. E. 227–228, 232

Names index 297

Shanley, M. 256, 272
Shaxson, N. 116, 121
Sheffrin, S. M. xx, xxv
Shefrin, H. M. 38, 49
Shehata, M. 199, 220
Shevlin, T. 253, 258, 273
Shiller R. J. 5–7, 14–15, 25, 35
Shiv, B. 171, 177
Shleifer, A. 6, 15, 155
Shroff, N. 253, 258, 273
Shuman, V. 160, 176
Siahaan, F. O. P. 130, 132, 134, 155
Sibieta, L. 127, 153
Sibley, W. M. 55, 78
Siegloch, S. 194
Siglé, M. 227–228, 232
Sikka, P. 253–254, 258, 275
Simmons, R. S. 227–228, 232
Simon, H. A. xv, xix, xxv, xxvi, 4, 15–19, 34, 36, 53, 78
Simonson, I. 40, 49
Slemrod, J. xviii, xx, xxv, 4, 8, 15, 91, 178, 180, 195, 227, 230, 288–289
Smith, H. 67, 78
Smith, K. W. 279, 289
Smith, V. L. xix, 6, 15, 64, 78
Solnick, S. 202, 219
Soriano, C. 160, 176
Sossin, L. 126, 155
Speklé, R. 227, 232
Spengel, C. 241, 252
Spicer, M. W. 279, 281, 289
Srinivasan, T. N. 157, 177–178, 195
Stanley, T. D. 25, 36
Staringer, P. 153
Stasavage, D. 116, 121
Steenbergen, M. R. 283, 289
Steffen, S. 60, 78
Steinmo, S. 197, 200–201, 219–221, 239, 252
Steiro, T. 256, 273
Stets, J. E. 159, 177
Stewart, H. 254, 274
Stiglitz, J. xv
Stillman, S. 10, 15
Stock, T. 196
Suchanek, G. L. 6, 15
Sugden, R. 5, 10, 15
Sukoharsono, E. G. 155
Summers, B. 254, 272
Summers, R. S. 106, 120
Sunder, S. 64, 77
Sunstein, C. R. xxi, xxvi, 6–8, 15, 19, 36, 39, 42, 44, 46, 49, 53, 55, 58–59, 78, 80, 91–92, 125, 155

Sussman, A. B. 178, 195
Sutter, M. 77

Takavarasha, K. 67, 77
Tankard, M. E. 130, 155
Tanzi, V. 3, 9, 11, 15
Taylor, W. B. 81, 83, 92
Tellegen, A. 159, 177
Temple-West, P. 253, 273
Thaler, R. H. xv, xix, xxi, xxvi, 6–8, 15, 19, 36, 38–39, 44, 46, 49, 58–59, 78, 125, 155
Thomas, D. 253, 275
Thompson, W. F. 163–164, 177
Thornock, J. 254, 258, 273
Titcomb, J. 269, 275
Todd, P. M. 18, 36, 53, 78
Torgler, B. 21, 35, 37, 53, 60–61, 77–78, 127–129, 132–135, 153, 155, 175, 180, 184, 196, 199–200, 219, 221, 224–225, 232
Tran, A. 180, 194
Tran-Nam, B. 130, 132, 155, 224, 230
Treneman, A. 267, 276
Trivedi, V. U. 201, 219
Tron, M. E. 111, 121
Turner, J. 267, 276
Turner, J. H. 159, 177
Tversky, A. xix, xxvi, 4, 14–15, 19–20, 36, 40–2, 49, 80, 92, 172, 175, 278–281, 288–289
Tyler, T. R. 131, 155, 158, 176

Ursprung, H. W. 234, 251
User, I. 153
Uslaner, E. M. 131–132, 134, 156

Vajjala, S. 61, 78
Valdesolo, P. 157, 176
Valente, P. 120
Valipour, A. 256, 276
van de Ven, N. 161, 177
van der Hel, L. 227, 232
van Gelder, J.- L. 175
Van Lange, P. A. M. 176, 221
Varian, H. R. 54, 78
Varma, K. N. 280, 289
Veldhuizen, R. 227, 232
Villeval, M. C. 158, 175, 178, 194
Vis, B. 80, 92
Vishny, R. 155
Vitell, S. 257, 276
Vitou, B. 182, 195
Vlaev, I. 9, 14
Voelpel, S. C. 221

298   *Names index*

Vohs, K. D. 171, 176
Volintiru, C. 197, 200–201, 220
Vollmayr, J. 260, 273
von Wright, G. H. 106, 120
Voracek, M. 201, 220
Voth, H. J. 239, 251
Vyncke, P. 261, 272

Wahl, I. xxi, xxv, 21, 36, 125, 154, 172–173,
    175, 223, 231
Wakker, P. 278, 289
Wakolbinger, F. 184, 196
Walker, J. M. 64, 78
Walker, M. 191, 193, 195
Wallace, S. 219
Wallschutzky, I. 21, 36
Walsh, D. 267, 276
Ward, H. 80, 91
Warneryd, K. 289
Wartick, M. L. 184, 196
Wartick, S. 253, 276
Watson, D. 159, 177
Webber, C. 239, 252
Webley, P. 279, 281, 289
Weigel, R. H. 289
Weiss, J. 191, 195
Wenig, A. 288
Weninger, M. 153
Wenzel, M. xx, xxv, 21, 37, 130, 156
Werdigier, J. 197, 221
Weyland, K. 80, 92
Whinston, M. D. 54, 78
White, E. L. 163, 177
Wicks, A. C. 259, 273
Wielhouwer, J. L. 173, 176
Wildavsky, A. B. 239, 252
Wilde, L. L. 199, 220
Williams, A. W. 6, 15
Williamson, O. E. 26, 37
Williamson, V. 21, 37
Willis, L. E. 53, 79
Willis, R. H. 256, 272
Wilson, A. M. 67, 79
Wilson, H. 266, 276
Wilson, R. J. J. 254, 258, 271
Witte, A. D. 278–279, 288–289
Wolf, N. 161, 174
Woodcock, A. 95, 121
Worstall, T. 267, 276
Wreschniok, R. 273
Wu, Q. 253, 258, 273
Wu, Z. 272
Wunder, H. F. 228, 232

Yahaya, N. 256, 276
Yaniv, G. 279–280, 289
Yılmaz, B. E. 153
Yip, R. W.Y. 228, 232
Yitzhaki, S. 178, 195–196
Yokum, D.V. 44, 49
Yoo, C.Y. 260, 273

Zardasti, L. 256, 276
Zeelenberg, M. 159–161, 175, 177,
    194
Zhang, H. 253, 258, 273
Zhang, K. 223, 230
Zhang, N. 200, 221
Zucman, G. 234, 245, 252
Zukauskas, S. 194, 230

Institution Names

ActionAid 127, 152
Australian Federal Parliament 115
Australian Parliament 113
Australian Securities and Investments
    Commission (ASIC) 76

Barclays Mercantile 98–100
Bowater Property Developments 96
British East India Company 242–243
Business Roundtable 253

Caffè Nero 267–268, 270
Center for Research in Securities and
    Prices (CRSP) 260–261

Daily Telegraph, The 266–269, 271–276
Deloitte 191, 194
Department for Work and Pensions
    192, 194
Department of Finance 223, 230

Economist, The 262, 266–267, 275
European Court of Justice 103

GAO 88, 91
GIB 135–136, 149, 154
Guardian, The 178, 229–230, 254, 256,
    274–275

Her Majesty's Revenue and Customs
    (HMRC) 116–117, 255–256, 259, 262,
    265–266, 269, 271
HM Revenue & Customs 226, 230

Names index   299

ICIJ 127, 154
Internal Revenue Service 233, 278
Italian Corte Suprema di Cassazione 103

JCT 85, 87, 91

Max Planck Institute for Tax Law and
  Public Finance 95, 98, 120
MoneyWeek 255, 274

National Audit Office 226, 231

OECD xxi, xxvi, 184, 191, 195, 248, 253

PricewaterhouseCoopers 228, 231
PSI 88–90, 92

Revenue Commissioners 96, 99, 223, 226,
  231

SEC 135, 155
Starbucks 247, 251; *see also* Chapter 13

TNS Political & Social 182, 195
Transparency International 193, 195–196
Treasury 86, 90, 92, 205
TÜİK 135, 137, 155

UNIDO 128, 155
United Nations 179, 196
US Executive Office of the President
  8, 15
US Supreme Court Justice 178

Subject index

abnormal returns 260–261, 263–265
abuse of law 103–104
accountability 85, 88, 133–134, 144, 287
accounting xvi, 8, 39, 59, 127, 170,
183–184, 234, 241, 254, 256–257, 266,
270; -based tax xxiv, 239–241, 244;
information 260; tricks 127, 234, 266
advance tax payment 279–280
aggressive tax planning 106, 116, 120, 258
altruism 43, 282, 287; altruistic
preferences 202
anti-avoidance rules: general 94, 96, 99–101,
104–105, 118–119, 120–121; specific
99–100, 105, 109
Anti Tax Avoidance Directive 104
appropriation 238, 244–245
asymmetric information 18, 25
audit 21, 63, 65–66, 157, 162–163, 166–167,
169–171, 201, 203, 226, 227; confusion
54, 61–62, 67–69, 72, 75; efficiency 172;
perceived 283, 285–286; probability
xx, 165, 172, 203, 224, 277, 279–281;
rate 173, 198–199, 278, 280–281, 285;
system 224
Australian National Credit Code 59
Austrian School 4–5

behaviour: contextual 202; instrumental 202
behavioural approach xx, xxii, 9–10, 17, 31,
33–34, 63, 223
behavioural assumptions 20, 25, 31
behavioural biases iii, xxi, 40, 42, 65, 80
behavioural consequences 160; behavioural
economics iii, 5–11, 13, 17, 19–20, 22,
33, 38–40, 43–45, 48, 53–54, 58–59, 76,
125; and education 46
behavioural economists 6, 10, 21, 23, 43, 59
behavioural models 20, 22, 28–29, 31–32,
39–40, 277

behavioural norms 17–20, 26
behavioural policy 42
behavioural public finance 7, 26–31, 34, 80,
94, 111, 119–120
behavioural tax compliance model 277
behavioural theory 20, 26, 30–31, 33
beliefs xix, 21, 116, 126, 130, 132–133,
173, 198, 225, 234, 256; moral 179,
278; personal 178–179, 188, 191–193;
positive 192
benefit: costs and 17, 38, 55–58, 66, 69,
80–81, 90, 125, 129; fraud 181, 192;
government 181, 183–184, 186, 188–189,
191–192; individual 201; labour 26–29;
of social cooperation 282; social 128, 131,
140, 152, 184; systems 193; tax 85,
99–100, 105, 110, 117; tourism 181
bodily symptoms 159
bounded rationality xix, 16–17, 19–20, 22,
24, 33, 35, 43
bribery 182
bureaucracies 233–234, 244

capital flows 89
cash flow 257, 259–260
celebrity endorsement 260
Chicago School 3, 5
choice architecture xxi, 7–8, 13, 20, 44, 46
civic duty 178, 193
classical economics 32, 111, 119
coercion xxi, 7, 13, 192
coercive power 126, 133, 173
cognitive: abilities 43, 126; appraisal 159;
biases 58; heuristic 80–81, 85–90;
load 53; processes 158; psychology 18;
shortcuts 80; skills task 162
collective action xviii, 29, 129, 282, 287
collective goods 128–129, 133–135, 140, 149
common good 126, 128, 225

Subject index 301

common needs 128
completeness 54–55
confusion index 62–63, 65, 75
consumer-based brand equity 258
controlled foreign company 110
cooperation 131, 161, 199–201, 218, 239, 241, 244, 248, 282
cooperative behavior 130, 199, 202
corporate value 259
corruption 4, 13, 132–134, 136, 138, 143, 145, 149, 152, 182, 193, 228
credence goods 61, 77
culturalist argument 125

deadweight loss 23–24
deceptive advertising 260
deduction 100, 102, 107, 109, 170, 245, 255, 269
democratic representation 128
demographic characteristics 136
Deposit Interest Retention Tax (DIRT) 223
depreciation 98
deterrence: effect 279–280; mechanism 151; model 125, 278; theory 277
developing countries 21, 126–127, 134
discrimination 129, 149
dishonesty 41, 197–198
distribution: bimodal 207; ethnic 135; fair 149, 152; of income 4, 127, 132; of national pie 11; power 127; price 42; resources 131; of tax compliance 209

economic substance 89, 102–103, 109, 117–118
economics of crime 157
Economist Historical Archive 262
education 24, 39, 42, 46–48, 60, 66, 129, 136–138, 149–150, 178, 183, 233, 246
efficiency: allocative 23–24, 27; economic 20, 27, 33; of institutions 198; of the market 5–6; of organisations 239; of public spending 9, 145; of taxation 33; of tax collection 22; x-efficiency 26, 28–30, 33–34
efficient market hypothesis 5, 43, 260
emotions: anger-related emotions 131, 170–172; anticipated emotions 161–162; composition of emotions 159; emotion categories 159–160; emotion qualities 159, 166; emotional experience 131, 159, 162–163, 171; emotional influences 161, 171; emotional state 41–42; emotions in cognitive processes 158; emotions toward behaviours of others 138, 141; Geneva

Emotion Wheel 159–160, 165–166; immediate emotions 161; incidental emotions 157–158, 161–163, 168, 171–172, 174; integral emotions 157–158, 161, 168–169, 171–172; negative emotions 126, 131, 149, 162–163, 166, 169, 173; negative feelings 161, 163; personal emotions 130, 146; positive emotions 161–162, 166, 168, 170, 173
enforcement 21, 81, 87, 104, 128, 130, 162, 173, 200, 228, 244, 248, 278, 282, 287
excessive profits 127
expected fine 278, 281–282
expected utility 157, 223, 277–278; Expected Utility Theory 224–225, 227, 229
experimental approach 54, 60
experimental economics 6, 202–203, 207
experimental economists xix, 5–6, 10
experimental methods 74
experimental survey 162, 169–170, 173, 211
experiment(s): choice 65; contribution game 161; controlled 6; field 59, 67–68, 70, 73; income-reporting game 161; investment 200; laboratory 6, 8–10, 58–59, 64–66, 70–74, 76, 161–163, 174, 201, 211; mystery shopping 67, 73, 76; natural 59–60, 62; public goods game 162; social dilemma games 217; tax 163, 197–198, 201, 207, 218; tax game 166–168, 203; ultimatum game 202

fairness: distributive 131; perception of 4, 126, 129–130, 136, 138, 149, 225; procedural 131; redistributive 131; tax 130; of tax system 21, 141, 225
fast and frugal 18, 20, 43
fictional transactions 102–104
fine rate 157, 173, 280, 283
fiscal capacity 22
fiscal exchange xviii, 129
fiscal illusion 11–13
fiscal privileges 233
fiscal psychology 223
flat rate 179
Foreign Investment in Real Property Tax Act (FIRPTA) 81–85
foreign ownership 81
free-rider 3, 129, 173, 180

gender 128, 136, 138, 170, 197–203, 209–211, 215–218, 283, 285–287

302　*Subject index*

government expenditure 16
governmental sector *see* public sector

heuristics and behavioural biases: anchoring 40–41; asymmetric dominance effect 40; availability 80–83, 86, 88–90, 281; compromise effect 40; default option 9, 39–40, 44–46, 48; framing 21, 41–44, 157, 224, 279–280; imperfect information 40; loss aversion 44–45; present bias 40; relative positioning 43; representativeness 80, 82, 86, 89–90; time-inconsistent preference 44–45
history of taxation 233–234, 243
homo economicus xix, 54
honesty-backed systems 192
horizontal equity 82–84
human capital 32–33, 234
human rights 128
hypothetical scenario 44, 277

incentives: distorting 20; economic 8, 16, 21–22, 44, 199; material 43; monetary 198; optimal 241; purely financial 171; social 129; tax 85–86, 127–128
incidental taxation 235–237, 239
individualistic state 12–13
inefficiency 134; allocative inefficiency 23, 27; *see also* x-inefficiency
inequality 83, 131–132, 178
inequality aversion 206
influential groups 127
information confidentiality principle 128
infrastructure services 136–137
institutional constraints 201
institutional context 126, 200, 217
institutional design 16, 20
institutional quality 133, 149
institutions 3, 43, 46, 62, 64, 127–128, 134, 198, 205–206; democratic 129, 282, 287; financial 59, 71, 88, 223; governing 126, 132, 136, 138, 140, 146, 149, 152; legal 117, 246; political 21 22, 128, 133; social 129, 135
insurance: health 43, 59, 85; products 70, 73; unemployment 32
intertemporal asymmetry 38
irrational behavior 4, 6–7
irrational exuberance 6, 8
irrationality 5–7, 11
irregular tribute 238

jurisdiction 22, 77, 97, 99–100, 103, 107, 114, 118–119, 191, 222, 253

justice: distributive 131; perception of 131; sense of 143, 151; tax 128, 151, 197

legal system 102–103, 112, 115, 132
legislative 90, 99–100, 103, 113, 118, 254; history 82, 84–85
legitimacy: of government 130; of local government 142; perceived 132; of the state 130, 132, 200; of tax collection 133
Leviathan 129
libertarian 7, 10, 13
life satisfaction 136–137
loophole 82, 84, 127, 132, 170, 254, 280
Lucas Critique 20, 24–26, 32–33

Magna Carta 245
major channel expansion 260
market failure 5, 7, 10
market fundamentalism 5, 10
masculine behavior 201
media: allegation 253; attention 253–254; coverage 260–261, 263, 283; effect of 277–278; influence of 259, 270; reports 81–82, 85, 254, 257, 259, 262, 270; social 271
mediating: mediating effect 197, 216; mediating variable 202; mediation analysis 213, 216–217
memory protocols 68
meta-analysis 53, 201
money illusion 19, 25, 30
moral concerns 178–180, 184–185, 188, 191, 193
moral costs 161
multinationals 127, 253–254
multiplier effect 223

National Insurance Contributions 115, 226
neoclassical economics 18
neurological factors 16
non-compliance 21, 125, 140–141, 146, 151, 157, 287
normative effect 223
norms: behavioral 17–20, 26; binding social 132; conventional economic 18–20; descriptive 45; personal 130; rationality 18; social 44, 129–130, 149, 171, 173, 199, 222; subjective 130
nudge(s) 7–13, 19–20, 39, 44–48, 120, 277, 283; bad 10–11; declarative 48; fake 10–11, 13

opportunity costs 31, 34, 43
out-of-pocket gains and losses 280

Subject index   303

parliament 98, 100, 113, 115, 119, 132, 135, 139, 144, 146, 151, 222, 244, 265
participation xviii, 83, 133, 208, 211, 213, 215–216
paternalism 40; benevolent 43; libertarian 7, 10
pay as you earn (PAYE) 226
peers 149, 180–181, 184, 198
performance index 65–67, 70, 74
Phillips Curve 30–31
plutocrats 127, 234, 240, 242–244, 246, 248, 250
political actors 80–81, 89–91; *see also* Chapter 5
political decisions 127
political economy *see* Chapter 7
political elites 80
political groups 258
political interactions xviii, 126–127, 138, 146
political landscape 127, 245
political opportunism 127
political rights 128
power: coercive 133, 173; legitimate 126, 133
preferential arrangements 127
privity of contract 119
probability of audit *see* audit, probability
progressive taxation 11, 179
prosociality 197–199, 202, 210, 218; prosocial behavior 197, 206; prosocial individuals 197, 199, 218
Prospect Theory 42–43, 224–225, 227, 229, 278–280
pseudo certainty effect 280
psychological costs 22
psychological factors 158, 172, 179
psychological motivations 198, 201
psycho-physiological reactions 159
public choice 3, 10–12, 48
public domain 128
public good 3, 128, 152, 162, 178–179, 181–182, 193, 200–203, 205–206, 233–234, 241, 283
public health 8, 39, 44–46, 48, 59, 118, 129
public interest 3–4, 7, 10–13
public policy xxi, 4, 16–17, 31–33, 98; behavioural economics and 38–48; behavioural labour and 31–33
public pressure 83–84, 86, 89, 127
public protest 254, 265, 270
public resources 127, 134, 139, 146
public sector 4, 113, 138, 143, 145, 149, 182, 193, 255, 268, 270

public services: cost of 127; quality 128, 134, 149, 151; satisfaction from 134, 142, 151; standards of 129, 134, 136
public spending xxi, 3, 7–12, 24, 145–146, 151
public transportation 193
punishment 22, 105, 133, 157, 178, 235, 249, 281–282, 287

quality of government 132, 134, 200
quality of life 178

race to the bottom 246
rational agent 25–26, 33, 38
rational behavior 5
rational choice 7, 56; paradigm 158; theory 277
rationality 4–5, 7, 18, 55, 90–91, 125, 171; assumption of xviii, xix, 4–6, 24, 38; bounded xix, 4, 16–17, 19–20, 22, 24, 33–35, 43, 171; collective 281
reciprocity 43, 128–129, 136, 138, 140, 199
recurrent taxation 234–235, 239
redistribution xxi, 131–132, 203, 205
reference point 224, 279–280, 287
regular tribute 238
regulation 3, 6–7, 54–55, 60–61, 64, 69–70, 74–75, 77, 127, 131, 173, 244; corrective 42; financial 53, 59, 246; performance-based 53, 58–59, 61; tax 173, 244
relationships: communal 201; dominance 55, 58, 60, 62–64, 66–67, 72–73; hierarchical 201, 235
religious preference 184
reputation: bad 161, 268; good 133, 157, 268
reputational loss 253, 254–260, 262–263, 265, 268, 270–271
revenue authority 222–226, 229
risk: attitudes 157, 211, 217; averse 200, 215; aversion 216–217, 224–225, 283; behaviour 157, 172; of detection 224–225; framing of 44; objective 44; perceived 201, 217, 281; tolerance 207, 212, 216–217
rule of law 105, 118, 128, 271

self-employed 86, 162, 164, 169–170, 173, 240, 283
self-interest xix, 198–199, 227, 281
slippery slope: extended 126, 133; framework xxi, 125–126, 158, 172–173, 199, 283; model 223, 225
smart agent 19, 24, 33, 35

304 Subject index

social amenities 134–135, 149
social benefit 128, 131, 140, 152, 184
social capital 282, 287
social contract xviii, 128, 134, 149, 152, 179, 225, 233
social factors 178, 222, 226–227
social inclusion 129
social life 128–129
social preferences 199, 207
social responsibility 103, 136, 138, 140–141, 227
social security 41, 193
social shaming 178
social utility 19
social value orientation 197–199, 206
social welfare 95
special interests 127–128
stakeholder theory 254, 258–259, 261, 265
status quo 163, 224
sustainability 259

tax: capital gains 81–84, 96–97, 226, 241; corporate 104, 127, 182, 227–228, 253–254, 271; corporation 247, 254, 269–271; custom 94, 242–243; death 94; dividend 88–90, 103, 107, 261; excise 9, 183, 226; exit 81, 85–86; fiduciary 222–223, 226, 228–229; income 9, 39–40, 94–95, 100, 105–106, 111–112, 114–116, 179, 182–183, 205, 222–224, 226, 239, 246, 278, 280; inheritance 226, 240, 245; international 80–81, 90, 106–108, 128, 245; land 96–97, 112, 233, 250; payroll tax 223, 239; seigniorage 235, 237–239; tribute 238; value added 9, 94, 183, 222, 226, 240–241, 244, 247, 284
tax amnesty 139, 142–143, 151, 280–281, 284, 287
tax arbitrage 245, 253
tax auditor 169, 171
tax authority 117, 126–127, 133, 169, 184, 225, 240–243, 248, 277–278, 280, 284–285
tax avoidance: aggressive 106, 116, 120, 254, 258; see also anti-avoidance rules
tax awareness 136, 138, 140, 283, 286–287
tax breaks 127
tax burden 22, 90, 101, 113, 126, 129, 131–132, 136, 149, 152, 228, 234
tax compliance: behaviour xxi, 125–128, 135, 149, 172, 225, 227–228; emotions in 158, 162–163, 168–169, 171–172;

fiduciary 222–223, 226–229; gender in 197–202, 211, 215–218; models 277; neoclassical 22; outcomes 228; prosocial behavior 197; role of executives on 228; socio-psychological in 158, 172; stimulus 228; theories xx, 125, 222–225, 227–229, 278; voluntary 129, 143–144, 149, 151–152
tax default 222, 226, 229
tax duty 281, 287
tax effort 134–135
tax ethics 283, 287
tax evaders 9, 125, 128, 149, 151, 172–173, 246, 281
tax evasion xx, 21, 41, 96–97, 102, 125, 130–134, 139–140, 142–143, 149, 151–152, 157, 161–162, 165, 172–173, 178–180, 182–185, 188, 190–191, 193, 197–199, 215, 223–224, 226–228, 234, 236, 244, 246–247, 253, 277–282, 284, 286–287
tax exemption 83–84, 127, 181
tax filing system 169
tax fraud 198, 226–227, 229, 281
tax gap 179, 183, 200
tax immunity 233
tax law 90, 95, 101–106, 109–111, 125, 131, 149, 162, 173, 180, 228, 246
tax liability 90, 104, 107, 118, 139, 240
tax minimization 94, 108, 116
tax morale xxi, 21–22, 111, 129, 132, 146, 180, 185, 199–200, 225, 227–229
tax payment shortfall 223
tax penalties: penalties 21–22, 102, 118, 199, 203, 223–225, 227, 250, 257, 265–266, 277–278, 285; penalty level 181; penalty rate 21; perceived fines 283, 285–286; punishment 22, 105, 133, 157, 178, 235, 249, 281–282, 287; severity of fine 172, 277
tax professionals 227
tax rate 21–22, 86, 116, 125, 157, 165, 178, 197, 201, 203, 205, 224, 258, 277–278
tax reconciliation 128, 151
tax reform 89, 279
tax refund 279
tax revolt 243–244
tax shaming 254
taxable income 95, 98–100, 102, 106, 110, 224, 247, 283
technological change 29, 31, 34
theory of social exchange 129

Subject index 305

theory of the firm 26, 30–31, 33
thin capitalization 110
time of filing 279–280
transfer pricing 253, 255
transitivity 54–56, 58, 62
transparency 63, 132–134, 193, 248
trust: in authorities xxi, 132, 143, 146,
149, 151–152, 168, 172, 199, 222, 225,
283, 287; in business 253, 259, 270;
between citizens and the state 129, 282;
in governing institutions 126, 132, 136,
138, 140, 149, 152; in government 21,
130, 132, 139, 143, 151, 208, 211–212,
215–217; horizontal 282, 287; implicit
126, 133; in judiciary 132; mutual 125,
133; in parliament 132, 144, 151; power
and 126, 199, 225; reason-based 126, 133;
socio-cognitive theory 133; in the state
146, 149; vertical 282, 287

uncertainty xvi, xix, 71, 106, 157, 169, 279
underground economy 183, 284, 286
underreporting 157, 161, 180, 203
United Kingdom Capital Allowances Act 98
unregistered economic activity 151

VAT *see* tax, value added
vested interests 127
voluntary-exchange 3, 12

welfare state 10
wellbeing 17, 24, 27–28, 30–32, 178,
199, 202
willingness to pay 41–42, 64, 132–133, 200,
203, 218
withholding 9, 81, 87–89, 169, 226,
247, 279

x-inefficiency 27–28, 30, 43

Taylor & Francis eBooks

www.taylorfrancis.com

A single destination for eBooks from Taylor & Francis with increased functionality and an improved user experience to meet the needs of our customers.

90,000+ eBooks of award-winning academic content in Humanities, Social Science, Science, Technology, Engineering, and Medical written by a global network of editors and authors.

TAYLOR & FRANCIS EBOOKS OFFERS:

- A streamlined experience for our library customers
- A single point of discovery for all of our eBook content
- Improved search and discovery of content at both book and chapter level

REQUEST A FREE TRIAL
support@taylorfrancis.com